The Hidden Millions

This book explores the extent, causes and characteristics of homelessness in developing countries. Bringing together a major review of literature and empirical case studies, it is invaluable for those studying, researching or working in housing, homelessness, social policy or urban poverty.

The Hidden Millions will challenge your preconceptions. Despite UN estimates of the number of homeless people being between 100 million and one billion, little is known about the true scale of homelessness, its causes, or the everyday experiences of homeless people in developing countries. This book highlights the very great differences between much current western theory and homelessness at a global scale, especially in developing country contexts, by:

- situating homelessness in the broader policy and housing context in developing countries;
- exploring the role of housing policy, supply systems and regulatory frameworks;
- breaking down socio-economic, cultural and political factors;
- looking at the effects of war and disaster on the levels of homelessness;
- reviewing the case of homeless children.

Drawing on local research in nine countries in the global south, this book offers an insight into the characteristics and lives of homeless people, public perceptions of homelessness and the policies and interventions which might variously increase or reduce homelessness. Exploring the human context as well as policy and planning, it combines quantitative estimates of homelessness with qualitative descriptions and real-life experience. This book will be of use to students, researchers, teachers, NGOs and policymakers in both developed and developing countries.

Graham Tipple is Reader in Housing Policy and Development at Newcastle University. He has over 30 years' experience in housing and urban development issues in developing countries at national and city level.

Suzanne Speak is Senior Lecturer in Planning at Newcastle University. She has 15 years' experience in social policy and planning research in the UK and developing countries.

Housing and society series
Edited by Ray Forrest
School for Policy Studies, University of Bristol

This series aims to situate housing within its wider social, political and economic context at both national and international level. In doing so it will draw on the full range of social science disciplines and on mainstream debate on the nature of contemporary social change. The books are intended to appeal to an international academic audience as well as to practitioners and policymakers – to be theoretically informed and policy relevant.

The Hidden Millions
Homelessness in developing countries
Graham Tipple and Suzanne Speak

Housing and Health in Europe
Edited by David Ormandy

Housing, Care and Inheritance
Misa Izuhara

Housing and Social Transition in Japan
Edited by Yosuke Hirayama and Richard Ronald

Housing Transformations
Shaping the space of 21st century living
Bridget Franklin

Housing and Social Policy
Contemporary themes and critical perspectives
Edited by Peter Somerville with Nigel Sprigings

Housing and Social Change
East–West perspectives
Edited by Ray Forrest and James Lee

Urban Poverty, Housing and Social Change in China
Ya Ping Wang

Gentrification in a Global Context
Edited by Rowland Atkinson and Gary Bridge

The Hidden Millions
Homelessness in developing countries

Graham Tipple and Suzanne Speak

Routledge
Taylor & Francis Group

LONDON AND NEW YORK

First published 2009 by Routledge
2 Park Square, Milton Park, Abingdon, Oxon OX14 4RN

Simultaneously published in the USA and Canada
by Routledge
270 Madison Avenue, New York, NY 10016, USA

Routledge is an imprint of the Taylor & Francis Group, an informa business

© 2009 Graham Tipple and Suzanne Speak

Typeset in Times and Frutiger by
HWA Text and Data Management, London
Printed and bound in Great Britain by
MPG Books Ltd, Bodmin

The publisher makes no representation, express or implied, with regard to the accuracy of the information contained in this book and cannot accept any legal responsibility or liability for any efforts or omissions that may be made.

British Library Cataloguing in Publication Data
A catalogue record for this book is available from the British Library

Library of Congress Cataloging in Publication Data
Tipple, A. Graham.
 The hidden millions : homelessness in developing countries / Graham Tipple & Suzanne Speak.
  p. cm. — (Housing and society series)
 Includes bibliographical references and index.
 1. Homelessness. 2. Homelessness—Developing countries. 3. Homeless persons—Housing—Developing countries. 4. Housing policy—Developing countries.
 I. Speak, Suzanne. II. Title.
 HV4493.T57 2009
 362.509172´4—dc22   2008034017

ISBN13: 978-0-415-42671-8 (hbk)
ISBN13: 978-0-415-42672-5 (pbk)
ISBN13: 978-0-203-88334-1 (ebk)

ISBN10: 0-415-42671-5 (hbk)
ISBN10: 0-415-42672-3 (pbk)
ISBN10: 0-203-88334-9 (ebk)

Contents

Tables

Figures

Foreword

Homelessness represents the most obvious and severe manifestation of the unfulfilment of the distinct human right to adequate housing. ... Few, if any, countries have entirely eliminated homelessness and in many nations this phenomenon is clearly increasing rather than declining.

(UNCHS, n.d.: para 44)

In 1999, UNCHS (as it then was) approached Graham Tipple to prepare the report from which *Strategies to Combat Homelessness* (UNCHS, 2000) was produced. In writing this, he noticed that there was very little written on homelessness in developing countries. Tipple applied for and received support from the ESCOR programme in DFID to carry out research on homelessness in ten (later nine) countries to flesh out the issues addressed in UNCHS (2000) for the developing world.[1] Suzanne Speak became the research associate in Newcastle and local researchers, mostly known to us already, were recruited in the nine countries. They were asked to write a report on homelessness in their countries using mainly existing sources and current local levels of understanding. Some carried out a few interviews with homeless people and agencies dealing with them. These reports, and the papers emanating from them, are collectively referred to in this book as the CARDO study. The country studies were; in Asia, China (Li, 2002), Bangladesh (Ghafur, 2002), India (Bannerjee Das, 2002), and Indonesia (Rahardjo, 2002); in Africa, Egypt (El-Sheikh, 2002), Ghana (Department of Housing and Planning Research, 2002), South Africa (Olufemi, 2001) and Zimbabwe (Kamete, 2001); and in Latin America, Peru (Miranda and Salazar, 2002).

Although these country reports are now quite dated, they still contain the most comprehensive information on homelessness in developing countries available anywhere. Using Google and Google Scholar, an internet search for literature generates surprisingly little from developing countries when 'homeless' is entered as the search word. Thus, the reports of our collaborating researchers, and their subsequent papers, are the main source of information in developing countries in this book. Throughout the book, currency conversions are given at the contemporary values pertaining when the data were collected. Since then, of course, many of the currencies have changed their value greatly. The Zimbabwe dollar has been both devalued many billion-fold and re-issued minus three noughts in 2006, and the Ghanaian cedi has been reintroduced minus five noughts. Thus, anyone checking our values against an internet currency calculator will be confounded!

In 2006, we held a conference in New Delhi to which about 30 academics and practitioners came. In the call and review procedure for papers, we tried to ensure that as many of the presentations as possible were addressing the poorest-housed people rather than just using homeless as a rubric for the inadequately housed households in their countries. It was obvious from the papers submitted in abstract form that very little understanding of homelessness exists in developing countries and that homelessness is still a very broad concept which can be used by serious writers when they are not even addressing the needs of the lowest 10 or 20 per cent of the population. Neither of these seem reasonable or healthy in the 21st century, 30 or more years since a focus on housing for the poorest in developing country cities first became mainstream through the Vancouver Declaration (UNCHS, 1976) and 40 or more years since the right to housing was legally enshrined in the International Covenant on Economic. Social and Cultural Rights (United Nations, 1966). Countering this lack of understanding is one of the purposes for this book.

This book is written from a strongly housing-oriented perspective. There are two reasons for this. Graham Tipple, who wrote the terms of reference for the CARDO study, is a housing specialist and saw the problem of homelessness in developing countries from that perspective. In addition, it is evident that housing shortages are large in developing countries, either in aggregate or in particular parts of the market, and form the major context which forces many people to live outside of conventional shelter and feature among the homeless population. These do not deny the place of other issues in causing homelessness. It is obvious that two households faced with the same socio-economic problems in the home may react differently so that one becomes homeless and the other does not. Not all low-income victims of domestic violence prefer to leave home and find comparative safety in the street. Equally, if insufficient provision is made for people with mental illness, many will roam the street, disowned by their kin and avoided by the general populace. Such issues will be included in the content but may be less central to the argument than some readers involved in more conventional homelessness studies would prefer.

We concentrate considerable attention on questions of definition and number because this is the first time homelessness as such has been addressed in the developing world in general and we find so little already in the literature that addresses them. 'Homelessness' and 'the homeless' are frequently used in the literature on housing in developing countries but they tend to be so loosely applied as to be meaningless; in this context, definition and counting stand as fundamental to making policy and framing interventions. If, for example, homelessness were defined very widely to include anyone with substandard housing, or lacking in water and sanitation services, or sharing with others not in their household, perhaps half the population would be included in many countries. If, on the other hand, only street sleepers were counted, there might only be a few thousand in each country. Furthermore, policies to address the issues raised would be exceedingly different. For these reasons, therefore, we make no apology for the considerable emphasis on definition and differentiation.

The form of the book reflects its housing bias. Following a brief review of current research on homelessness in industrialised countries, in the first six chapters we review the policy context and nature of the housing shortage which exists in most of the world; examine its relationship to homelessness; define homelessness in developing countries' contexts; differentiate between what constitutes homelessness and what is 'merely' inadequate housing and attempt to estimate the extent of homelessness defined in different ways.

In the following three chapters, we examine the characteristics of homeless people and what socio-economic, cultural, political and legal circumstances might have led them to be homeless. There are then three chapters on specific topics concerning homelessness: disasters and conflicts, isolation and exclusion, and children. Finally, we examine current interventions being attempted by governments and NGOs and suggest a palette of interventions in both housing and non-housing fields which would improve life for homeless people in developing countries.

Acknowledgements

The CARDO study was carried out under a UK Department for International Development (DFID) ESCOR Research Grant, No.ESA343, 2001-2003. DFID supports policies, programmes and projects to promote international development. DFID provided funds for this study as part of that objective but the views and opinions expressed are those of the authors alone. The country studies were researched and written as follows:

Bangladesh, Shayer Ghafur
China, Hou Li
Egypt, Tarek El-Sheikh
Ghana, Department of Housing and Planning, KNUST, Kumasi
India, Peu Banerjee Das, with Trudy Brasell-Jones and Jaishree
Indonesia, Tjahjono Rahardjo
Peru, Liliana Miranda Sara and Luis Salazar Ochoa
South Africa, Olusola Olafemi
Zimbabwe, Amin Kamete

The authors also wish to acknowledge the contribution to their understanding of homelessness gained from those who took part in the international conference on homelessness in developing countries held by Newcastle University in Delhi, January 2006.

1 Current understandings of homelessness

The developing world is urbanising at a rapid rate. In 1990 only 35 per cent of people in developing countries lived in cities. In 2006, however, UN-Habitat predicted that someone would move to, or be born in, a city in 2007 who would cause the balance to tip from a majority rural world to one in which most people live in cities. In the same year, it predicted, the number of people living in slums would reach one billion (UN-Habitat, 2006b). The majority of the growth in cities and in the slums therein will be made up of people living in poverty. This rapid urbanisation of poverty is having a significant impact on poor people as they migrate from rural areas in search of paid employment in cities and towns and become homelessness.

There is a lack of literature on homelessness in developing countries, as attested in UNCHS (2000)[1] which specifically set out to give the developing world an equal focus but could not locate enough literature except on street children. Current international reviews of homelessness tend to concentrate on industrialised countries only (e.g. Christian, 2003) with a very few developing countries case studies within volumes heavily focused on industrialised countries' contexts and issues (e.g. Glasser, 1994). In the few cases where homelessness in developing countries is explored, it tends to look at individual countries or individual aspects of homelessness within a single country or a small number of countries. At the time of UNCHS (2000), there was a little on South Africa (Olufemi, 1997, 1998, 1999), India (Swaminathan, 1995) and Nigeria (Labeodan, 1989),[2] but almost all the literature on developing countries concentrated on street children. The adults were nowhere to be seen and nor were the children living with those homeless adults. Furthermore, the literature on homelessness, being so concentrated in industrialised countries, had little relevance to what seemed, intuitively, to be the main problem in developing countries; namely that there just was not enough housing to go round and that it was much too expensive for quite a large portion of the population. In addition, it concentrated on issues which seemed to be much less central in developing countries: social isolation, substance abuse, mental illness and the design of welfare interventions. This book attempts to redress the balance between industrialised and developing countries' experiences a little by bringing together both empirical evidence and literature on homelessness in a broader range of countries.

It is particularly important that we set out, at the beginning of this work, the theoretical context within which most of the existing literature on homelessness in industrialised countries is based. In doing this we highlight that, to a great degree, the theoretical building blocks for our understanding of homelessness in industrialised countries do not prepare us well to understand the realities in developing countries.

This chapter establishes the context for what follows by briefly exploring our current understanding of homelessness in terms of theories, typologies and rights. Two concepts which underpin an understanding of homelessness are those of citizenship and human rights. As it is bound up with notions of rights and responsibilities, the concept of citizenship suggests ideas of deserving and undeserving. Moreover, not all those living in a country will be seen as its citizens, thus, however deserving they might be, they may not be entitled to the same rights as those who are citizens. This is becoming ever more evident in the context of migration and asylum seeking. Thus, the concept of citizenship does not suffice as a framework for understanding or addressing homelessness. As Turner (1993) notes, human rights can be grounded in the sociological concept of human frailty, especially the vulnerability of the body and the idea of moral sympathy. It is, perhaps, this moral sympathy which drives much of the work on homelessness and argues that all people are entitled to an adequate home irrespective of their deserving it.

Theoretical contexts within which homelessness is studied in industrialised countries include those from the interface between health and criminal behaviour (e.g. Martell, 2005), deviance and risk amplification (Whitbeck et al., 1999, 2001), subcultures (e.g. Tait, 1993) and feminist theory (Neale, 1997). Not all of these contexts can be covered in this work. Nevertheless, here we highlight some of the theoretical issues surrounding homelessness which arise throughout this book.

Theoretical concepts of home

> Home is the place where,
> When you have to go there,
> They have to take you in.
> (Robert Frost, 'The Death of the Hired Man')

Home is a very rich concept, embodying many ideas such as comfort, belonging, identity and security. Kellett and Moore (2003: 216) stress the need to examine the context of homelessness in the 'wider processes of home-making and belonging in society'. Writers such as Dovey (1985), Somerville (1992), Watson and Austerberry

(1986) and Kellett and Moore (2003) have explored the meaning of home and homelessness in depth. Home can be defined as a relationship between people and a place, 'an emotionally based and meaningful relationship between dwellers and their dwelling places' (Dovey, 1985). From qualitative evidence in Colombia, Kellett and Moore (2003) suggest that the owning of some tangible structure called home, no matter how poorly constructed it may be, is very important for a household's security, freedom, autonomy, well-being and opportunity.

Somerville (1992) suggests that home is 'physically, psychologically and socially constructed in both "real" and "ideal" forms. It is where we construct and manage our relationship with the physical and social worlds. It represents not only how we live but who we are'. Fuhrer and Kaiser (1992: 105; quoted in Oswald and Wahl, 2005) describe home as the 'extension of self through place'. If this is true, does the loss of home, especially through eviction or crisis, represent the loss of self? This is important in developing an understanding of the implications of evictions, even from the very poorest settlements of the lowest quality dwellings.

Despres (1991) distinguishes ten characteristics of home, as follows:

1   permanence and continuity;
2   centre for family relationships;
3   security and control;
4   mirror of personal views;
5   influence and place for change;
6   retreat from the surrounding world;
7   personal status indicator;
8   centre for activity;
9   concrete structure; and
10 (a place to own).

Somerville (1992: 532-4) also attempts to tease out the multi-dimensional nature of the meaning of home and its converse, homelessness. He presents seven key signifiers of home – 'shelter, hearth, heart, privacy, roots, abode and paradise'. To these, are added the connotations they have for dwellers (warmth, love, etc.), the nature of the security they give (physiological, emotional, etc.) and how these affect them in relation to themselves (relaxation, happiness, etc.) and others (homeliness, stability, etc.). Homelessness is the condition that represents the opposite of these, expressed in connotations of coldness, indifference, etc., presenting stress, misery, alienation, instability, etc. These are similar to the characteristics listed by Despres (1991) but expressed in different ways. For example, Despres's permanence and continuity is contained within Somerville's 'source of identity' and, perhaps, 'materiality'. Somerville's concept of home presents a very positive and optimistic view of life. In contrast, Somerville's concept of homelessness presents a dark and pessimistic view of the absence of home, one in which anomie, indifference, stress, powerlessness, vulnerability and a denial of individuality dominates.

Both Despres (1991) and Somerville (1992), therefore, express 'home' as a place where a person is able to establish meaningful social relations with others through entertaining them in his/her own space, or where the person is able to withdraw from such relationships. 'Home' should be a place where a person is able to define the space as their own, where they are able to control its form and shape. This may be through control of activities and of defining their privacy in terms of access to their space. When this is done, they have made a home with a sense of their identity (Cooper, 1995).

However, based on some of the characteristics of home, suggested by both Somerville (1992) and Despres (1991) – for example, concrete structure, a place to own or security and control – much of the world's adequately housed population would be classed as homeless. By virtue of not owning their home, it offers them little security, they cannot exercise control over it nor is it a mirror of their personal views. This might be the case for those living in perfectly adequate rented accommodation with strict conditions, or for those sharing with others who dominate the space.

Moreover, in developing countries, many people live in the most physically inadequate forms of shelter, for example, rag pickers living under very makeshift shelter in the cities of India. Even so, they form lasting social relations with those around them, entertain them in their meagre dwellings and can withdraw into their shelters where their privacy is respected by those around.

In the context of defining homelessness, it might be argued that *home* is qualitatively different from *adequate shelter* in that it provides a set of essential social and emotional requirements separate from shelter and which cannot be provided by adequate shelter alone. Indeed, in some cases, it may be necessary to forfeit adequate accommodation in order to achieve these social and emotional requirements. Such is the case for women and children made homeless through fleeing familial violence (Brown, 1997; Browne and Bassuk, 1997). Conversely, in the context of defining adequate shelter, it could be argued that shelter is not adequate unless it provides such essential requirements. These interlinked arguments have relevance for definitions of homelessness that we discuss in Chapter 4.

Debating the causes of homelessness

As our understanding of the meaning of home has grown, so too has our insight into the causes of homelessness. Two main approaches dominate the debate. The first suggests that homelessness is the result of an individual's actions and choices. The second, that it is the result of wider structural problems outside their control. This sets up a dichotomy between what Jacobs et al. (1999) termed 'minimalist' and 'maximalist' approaches and what Neale (1997) refered to as 'agency' or 'structural' explanations.

From the mid-1970s to the late 1990s, at a political level, the causes of homelessness were increasingly associated with the minimalist approach and cited individual pathology of the homeless person as the main underlying cause (Jacobs et al., 1999). The 'agency' explanation locates causes of homelessness either in an individual's inadequacy, for example, learning difficulty or mental health problems, or in their behaviour, such as drinking or drug abuse. The agency explanation seems to have been something of a preoccupation amongst academics, at least until the late 1990s, with ten times more reports on homelessness with a focus on mental illness than with a focus on poverty or housing (Juliá and Hartnett, 1999).

Individual pathology approaches hint at the notion of deserving and undeserving homeless and has found its way into homelessness legislation in the UK in the form of 'intentionality'. That is to say, some people might be without shelter but would not be considered eligible for support or housing if they were perceived to have brought their homelessness about by their own actions.

Since the arrival of social exclusion as a basis for policy development, there has been a return to a focus on structural causes. Recently, therefore, a structural view, which places the responsibility for homelessness outside the control of the homeless person has been increasingly dominant in the theoretical debates around homelessness (Neale, 1997; Kennett and Marsh, 1999).

For those who prefer the structural explanation, understanding is complicated further by disagreement over the nature of structural causes. It remains unclear whether they are a result of the failure of the housing market to provide adequate, affordable housing, or are underpinned by wider, global economic factors, linked to what Kennett and Marsh (1999) consider the 'new terrain' of homelessness. The fiscal crisis affecting local, national and global economies has brought about major structural changes with resultant reshaping of welfare policies, ostensibly in an unavoidable attempt to curb public spending (Foster and Plowden, 1996). These structural changes have led to a weakening of the welfare support system in many developing countries and an increased risk of poverty and homelessness for the mass of the population (Kennett and Marsh, 1999). As we will see in Chapter 8, this new understanding of increasing vulnerability for the mass of the population in industrialised and transitional countries has resonance with homelessness in developing countries, where state-run welfare safety-nets have never existed.[3] Thus, developing countries might offer an insight into things to come in industrialised countries.

Whilst this vulnerability could affect most people, it does not affect them constantly or equally. As Forrest (1999: 17) notes, 'there is a continuum of security and insecurity in terms of factors such as employment, income, family life and social networks'. One could argue that such a continuum always existed. What is new is the degree to which many more households find themselves moving, both backwards and forwards, along it as the social networks and welfare regimes, which once kept them constant, decay.

Just as households are subjected differently to the risk of homelessness, so they also experience and perceive their place on the risk continuum differently. Even at the extreme end of the continuum, for example, in local authority shelter, different households experience homelessness differently, depending on a range of factors, including whether they see their life chances as being in an upwards or downwards trajectory. In Chapter 5, we posit that having the possibility of an upward trajectory identifies the boundary between homelessness and inadequate housing.

An alternative view of the structural approach suggests that a fundamental failure of the housing market to deliver adequate, affordable housing plays a major part in the increase in homelessness. Most industrialised countries have relatively well-functioning housing markets and housing finance markets. Except for a few years following the massive displacements and urban destruction of the Second World War, not since the 19th century could homelessness be attributed to an acute housing shortage. However, in the UK, and to an extent the USA, inflation in house prices, coupled with a reduction in building, particularly of social housing by local authorities, have impacted on the availability of affordable housing. This impact has not been felt equally in all places. In the USA, Honig and Filer (1993) suggest that the local variations in homelessness are linked to an imbalance between the cost of available housing and a household's income. It is intuitively evident that, if a household has insufficient income or capital to afford whatever housing is available when they need it, they are in danger of having nowhere to live and thus will become homeless unless helped by welfare measures. While this rather narrow housing market view does not account for all homelessness, it is a factor in regional and local differences, and in the existence of homeless people and empty housing stock in the same locality.

These two main approaches to the causes of homelessness raise dilemmas for governments. The structural approach requires wider societal and economic change, such as improved housing supply or increased employment. The agency approach, however, requires assistance that is more individually directed at the homeless person. Moreover, within these two approaches, we see the emergence of the binary concept of 'deserving' and 'undeserving' homeless people. This is critical to our understanding of the development of welfare policy. If the structural approach is adopted, it could be argued that most homelessness is beyond individual control. Therefore all homeless people are equally deserving of support. If an agency approach is accepted, governments must then decide how to prioritise assistance. It would seem inappropriate to treat someone suffering mental illness, or fleeing an unsafe home, in the same way as someone perceived simply to be willingly vagrant.

Whether the structural or agency explanation is adopted, it is clear that homelessness is a dynamic process rather than a static state. Fitzpatrick (1999) and Anderson and Tulloch (2000) amongst others have sought to explore it using a pathways framework. The metaphor of a 'pathway' was first introduced to help understand peoples' engagement with housing, rather than homelessness. Clapham (2002: 122) suggests that the housing pathway of a household is 'the continually changing set of relationships and interactions which it experiences over time in its consumption of housing'. The strength of the pathways framework for homelessness is that it acknowledges that people move in and out of homelessness, sometimes on numerous occasions, and that it cannot be understood in isolation from issues and relationships before and after a period of homelessness. Thus, homelessness is seen as an episode within a person's housing pathway (Clapham, 2003). This is a particularly valuable framework for understanding homelessness in developing countries because, as this work will show, for many in the developing world homelessness is an integral, necessary and even accepted element of a range of survival and housing strategies (Speak, 2004). Moreover, the pathway approach allows us to see how both agency and structural explanations play their part in homelessness. For example, while wider structural issues of housing shortage or poverty underpin homelessness in developing countries, not all people experiencing these things are homeless. Understanding the pathways of those people who are homeless helps us to understand what it is about their individual action or agency which makes some more vulnerable to homelessness than others.

In contrast to industrialised countries, as will be shown later, homelessness in developing countries is much more associated with housing market deficiencies. In most developing countries, there is a quantitative shortfall in housing, at least in urban areas, often of quite large proportions. In addition, the housing supply is lumpy in terms of cost and quality so that there may be large gaps in particular parts of the cost and quality ranges and oversupply in others. Furthermore, there is a fundamental problem that many households, sometimes half or more of the population, cannot afford a dwelling of any sort and have to share or multi-occupy housing, or build informal dwellings on land they do not own. Each of these solutions leads to a risk that the housing conditions experienced by these large numbers of households might constitute homelessness. The supply issues will be discussed in detail in Chapter 3 and the definitional issues in Chapters 4 and 5, but it is evident from just these few sentences that inefficiencies in the housing supply market have much greater influence on homelessness in developing countries than in industrialised countries.

Regardless of the underlying causes of homelessness in either industrialised or developing countries, some groups of people, especially women and children, are significantly more vulnerable. The gendering of homelessness and housing policy, and the differing effects on men and women of changes to the housing market have been well documented in industrialised countries (see e.g. Novac et al., 1996; Edgar, 2001). Early feminist theory argued that women were at a disadvantage in the housing market, being less able to house themselves independently of men. There remains some truth in the assumption that patriarchal values condition the production of and access to housing for owner occupation and renting, even in industrialised countries (Watson, 1987; Watson, 1988, cited in Neale, 1997). However, welfare policy, including social housing policy in many industrialised countries, has favoured women over men (Pascall, 1991, cited in Neale 1997; MacGregor, 1999).

Even without welfare support systems, women of industrialised countries are considerably better able to establish independent housing than many of their counterparts in developing countries. Marriage and a male breadwinner is no longer the only, or even the main route, to a home for women in industrialised countries, since the second feminist movement of the latter part of the 20th century (Gonzalez Lopez and Solsona, 2000; Doherty, 2001). This is not the case for most women in developing countries, who still rely on marriage as their only route to a home independent from their birth families (Speak, 2005). Thus, some of the early feminist arguments about patriarchal dominance are most strongly realised in the housing and homelessness of women in developing countries.

Theory on the feminisation of poverty also offers a valuable perspective on women's homelessness. Glendinning and Millar (1992), Daly (2002) and Ungerson (1990) all argue that women are disproportionately at risk of poverty, in part because patriarchal society and institutions work to reinforce women's dependency on men, particularly within the domestic sphere and partly because of the state's dependence on them as carers. This may be particularly true in very patriarchal societies, such as Bangladesh (Schuler et al., 1996) as we will discuss in Chapter 8.

Defining and counting homelessness

Controversy abounds about the value of trying to define, and subsequently count, homeless people. As we will show in Chapter 6, the very act of counting implies that a government is acknowledging homelessness as a problem. Moreover, where that government is presenting itself to the international community as modernising and progressive, to highlight homelessness is to highlight its own failure to provide adequately for its citizens and uphold human rights (Jacobs et al., 1999). This is at the heart of the services–statistics paradox in which countries with services directed at mitigating or eradicating homelessness tend to have more homeless people than those which do not (FEANTSA, 1999).

Any definition of homelessness which is not too all encompassing to be of value immediately identifies some people as high priority for assistance. This may be because they are seen as being in greater need than others, even those in very similar situations. Alternatively, it may be because they are seen as more 'deserving' (Rosenthal, 2000): see Chapter 11. We discuss the issues of definition in detail in Chapter 4.

Definitions are a means of identifying who is, and conversely who is not, homelessness. Thus, they tend to be absolute, people are either defined as being homeless or not homeless. Typologies, however, are somewhat different, seeking to categorise homeless people, for example, by their characteristics or needs. Such typologies could be useful in assisting governments and NGOs in allocating limited resources to support homeless people to improve their own situation.

Our increased understanding of the 'new terrain' of homelessness in industrialised countries shows it to be underpinned by a greater vulnerability to unemployment and poverty and increased insecurity for the masses. One might expect, then, that Western typologies might be useful in defining and describing homelessness in developing countries, where poverty is so deeply entrenched. Indeed, in the CARDO survey, researchers in the nine countries were asked to comment specifically on the applicability of the Western typologies which, we had written about in preparing UNCHS (2000), to homelessness in their countries. This provides the only detailed comparative study of this sort and one of the few occasions where homelessness in industrialised and developing countries have been subjected to such analysis. Because of its helpfulness in comparing the well-researched circumstances in the industrialised world with the under-researched conditions in the developing world, it provides a useful introductory analysis within this book. Thus, we present it in some detail in Chapter 4 as part of the long process of trying to identify, define and categorise homelessness in developing countries which takes up the first half of the book.

Because of the complexity and progression of homelessness, continuums feature in typologies and definitions, two layers being described by commentators:

1   typologies as continuums (Watson and Austerberry, 1986; Neale, 1997), and
2   continuums of definitions (Williams and Cheal, 2001).

We deal briefly with the former here and with the latter in Chapter 4. In a context of insecurity, one approach to understanding is that of a continuum of homelessness or of a continuum from home to homelessness (Watson and Austerberry, 1986; Neale, 1997). Looking at homelessness in this way enables it to be defined as something other than an absolute which places people in a simple administrative category.

At one end of the latter, more all encompassing, continuum lie satisfactory and secure forms of housing and at the other lies sleeping rough. Similarly, Neale (1997) sees homelessness as a highly ambiguous and intangible phenomenon that is integral to the housing system and inseparable from other aspects of housing need. Thus, she argues, theories of homelessness and policies to tackle it cannot be separated from other aspects of housing policy.

This lends itself reasonably well to a developing countries context because of the vast span of housing quality and security which is evident in those countries and because much of what might be considered as housing in those countries would be considered inadequate or even homelessness by Western standards (see Chapter 4). Thus, we can view inadequately housed people in developing countries as being somewhere along the continuum. The continuum approach also allows us to recognise the fluidity of people's housing and homelessness situations in developing countries over time, often as a consequence of their conscious decision to move between poor housing and the street (Speak, 2004).

Conclusions

There is a need to develop knowledge and understanding of homelessness in the particular circumstances of acute housing shortages, urbanisation of poverty, rapid population growth, and weak governance and fiscal systems found in developing countries. Just as there is a housing literature specific to developing countries, so there is a need for a homelessness literature focusing on developing countries' circumstances

Our current understanding of homelessness, and the factors leading to it, has mainly been developed in the context of industrialised countries. In this context, homelessness fits within a general welfare agenda. Where it occurs it is seen as the most abject manifestation of poverty and societal failing and something about which governments or local authorities should act. Action is expected, either at a macro level, in terms of ensuring adequate housing is available, or at an individual level, in ensuring that individuals are able to access and afford housing, and are capable of living in it.

However, the context in developing countries is completely different. The scale is, by any definition, huge and homelessness is just one of a multitude of equally pressing social problems governments are trying to address. The linking of home to kinship, the role of the extended family, the weaker position of women in society, the different attitudes to ownership and the broad range of political contexts in developing countries all serve to make our current understanding, based on industrialised perceptions, values, culture and society, inappropriate for the developing countries context.

2 Homelessness and international housing policy

Introduction

In developing countries, it is impossible to separate homelessness from the context of housing supply policy as there is a severe shortage of accommodation for low-income households. This is in contrast to most industrialised countries where housing shortage and supply failure are not major contributors to homelessness. Edgar et al. (2002), however, note that, although European countries have no overall housing shortage, in some regions the operation of both private and public sectors leads to effective shortages for more vulnerable people. In this chapter, we deal with the international policy context within which governments work to formulate their priorities for housing policy and practice and how they impact on homelessness. Shortages in housing supply are universal in the nine countries in the CARDO study and elsewhere. For example, India lacked nearly 19 million dwellings in 2002 (Government of India, 1996). We will focus on the shortages and their national policy backgrounds in detail in Chapter 3.

Two main strands of international policy have impacted homeless people: housing supply policy and human rights policy. The former has addressed the scale and nature of the housing supply system which has failed to provide sufficient low-cost dwellings in the appropriate locations for all households. The latter has provided the international pressure on governments to improve their housing supply systems to provide for the poorest households and to consider separate streams of housing supply for them.

Housing policy: the international context

The context in which housing is provided has progressed from welfare provision through to housing as a basic human right. Programmes have moved from subsidising the cost of a few high-quality (but usually small) dwellings in well-serviced neighbourhoods to policies aimed at enabling the markets to provide

Table 2.1 The evolution of housing policies promoted by international agencies for developing countries

Phase and Approximate Dates	Focus of attention	Major instruments used	Key documents
Modernisation and urban growth: 1960s–early 1970s	Physical planning and production of shelter by public agencies	Blueprint planning: direct construction Eradication of informal settlements	Vancouver Declaration (UNCHS 1976);
Redistribution with growth/basic needs: mid 1970s–mid 1980s	State support to self-help ownership on a project-by-project basis	Recognition of informal sector Squatter upgrading and sites-and-services Subsidies to land and housing	Shelter, Poverty and Basic Needs (World Bank, 1980); World Bank evaluations of sites and services: 1981–3 (e.g. Bamberger et al., 1982; Keare and Parris, 1982; Mayo et al., 1986; Mayo and Gross, 1987) UNICEF Urban Basic Services
The enabling approach/ urban management: late 1980s–early 1990s	Securing an enabling framework for action by people, the private sector and markets	Public/private partnership; Community participation; Land assembly and housing finance; capacity-building	Global Shelter Strategy to the Year 2000 (UNCHS, 1990); Urban Policy and Economic Development (World Bank, 1991); Cities, Poverty and People (UNDP, 1991); Agenda 21 (UNCED, 1992); Housing: Enabling Markets to Work (World Bank, 1993)
Sustainable urban development: mid 1990s onwards	Holistic planning to balance efficiency, equity and sustainability	As above, with more emphasis on environmental management and poverty-alleviation	Sustainable Human Settlements Development: Implementing Agenda 21 (UNCHS, 1994)

HABITAT II: 1996	'Adequate shelter for all' and 'sustainable human settlements development'	*The Habitat Agenda* (UNCHS, 1997); *Global Report on Human Settlements* (UNCHS, 1996)
Millennium Summit 2000	Culmination and integration of all previous policy improvements	United Nations Millennium Declaration (United Nations, 2000); Millennium Development Goals
Istanbul+5: 2001	Review of the Habitat Agenda Process; Renewal of the Habitat Agenda commitments and seeking/devising more effective strategies	Declaration on cities and other human settlements in the new millennium (UN-Habitat, 2001); *Cities in a Globalizing World* (UNCHS, 2001a); *The State of the World's Cities* (UNCHS, 2001b); *Implementing the Habitat Agenda: The 1996-2001* Experience (UNCHS, 2001)

Source: UN-Habitat (2006)

for most people. Table 2.1. shows the evolution of housing policies promoted by international agencies for developing countries since 1960.[1]

International housing policy affecting developing countries has its roots in the search for low-cost solutions to housing for the majority of people who flooded to their cities from the end of the Second World War onwards. In the early post-Second World War years, house building was regarded as a social overhead cost to economic development. It was assumed that good housing assisted economic development and, therefore, investments in housing were worth making. As such, it became a suitable case for treatment by international aid organisations and lenders. Separate strands of funding of developments in Latin America by USAID (Harris and Arku, 2007), a growing interest in designing housing for tropical conditions (e.g. Fry and Drew, 1964; Koenigsberger, 1973), and the establishment of building research institutes in the colonies came together in an effort to provide low-cost housing of high physical quality. The dwellings resulting were inevitably small and had to be heavily subsidised to reach low-income people.

In the late 1960s and early 1970s, John Turner's writings (1968, 1972, 1976) arising from his experiences of squatter invasions in Peru, established self-help housing as a dominant concept for the next decades. His arguments were timely, coming as they did when city administrations were being swamped by the pace of urban growth, and became conventional wisdom in international circles if not in country policies. Turner's arguments were:

- that housing did something for its occupants' welfare and social and economic progress;
- that people were able to provide it for themselves incrementally;
- that informal suburbs could be the solution rather than the problem; and
- that improving and servicing what was there was the way forward, rather than bulldozing it away and starting again.

Turner's theories have been heavily criticised (Burgess, 1982, 1985; Ward, 1982) but the idea that relatively poor people can be responsible for their own housing solutions has been hugely influential ever since.

In 1976, in response to the growing development challenges arising in human settlements, the United Nations convened the first UN Habitat Conference in Vancouver (United Nations, 1976). This led to the Vancouver Declaration on Human Settlements and the setting up of UNCHS (Habitat). The Vancouver Declaration affirmed that:

> Adequate shelter and services are a basic human right which places an obligation on Governments to ensure their attainment by all people … Governments should endeavour to remove all impediments hindering attainment of these goals.
>
> (UNCHS, 1976: III, para. 8)

and

> The highest priority should be placed on the rehabilitation of expelled and homeless people who have been displaced by natural or man-made catastrophes, and especially by the act of foreign aggression.
>
> (UNCHS, 1976: II, para. 15)

In 1982, the General Assembly included homeless people in its resolution to 'Consolidate and share knowledge and relevant experience gained since Habitat I, so as to provide "tested and practical alternatives for improving the shelter and neighbourhoods of the poor and disadvantaged and for providing shelter for the homeless"' (United Nations, 1982: para. 3b).

The United Nations Centre for Human Settlements, UNCHS (Habitat – now UN-Habitat), was established in 1978 to promote the Vancouver Action Plan and monitor the implementation of housing policies around the world. It is the main agency for policies to eradicate homelessness but has, so far, paid only limited attention to homeless people, mainly through the publication of *Strategies to Combat Homelessness* (UNCHS, 2000).

International Year of Shelter for the Homeless (IYSH), 1987

The IYSH was intended to focus international attention on the problems of homelessness and inadequate housing in developing countries at a time when there was great concern that the shelter conditions of the majority of people were continuing to deteriorate.

The objective of activities connected with the IYSH was, thus,

> to improve the shelter and neighbourhoods of some of the poor and disadvantaged by the end of 1987, particularly in the developing countries, according to national priorities, and to demonstrate by the year 2000 ways and means of improving the shelter and neighbourhoods of the poor and disadvantaged.
>
> (United Nations, 1982: para. 2)

> Develop and demonstrate new ways of supporting the efforts of the homeless, poor and disadvantaged to secure their own shelter as a basis for formulating new national policies and strategies for improving their shelter conditions by the year 2000.
>
> (United Nations, 1982: para. 3c)

15

IYSH stimulated a wide range of international and national initiatives aimed at improving the shelter conditions of the poor but not, generally, people without shelter or neighbourhoods, despite its name.

The grouping of poor housing together with homelessness in this and other international initiatives allows the more organised and easier-to-reach groups (those who are in organised neighbourhoods with community-based organisations) to dominate the agenda. One of the arguments of this book, and our work in general, is that homeless people need to be separated conceptually from those who are merely inadequately housed for some policy initiatives to prevent this hijacking of the assistance available away from those most in need. In Chapter 5 we attempt to draw a somewhat fuzzy boundary between the people whose inadequate housing should be considered as so poor as to render them homeless and those who should not be included in the homeless population.

The Global Strategy for Shelter to the Year 2000 (GSS) and the enabling approach

The experiences of the IYSH led to the GSS, which the UN General Assembly formally adopted in 1988. The GSS provided 'the framework for a continuous process towards the goal of facilitating adequate shelter for all by the year 2000' (UNCHS, 1990: para. 22). The fundamental policy change put forward in the GSS was:

> the adoption of an enabling approach whereby the full potential and resources of all actors in the shelter production and improvement process are mobilized; but the final decision on how to house themselves is left to the people concerned.
> (UNCHS, 1990: para. 14)

The enabling approach had first been described in detail in the World Bank Housing Sector Paper, appropriately subtitled 'Enabling markets to work' (World Bank, 1993). It theorises that the six inputs to the housing supply process present bottlenecks to supply in most developing countries and that they should be freed up by government action. Five of the six are expressed as markets: land, finance, labour (the construction industry), building materials and infrastructure. The sixth is the government's regulatory framework.

The underlying philosophy of the enabling approach is that governments should withdraw from direct provision of housing. In the neo-liberal approach of the World Bank's housing researchers at the time, the thinking was that, if governments took their part in influencing the inputs, the market would provide all the housing needed (Malpezzi, 1990). Thus, the enabling approach to shelter development and improvement calls for a policy environment in which the government, for the most part, does not supply housing directly. Rather, it facilitates production by other actors in the sector: private developers, non-governmental organisations and community groups. It enables them to contribute fully, and in their most appropriate roles, in the achievement of adequate shelter for all (World Bank, 1993; UN-Habitat, 2006). This paradigm rejects the interventionist provision of public housing by the state which presupposes that the other actors in the housing sector cannot fulfil the right to adequate housing (Angel, 2000). Thus, while the other actors develop and improve housing in the most efficient manner possible, governments should target their limited resources more effectively where they are most needed (UN-Habitat, 2006). One such area is in direct interventions to enable the poorest to gain access to adequate housing.

The enabling approach does not, however, mean a lesser role, or no role at all, for government, as is commonly misconceived. Decisive and coherent action on the part of government is required. The intention was not to reduce governmental responsibility but rather to change it: to rationalise and optimise the activities and resources of all the actors in housing development. Indeed, the enabling approach works within a context of housing rights, affirming '[t]he right to adequate shelter is recognised universally and constitutes the basis for national obligations to meet shelter needs' (UNCHS, 1990: para. 13). In serving as 'enablers' in the housing sector, governments should withdraw from a role of providers of housing and, instead, play a more effective role in facilitating the construction and improvement of housing, especially by and for the poor. Within this enabling environment, all the actors in the housing supply process should be able to function more effectively, and in ways which are compatible with the needs of the poor. The institutional arrangements underpinning housing development and improvement are thus a critical element of the enabling approach (UNCHS, 1991; UN-Habitat, 2006).

Although the enabling approach is strongly market-oriented, the GSS underlines that

> governmental intervention may be required, in many instances to remove or offset market imperfections, and, in some specific cases, a policy may be justified to meet the social welfare requirements of the very poor and destitute.
>
> (UNCHS, 1990: para. 54)

This legitimises direct provision for households for whom any market solution is inappropriate, including, we would contend, many homeless people. Indeed, the enabling approach should liberate government resources from direct provision of housing for ordinary households. Instead they should be used for more urgent housing issues such as relief of homelessness.

There was not intended to be any blueprint for the enabling approach – countries should adapt the concept to their local circumstances and prioritise different elements in locally relevant ways. This was a risky strategy, however, and though many countries adopted enabling shelter strategies, they often failed in implementation. Furthermore, with the less direct role for government in housing supply, housing issues slowly disappeared from many national strategies and from the international development agenda (UN-Habitat, 2006).

The Millennium Development Goals

The United Nations Millennium Development Goals (MDGs) are included in the Millennium Declaration of 2000 (United Nations, 2000). It is claimed by the United Nations (2005) that they 'have galvanised unprecedented efforts to meet the needs of the world's poorest'. It is true that they have become the major drivers of international development policy, especially donor funding, since that time. However, we would argue that the poorest people may be left out of the benefits.

MDG No. 7 seeks to ensure environmental sustainability. Within it, target 10 focuses on halving the gross shortfalls in servicing and target 11 seeks to achieve significant improvement in the lives of at least 100 million slum dwellers by 2020. Its only indicator (32) is tenure, but there are many other ways in which improvements could be made. MDGs are the context for most international and donor efforts in the human settlements field since 2000. However, it is easy for governments, donors and international agencies to exclude homeless people as they do not live in slums. Furthermore, countries are likely to 'cherry-pick' the households who are easy to help. Yet, if the trouble is taken to reach homeless people, a significant improvement in their lives may be more effective for less cost than in the case of those people who are already housed, albeit inadequately. Such improvements can be achieved, for example, by opening disused buildings, or upper floors of buildings, in city centres as hostel accommodation, leading to significant improvements in shelter and safety. These will be dealt with further in Chapter 13.

Table 2.2 Millennium Development Goal 7: *Ensure environmental sustainability* and targets most directly relevant to Enabling Shelter Strategies

Target	Indicators
Target 10: Halve, by 2015, the proportion of people without sustainable access to safe drinking water and sanitation	Indicator 30: Proportion of population with sustainable access to improved water source
	Indicator 31: Proportion of people with access to improved sanitation
Target 11: By 2020, to have achieved a significant improvement in the lives of at least 100 million slum dwellers	Indicator 32: Proportion of people with access to secure tenure

Source of indicators: United Nations (2005)

Human rights and the right to housing

Human rights are defined and established in the International Bill of Rights, which consists of three instruments: the Universal Declaration of Human Rights (United Nations, 1948), the International Covenant on Economic, Social and Cultural Rights (United Nations, 1966) and the International Covenant on Civil and Political Rights (United Nations, 1966). Through Article 25.1 of the Universal Declaration of Human Rights (United Nations, 1948) everyone has the right to a standard of living adequate for health and well-being, including housing. The International Covenant on Economic, Social and Cultural Rights (United Nations, 1966) contains perhaps the most significant foundation of the right to housing found in international human rights law. Through article 11.1:

> [states] recognize the right of everyone to an adequate standard of living … including adequate food, clothing and housing, and to the continuous improvement of living conditions. The States Parties will take appropriate steps to ensure the realization of this right.

All women are accorded the right to housing and to enjoy adequate living conditions, particularly in relation to housing, sanitation, electricity and water supply, under article 14 of the Convention on the Elimination of All Forms of Discrimination Against Women (United Nations, 1979).

The particular housing rights of children are addressed by both the United Nations Declaration of the Rights of the Child (United Nations, 1959) and the Convention on the Rights of the Child (UNHCHR, 1989). Article 27 of the latter requires that, where parents are in need, states should 'provide material assistance and support programmes, particularly with regard to nutrition, clothing and housing' (UNHCHR, n.d.). The right to adequate housing forms a cornerstone of the Global Shelter Strategy. All citizens of all states, however poor, have a right to expect their governments to accept a fundamental obligation to protect and improve houses and neighbourhoods, rather than damage or destroy them. Adequate housing is defined as meaning: 'adequate privacy, adequate space, adequate security, adequate lighting and ventilation, adequate basic infrastructure and adequate location with regard to work and basic facilities – all at a reasonable cost' (UNCHS, 1990).

Chapter 7 of Agenda 21 adopted by the UN Conference on Environment and Development (UNCED, 1992) contains clauses referring to aspects of the human right to adequate housing. These include the recognition that 'access to safe and healthy shelter is essential to a person's physical, psychological, social and economic well-being and should be a fundamental part of national and international action' (UNCED, 1992: para. 7.6). The writers of Agenda 21 acknowledged that there were at least one billion people (and rising) without access to safe and healthy shelter in

1992. They stressed that all countries should take immediate measures to provide shelter to their homeless poor (UNCED, 1992: para. 9a).

Agenda 21 also calls on governments to accelerate efforts to help the poorest people in cities by 'Providing specific assistance to the poorest of the urban poor through, *inter alia*, the creation of urban infrastructure in order to reduce hunger and homelessness, and the provision of adequate community services' (UNCED, 1992: para. 16.b.ii).

The Universal Declaration of Human Rights (paragraph 15) places the highest priority on the rehabilitation of expelled and homeless people who have been displaced by natural or human-made catastrophes. All countries have the duty to cooperate fully in order to guarantee that such displaced people are allowed to return to their homes and given the right to enjoy their properties without interference (UNCHS, n.d.).

It is clear that human rights are interdependent so that the full enjoyment of a right to housing is connected with many other rights such as human dignity, non-discrimination, an adequate standard of living, freedom to choose one's residence, freedom of association and expression, and security of person.

> [N]ot to be subjected to arbitrary interference with one's privacy, family, home or correspondence is indispensable for the right to adequate housing to be realized, possessed and maintained by all groups in society.
>
> At the same time, having access to adequate, safe and secure housing substantially strengthens the likelihood of people being able to enjoy certain additional rights. (UNHCHR, n.d.)

As such, housing is a foundation from which other legal entitlements to housing and living conditions, to environmental hygiene and mental and physical health, can be achieved (UNHCHR, n.d.).

Other international organisations have also formulated statutes addressing housing rights. The revised European Social Charter (1996), article 31, takes up housing rights, as follows:

> With a view to ensuring the effective exercise of the right to housing, the parties undertake to take measures designed: (1) to promote access to housing of an adequate standard; (2) to prevent and reduce homelessness with a view to its gradual elimination; (3) to make the price of housing accessible to those without adequate resources. (UNCHS, 2000)

Realising the right to housing

The United Nations Housing Rights Programme (UNHRP) and resolution 16/7 of the Commission on Human Settlements recognise that the realisation of the right to housing will be a progressive process extending over decades (UNCHS, n.d.). The basic human right to adequate shelter and services places an obligation on governments to ensure that all people can attain them. This begins with direct assistance to the least advantaged through guided programmes of self-help and community action. Governments should, therefore, endeavour to remove all impediments and involve people directly in shaping the policies and programmes affecting their lives (UNCHS, n.d.).

The Habitat Agenda (UNCHS, 1997: para. 60) defines adequate shelter at some length as follows:

> Adequate shelter means more than a roof over one's head. It also means adequate privacy; adequate space; physical accessibility; adequate security; security of tenure; structural stability and durability; adequate lighting, heating and ventilation; adequate basic infrastructure, such as water-supply, sanitation and waste-management facilities; suitable environmental quality and health-related factors; and adequate and accessible location with regard to work and basic facilities: all of which should be available at an affordable cost. Adequacy should be determined together with the people concerned, bearing in mind the prospect for gradual development. Adequacy often varies from country to country, since it depends on specific cultural, social, environmental and economic factors. Gender-specific and age-specific factors, such as the exposure of children and women to toxic substances, should be considered in this context.

The Programme of Action of the World Summit on Social Development (United Nations, 1995: para. 34.h) stresses that urban poverty should be addressed through special measures to protect, among others, homeless people, and to ensure that they are integrated into their communities.

The Habitat Agenda, the main political document from the Istanbul Habitat II Summit in 1996 and adopted by 171 governments, addresses the realisation of the right to adequate housing. Paragraphs 26, 39 and 61 are the most focused on housing rights.[2] Paragraph 26 reaffirms a commitment to ensuring the full and progressive realisation of human rights in housing. It recognises an obligation on governments to enable people to obtain shelter and to protect and improve dwellings and neighbourhoods. It commits signatory governments to improving living and working conditions equitably and sustainably so that everyone will have shelter that is adequate, is free from discrimination and has legal security of tenure (UNCHS, n.d.).

Paragraph 39 commits governments to enabling people to obtain shelter, and to protect and improve dwellings and neighbourhoods so that everyone will have access to adequate shelter. Paragraph 61 reiterates that the provision of adequate housing for everyone requires action not only by governments but by all sectors of society. Within an enabling approach, governments should:

- promote, protect and ensure the full and progressive realisation of the right to adequate housing through laws that prohibit any discrimination on any ground;
- provide legal security of tenure and equal access to land for all, as well as effective protection from forced evictions;
- adopt policies aimed at making housing habitable, affordable and accessible, monitoring and evaluating housing conditions, including the extent of homelessness and inadequate housing and, in consultation with the people, formulate, adopt and implement appropriate housing policies to address the problems. (UNCHS, n.d.)

According to UNCHS (n.d.), about half of the world's national constitutions refer to general obligations within the housing sphere or specifically to the right to adequate housing. The overwhelming majority of constitutions make reference to rights related to housing rights. These include the right to freedom of movement and to choose one's residence, the right to privacy and respect for the home, the right to equal treatment under the law, the right to dignity, the right to security of the person, some rights to property or the peaceful enjoyment of possessions. Perhaps the most recently developed is the Constitution of Iraq agreed in October 2005 (Iraqi Constitutional Committee, 2005). In it, each person has the right to personal privacy as long as it does not violate the rights of others and general morality (article 17(1)) and the sanctity of the home is protected (article 17(2)). There are also provisions to protect private property in article 23. The existence of such provisions does not necessarily mean that they are translated into performance.

Governments' responsibilities in housing rights

The main document for understanding governments' responsibilities in housing rights is the International Covenant on Economic, Social and Cultural Rights (United Nations, 1966). Article 2.1 reads as follows:

Each State Party to the present Covenant undertakes to take steps, individually and through international assistance and co-operation, especially economic and technical, to the maximum of its available resources, with a view to achieving progressively the full realization of the rights recognized in the present Covenant by all appropriate means, including particularly the adoption of legislative measures.

As UNHCHR (n.d.) explains, three phrases in this article are particularly important for our understanding of the obligations of governments. These are: 'undertakes to take steps … by all appropriate means'; 'to the maximum of its available resources'; and 'to achieving progressively'. In this, 'undertakes to take steps

… by all appropriate means' means that deliberate, concrete and clearly targeted legislative, administrative, judicial, economic, social and educational steps must be undertaken immediately towards meeting the states' obligations. Each state should adopt a national housing strategy reflecting extensive and genuine consultation with, and participation by, all social sectors, including the homeless and the inadequately housed and their representatives and organisations. 'To the maximum of its available resources' means that both the resources within a state and those provided internationally must be utilised equitably and effectively. Even when they are demonstrably inadequate, and even in times of severe economic contraction or structural adjustment, vulnerable members of society must be protected by the adoption of relatively low-cost targeted programmes. The 'to achieving progressively' means that states should move as quickly and effectively as possible to ensure full realisation of housing rights. There must be a 'continuous improvement of living conditions' (article 11(1I)). Any deliberately retrogressive measures would be difficult to justify (UNHCHR, n.d.). These measures mean that no state can plead lack of capability and ignore housing rights-based actions.

The right to housing has been interpreted by the first Special Rapporteur for UN-Habitat as implying that a claim can be made upon society for housing resources for homeless people and those inadequately housed or lacking the bundle of entitlements implicitly linked with housing rights (UNCHS, 1995).

But the right to housing does *not* imply that

- states are required to build housing for the entire population;
- states should provide housing free of charge to all who request it;
- states must necessarily fulfil all aspects of this right immediately;
- states should exclusively entrust either themselves or the unregulated market to ensuring this right to all; or
- this right will manifest itself in precisely the same manner in all circumstances and locations (UNCHS, 1995).

It is clear from the International Covenant (United Nations, 1966) that states cannot wait until economic conditions are conducive for fulfilment of housing rights. All states are expected to provide at least for a minimum level of each human right and states within which any significant number of individuals is deprived of basic shelter are *prima facie* failing their obligations under the covenant (UN-Habitat, 2002).

National interpretations of the right to housing: the case of South Africa

The South African government wrote the new constitution at a time when rights were becoming a prominent part of the international discourse on housing, so its interpretation is a useful model of the internationally agreed role of the state translated into local intention. Chapter 2 of the 1996 Constitution of South Africa forms a Bill of Rights. Section 26 deals with housing and defines the right to housing as follows:

1 Everyone has a right to adequate housing.
2 The State must take reasonable legislative and other measures, within its available resources, to achieve the progressive realisation of this right.
3 No one may be evicted from their home, or have their home demolished, without an order of court made after considering all the relevant circumstances. No legislation may permit arbitrary evictions.

(Republic of South Africa, 1996)

The rights of children are also defined with reference to housing as follows in section 27: every child has the right: 'c) to basic nutrition, shelter, basic health care services and social services'. There is also provision for equitable access to land (section 25) and equality of treatment (section 9), unpicking the apartheid system. In its contrast to that discredited system, the new constitution was radical and, as de Vos (2001: 260) calls it, 'transformative'. However, the interpretations added by the courts in connection with housing the poor have not been as radical and transformative as might have been hoped. The key case in this, and the one which is now referred to all over the world, is that involving Mrs Irene Grootboom[3] and her fellow squatters of Wallacedene near Cape Town.

The Grootboom case

In 1998, about 900 residents of Wallacedene squatter settlement on the edge of Cape Town had moved to occupy neighbouring land whose owner applied to the court for eviction. This was agreed and a date set. However, those who had moved found that their former living space had been occupied by someone else and they had nowhere to which to return. When their new homes were bulldozed following the court order, they moved on to a sports field and erected shelters. The shelters and services there were entirely inadequate for the 350 adults and 510 children so, on behalf of the others, Mrs Grootboom appealed to the Cape of Good Hope High Court on the grounds that their right to adequate housing and their children's right to basic shelter had been denied. This court decided that the state had a rational housing programme in place designed to solve a pressing need in the context of few resources. It was too soon after the constitution had come into place to expect it to be implemented fully and the court agreed with the provincial and national government that providing adequate shelter for the appellant and her group would divert scarce resources from the main housing task (Huchzermeyer, 2003). This was a 'flood-gates' argument, conjuring up images of hordes of desperate people besieging municipal offices demanding housing if the most needy were prioritised through a court ruling. The judge felt that Mrs Grootboom and her neighbours had no claim on the authorities with respect to their housing rights. The rights of the children to shelter, however, was found to have been breached so the court recommended that a bare minimum of tents, portable latrines and regular supply of water (in this case by tanker) should be supplied until such time as the parents could house their children themselves (Huchzermeyer, 2003).

The municipality challenged this ruling in the Constitutional Court. In preparation, the Legal Resources Centre appointed an adviser, Geoff Budlender, as an attorney to the 'friends of the court' (*amici curiae*) to prepare an analysis of the case. In it, *inter alia*, he questioned the government's excuse about whether helping people in dire need would divert resources from the medium- and long-term housing delivery programme. He argued that not only did the government have no data as to the scale of the urgent need but also that the known scale of the backlog did not excuse the government from addressing the needs of the most desperate and vulnerable (Budlender, 2001, quoted in Huchzermeyer, 2003). Budlender's argument seems to have carried the day. The judge in the Constitutional Court ruled that the housing programme must not only serve the medium- and long-term needs but also fulfil the immediate needs arising from crises so that a significant number of desperate people could be afforded relief even though all of them do not receive it immediately (Huchzermeyer, 2003). Thus, the ruling in the Grootboom case gives the government two duties with respect to human rights within its housing policy:

1 to provide for medium- and long-term need through a rational housing delivery system;
2 to provide for at least a substantial proportion of emergency and crisis needs with basic housing and servicing.

The first is currently addressed through the international adoption of the enabling approach. The second establishes an important principle of special case provision for those in crisis need upon which we wish to build in this book.

Donor policies

The concerns and needs of homeless people tend to disappear down inter-agency cracks. In the UN system, UN-Habitat has responsibility for the housing issues involved in homelessness and has an international rapporteur with responsibility for keeping homelessness on the agency's agenda and reporting progress or lack thereof. In addition, the publication of a report on strategies to combat homelessness (UNCHS, 2000) raised the profile of homelessness in the agency for a short while. At other levels, however, homelessness tends to be missed out. The Urban Indicators Programme lacks an indicator for homelessness and so it does not feature in the work of the Global Urban Observatory. The 'durable structures' indicator talks of non-hazardous locations for housing and includes many of the locations of inadequately housed households whom we might consider homeless (see Chapter 5), for example, on garbage tips, highly polluted land and railroads. But this is the only approach the indicators make to homelessness.

There is, however, a strong philosophical pull towards the worst-housed people among the personnel in UN-Habitat. For example, international NGOs representing very poorly housed groups, such as Slum/Shack Dwellers International (SDI), are held in high regard by the senior staff of UN-Habitat, as evidenced by the closeness with which SDI and UN-Habitat work in arranging recent major events such as the first three World Urban Forums in Nairobi in 2002, Barcelona in 2004 and Vancouver in 2006.

Structural Adjustment Programmes

Economic reforms and Structural Adjustment Programmes (SAPs) imposed by the World Bank on borrowing countries between the late 1970s and early 1990s have been blamed for increasing poverty and the growth of the informal sector (e.g. in Berner, 2001). It is self-evident that, in the short term, the reduction of government jobs and spending, and liberalising markets are bound to create unemployment for many and economic uncertainties for most. In Jamaica, for example, the proportion of wage earners whose incomes failed to keep a family increased from 10 per cent in 1977 (before SAP) to 48 per cent in 1985 (after SAP) (Clarke and Howard, 2006). It was expected that people living in poverty would be particularly affected and some country programmes included measures to mitigate the harmful effects of SAP on the poorest households, for example, the PAMSCAD (the Programme of Action to Mitigate the Social Cost of Adjustment and Development),[4] the Emergency Social Relief Programme (ESRP)[5] and Rural Housing Improvement Scheme (RHIS) measures, all in Ghana (Subbarao et al., 1995).

Undoubtedly, many individuals and households whose livelihoods were fundamentally affected by restructuring will have been extremely vulnerable, so increases in homelessness were inevitable. Effects have differed between regions. Subbarao et al. (1995) report that, in South Asia, for example, the landless poor and homeless urban poor (such as construction workers) have been the hardest hit in the short term, while, in Sub-Saharan Africa, the rural and urban informal sectors and marginal farmers suffered most in the short term.

The long-term effects of SAP appear to have been less negative than early predictions feared. They have failed to have strong positive effects on many economies but the harm seems to have been shorter lived and less serious than many commentators predicted. In Jamaica, for example, the proportion of Kingston's population living in poverty and unable to meet minimum food standards was down to 11 per cent by 1999, following the rise up to 1985 (above) during SAP's early years, (Clarke and Howard, 2006). This agrees with Handa and King (1997) who found that, after an initial period of increase, inequality and poverty declined following SAP. However, the decline in poverty may be difficult to sustain in Jamaica as it is partly founded on remittances from overseas.

It is, however, difficult to chart the effects of SAP as they are often combined with other changes and events which affect poverty and inequality. In Zimbabwe, for example, Marquette (1997) discusses the combined and separate effects of SAP and drought in Zimbabwe. She determines that the liberalisation of the economy, leading to loss of public-sector jobs and increased competition from foreign goods, increased poverty. As it coincided with drought, the combined trauma had a negative effect overall and, certainly, badly affected many low-income households in the short term – enough to threaten their housing viability, no doubt.

The lack of negative effects on the poor found by Sahn et al. (1996),[6] contrary to popular belief, comes partly from their separating SAP effects from those of the economic recession or failure to implement adjustment policies, and partly from the effects of the way the poor operate in cities. As they tend to use the informal markets, the poor have rarely benefited from subsidised official prices so do not notice their withdrawal very much. For this and other reasons, the effects of SAP have been uneven across income groups.

Some of the greatest losers from SAPs are the urban elites (Sahn et al., 1996), those for whom government provided easy, relatively well-paid jobs and access to perks such as subsidised housing. When governments cut their workforces, many civil servants and employees of quasi-government enterprises found themselves out of work and required to vacate their homes. Although some received golden handshakes, which could be used to start businesses, many did not have the skills or entrepreneurial spirit and soon became impoverished.

In Mexico, under SAP, the economy improved but there was an increase in poverty for 35 per cent of the population as benefits for society as a whole took place alongside regressive transfers from the poorest groups. It is argued that reductions in inequality are more important for the poor than economic growth (Szekely, 1995). Where structural adjustment has been demonstrated to be very effective in lifting people out of poverty, the very poorest often miss out and see their livelihoods worsened because of their lack or education and skills (Ferreira, 1996).

Structural adjustment was found to increase feminisation of the labour force[7] through worsening income distribution and an increase in export industries (Çagatay and Özler, 1995). In Wisconsin, USA, where SAP-like welfare reform was implemented very suddenly, many women were plunged into crisis, including homelessness (Schleiter and Statham, 2002).

Homelessness in Poverty Reduction Strategy Papers (PRSPs)

In contrast to UN-Habitat's interest in homelessness, the World Bank's urban programmes seem to be less focused on the very poor. A quick survey of the completed PRSPs on the World Bank's website (World Bank, 2007) reveals that homelessness is not a major preoccupation of the officers developing poverty strategies in developing countries. Of the 'Latest Country Papers' on the website in early 2007, those of Burkina Faso, Burundi, Central African Republic, Dominica, Lesotho, Madagascar, Malawi, Nicaragua, Nigeria, São Tomé and Principe, Senegal, Tanzania and Uganda made no mention of homeless people or homelessness. Only those of Bangladesh, Ghana, Mozambique, Sierra Leone and Vietnam made any mention of homeless people. This balance is continued in the interim PRSPs on the same website in which those of Comoros, Grenada, Guinea, Haiti and Liberia did not mention homelessness and those of Cambodia and Uzbekistan did, albeit only in passing.

In PRSPs, homeless people are generally mentioned only to include them among other groups of vulnerable people who need help. In its plan for human capital, Mozambique's PRSP proposes children's homes as the solution to the problems of homeless children (Republic of Mozambique, 2006). The Bangladesh report (Government of Bangladesh, 2005) reports on the *Asrayan* and *Abashan* Programmes which combine shelter and employment benefits for the poorest, including homeless, people (see Ch. 13).

Making Markets Work for the Poor (MMW4P)

MMW4P has been adopted by international agencies including the World Bank, DFID and SIDA as a way of redefining their private sector strategies in development. Recognising that the enabling approach is basically about markets, MMW4P focuses, first, on the market as an institution and, second, on ways to intervene in particular markets to direct them towards pro-poor development. South Africa has been the scene of much MMW4P activity, especially through DFID, as it fits well with President Thabo Mbeki's 'Developmental State'.

It has previously been assumed that markets are only indirectly relevant or actually detrimental to the poor. While operating to generate economic growth, some of which trickles down to the poor, the action of markets has, nevertheless, been seen to exploit people living in poverty. Thus, the state has a role in protecting the poor from markets. MMW4P, however, asserts that markets can and should work for them both as consumers and producers (Porteous, 2004). In MMW4P, three features of markets are seen to be of particular interest (Porteous, 2004):

1 Price discrimination, where producers charge more to those prepared to pay more and less to those less able to pay. This allows market-determined cross-subsidisation.
2 The lumpiness of the market, where up-front cost which is a major hurdle to purchase can be mitigated through credit or reducing fixed prices. The market in cars has shown how this operates; when instalment finance became available, this was a major boost to sales.

3 The scale of possible production and distribution determines whether there can be economies of scale.

Through actions in these three, some increase in the reach of a market may be achieved, moving the frontier of the market downwards through developing it. However, ultimately, there may be many people who cannot be touched by the market; those whom Porteous (2004) describes as in the supra-market zone. They can only be reached by redistributive policies. In housing, the large size and cost of the product, compared with a cell-phone, for example, is a major constraint to market spread.

There are four conventional strategies which can be used to extend the usage of services to those who would normally not be able to participate in the market. These are:

1 providing the service directly through government agencies;
2 paying others to provide the service;
3 transferring the means to buy the service to consumers, for example, through vouchers; or
4 requiring providers to cross-subsidise the poorer households

(Porteous, 2004).

A fifth intervention has proved effective in the telephony sector in South Africa which may have relevance to housing. In it, industrial providers have to pay a levy on all products which is then used to extend the market more effectively to poorer users than would a requirement for producers to extend their markets to non-profitable customers (Porteous, 2004). In housing, this could take the form of a levy on each dwelling built, which is then used to build housing for the poorest households.

However, policy tends to increase the barrier in the housing market by raising the threshold of what is traded – what the minimum accommodation available consists of. Even at the lowest level, a single room can cost too much to build and service because of building regulations and planning laws which, for example, specify minimum size and type of construction. In addition, many governments assume that every household should occupy a dwelling on a plot and act to prevent shared accommodation being made available. Thus, households who build extra rooms to rent may find that their actions are illegal. The discouragement of rooming accommodation shifts the boundary between the market and supra-market zones (the access frontier) (Porteous, 2004) in a direction damaging to the poor. Thus, well-intentioned government policy makes the threshold an increasing obstacle to those most in need.

With respect to homelessness, we will argue later that many are likely to be in the supra-market zone, unreachable by market adjustments and efficiencies and requiring special treatment through welfare-related interventions in the markets.

Conclusions

There has been almost half a century of housing policies designed to help the lower income groups with their housing since the breakdown of colonial rule and increased rates of population growth ushered in the age of rapid city growth in developing countries. Despite the best efforts of policymakers, the poorest households in society tend to have been by-passed by the new housing provided and have had to find niches in the worst housing. The new emphasis on housing rights has allowed for a process to start which may clarify the relationship between governments and housing supply for people living in poverty and which may eventually serve to combat homelessness through housing policy. Meanwhile, however, governments can escape from directly assisting most homeless people unless groups can find the resources to take them to court. Internationally promoted policies specifically targeted at the poor are a good starting point for dealing with homeless people as part of the whole housing system. MMW4P has great potential if it can be rolled out in many countries. Up to now, however, homeless people have had low visibility on international housing and social policy agendas. They remain the hidden millions.

In the next chapter we look at the policies which have been promulgated in developing countries within the international context reviewed in this chapter and demonstrate how housing is not only in short supply but also is provided unevenly and is not affordable to many millions of households.

3 The continuing urban housing shortfall and affordability crisis

In developing countries, there is a cogent case for arguing that housing shortages are structurally important in homelessness. Over the last several decades, especially since the flood of independences from colonial rule during the first 20 post-Second World War years, the demand for housing in urban areas has outstripped formal supply in most developing countries. As a result of the shortfall in supply, many households have resorted to informal settlements for their accommodation. In calculations of housing stock and its corollary, housing need, such informal housing is often discounted. Thus, in some official eyes, all inhabitants of informal housing are homeless. So important is the lack of housing in relation to homelessness in developing countries that we will devote some time to the housing context – assessing the scale of the shortfalls in supply, aspects of the housing policy context which have allowed it to occur and the incongruence between housing supplied and the ability of people to afford it.

Calculating housing shortfalls

The way housing is counted complicates the supply shortfall issue in both assessing homelessness and determining how far it is a cause of homelessness. When a country's housing policymakers attempt to generate a figure for the shortfall in supply, they estimate numbers of households and compare these with the number of accommodation units that exist. This is usually adjusted to include some figures for stock that is currently unacceptable for reasons of poor condition (where non-permanent materials are used for floors and walls, roofs leak, etc.), crowding (either as people per room measures or as households per unit) and obsolescence (where units have passed an arbitrary lifespan date). The aggregate number of acceptable units is then compared with the current number of households from the census and an estimate of shortfall or excess generated. The numbers of accommodation units required immediately is then usually divided into a number of years in which extra supply is required at a level to catch up on the shortfall.

Further calculations are made for additional units required annually to cope with new households, generated by both natural growth and in-migration, and the need to replace units becoming obsolete by the passage of time. The need for new units is then added to the catch-up amount to generate annual needs. These are, usually, way beyond the ability of the formal suppliers to provide. Further problems arise when there is no clarity in the accommodation units used in the calculations, especially when they are not the equivalent of a dwelling (the unit occupied by a household).[1] Some countries then use the shortfall figure as a proxy for homelessness. However, these calculations seldom include people sleeping on the streets or others who might be considered homeless.

Other housing shortage issues

The problems of finding accommodation can be exacerbated by lumpiness in supply. For those who can afford the best-quality housing, there is often enough and to spare. At the lower end of the market, however, there might be a complete dearth and households have to occupy only part of a unit, sharing with another household. In between, the supply might well not be consistent with demand; some types and costs of housing are in good supply and others non-existent. Locational factors also affect the availability of housing.

As we suggested in Chapter 2, one major contributor to both dearth and lumpiness in supply is the regulatory framework in use. As has been argued by many influential commentators, from work in the early 1970s (Turner, 1972) to recent work (Payne and Majale, 2004), building and planning regulations set minimum standards for formal housing that are too high for most households. To be formal is important as it opens the way for bankable levels of land tenure, market-rate loans (or even subsidised ones), servicing, and all the status benefits derived from being in a formal and well-built neighbourhood. The cost of not being formal is a lack of security, credit and servicing which, together, reduce the standards to which the household is willing to build. Even quite low-income households are more than happy to invest three or four years' income on building a dwelling that they are confident will serve them and pass on to their children (Tipple et al., 1999). But households are not likely to invest more than a few months' income if there is a threat of removal and loss of the dwelling.

In countries where governments have sent any signals that informal settlements are not secure, for example, by evicting occupants of government land, there is often a major difference between the standard and cost of informal and formal housing, resulting in even more lumpiness in supply. Where there is no eviction or some squatter settlements are legalised, the *de facto* security may allow residents of informal neighbourhoods to improve them so that they resemble formal ones in standards and costs. Unfortunately, such indicators of *de facto* security might be subject to sudden and serious change. For example, incidences of evictions in

India have been generally low, suggesting that the cities have been taking up in situ upgrading of slums, leading to an increase in confidence among residents of even unrecognised settlements.[2] In 2006, however, there was a surge of evictions of households, mainly from squatter settlements in locations needed for some essential public use such as provision of basic services to the surrounding areas and for public projects. These evictions are directly linked with the provision of alternate sites, which provide shelter and services but rarely replicate the locational advantages of the previous settlement. Some instances of squatters being removed to make way for high-value shopping malls and similar private developments are occurring and seemingly on the increase. There has also been a spate of evictions connected with cleaning up Delhi for the 2010 Commonwealth Games.

Over many years, there has been an effort to help lower income households in the guise of 'affordable housing'. This has served to create or encourage a myth that housing is being provided for people living in poverty. Instead, it is often only affordable to those who are just under the usual affordability threshold for the small formal sector housing stock. Part of the reason for this is that governments are caught in the bind of having to fulfil their own regulations in any housing they provide directly or are seen to sponsor.

The issues touched on above are dealt with in more detail below.

Housing supply shortfalls

In many industrialised countries, homelessness has little directly to do with housing shortages. In Japan, for example, unemployment arising from a downturn in the economy led to a sudden growth of homelessness (Ezawa, 2002). In the UK, while there is an increasing shortage of affordable housing, homelessness is largely the result of personal crisis underpinned by wider structural change, diminution of social welfare and reducing family and social support networks.

In developing countries, however, housing supply shortfalls in absolute terms are undoubtedly a structural cause of homelessness. Almost all rapidly developing countries share problems of supplying enough housing for all their people in urban areas. Against international trends, however, China steadily increased the amount of urban housing space per person during the last years of the 20th century. According to Wang (2004), living space per person was consistently around 3 square metres between 1949 and 1980. Wu (2002) reports that it had risen to 6.7 square metres in 1990 and to 9.3 square metres by 1999, a truly heroic achievement. By 2000, over 70 per cent of urban residents owned their own homes and the mean floor space per person had reached 10 square metres (Wang, 2004). A study of nine cities in China shows an even more notable achievement – an almost doubling of living space per household member in eleven years from 8.0 square metres in 1988 to 15.8 square metres in 1999 (Sato, 2006). The only way to have achieved this was to have built huge amounts of new housing.

The housing shortfall and affordability crisis

The more common story of large and increasing housing shortfall, however, can be well illustrated by information from Africa and Asia (excluding the Former Soviet Union – FSU). Almost every country in Sub-Saharan Africa is experiencing an increasing housing shortage; in North Africa and the Middle East, deteriorating economic conditions have led to poorer housing conditions, in particular for the urban poor; and in South-Central Asia, there is a growing housing need in most countries. Formal housing delivery in most of South-Eastern Asia kept pace with the increased demand in the 1990s but the financial and currency crisis of 1997 caused the economies of many countries in the region to decline quite sharply. Estimates available show the following housing shortfalls in Africa and Asia (excluding the FSU)

- In Angola, 700,000 units were needed in 2000, but this figure could double to 1.4 million by 2015 (UN-Habitat, 2006a).
- Cameroon's shortfall is close to 70,000 units (UN-Habitat, 2006a).
- In Zambia, 846,000 units were needed according to the National Housing Policy of 1996 but now the general consensus is that it is over a million units (at five people per household, roughly half the population) (Gardner, 2007).
- In Iraq, in Baghdad alone, 377,000 are needed after 30 years of wars and UN Sanctions (UN-Habitat, 2007b).
- In Libya, 165,000 dwellings and around 492,000 dwellings are needed between 2002 and 2011, even though it is relatively prosperous and the government is strong and active (Grifa, 2006).
- Morocco's shortfall is one million units (UN-Habitat, 2006a).
- Malaysia is expected to need about 709,400 units for the period 2006 to 2010 (Government of Malaysia, 2006).
- Pakistan currently needs 7.3 million units, increasing by 270,000 units a year (UN-Habitat, 2006a).
- In the Philippines, the shortfall is 3.75 million units for the period 2005 to 2010 (Uy, 2006).
- Sri Lanka needed 400,000 units in 2002, rising to 650,000 in 2010 (UN-Habitat, 2006a).

Examples of deficits expressed in annual needs are as follows:

- Algeria, an estimated 175,000 new housing units annually between 2002 and 2012 to absorb the current housing deficit and to satisfy future demand in (World Bank, 2002);
- Bangladesh, 659,000 units (UN-Habitat, 2006a);
- The Democratic Republic of Congo, an 240,000 units annually (DRC, 2007);
- Ethiopia, between 73,000 and 151,000 housing units annually (UN-Habitat, 2006a).

The story told by these examples is one of near-universal failure to supply the housing needed. Some of the countries in the CARDO study are quite good examples of the housing supply crisis facing developing countries. In most of the study countries, the officially accepted housing deficit is very large. It does not mean, however, that these dwellings simply do not exist. In many cases, the deficit stated includes replacements for deteriorating housing and that which fails to meet national standards. It may also predict the need for new housing arising in the immediate future. These are often featured as percentages of the current stock. For example, deterioration replacement figures are often calculated using an expected lifespan and translating that into the percentage of the stock needing replacement each year. For a 50-year dwelling lifespan, 2 per cent of the stock is regarded as requiring replacement each year.

As lifespan and other estimates are usually fairly arbitrary, and actual obsolescence or collapse may be much less predictable, the calculation of annual needs can be a very inexact science and highly influenced by the politics of housing supply. As it is expressed numerically, however, it tends to take on a specious credibility. Lobbying NGOs will calculate much higher housing need figures than national governments for whom low figures are beneficial. In the cases in the CARDO study, however, allowances for even quite large measures of calculation error cannot hide the gross shortage of housing, especially of that affordable by the poorer echelons of society.

The question arises of how these shortfalls have occurred. Like many of its counterparts in the CARDO study, the Government of Bangladesh accepts some responsibility for housing its people. The national population more than doubled between 1961 and 2001 from 55 million to 129 million. At the same time, the urban population rose from 3 million (6 per cent of the total) to 29 million (23 per cent) and the share of urban housing in the national housing stock rose almost in parallel from 460,000 (5 per cent) to 5.6 million (23 per cent) in 2001 (Ghafur, 2002).

In common with most developing countries, the Bangladesh government's role in direct supply has produced quite a small proportion of the stock – 3 to 4 per cent including serviced sites (UNDP-GOB, 1993) – even though the numbers may be quite large. In line with international best practice, however, Bangladesh has had a published Housing Policy document since 1993. Even before this policy was in place, a paradigm shift had taken place from housing provision and supports (sites and services schemes, squatter upgrading, etc.) to an 'enabling approach', facilitating the activities of the private sector, and limiting its own activities within broad infrastructure development. Like many other governments, it may have made this shift gladly as a way of easing acute resource constraints on a more active role in housing supply. This is less in line with international best practice but typical of many governments' response (Ghafur, 2002).[3]

The Bangladesh National Housing Policy has an explicitly pro-poor focus; it is inclusive of all income groups but makes the 'disadvantaged, the destitute and the shelterless poor' priority target groups (clause 3.1). It commits the government to conferring occupancy rights in areas where improvement is feasible and to relocation of squatter settlements from sites that need to be cleared in the public interest (clause 5.10.1). It also aims to provide credit to help improve incomes and buy housing (clause 4.3) (Ghafur, 2002).

By 2001, however, the shelter deficit in Bangladesh was about 5.6 million dwellings, about one quarter of the total stock. Indeed, if the needs of all the population below the 45th percentile are included, the housing need was 659,000 dwellings (12 per cent of the existing urban stock) or 44 dwellings per thousand of the urban population (of 29 million) per year[4] (Ghafur, 2001). Such a figure is virtually impossible to achieve, especially when special agencies set up to construct housing tend only to cater for the elite.

As in many other countries, the Bangladesh government has failed to match policies with promises. The parts of the policy palette that benefit the elite are more likely to be effected than those positively assisting people living in poverty and powerlessness. Thus, clearing sites in the public interest through evictions continues to occur and even proliferate while the secure land needed for poverty reduction programmes has not been provided. In addition, the government continues to use meagre housing sector resources to house its own staff and favours the rich through its city development authorities, for example, RAJUK, which provide the ruling elite with building plots and flats.

On the positive side, some progress has been made through the enabling strategies. Housing has lately been seen in a more holistic context of poverty alleviation and gender (Ghafur, 2002, 2001). In 1997–8, for the first time in Bangladesh, the annual budget made provisions for programmes to help destitute people. These included:

- a monthly allowance to poor elderly people;
- funds to provide loans for housing homeless people;
- the establishment of a bank which would offer loans to unemployed young people who are willing to start any income-generating activity (MOF, 2000);
- allowances for destitute women;
- homes for the aged destitute; and
- setting up *Ashrayan* (formerly known as Ideal/Cluster Villages) (Ghafur, 2002).

However, a recent study by Asfar (2001) concludes that there is very little tangible improvement. People living in poverty still miss out on access to urban land (McAuslan, 2000).

In Egypt, the figures for 1996 for total households (12.7 million) and total 'residential units' (16.2 million) (CAPMAS, 1996) suggest that there is no housing problem in terms of quantity. However, there are hidden problems within these figures. In many cases, married children live with their parents owing to their inability to find or afford their own homes (El-Sheikh, 2002). In addition, there is a serious mismatch between supply and affordability and there has been a long-held practice of keeping flats empty against the time when grown-up children will need them (Wheaton, 1980). A combination of the rent control laws and the scale of key-money paid (Malpezzi, 1986)[5] make it so difficult to remove tenants that such flats have been left empty for years. The formal low-income housing supply ceased in about 1980, leaving only informal settlements to accommodate the majority of the population. Occupants of many settlements have lobbied for and received official recognition and services, even though the process took years (El-Sheikh, 2002).

In Ghana, the national housing deficit is put at 800,000 units and the annual need over supply is variously estimated to be at least 70,000 housing units annually (Republic of Ghana, 2006) or 53,000 units (Abdulai and Ndekugri, 2007), with the differences probably arising from using different units in the calculations.[6] The national supply is currently about 25,000 per annum (Republic of Ghana, 2006). The State Housing Corporation and other state and para-statal agencies have built a few thousand dwellings to the accompaniment of much political noise without making significant inroads into the supply of housing for the majority.

In India, through the succession of Five-Year Plans, the National Housing Policy has followed international trends and changed from a project-based approach to a sectoral approach, in which housing is seen as an integral part of economic development. The public sector is relinquishing the role of house builder and instead acting as a promoter and facilitator to create an enabling environment for other partners in the housing sector to add successfully to the national housing stock (which is 'textbook' enabling approach).

On paper, the Indian National Housing Policy gives priority to the economically weaker groups, homeless and disadvantaged people. Policies and projects have been adopted which have set up specialised institutions to provide housing finance, experimented in land banking (e.g. by the Delhi Development Authority) and limited the amount of land any individual can own (through the Urban Land Ceiling Act). They have given secure tenure to some slum dwellers, attempted to integrate housing projects with urban development and employment projects, and provided some homeless people with night shelters and sanitary facilities (Bannerjee Das, 2002).

Despite all these and other well-meaning policies, however, there was a net housing shortage between 1997 and 2002 of 18.77 million, of which 8.46 million are additional dwellings to be built and 10.31 million are for replacement of 'non-serviceable *kutcha*' dwellings[7] (Government of India, 2000). Of course, these figures do not account for the physical deterioration of existing houses in the last decade nor the damage from floods and other disasters which plague the country (Bannerjee Das, 2002).

In Peru, the state takes no part in housing supply, leaving the solution of housing and other basic needs in the hands of the people. Land is easily obtained in the desert fringes of Lima so the people have responded by building individually or through supportive social organisations.[8] The government has put in place relatively easy (but slow) means of obtaining title to a plot, often after many years' residence. Once title is acquired, residents of such areas are not regarded as homeless even though they may have no structure or only a very rudimentary shelter and no services.

There is no clarity regarding the amount of housing deficit in Peru. According to the last national census (INEI, 1998), the housing shortfall was 335,000 units, enough for about 7 per cent of households at the time. Taking account of further units which do not fulfil quality requirements (owing to physical deterioration, dangerous location, lack of basic services, overcrowding, poor materials, insecure tenure, etc.), the deficit could be as high as 1.5 million units, which is 35 per cent of the current housing stock (Government of Peru, 2001). According to the estimates of the Habitat Commission (Government of Peru, 1998), the total housing deficit in Metropolitan Lima was 410,000 in 1997 (Miranda and Salazar, 2002).

In South Africa, most housing policies after 1994 have been within the ANC's Reconstruction and Development Programme (RDP) subsidy programme for low-income households which sought to provide one million dwellings after the democratic elections of 1994. It successfully delivered just over two million owner-occupied dwellings and 35,000 for rental between 1994 and 2006 (Department of Housing, 2006; Rust, 2007).[9] Even so, the housing backlog in South Africa is said to be 2.2 million dwellings (IRIN, 2007) which is very close to the number of households in the 2002 Census who do not live in formal or traditional housing.

During the 1990s, the Government of Zimbabwe enthusiastically embraced the Global Strategy for Shelter and produced a series of national plans and strategies that culminated in the National Housing Policy for Zimbabwe (NHTF, 2000). It is notable that the government participated in all major Habitat forums and produced impressive national reports for most of these (see Ministry of Public Construction and National Housing, 1991). During the 1990s, considerable progress was made in the housing sector. Among the major developments were the creation of Government Construction Units directly to build houses; the downward revision of housing standards; and the introduction of Pay Schemes.[10] In addition, a multi-stakeholder coordinating body responsible for housing (the Zimbabwe National Co-ordination Committee on Human Settlements) and a multi-stakeholder task force (the National Housing Task Force) to oversee developments in the housing sector and formulate policy and strategies were set up in 1994, along with tax allowances for employers who provide housing to their employees (in 1995). Between 1997 and 2000, a National Housing Policy was drawn up and approved (Kamete, 2001).

In Zimbabwe, the total urban population of over 4.6 million, in 2000, was housed in an estimated stock of around 600,000 housing units.[11] There is some consensus that one million dwellings were needed for the planning period 2001–5 to make up for the shortfall.[12] The annual production needed to satisfy this shortfall was 200,000 units for the period 2001 to 2005, but the average annual production for the period to 2000 was no more than 15,000 (Kamete, 2000; National Housing Task Force (Zimbabwe), 2000). The highest output – at one time as high as 25,000 units per year – was realised between 1992 and 1997 during the period when central government intervened in the housing sector by building housing through Government Construction Units (GCUs) created in July 1992 (MIPTC (Zimbabwe), 1992; Kamete, 2001).

It is agreed that the shortfall is a result of supply bottlenecks, which themselves are linked to macro-economic instabilities that have plagued the country during most of its post-independence existence. This in turn has affected important housing-related sectors such as finance, construction, income and building materials manufacturing (National Housing Task Force (Zimbabwe), 1998; Mubvami and Kamete, 2000). In addition to the state of the economy, the bottlenecks have also been linked to legislative and policy inadequacies and impediments (Mubvami and Musandu-Nyamayaro, 1996; Kamete, 1997).

From the above national experiences, we see that there are widespread shortfalls in housing, both nationally and in urban areas, particularly capital cities, resulting from ineffective supply and policies that are not optimal for satisfying supply, especially for the poor. With shortfalls of these dimensions persisting, it is intuitively inescapable that homelessness in developing countries is closely related to lack of housing supply. Thus, attention to housing supply policies is essential in reducing homelessness.

Regulatory frameworks and the informal sector

Regulatory frameworks are important in influencing decisions to supply housing, especially by the private sector, including small landlords. They govern what type of housing is fully legitimate and, therefore, entitled to receive services and 'bankable' for the purpose of raising housing finance. Where the threshold of legitimacy is too high for the majority of the population, they will build outside of controls and the informal sector will grow as a proportion of total stock. Irrespective of definitions, it is indisputable that the scale of informal housing activity is massive and is increasing (Hernandez and Kellett, 2008).

Durand-Lasserve (1997) estimates that between 30 and 70 per cent of the population of developing countries live in informal housing. Furthermore, 85 per cent of new housing worldwide is estimated to be produced in an extra-legal manner (Berner, 2001). So great has been the contribution of the informal sector in Sub-Saharan Africa during the last 40 or more years that Fekade (2000) estimates that between 50 and 75 per cent of households there have obtained their land informally.

According to UN-Habitat (2003), the proportion of the urban population living in slum housing[13] varies from 72 per cent in Sub-Saharan Africa through 59 per cent in South-Central Asia, and 32–6 per cent in Latin America and Caribbean, Western Asia and Eastern Asia, to 28 per cent in both Northern Africa and Oceania. These are very subjective figures; many other estimates are available and not always consistent with regional generalisations. For example, Hernandez and Kellett (2008) point out that, as 70 per cent of the city of Lima can be defined as informal and 80 per cent of new housing in Caracas is self-built, squatters, *favelados* and ordinary citizens are the real city builders. Whatever figures we use, the lesson is much the same: the contribution to housing made by the informal sector is too large and important to write off as worthless because of its not fulfilling regulations.

Land-use and building regulations often exacerbate the difficulties of households low down in the market by insisting on large plots and low building coverage in an effort to develop utopian cities. Regulations limiting development to one dwelling per plot and discouraging multi-habitation remove valuable opportunities to increase housing supply without extending the urban footprint or having to pay the price of land as an overhead for the additional housing goods. In Zimbabwe, reducing plot sizes has reduced costs by 29 per cent (UN-Habitat, 2006a).

It is governments' role, under the enabling approach, to ensure that the right incentives and controls are in place to maximise housing supply for the urban poor. This role includes removing impediments and disincentives in housing supply (such as rent controls and transaction costs) and enabling the poor to have recourse to law, especially in land title disputes. It also includes legitimising incremental building so that a dwelling may fulfil regulations over a long construction-and-occupancy period rather than initially. As globalisation has quickened the pace of land price inflation, it is increasingly important that costs other than land are minimised. This is particularly true of transaction costs which are often generated by governments, and include the cost of cadastral surveys, the need to develop the land quickly and the length of time it takes to gain the rights being applied for. It is equally important that other outlets for sound investment are encouraged to lessen the pressure on land, including stocks and shares, savings accounts and business opportunities.

Similarly, property rights, developed through laws and regulations, are often also granted on conditions that the poor cannot satisfy, especially with respect to transaction costs. Thus, poor households can be excluded from property rights, especially in countries where women have no rights to own property.

Lumpiness in supply

In a well-developed housing market, a buyer or renter should be able to find housing at more or less any price from the minimum cost of a dwelling up to the maximum for that city or country. This is not the case in cities in many developing countries. Instead of a smooth supply by size, cost, etc., there is usually considerable lumpiness, notwithstanding very active alteration and extension (transformation) activity in many cities (Tipple, 2000). The result of lumpiness is often that households do not occupy dwellings which reflect their potential demand. Those in cheap housing cannot easily move up the market because suitable housing is unavailable or there is too much of a gap between what they could sell the current dwelling for and what would be needed to buy one any further up the market. Similarly, moving down the market may involve so large a change in conditions that those who want to pay less for housing could not consider moving into the much poorer accommodation available for their preferred price.

Probably the greatest source of lumpiness is the gap between the formal sector and the informal sector. The massive housing shortfall that results from inadequate formal supply tends in part to be taken up by the informal sector; activities of small-scale builders and developers, self-help owner-builders, small-scale landlords and their intermediaries. These are the largest suppliers of shelter in most developing countries, supplying housing without any incentives and recognition from the public authorities. Indeed they usually operate under heavy constraints.

Under some circumstances, informally developed housing may be indistinguish-able from formal, especially if it is developed on land which gives the occupier a reasonably secure tenure with many of the bundle of rights available in fully secure land (Payne, 2001). Thus, housing on plots with reliable protection from eviction and the ability to transfer, especially through inheritance, may be apparently of similar quality to that in fully serviced formally developed neighbourhoods. However, at the other end of the spectrum, informally developed, unserviced neighbourhoods may be little more than shacks of recycled materials clinging to land on which the 'owners' only have tenuous property rights and which is liable to flooding, landslip or other disaster.

Typically for developing countries, the formal housing supply system in Bangladesh has completely failed to reach the bottom 15 per cent of urban households in Dhaka. The informal sector's contribution (as much as 97 per cent of supply) completely dominates the lower end where the mass of people living in poverty are its clientele. About two-thirds of the stock is regarded as structurally temporary (known as '*kutcha*' in both Bangladesh and India), a circumstance that would qualify its occupants as homeless in industrialised countries (Ghafur, 2002).

Though housing tenure is much more complex than the dichotomous owning and renting that dominate the literature, with lodgers, subtenants, rent-free tenants, owners of structures who do not own the land, etc., most statistics concentrate on owning and renting, with the former regarded as preferable. In Bangladesh's urban areas, 60 per cent of dwellings are regarded as owner-occupied but, in Dhaka, as much as 70 per cent contain rooms that are rented to others (GOB and ADB, 1993; Shafi, 1998).

South Africa's housing stock was developed in the apartheid era when lumpiness in supply was enshrined in law; with a separate and unrelated supply system for each of four racial groups. There was a huge disparity between races and the poor majority were radically underprovided for.

Most countries have markets in high-cost housing, especially that which appeals to expatriates, investors and diplomats. However, Gilbert (1999) and others have shown that most low-income households are not in market contexts. The reasons for this include lack of market information, few alternative dwellings being available and an inability to raise finance to cover the difference in cost when moving up the market. In some countries, notably in Sub-Saharan Africa north of the Zambezi River, there are many cultural barriers to the sale of real property outside of a family so no market is likely to develop except among the elite who are heavily affected by Western values.[14]

Contrary to expectations, however, several cities are known to have more dwellings than households and could house everyone if distribution mechanisms were more efficient. In 1996, Delhi had 280,000 dwellings lying vacant, with an expected increase to 342,000 by 2002 (Bannerjee Das, 2002). Indeed, recent years have seen the development of Non-Resident Indian (NRI) estates. Dwellings in these estates, bought for investment purposes by Indians living in USA and Europe, remain empty most of the time. Housing is, therefore, not distributed according to the demand as there is an oversupply of private sector high- and medium-cost housing but an undersupply of low-cost dwellings; a supply task left to the government but taken up by the informal sector. This is a long-lived issue, as similar lumpiness in supply was reported by Wheaton (1980) almost 30 years ago when the oil boom in the Middle East was boosting supply in Cairo.

The myth of 'affordable housing'

In 1999, according to UN-Habitat (2003), half the world's population, three billion people, lived on less than $2 per day and about 1.2 billion people (23 per cent of the world) lived on less than $1 per day. In most developing countries, therefore, poverty is a major structural issue in homelessness; there is a gap between what many households can afford to spend on housing and what the lowest-priced accommodation available to them costs. This is what MMW4P calls the 'supra-market zone' within which the market cannot operate (Porteous, 2004). We will focus more attention on poverty in relationship to homelessness in Chapter 7.

> The provision of affordable housing at scale remains a challenge to most countries, particularly in the developing world and in transition countries. Currently, more than one billion people are living in slums. Over the next 25 years, more than two billion people will add to the growing demand for housing and basic infrastructure services. The situation is particularly serious in developing countries where governments at central and local levels often lack the resources adequately to address this challenge.
>
> (Majale and Tipple, 2007)

Affordability is defined in UN General Comment 4 as: 'Personal or household financial costs associated with housing should be at such a level that the attainment and satisfaction of other basic needs are not threatened or compromised'. The unwritten subtext in this is that affordable housing should be 'adequate' as defined by the Habitat Agenda (UNCHS, 1997 and above) including spaciousness, durability and servicing, which are usually only found together in the formal sector. In defining it thus, so-called 'affordable housing' in developing countries is positioned between informally provided, poorly serviced housing on the one hand and the conventional, market-driven, formal housing supply on the other. Figures 3.1 to 3.3 are graphic presentations of this, showing that the informal sector occurs where costs and standards of construction are both relatively low. The formal sector tends to occupy the ground where more expensive and higher standard housing occurs; the affordable housing stock is at the lowest end of this. The boundary between the informal and formal sectors tends to be at varying positions on the supply curve in different regions and one of the aims of housing policy is to increase the proportion of the curve occupied by the formal sector. In South-East Asia, the informal/formal boundary tends to be quite low down in the curve (Figure 3.1), in Sub-Saharan Africa it is quite high (Figure 3.2). Similarly, the affordable area is relatively large in South-East Asia and small in Sub-Saharan Africa (Majale and Tipple, 2007). There may be a supply gap between the sectors (Figure 3.2) which could be better represented in some places by a step in the supply curve as the informal sector provides some dwellings of similar quality to the formal sector but at lower cost. Thus, there might be no standards gap though there is a cost gap (Figure 3.3).

In South Africa, Rust (2007) points out two very wide gaps in what she calls the 'housing ladder' expressed in terms of incomes and costs. She reports that there are three unconnected housing programmes: the subsidy housing, so-called 'affordable

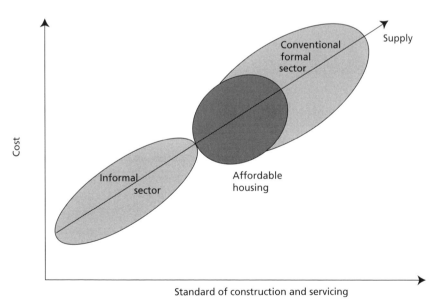

3.1 The place of affordable housing in the cost/standards locus in South-East Asian countries cases

The housing shortfall and affordability crisis

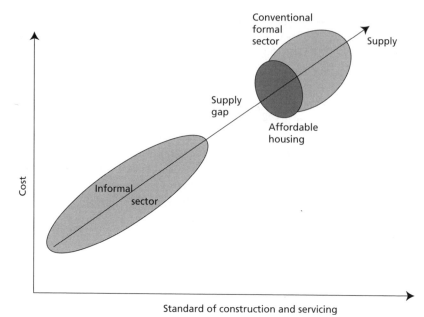

3.2 The place of affordable housing in the cost/standards locus in Sub-Saharan African countries

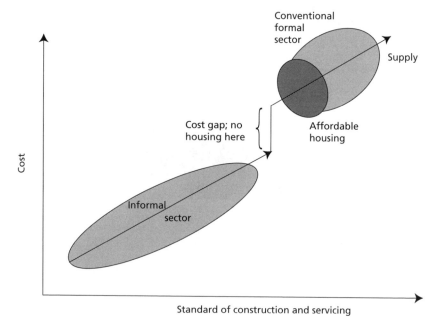

3.3 The cost gap may not be reflected in differences in standard of construction and servicing

housing' and the long-standing formal market which was only open to whites in the apartheid years. The first gap is, then, above the subsidy houses costing up to R36,700[15] for which households earning less than R3,500 per month are eligible. From there up to 'affordable' units costing about R150,000 in 2006, affordable by households with incomes of more than R5,250 per month, there is no supply. This is a gap of R115,000. Above the affordable housing, however, the gulf is frighteningly large. A small (80–140 square metres) dwelling in the formal (open) market averaged about R600,000 in 2006. Rust (2007) emphasises how difficult it is, therefore, for a household to progress from one part of the market to the next and how this negates any 'starter home' role for either the subsidised supply or the affordable supply. Even if a household with an affordable dwelling to sell could realise all of its value in equity, they would still need an income of R19,000 per month to make the leap from the affordable market to the open (formerly whites-only) market in housing. She also points out that the supply trend is widening the gaps rather than narrowing them.

Finance and housing affordability

Finance is an important component of affordability. Where housing finance is present and accessible to most households, affordability tends to be much higher than where households must rely on savings; both less wealthy and younger households can achieve home-ownership. Mortgages, however, are often not suitable for the lower-income groups as they need to be relatively large and, therefore, repaid over a long period to be attractive to lenders. Few low-income households have the resources to undertake mortgages, particularly with respect to stable incomes and being able to raise the down-payments. In addition, they are unattractive to lenders. Thus, only housing micro-loans (probably less than US$10,000, repaid over five years or so) are likely to appeal to, and be suitable for, households at risk of becoming homeless.

Two of the major factors in affordability in Indonesia are relatively high interest rates (20 per cent per annum is not unusual) and the high down-payment (around 30 per cent) demanded by mortgagors. Mainstream lenders do not make loans on property worth less than Rp.40 million (c.£3,3000), affordable to only the richest 25 per cent of the population. Unsecured housing loans at 30 per cent per annum are a last-resort borrowing option through which households at the 20th percentile (earning about Rp.500,000 a month (£42) can afford to borrow Rp.2.4 million (£200) (Hoek-Smit, 2002; Rahardjo, 2002). The high interest rates are, however, potential causes of vulnerability for those using such loans.

Conclusions

The current international housing policy environment comes very close to mandating governments to address the problems of homeless people in housing terms. Although the housing rights legislation does not give governments the duty to house all-comers, the needs of homeless people are more in focus than ever before. As fiscal poverty is no excuse for expending the maximum possible resources on housing vulnerable groups, governments could be held much more accountable for homeless populations than they are currently. Instruments such as PRSPs have the potential to be used to focus attention on homeless people. In addition, initiatives such as MMW4P could be the way to reach the groups that have not been reached by previous policies. Little is currently being made of these potential routes to better understanding of the needs of people living in poverty and to focus investment on their housing needs.

In this context, however, the housing shortfalls are still huge and, in most developing countries, rising. Despite much rhetoric showing that governments are aware that housing for people living in poverty is a priority and close to the heart of their policies, few measures have been installed which succeed in improving housing supply at the bottom of the market. China and South Africa have both improved upon past performance through heavy government involvement and supply-side subsidies but few governments have the stomach for such intervention and the current international policy wisdom points away from them. The enabling approach has encouraged governments to keep housing supply at arms length but many have taken this as a signal to remove themselves from the game entirely. Lumpy supply has exacerbated the situation for many of the poorest households and kept so-called 'affordable housing' out of reach for most households. The root cause of the affordability problem, poverty, is still endemic in much of the developing world. It is unlikely that most households in the poorer echelons in the world will be able to afford a self-contained dwelling in the medium term. There is a limit to how cheaply housing can be built, especially if it contains internationally traded materials such as cement, iron rods, timber and glass. Even in contexts where housing cost to income ratios are declining, many households must make do with less than a complete dwelling. Indeed, Tipple (1994b) has argued that ownership of the standard unit of a self-contained dwelling on a plot is unaffordable by the majority of households in urban Africa. Thus, occupying a room or rooms, in the shared housing so common in traditional societies and many current neighbourhoods in rapidly developing cities, is likely to remain the only viable housing solution for many households.

4 Defining homelessness in developing countries[1]

The need for definition(s)

A definition is a statement expressing the essential nature of something, a statement of the meaning of a word or word group, or a sign or symbol. Definition is the action or process of defining; the action or the power of describing, explaining, or making definite and clear (Merriam-Webster Online Dictionary). In this chapter, we attempt to describe homelessness and examine definitions attempted in theory and policy. In Chapter 1, we made the link between home and homelessness because the word we choose to use in English to describe homelessness has, as its root, the value-laden term 'home'. In this chapter, we examine the range of definitions used worldwide and in the CARDO study countries, beginning by probing the English language for suitable terms. The definitions of homelessness used in industrialised countries offer some guidance but tend to include almost everyone who is inadequately housed. We examine the definitions used by governments in developing countries, focusing on particular criteria. We end by looking at working definitions used by NGOs who are active with homeless people, whose definitions tend to be backed by actions.

Several commentators, and UN-Habitat, have attempted to find a better term than 'homelessness', at least partly in order to remove the deeper meanings embodied in the word 'home' and the implicit inclusion of these in what the homeless person lacks, including social ties and relations, which imply social exclusion or marginalisation (Edgar et al., 1999). Further, they attempt to differentiate between conditions of homelessness, as we will do a little later. The universality of the English language in international development policy discussions, research and teaching means that it is important to recognise that English wording will influence other language-speakers' views of homelessness.[2] Other European languages may have been more useful starting points for an internationally helpful root word. For example, there are three phrases used in French: *sans abri* 'roofless' and *sans domicile fixe* (*SDF*), which carry no undertones of 'home', and *sans logis* which does. In Spanish, *sin techo*, 'roofless', carries no deeper meaning of home. The Scandinavians are particularly careful not to apply terms that confuse matters. In Finland, the term for homeless, *kodito*, which contains meanings of having no established relationships, has been replaced by *assunnoton*, 'having no dwelling'. In Norwegian, the term *hjemløshet*, 'homelessness' has been replaced by *bostedsløshet* 'having no dwelling' and official documents use the term *uten fast bolig* (*UFB*) 'having no permanent dwelling' (UNCHS, 2000: 10).

The terms 'homeless', 'houseless', 'roofless', 'shelterless' people, and 'street-sleepers' and 'pavement dwellers' do not always cover the same people. Indeed, Dupont (1998) deliberately avoids the use of the term 'homeless' in her work in India because it adds the loss of familial roots to a lack of shelter. In Hindi, for example, the word *ghar* 'home' includes all the dimensions of affection, attachment, loyalty, memory, in the English word 'home' (Chapter 1) and also includes 'family' and 'household' (Mital, 2006). Dupont's stand would also be relevant in many cultures in which everyone has a home, in their family's place of origin, in which, should they go, they have an unquestioned right of abode. Arguing from the reality of Indian streets, Dupont (1998) argues that many people who live a life on the street actually have a house and/or a home somewhere else, most likely in a rural area. In addition, the spatially scattered family provides support and emotional ties or, indeed, imposes duties and obligations whose existence the usual image of homelessness would deny. Bannerjee Das (2002) differentiates between 'street sleepers' (men who decamp from their crowded dwellings at night to sleep on adjacent pavement space) and pavement dwellers (individuals or households who live on the streets).

Theoretical and functional definitions of homelessnesss

> [T]here are as many classifications and definitions of homelessness as there are different [points of view]. A definition of homelessness might refer to a special housing situation, to a special minimum standard, to the duration and the frequency of a stay without shelter, to lifestyle questions, to the use of the welfare system and to the being part of a certain group of the population, to the risk of becoming houseless and to the possibility to move or not if desired.
>
> (Springer, 2000: 479)

Williams and Cheal (2001), working in an industrialised world context, argue that homelessness is such a complex and heterogeneous concept that it is not appropriate to try to make it a single issue. They talk of a paradoxical situation in which there is a need for a definition of homelessness in order to know how many people are involved. The resulting data must then come with so many caveats and conditions that the definition is obviously 'ontologically slippery' but necessary in order to gain the results that 'demonstrate its slipperiness' (Williams and Cheal, 2001: 240). In addition, it is a dynamic process, with people moving in and out of homelessness over a period that could amount to many years (Williams and Cheal, 2001).

The complexity of homelessness and its definitions have led to two layers of continuums being described by commentators:

1 typologies as continuums (Watson and Austerberry, 1986; Neale, 1997);
2 continuums of definitions (Williams and Cheal, 2001).

Williams (2005) argues that homelessness is not a state that is the corollary of not-homeless; rather it is one end of a housing continuum. Indeed, definitions of homelessness attempted can be fitted along two different continuums (Figure 4.1), one based on ideology and one on complexity (Williams and Cheal, 2001: 240).

•   The ideological (or political) continuum has, at one extreme, the 'individualistic explanations of homelessness that accept the heterogeneity of the problem, but blame it on individual fecklessness'. This is described as a minimalist construction of homelessness by Jacobs et al. (1999). This falls on the political right. Neale (1997) adds a qualification to this end of the continuum in that individualistic or 'agency' explanations can include not only the 'victim blaming' approach, regarding people as homeless because of their personal inadequacy (substance abuse, unwillingness to work – the stereotypical dossers, deviants, alcoholics, etc.) – but also the approach that maintains that people are homeless because of endogenous characteristics that lead them into homelessness (e.g., psychiatric problems). At the other extreme of the ideological continuum is the structural definition. In it some characteristics of society, as well as major fiscal change, are to blame and broad welfare measures are seen to be the solutions. This falls on the political left; it recognises the heterogeneity of the antecedents of homelessness and encompasses a wider range of housing need (Chamberlain, 1999, cited in Williams, 2005).

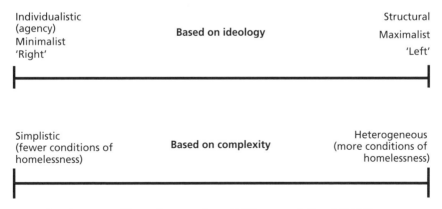

4.1 Continuums of homelessness from Williams and Cheal (2001)

Jacobs et al. (1999) refer to it as a maximalist construction of homelessness. As focus shifts along the continuum, different definitions include and exclude people from the homelessness definition.

• The complexity continuum of definitions ranges from the simplistic to the heterogeneous. Although political right and left can map onto this continuum also, 'the simpler definitions usually arise from administrative necessity, whilst heterogeneous ones are often the result of attempts at sociological improvement and comprehensiveness' (Williams and Cheal, 2001: 240–1). The simpler definitions might focus only on rough sleepers while the heterogeneous definitions try to include many conditions from street sleeping through to inadequate housing. The continuum of definitions of homelessness (described below) maps quite well onto the heterogeneous end of this definitional continuum and the research which has led this book to take the heterogeneous approach to definition.

Williams and Cheal (2001: 251) conclude that 'homelessness is not a thing but a process of different kinds of severe housing need resulting in a wide range of individual circumstances'. In response to this, they recommend a policy approach that concentrates on the housing pathways upon which homeless people are embarked and the non-housing events and circumstances (family violence, unemployment, bereavement, debt) that have brought them there.

FEANTSA[3] uses a fourfold quality-oriented typology both to define the condition of homelessness and evaluate its extent:

• rooflessness (i.e. sleeping rough);
• houselessness (i.e. living in institutions or short-term 'guest' accommodation);
• insecure accommodation; and
• inferior or substandard housing

(Daly, 1994).

Springer (2000) points out that 'insecure accommodation' and 'inferior or substandard housing' overlap, as accommodation might be both insecure and substandard.

Some recent attempts to study homelessness have expressed its dynamic nature through the 'housing careers'[4] or 'housing pathways' approaches (Fitzpatrick and Clapham, 1999). In these, the life-course trajectories of homeless people, following their route into homelessness, their experiences while homeless and their route out of homelessness, provide insight into the interplay of agency and structural aspects of homelessness.

Structural changes provide both threats and opportunities in developing countries. People respond to, and are affected by, these threats and opportunities in a variety of ways. For example, as we will see below, some people seize the opportunities for employment in the city (provided by structural change) by accepting homelessness and living on the street, rent-free, in central locations as a way to improve their lives. In doing so they may be able to improve their rural homes and benefit the entire household. This is especially the case in India (Bannerjee Das, 2002) and Bangladesh (Ghafur, 2002). Thus, their homelessness is part of a housing career and may not be more than a temporary strategy in a generally hopeful life-course. Others, however, are likely to be on a downward trajectory and their homelessness carries hopelessness in its wake. This is embodied in the sense that homelessness separates people from society, especially after the first flush of optimism and resistance wears off and hopelessness and acceptance of the homeless state takes hold (Hertzberg, 1992). Thus, in industrialised countries,'[h]omelessness is a condition of detachment from society characterised by the absence or attenuation of the affiliative bonds that link settled persons to a network of interconnected social structures' (Caplow et al., 1968: 494; quoted by Glasser, 1994: 3), the Australian Institute of Health and Welfare (1999) points out that definitions of homelessness usually focus on five circumstances. These are:

- living on the street;
- living in crisis or refuge accommodation;
- living in temporary arrangements without security of tenure, for example, moving between the residences of friends or relatives, living in squats, caravans or improvised dwellings, or living in boarding houses;
- living in unsafe family circumstances, for example, families in which child abuse or domestic violence is a threat or has occurred;
- living on very low incomes and facing extraordinary expenses or personal crisis .

(quoted in McIntosh and Phillips, 2000: 2).

Many national definitions do not progress beyond the first two categories. For example, in the USA, the Stewart B. McKinney Homeless Assistance Act of 1987, defined 'homeless' to mean:

1 An individual who lacks a fixed, regular, and adequate night-time residence; and
2 An individual who has a primary night-time residence that is:
   A supervised publicly or privately operated shelter designed to provide temporary living accommodations (including welfare hotels, congregate shelter, and transitional housing for the mentally ill);
   An institution that provides a temporary residence for individuals intended to be institutionalized; or
   A public or private place not designed for, or ordinarily used as, regular sleeping accommodations for human beings.
3 This term does not include any individual imprisoned or otherwise detained under an Act of Congress or state law.

(USA, 1994: 22)

This is the definition used by the US Department of Housing and Urban Development for defining homelessness. Similarly, in Hungary, the Social Law of 1993 states:

> Somebody is homeless if he/she does not have a registered permanent address or his/her permanent address is in one of the institutions provided for the homeless.
> Somebody is homeless if he/she spends the nights in public spaces or in places improper for living.
>
> (Beata and Snijders, 2002)

In the UN System, the 'Compendium of Human Settlement Statistics', concentrates on living on the streets and not in conventional housing. There, the expression 'Homeless household' refers to:

> households without a shelter that would fall within the scope of living quarters. They carry their few possessions with them sleeping in the streets, in doorways or on piers, or in any other space, on a more or less random basis.
>
> (United Nations, 1998: 50)

This definition, suggesting visibly dishevelled figures tramping city streets and carrying their possessions to random sleeping places, is universally recognised and simple. However, such 'accommodation-oriented' definitions have been criticised because they have restricted the issue of homelessness to not having a house – 'houselessness'. They do not do justice to the complexity of homelessness nor are they sufficient to describe the different realities of homelessness in every country (Cooper, 1995).

In Japan, homelessness is usually defined very tightly as only those visible sleeping on the streets (Aoki, 2003). Indeed Kakita (n.d.) points out that the words *hōmuresu* (homeless) and *nojuku seikatsusha* (rough sleepers) are used in a similar way. They exclude people who sleep in cheap lodgings or rely on friends or relatives to find somewhere to sleep, who might fairly be considered to be homeless.

In featuring the lack of a right of access to secure and minimally adequate housing, Edgar et al. (1999: 22) refer to a threefold division of homelessness as 'rooflessness (living rough), houselessness (relying on emergency accommodation or long-term institutions), or inadequate housing (including insecure accommodation, intolerable housing conditions or involuntary sharing)'. Within the property-based definitions, Cooper (1995) discusses the ideas of 'relative' and 'absolute' homelessness. Absolute homelessness occurs when there is neither access to shelter nor the elements of home. Relative homelessness occurs when a person has a shelter but not a home, as is the case for those in institutions.

In the context of Western writing in which social exclusion is a major component of the concept of homelessness, Somerville (1992) uses perhaps the clumsiest word in this vein, 'propertylessness'; the state of having no real property. Somerville

(1992) also posits that homelessness is likely to have rather different meanings for women and men. Men would be expected to feel deprived of property rights, whereas women would miss exclusive possession, users' rights and the implications that has for the day-to-day discharge of domestic responsibilities.

> Thus, although homelessness means lack of privacy and dispossession for both men and women, for men it seems more likely to take the form of propertylessness, whereas for women it is more likely to mean the disruption of everyday routines. Again, this could mean that homelessness is more serious for women than for men.
>
> (Somerville, 1992: 535)

It should be noted, however, that this idea may seem somewhat outdated for many women in contemporary, industrialised societies. It assumes the way in which women might view property and home has not changed in line with other changes to women's lives and sees them primarily in a domestic role.

Springer (2000) refers to the Austrian quality-oriented criteria for assessing homelessness (BAWO Projekt Büro, n.d.). Criteria used are the minimum standard of the housing unit; the infrastructure, including schools, shopping opportunities and transport, psychological and health criteria; and the juridical security of the housing situation.

Such narrow definitions of homelessness equate to the two groups in Europe who would be sleeping rough or in a public shelter. The Council of Europe (1992) took its lead from these but also added some detail as to what 'lacking adequate accommodation' might mean. It has defined as homeless:

> persons or families that are socially excluded from permanently occupying a personal and adequate home. Persons or families that:
> - have no roof over their head and are condemned to live in the street as vagrants;
> - are temporarily housed in hostels or centres for the homeless, especially created by public authorities or the private sector;
> - are temporarily housed in the private sector, in bed and breakfasts, cheap hotels or private hostels, or with friends or relatives with whom they may be obliged to live;
> - occupy, legally or illegally, unsafe housing, shacks, abandoned houses, etc.
> - live in institutions, children's homes, hospitals, prisons or psychiatric units, and have no home to go to when they leave;
> - live in a dwelling that cannot be considered adequate or socially acceptable, thus converting them into poorly housed persons or families.
>
> (Quoted in Munoz and Vazquez, 1999: 3)

This definition includes whether the shelter is safe and secure, as does the Supported Accommodation Assistance Program (SAAP) Act 1994 for Australia which defines a homeless person as one who has inadequate access to safe and secure housing (s. 4). Inadequate access to safe and secure housing is, in turn, defined as having access only to housing which damages, or is likely to damage, the person's health; or threatens their safety; or marginalises them personally, economically and socially; or adversely affects the adequacy, safety, security and affordability of that housing (McIntosh and Phillips, 2000).

Resource Information Services (2000) call the segment of homeless people in industrialised countries who are not literally 'roofless' the 'hidden homeless'. This includes people in personal danger in the context of domestic violence as well as in unfit housing or dangerous sites. These are people who

> are forced to live in insecure, overcrowded, dangerous, illegal or very temporary accommodation (e.g., bed and breakfast hotels, women's refuges, hostels, friend's/relative's floors, squats, and women forced through lack of alternatives to remain in abusive situations).

Beavis et al. (1997) add the use of the time component in their study of homelessness among Australian aborigines. They distinguish among situational or temporary, episodic and chronic forms of homelessness. Holmes (2006) follows the life of an aborigine woman who has episodes in 'the long grass', referring to homelessness, and periods when she is settled in welfare accommodation. She is under pressure from her homeless relatives to resume drinking, using unconventional and menacing behaviour around and within her home which brings complaints from neighbours and threats of eviction, or to return to the long grass. This demonstrates how interlinked may be the worlds of homelessness and welfare housing for some people.

Other definitions include lack of links with the community or other social disruption. The United States Alcohol, Drugs Abuse and Mental Health Administration (ADAMHA, 1983), defines a homeless person as 'any person that lacks adequate accommodation, resources or links with the community'. This definition goes beyond McKinney in that it adds social isolation to housing poverty (Munoz and Vazquez, 1999). It corresponds mostly to a narrow or literal definition of homelessness but qualifies it with the absence of community and family ties, privacy, security and the lack of shelter against the elements.

Many of the definitions above included 'adequate' to extend the focus of homelessness to those whose housing can be deemed to be inadequate. FEANTSA and the European Observatory of the Homeless (Daly, 1994; Avramov, 1995) reach a similar conclusion:

The [homeless person] is that person who is incapable of acceding to and maintaining an adequate personal dwelling through his/her own means, or incapable of maintaining a dwelling with the aid of Social Services.

(Quoted in Munoz and Vazquez, 1999: 3)

However, writing on behalf of FEANTSA, Avramov (1996: 71) prefers a wider, but still accommodation-based definition which also includes the value-laden term 'adequate':

Homelessness is the absence of a personal, permanent, adequate dwelling. Homeless people are those who are unable to access a personal, permanent, adequate dwelling or to maintain such a dwelling due to financial constraints and other social barriers.

(In FEANTSA, 1999: 10)

Adequate housing was defined by the United Nations Committee on Economic, Social and Cultural Rights in the following terms:

As both the Commission on Human Settlements and the Global Strategy for Shelter to the Year 2000 have stated: 'Adequate shelter means ... adequate privacy, adequate space, adequate security, adequate lighting and ventilation, adequate basic infrastructure and adequate location with regard to work and basic facilities – all at reasonable cost.'

(UNCESCR, 1991: art. 11(1))

As we have seen in Chapter 2, a later definition in the Habitat Agenda (UNCHS, 1997) defines adequate shelter more comprehensively to include physical accessibility, security of tenure, structural stability and durability, adequate heating, and suitable environmental quality and health-related factors. It continues:

Adequacy should be determined together with the people concerned, bearing in mind the prospect for gradual development. Adequacy often varies from country to country, since it depends on specific cultural, social, environmental and economic factors. Gender-specific and age-specific factors, such as the exposure of children and women to toxic substances, should be considered in this context.

(UNCHS, 1997: para. 60)

The definition used by the US Department of Education for homeless children and youth includes living in motels, hotels, trailer parks, camping grounds, cars, parks, public spaces, abandoned buildings, substandard housing, bus or train stations, or similar settings, or emergency or transitional shelters. It also includes those who are sharing the housing of other persons owing to loss of housing, economic hardship or a similar reason and those who are abandoned in hospitals or are awaiting foster care placement (Chicago Coalition for the Homeless, 2006).

Chamberlain (1999) suggests that there are two main forms of definitions: 'service delivery definitions', such as the one used by SAAP (above) and 'advocacy definitions', such as the one used by the Australian Council for Homeless Persons in 1995:

> A homeless person is without a conventional home and lacks most of the economic and social supports that a home normally affords. She/he is often cut off from the support of relatives and friends, she/he has few independent resources and often has no immediate means and in some cases little prospect of self support. She/he is in danger of falling below the poverty line, at least from time to time.
>
> (McIntosh and Phillips, 2000: 2)

It is intuitively evident that the social exclusion and detachment implied in many definitions may apply to men sleeping rough in the United States and Europe. It may not, however, apply to pavement-dwelling households in developing countries and is unlikely to apply to the many millions of people living in informal settlements throughout the world (Glasser, 1994) if we define them as homeless.

Typologies of homelessness

One way of understanding homelessness is through typologies, grouping the population into sectors with similar behaviour or characteristics based on some parameter. Typologies are valuable, particularly in the context of the more all-encompassing definitions, as they help us differentiate between and prioritise different subgroups of people who might all be defined as homeless. In the following, we examine some of these based mainly on industrialised countries' experience.

Based on quality and type of accommodation

The European Federation of National Organisations Working with the Homeless (FEANTSA) suggests a typology based on a combination of high or low quality and security (FEANTSA, 1999).

As presented in Figure 4.2, an adequate home (square 1) is one which is secure and where available space and amenities (quality) provide a good environment for the satisfaction of physical, social, psychological and cultural needs.[5]

Low quality (squares 3 and 4) would be manifest by overcrowding, high levels of noise and pollution or infestation. These are at odds with the need for and right to personal privacy, health and comfort. Low security, for example, temporary

Security

		High	Low
	High	1	2
Quality			
	Low	3	4

4.2 Types of housing adequacy (source: FEANTSA, 1999)

lodgings, a lack of community belonging or family exclusion and/or poor tenure rights and risk of evictions, are signs of households at risk of homelessness in a narrow sense (squares 2 and 4).

Any categorisation based so strongly upon the concept of low quality or security would include the vast majority of the developing world's population and would offer little differentiation between their individual circumstances and stress. It would not help to differentiate the potentially greater needs of street sleepers, without any form of shelter, from those of the millions of squatters around the world (see Chapter 5). As FEANTSA notes, in such a broad category, 'the unique distress and urgent needs of those people who are identified by a narrow definition (square 4) are lost and neglected' (FEANTSA, 1999: 10).

Even within the category of street sleepers, it would not assist us to prioritise those without any form of alternative place to sleep from those who have access to accommodation elsewhere, whether in the home village or in some less accessible location for other needs such as daily work.

When asked to fit their housing conditions into the FEANTSA four-way grid, five of the CARDO country researchers attempted to identify housing types in each cell. Anyone familiar with housing in developing countries will recognise from Table 4.1. that the high-quality/high-security cell (1) is occupied by only a small proportion of the housing extant: that which is in the formal sector, well-serviced, and still in good condition. The opposing cell (4) contains much of the housing stock occupied by the lowest-income groups. The aggregate of cells 2, 3 and 4 represent what are referred to by UN-Habitat (2003) as slums.

Cooper (1995) offers us a typology based again on accommodation or shelter but one which is structured by degrees. The worst degree, 'absolute homelessness', includes those living on the streets, under bridges and in deserted buildings. Even lesser degrees within Cooper's typology would certainly include millions of squatters and the CARDO study researchers regarded it to be of little use in their countries for developing interventions or apportioning resources.

Whilst this approach does allow a focus on absolute homelessness which would prioritise the worst cases, it lacks the cultural dimension within which people experience their homeless state. As we will show in Chapters 7 and 8, the social

Table 4.1 FEANTSA's model applied to circumstances in five developing countries in the CARDO study

	High security	Low security
High quality	1. Owner-occupied and formally rented housing in permanent materials, in low-, medium- and high-income areas, with at least some mains services.	2. Informal-sector rented housing. Owner-occupied or rented housing, and housing on lease,[a] built of permanent materials but on land that is not owned by the owner of the structure (squatters), or is on a short lease (Indonesia), or is threatened by flood (Bangladesh), landslide, and other natural disasters. Lodgers in good-quality housing (Indonesia, Zimbabwe, South Africa). Occupants of graveyards (Egypt).
Low quality	3. Housing in established areas where services are poorly provided or absent. Congested private slums, refugee settlements and old-city tenement houses (Bangladesh, India), *kampung* areas, especially *kampung kumuh* (Indonesia), old suburbs[b] and transit camps (Zimbabwe, South Africa), temporarily converted shops and emergency housing (Egypt).	4. Housing in unserviced and illegal squatter settlements with threat of eviction, violence and extortion. *Permukiman liar* (Indonesia), backyard or other shacks (Egypt, Zimbabwe, South Africa). Sleeping rough, pavement dwelling. Living under staircases, in boats and Zabbaleen settlements (Egypt).

Sources: Bannerjee Das (2002), El-Sheikh (2002), Kamete (2001), Olufemi (2001) and Rahardjo (2002)

Notes:
a In 21st-century Indonesia, the lease system is common; more than 30 per cent of urban and about 18 per cent of rural housing. A lease contract is usually for at least two years, after which a new contract is made, usually at a higher price in advance. If a new agreement is not reached, the lessee will have to leave the house and find a new place to stay (Rahardjo, 2002).
b In Zimbabwe, these include residential areas established in the colonial era for limited populations (mostly single men), which experienced great increases in population after independence. A fuller analysis can be found in Kamete (2000).

Table 4.2 Cooper's categories of homelessness

Characteristics	Degree of homelessness
Housed but without conditions of 'home', e.g. security, safety, or inadequate standards.	Third-degree relative homelessness: inadequate housing/incipient homelessness.
People constrained to live permanently in single rooms in private boarding houses.	Second-degree relative homelessness.
People moving between various forms of temporary or medium-term shelter such as refuges, boarding houses, hostels or friends.	First-degree relative homelessness.
People without an acceptable roof over their heads, living on the streets, under bridges and deserted buildings.	Absolute homelessness.

Source: Cooper (1995).

and cultural context for homelessness in developing countries is radically different from that in industrialised countries.

Based on risk

Daly (1996), from work in Britain, USA and Canada, posits a five-point classification based on the people's potential for homelessness:

1 People who are at risk or vulnerable to homelessness soon, perhaps within the next month, who need short-term assistance to keep them off the streets.
2 People whose primary or sole need is housing. They are usually working people who may be temporarily or episodically without homes and really need some financial or other assistance but do not have serious problems otherwise.
3 People who can become quasi-independent but need help with life skills so that they can manage on their own.
4 People with substantial and/or multiple difficulties but who, with help, could live in group or sheltered housing. These include those who have been institutionalised or abused and who need time before setting up independently.
5 People who need permanent institutional care or who may graduate on to some supportive or sheltered housing.

This risk or potential for homelessness echoes the understanding in Austria where, the 'Bundesarbeitsgemeinschaft Wohnungslosenhilfe' (BAWO) defines these as follows:

- 'Potential houselessness' includes those where the housing loss is not imminent but may be approaching because of inadequate housing or income.
- 'Imminent houselessness' concerns those who are threatened with the loss of their current abode, who are incapable of keeping it, or who cannot provide a replacement for themselves.
- 'Acute houselessness' includes living in the streets; in buildings meant for demolition, subway tunnels, railway wagons; in asylums, emergency shelters, institutions, inns and pensions; and people evicted from their former residence, staying with friends or relatives, and living in housing that is an acute health hazard.

(BAWO Projekt Büro, n.d.).

However, within this structure, the category of 'acute homelessness' is very broad and, in a developing countries context, would include too may people to be of use in prioritising resources for the most needy. Moreover, the categories of potentially houseless would include all those in informal settlements, in potential danger of eviction.

Based on homeless people's perceptions

What is noticeable about the typologies discussed thus far is that they do not take account of the way in which homeless people themselves would classify their situation. An approach which includes an understanding of the lived experience of homelessness in the United States is offered by Hertzberg (1992). She offers three groups of people, 'teeterers', 'resistors' and 'accommodators', defined by their characteristics, their perceptions of their homelessness and the length of time they have been homeless. It suggests that 'resistors' are fighting against homelessness, 'teeterers' are ambivalent to it and 'accommodators' have accepted it.

As Table 4.3 shows, people in each group share certain characteristics in relation to their accommodation and, more importantly, to their attitude to their situation. While acknowledging the importance of the homeless person's perception of their situation, Hertzberg's typology is generally inappropriate for developing countries for at least two reasons.

- She begins by categorising those people who are already recognised as homeless by other classifications.
- The timeframe she uses to identify each group and the places they are most likely to stay are inappropriate for developing countries. For example, many people in developing countries who have been homeless for up to ten years share few of the significant personal barriers to stability (mental illness, alcoholism, severe family dysfunction) of her teeterers.

Table 4.3 Hertzberg's threefold classification of homeless people

Characteristic	Resistors	Teeterers	Accommodators
Length of homelessness	Brief (2–4 years)	Longer (4–10 years)	Long-term (10+ years)
Attitude to condition	Fighting against	Ambivalent	Accepting
Staying where?	Inside	Most outside	Outside
Reason for homelessness	Not own decision	Not own decision	Some own decision
Desire for more education	Most want	Some want	Few want
Literate	National average	Most	Half
Severe family dysfunction	Some	Almost all	Most
View childhood positively	Almost all	Most	Almost none
Desire for own place	Almost all	Some	Few
Realistic hopes for the future	Most	Few	None

Source: Hertzberg (1992)

Based on exclusion

In industrialised countries, home and housing play an important role in people's place in society, potentially more so than they do in developing countries. Thus, exclusion from home and housing links directly to exclusion from society. Building upon this, Edgar and Meert (2005) present a typology of homelessness based upon exclusion from three domains – physical, legal and social. The physical domain is the adequate and appropriate physical dwelling. The social domain relates to having privacy and development of social relations. The legal domain is concerned with security and legal title. They present seven theoretical types or degrees of homelessness and housing exclusion, across three major domains, ranging from rough sleeping to living within a physically adequate, legally occupied dwelling but being in danger of personal violence, such as from an abusive partner. See Figure 4.3.

Based on choice and trajectory

From a Western viewpoint, it is particularly difficult to see homelessness, especially street sleeping, as anything other than negative and the most abject manifestation of destitution. However, this assumes a greater linkage between shelter and home

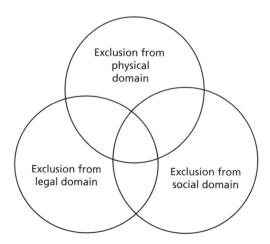

Exclusion from physical domain

Exclusion from legal domain

Exclusion from social domain

4.3 Domains of exclusion (source: Edger and Meert, 2005)

than is necessarily the case. Moreover, it prioritises what can be provided by shelter over what is provided by home.

Using the material in the CARDO study, Speak (2004) presents a typology which seeks to categorise homeless people not by their shelter situation but by the degree of choice they have over that situation and by how they exercise that choice in relation to improving other aspects of their lives. She suggests three categories of 'Supplementary', 'Survival' and 'Crisis' homelessness. As Table 4.4 shows, each has arrived at a state of homelessness via a different route and, thus, needs different approaches to support.

Based on responsibility for alleviating action

In the UK, the legislation provides a safety net but not for all. The UK Housing (Homeless Persons) Act of 1977 created a complex system of sequential tests designed to screen out the undeserving. As such its spirit can be traced back to earlier times and the Poor Law which offered relief for the deserving poor. The legislation places a duty on local authority housing departments to rehouse those applicants who are homeless or threatened with homelessness, who are eligible for rehousing, who are in priority need, who have not made themselves intentionally homeless and who have a local connection with that borough. The law, up to the 2002 amendment, is outlined in Tables 4.5 and 4.6.

Definitions of homelessness in developing countries

This section explores the different definitions of homelessness used in developing countries, and definitions which may form models for them. Definition is important

Table 4.4 Degrees and trajectories of homelessness

	Supplementary	*Survival*	*Crisis*
Reason	To supplement livelihood in existing home or for specific short term financial need (daughter's wedding)	To maintain personal or household basic needs	For immediate safety of own or household lives/ livelihoods
Degree of choice	Moderate to High	Low	None
Circumstances	Often lone males Has relatively stable home in other location Working Temporary or sporadic homeless	Includes women and children Losing or lost previous home Working or not working Longer term	Includes all groups
Trajectory	Upward – homeless situation improves living	Horizontal/ balanced – economic improvement at cost of home/ housing	Downward
Needs	Temporary, basic shelter, secure storage for earnings, medical treatment	Longer-term housing, economic assistance, training and education in city or diversity opportunities in rural location	Emergency shelter, food/ medical care/ education Resource to rebuild home, land, training
Example	Lone working male migrant remitting money to rural home (India)	Working man and wife, leaving children with elderly relatives in rural village (China)	Woman and/or children fleeing violence. Disaster victims (tsunami-hit coastal Sumatra, Indonesia)

Source: after Speak (2004)

Table 4.5 Conditions for housing under 2002 amendments to the UK Housing (Homeless Persons) Act of 1977

Status	Conditions
Homelessness	No legal right to occupy any accommodation.
	Has accommodation but may not occupy because of violence or actual threat of violence.
	Has moveable accommodation, e.g., boat or caravan but nowhere to moor/park.
Eligibility	Is a qualifying person in respect of immigration status.
	Has not been guilty of 'unacceptable behaviour' that makes them unsuitable to be a tenant.
Priority need	A person who has dependent children who would reasonably expect to reside with that person.
	A pregnant woman.
	A person who is homeless through fire, flood or other disaster.
	A person aged 16 or 17.
	A care leaver under 21.
	A person who is vulnerable because of old age, disability, mental illness, violence from another person, having served a custodial sentence, having been a member of the armed forces.
Intentionality	Has the applicant left accommodation they had legal right to or lost their accommodation through a deliberate act or failure to act?
Local connection	Is or was resident in the borough, is employed there, has family associations, must be near medical support.

Table 4.6 Legal entitlements to homelessness assistance

Status	Legal entitlements
Not homeless	No duty owed
Homeless, but not eligible	Advice and assistance
Homeless, eligible but not priority need	Advice and assistance
Homeless, eligible and priority need and not intentionality homeless	Secure accommodation
Homeless, eligible, priority need and intentionally homeless	Advice, assistance and secure accommodation for a reasonable period so that the applicant may find accommodation for themselves
Homeless, eligible, priority need, not intentional, local connection elsewhere	Secure accommodation requested from that authority

because 'most researchers agree on one fact: who we define as homeless determines how we count them' (Peressini et al., 1995).

The lack of data on homelessness in developing countries means that much of the current debate lacks an empirical foundation, without which the suitability of Western definitions and typologies cannot be assessed. We have difficulty, for example, in accepting that all who are not 'adequately housed' could be regarded as homeless in developing country contexts.

Estimates of people living in inadequate housing are quite varied as they tend to be based on examples and then factored up to a world scale. According to UN-Habitat (2006b), for example, 924 million people (about 300 per thousand of the world's urban population and about 143 per thousand of the total world population[6]) live in slums. According to UN-Habitat (2003), about half the housing in cities in the least developed countries is made of non-permanent materials and would have a lifespan of less than ten years; approximately 1.8 billion people (300 per thousand) lack access to improved water supply and 2.3 billion (383 per thousand) lack access to sanitation (UN-Habitat, 2003: extrapolated from table B.4). According to the World Bank (2003: 129), in 2000, developing world statistics show 'about 200 per thousand people without access to safe drinking water, 500 per thousand lived without adequate sanitation, and 900 per thousand lived without their wastewater treated in any way' (cited in UN-Habitat, 2006a: 117).[7]

Though there is much uncertainty about the numbers, the scale is clear enough. If this process were continued for each measure of inadequacy, and all households whose accommodation could be classified as inadequate[8] were included in the homelessness totals, most households in developing countries would be homeless. In Indonesia, for example, an estimated 62 per cent of urban households and 92 per cent of all rural households do not have access to piped water and have to depend on wells, springs, rivers or water vendors for their water supply. In Jakarta, Indonesia's capital and economic centre, only half of the population have connections to the municipal water supply (Badan Pusat Statistik, 2000). However, these people are unlikely to be thought of as homeless, nor to feel themselves to be homeless.

Similarly, just because a household is crowded by some definition does not automatically and universally render it homeless. For example, we found in previous work that 73 per cent of all households in Kumasi, Ghana, live in single rooms and there is a city-wide mean occupancy rate of 3.3 persons per room (Tipple and Willis, 1991). Although most households at or near the mean might regard their housing as inadequate, residents of Kumasi would not generally regard themselves, nor would they be regarded, as homeless because of the crowding. Similarly, the sharing of accommodation because of some hardship is one of the criteria for homelessness that may hold good in industrialised countries but may be contentious if used in the same way in developing countries. Sharing is so common, and accepted in societies there (e.g. Gilbert et al., 1993), that it cannot reasonably be regarded as homelessness unless it is accompanied by some other problem such as overcrowding, poor physical condition, lack of services or dangerous location.

The discussions on the validity of any definition of homelessness (above) are undoubtedly keenly contested in the industrialised world, where homelessness is accepted as an issue, however poorly it might be handled in policy. In the developing world, however, states are in a very different stage of development with respect to accepting that they have any role in dealing with those who are in housing crisis. In addition, states and NGOs have such a major task helping people who are very badly housed indeed that they tend to ignore people who are not accommodated at all. Indeed, NGOs such as Homeless International, based in the UK, and Shack/ Slum Dwellers International, operating in many countries, tend to work through location-specific communities in which the most poorly housed and unsheltered are unlikely to be found. Thus, while the focus in industrialised countries may be privileging the rough sleepers ahead of the very poorly housed, the opposite is more likely in developing countries. Furthermore, the further up the poorly housed range a household is, the more likely it is to be helped, especially as audits of states' performances towards the Millennium Development Goals show the need for easy targets for assistance. Thus, we make no apology for going back to basics in exploring what efforts are being made to define homelessness and homeless people in developing countries, however crude they may appear following the discussion above.

The lack of a definition of homelessness has serious implication for homeless people, particularly as it leaves them in a legal vacuum (Munoz and Vazquez, 1999). Recent events in Zimbabwe demonstrate why it is important both to define homelessness and to differentiate between housing which is acceptable in policy and that which is not and, thus, constitutes homelessness for its occupants. In May 2005, thousands of shacks and informal dwellings were destroyed in Zimbabwe's Operation Murambatsvina (Shona for 'Drive out the rubbish'), launched by President Mugabe and his ruling ZANU PF party. In the logic of this operation, it was argued that no one was being made homeless because the occupants of the targeted settlements were already homeless. Their structures were illegal shacks ('rubbish'), encroaching on public land, and so had no right to exist (Institute for War and Peace Reporting (IWPR), 2005).

Similarly, muddled thinking about housing can increase homelessness in the guise of improving housing conditions. Several years ago, one of the authors (Graham Tipple) was talking to the 'squatter control officer' in the City of Kitwe, Zambia, where he had worked as a planner more than a decade previously. They were discussing plans the Squatter Control Unit had for a settlement near the City Council's Ndeke estate. There was a policy at that time to clear the informal settlements and build formal residential areas. Being subversive, Tipple asked the officer if she felt it was reasonable to clear housing to build other housing. Her reply was that the current housing was not of a good enough standard and should be cleared to make way for some which was. In response, Tipple argued that he knew of several very well-built houses there. The officer responded that, if the houses were good enough, they would be left intact. Tipple suggested that it would be in the people's interests, therefore, to improve their homes quickly, so that they would retain their place there. To this, the officer responded that only those good enough by a certain date in the recent past should be accepted.[9]

Such real or intended clearances in Zimbabwe and Zambia demonstrate the extreme end of a continuum of muddled thinking about what constitutes being housed: which dwellings are valid as housing supply, whose dwelling is counted and whose is not in a statistical representation of the housing stock in a country. In calculating the current housing stock in India, for example, the statistics distinguish between serviceable units (in *pucca*, semi-*pucca* and *kutcha* categories),[10] which are included, and non-serviceable[11] *kutcha* housing of which there were 11 million in 1991 (Government of India, 1996), which are not included. This makes clear that the Government of India regards people in non-serviceable *kutcha* dwellings to be in need of housing but it does not mean that it necessarily regards them as homeless.

Definitions of homelessness from the CARDO survey[12]

Because there seems to be a broad margin of housing inadequacy that cannot easily be assumed to constitute homelessness, we asked all the nine country survey collaborators in the CARDO survey, how homelessness is defined in their country context. The following is a discussion of these definitions.

Official or government definitions vary widely among the countries in the CARDO study. They range from non-existent to virtually all-encompassing. Despite using the term 'homeless' widely in policy, a number of countries, including Peru, Ghana and China, have no single official governmental definition of homelessness. The way in which the term is used in housing development policy and in censuses, however, gives an indication of how some governments use the term 'homeless'. In the following, we divide the definitions into those using the criteria of location, permanence of occupation or security of tenure, welfare entitlement and quality.

Location

The group most easily defined as homeless are those living on the streets. In earlier analysis (Tipple and Speak, 2005), we have separated this category into two, the second of which is 'lifestyle' (transience, vagrancy). However it seems more reasonable now to subsume the two into a definition of homelessness based on where people are: 'on the streets or other open spaces'; mobile or temporary rather than settled. Thus, if someone lives on the streets or other open spaces and does not regularly sleep within a recognised dwelling, they are defined as homeless. These are in FEANTSA's state of 'rooflessness' (FEANTSA, 1999), Cooper's absolute homelessness (Cooper, 1995), at the extreme end of both homelessness and home-to-homelessness continuums (Watson and Austerberry, 1986), and within the UN's (1998) definition of 'homeless households'.

Many countries define homelessness as not living in recognised dwellings and then go on to stipulate the sort of places homeless people are found. Thus, those living on the streets (a location as well as a lifestyle) are usually included. In Bangladesh, the definition includes locations where the homeless people 'are found on the census night … in the rail station, launch *ghat* (terminal*)*, bus station, *hat-bazaar* (market), *mazar* (shrine), staircase of public/government buildings, open space, etc.' (BBS, 1999: 3; cited by Ghafur, 2002). The common thread in these locations is that they are public places not intended for residence. Thus, there is a strong connection between expressions of homelessness based on the adequacy of housing and those based on location. In South Africa, officials of the Gauteng Provincial Housing Department and the Greater Johannesburg Metropolitan Council base their definition on quality[13] but tend, in part, to express it locationally as they consider homelessness to be:

> People without … adequate shelter [or] secure tenure, … living in squatter settlements, … living in backrooms in townships and elsewhere,[14] [and] living in slum conditions. … a cardboard house under the bridge, occupation of metropolitan open spaces, parks, vacant land, a couple of dirt-stained blankets on the corners of high-rise building, occupation of unused buildings.
>
> … The definition of homelessness includes the unavailability of adequate shelter, land and security of tenure. It is a result of unfavourable financial conditions and other conditions beyond the control of the homeless people …
>
> (Olufemi, 2001)

In the above, some of the locations are within residential areas and in structures which are built as residences, albeit to a standard lower than is formally approved. The backrooms in townships are structures of timber or masonry built to the rear of formal high-density[15] (former 'black') township housing plots. The tenants usually share the services of the plot with the other occupants. However, there is no differentiation in this between renters in flimsy wooden sheds sharing bathing and sanitation facilities with twenty or more occupants of the plot and married children of a plot holder occupying rooms built in cement and iron with self-contained bathroom and toilet.

Even though adequacy appears to be important in the definitions used by the interviewees, no distinction is made amongst shack dwellers, people in informal settlements and homeless pavement dwellers. The result is that shack dwellers and people in informal settlements, arguably somewhat better off than pavement dwellers, benefit most from the various housing delivery policies and programmes such as subsidies and informal settlement upgrading programmes.

The interviewees also appear to have yielded to the temptation of adding detail to imply neglect of conventional values and personal inadequacy; the 'couple of dirt-stained blankets' contrasted directly with the 'high-rise building', to place the occupant firmly outside of respectable society. We can feel the opprobrium of 'respectable' Johannesburg as we read the words.

Transience, impermanence of occupation, insecurity of tenure

It might appear that people living in unconventional locations, such as steep river banks or derelict buildings are transient or impermanent. This is not necessarily so and there are many people around the world who reside in such locations for lengthy periods. They are, however, extremely insecure and eventually forced to leave through eviction or disaster, for example, flood or landslide. Nevertheless, many homeless people are transient. In Bangladesh, many homeless people are landless or have become so by losing their original homestead. Thus, they have no permanent place to set up home. This is reflected in the Bangladesh Bureau of Statistics (BBS) official definition of homelessness, which it uses for census purposes, as: '[The] floating population are the mobile and vagrant category of rootless people who have no permanent dwelling units whatever' (1999: 3; cited by Ghafur, 2002).

This definition was refined from an earlier one which included the term 'transient population', when it was agreed that many of them may have homes elsewhere which they had temporarily abandoned. They are characterised as 'floating', a term also used in China (see below), and 'rootless' (implying separation from family and familiar places). This is further reinforced using the terms 'mobile' and 'vagrant'; both implying moving about on a regular basis but the first being value-free, the second laden with judgements about worth and desert. In dictionary definitions of 'vagrant', the concept of idleness is conjoined with wandering and is compounded by links with 'vagabondage' which 'emphasizes the idea of worthless living, often by trickery, thieving, or other disreputable means' (Dictionary.com). This is further underlined by translations of vagrant as 'vagabond' or similar in the major international languages of French, Portuguese and Spanish. Together they suggest the rootless, irresponsible and reprehensible lifestyle at odds with settled society.

Permanence of occupation, or the level of security of tenure, is another criterion often used in definitions. It appears early on in the Johannesburg definition (above) and is adopted by many countries in their definitions of homelessness. Those involved can range from people who are rootless, moving from one rough-sleeping location to another, to those in dwellings that may be of varying quality but share a lack of secure tenure – reflecting FEANTSA's (1999) 'insecure accommodation', part of Cooper's (1995) criteria of relative homelessness and Springer's (2000) risk of becoming homeless. In the CARDO samples, it is the most frequently used criterion.

In Peru, people without legal title to land are regarded as homeless, unlike occupants of legally owned but poor-quality buildings. They are included in the land registration programme which focuses on formalising land title for people in informal settlements without a registered plot or property, who are below the poverty level, and can claim a plot from the government. It is officially thought, in line with De Soto (2000), that their problem can be solved by increasing security through legal title. Figure 4.4 shows the process of formal plot allocation and regularisation under way in one illegally settled area of the desert outside Lima. The municipality will take no further role in improving the settlement but the settlers now have legal title. Households' ability to consolidate their dwelling varies from simple woven palm fronds or plywood or corrugated iron rooms to rendered brick villas. Figure 4.5 shows the range of housing.

In Indonesia, the closest translation of homelessness in the national language is *tunawisma* (from Old Javanese meaning 'no house'). The Indonesian language does not distinguish between house and home (both words translating into *rumah*). This might suggest that Indonesians would have difficulty differentiating between

4.4 Lines in the sand, drawn by the local municipality, show the regularisation process under way. Individual plots have been allocated and areas have been cleared for 'roads' in an informal settlement in the desert near Lima.

4.5 Households who invaded at the same time consolidate their dwellings differently over time depending on their abilities, resources and priorities

houselessness and homelessness. However, the official definition, as used in the national census of 2000, is based not on houselessness, rooflessness, rootlessness or landlessness, but on permanence.

The Indonesian census of 2000 divides the population into two main categories, those having a permanent place to stay (*mempunyai tempat tinggal tetap*) and those not having a permanent place to stay (*tidak mempunyai tempat tinggal tetap*). The latter included ship's crewmen, nomadic people and people living in houseboats or floating houses,[16] as well as the more obvious *tunawisma* – houseless (Rahardjo, 2002).

The importance of tenure is seen again in a somewhat extreme form in Zimbabwe. The definition used by the National Housing Taskforce of Zimbabwe is based on the assumption that anyone who does not own their own home in an officially approved residential area is homeless. Thus, as we saw above, the people in informal settlements evicted in the violent demolitions of May 2005, could be ignored by the government as their state of homelessness had not been caused by the evictions; it had pre-existed them. So embedded is this concept of homelessness being related to ownership in Zimbabwe that government housing policy prescribes that 90 per cent of all new housing should be for home ownership and only 10 per cent for rent. Furthermore, in a policy reminiscent of the UK's Right to Buy policy, all urban local authorities are required to sell their housing to tenants.

However, this is only a precursor to a second classification of welfare entitlement (see below), in that everyone in Zimbabwe who does not own a publicly provided dwelling is entitled to register on the Official Housing Waiting List (OHWL). Government housing is available to all those on the official waiting lists under this definition, on a 'first-come, first-served' basis. No priority is given on the basis of need; their insecurity of tenure is sufficient (Kamete, 2001).

The clearest case of transience being considered as homelessness is in China. During the planned economy in China, under the domiciliary registration system, the government only allowed rural people to migrate to the city if they were transferring officially from their place of registration (*hukou*) to a receiving work unit (*danwei*). They would then be registered in the receiving *hukou* and it would appear on a reissued identity card as their official place of registration.[17] Any migration outside of this registration system was considered as disorganised and unplanned and was forbidden under a State Council decision of 1953 to prevent rural migrants from flowing aimlessly into cities. The word '盲流', *mangliu*, coming from the phrase '盲目流动' meaning 'aimlessly flowing',[18] has been used since then, in a discriminatory way, about the unemployed, unregistered migrant population in PR China. Importantly for us, *mangliu* has strong pejorative undertones; indeed, there have been posters in public places urging people to stamp out the *mangliu*.[19] It is now regarded as rather dated as the state increases its stress on a harmonious society with protection of the rights of the poor.

Another term used for poor people in the cities is '三无人员' *sanwurenyuan*, meaning 'three "no" people' as they have no ability to work, no source of income and no relatives or dependants. These people may not be migrants, however, as elderly or disabled people may be included (Wang, 2004). There have also been references to three other 'nos' of no ID cards, no temporary residence cards and no work approval cards (*China Daily*, 2005). 'Floating' employed people are called '民工' *mingong* (civilian worker). The word *mingong* has less of a derogatory sense than *mangliu* (personal communication, Ying Chang, 16 January 2007). Other derogatory terms used include *liulanghan*, people who sleep on the street, and *jiaohuazi*, beggar.

The development of a market economy in China and the relaxation of some controls, including control over movement, has meant that China is experiencing a growth in the number of people moving away from their *hukou*, where housing is assured. These *mangliu* or *sanwurenyuan* appear to be the closest to being officially defined as homeless people that can be found in China. They may not be without shelter but they have some of the characteristics of homeless people in that they suffer multiple exclusions, they do not have access to (subsidised) housing through the normal channels and, like most households, find themselves unable to afford housing on the open market. They collect in *chengzhongcun*; villages which have been consolidated into expanding cities where the housing tends to be of poor quality and overcrowded. They tend to be dislocated from mainstream society in that they are not locally entitled to school places, welfare payments, etc. This reflects Edgar et al.'s (1999) state of social exclusion and marginalisation, and Caplow et al.'s (1968) absence or attenuation of affiliative bonds. However, China still has no official definition of homelessness and regards those without housing, especially

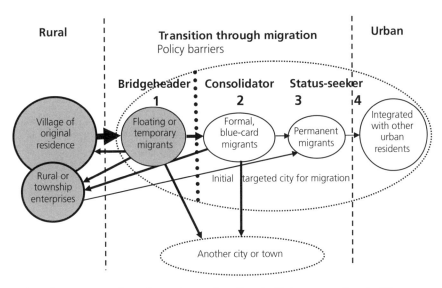

Rural

Transition through migration
Policy barriers

Urban

Bridgeheader ⋮ Consolidator   Status-seeker
        1   ⋮   2   3   ¦4

Village of original residence

Floating or temporary migrants

Formal, blue-card migrants

Permanent migrants

Integrated with other urban residents

Rural or township enterprises

Initial targeted city for migration

Another city or town

4.6   The process of rural to urban migration in China according to Wang
       (2004: 121)

squatters, as illegal rather than as a category of people to be supported by policy.
No differentiation appears to be made between the few *mangliu/sanwurenyuan*
who live on the street and those in *chengzhongcun* village accommodation with
respect to citizenship rights.

Wang (2004) attempts to explain the migration to Chinese cities in a
diagram which is quite helpful for understanding where the floating migrants
(*mangliu/sanwurenyuan*) fit within the system (Figure 4.6). Wang (2004) uses
the bridgeheader–consolidator–status-seeker typology from Turner (1976) to
differentiate migrants with different statuses. Unlike Turner, who posited a progress
from bridgeheader, through consolidator, to status-seeker, Wang shows that the
migration process is not simply one-way. He shows that only some of the groups
progress to the next stage while others move back to the rural area. Indeed, the
floating or temporary migrants are restricted from settling permanently by the
process of gaining the blue-stamped residence card (the urban *hukuo*) unless they
have been very successful in business. All homeless people in urban China will
fall into Wang's 'bridgeheader' category but not all people in this category will
be homeless.

However, one of the main issues facing people in China is forced sharing,
leading to severe overcrowding, which is not considered as homelessness but
would be in an industrialised context. None of the CARDO study countries defined
those involuntarily sharing accommodation or those living in institutions (except
shelters specifically for homeless people) as homeless, except when they qualify
for other reasons.

4.7 Rooftop rooms in Egypt built in masonry but poorly roofed and without planning permission. Occupants are defined as homeless. (Photograph by Suzanne Speak)

Quality

The definitions which have gone before have included some qualitative measures; they seem unavoidable – in Bangladesh and Indonesia, the lack of a permanent dwelling; in South Africa, the lack of adequate shelter and references to a 'cardboard house'. Others, however, appear to be almost totally quality-based. Egypt categorises people as homeless by the quality of their housing. People living in 'marginal housing' (*iskan gawazi*) and 'unsuitable housing' are regarded as homeless. These are then expressed through locational categories to imply quality of accommodation; residents of shacks, kiosks, staircases, rooftops (Figure 4.7), public institutions and cemeteries (El-Sheikh, 2002).[20] In addition to its welfare criterion (below), the Census of India defines homeless people as those not living in 'census houses', i.e. a structure with a roof.

In Ghana, the very concept of homelessness is new and it sits uneasily within a context of traditional extended family responsibility. There is, in fact, no word for homelessness in the main Ghanaian languages, reflecting that the phenomenon is relatively recent and contrary to Ghanaian culture.[21] In its attempt to rise to the new challenge of homelessness, the Ghana Statistical Service (GSS) uses a standard of accommodation criterion by accepting that anyone who lives in a structure with a roof is not homeless. No other issues of structural quality or suitability are considered. Thus, 'homes' in Ghana include sales kiosks, abandoned warehouses, offices or shops (Department of Housing and Planning Research, 2002). There is some logic to this as the main cities in Ghana (Greater Accra, Kumasi and Cape Coast) are never cold and there is a high level of personal safety in its ordered society. Thus, as long as one can keep out of the torrential rain, little other shelter is required. In addition, however, for the 2000 population and housing census, the GSS defines homelessness not only in shelter terms but also in social terms as 'people not belonging to a household'.[22] This means that only the most destitute, without any form of shelter or roof and without kin or friends anywhere nearby to take responsibility for them, are considered as officially homeless. In the main cities in the south, many of these will be northerners dispossessed and orphaned by inter-ethnic conflicts.

We offer tabular forms of the above discussion in Table 4.7.

Working definitions

The official definitions discussed thus far are those used by governments, predominantly in their land and housing policies and censuses. However, arguably more appropriate, working definitions are adopted by NGOs to bring priorities to their work. In some cases working definitions are tighter than official ones, in order to focus the NGOs' work on those most in need. In other cases, an NGO's definition can be much more all-encompassing, in order to provide for those who would not be considered homeless officially, and for whom government support is not available.

In South Africa, the government view seems to be widely accepted. NGOs such as the South African Homeless People's Federation regard shack dwellers and squatters as homeless people. The Federation states that it is a network of organisations that are 'rooted in shack settlements, backyard shacks or hostels' (Bolnick, 1996).[23] It operates on a wider definition to support those living in conditions which would not otherwise be considered as homelessness in many countries. Furthermore, by including these, the Federation opens its remit to about one-fifth of all residential units in areas built under apartheid for members of the majority black population (Crankshaw et al., 2000).

Three distinct groups of homeless street people were identified by NGOs in the Johannesburg inner city (Olufemi, 1997, 1998):

- pavement or street dwellers – for example, those who live on bare floors, pavements, in cardboard boxes, etc.;
- those who live in temporary shelters such as bus or railway stations, open halls, taxi ranks, etc.
- those who live in city shelters (shelters provided by NGOs or faith-based organisations).

These are based on quality (or adequacy) and location, just as the ones used by officials in local government are.

Table 4.7 Criteria for homelessness by country studied

	Location	Transience, impermanence of occupation or insecurity of tenure	Housing quality
Bangladesh	In rail station, launch terminal, bus station, market, shrine, staircase of public/ government buildings, open space, etc.	Floating, mobile, vagrant, rootless people	
China		Floating people without residence permit	
Egypt			In marginal and unsuitable housing, including shacks, kiosks, staircases, rooftops, public institutions, open boats and cemeteries
Ghana			Lacking a roof
India			Not living in 'census houses', i.e. a structure with a roof
Indonesia		Without a permanent place to stay	
Peru	Living on the streets: alcoholics, addicts, vagrants, criminals and mentally ill	Without legal title to land	
South Africa	In squatter settlements, in backrooms in townships and elsewhere	Without secure tenure, in squatter settlements, in rented backrooms in townships and elsewhere	
Zimbabwe		In informal residential areas	

As we have seen, in Zimbabwe, the government's definition of homelessness is very broadly based and includes everyone 'without a house to his name'. Even some NGOs there, such as Dialogue on Shelter for the Homeless in Zimbabwe (DSHZ) and the Zimbabwe Homeless People's Federation (ZIHOPFE), subscribe to this definition. However, among many relief NGOs, this definition is narrowed to focus on those in greatest need, such as people on the streets, displaced people and farm workers recently evicted by the government in the land reallocations. Some NGOs such as Bulawayo Shelter, the Scripture Union and Zimbabwe Red Cross Society include displaced persons in their client group (Kamete, 2001). Even these groups will not, however, support anyone with family willing to take them in. In this they use a definition based on familial connections comparable with the Ghana definition (Department of Housing and Planning Research, 2002).

In India, NGOs operate on a wider definition of homelessness than the government. This is either to draw attention to the poor and unsafe housing conditions in which many people live, or actively to support those people who would not be eligible to receive government help. The National Campaign for Housing Rights uses a broad, holistic, definition of home as a place where one is

> able to live with dignity in social, legal and environmental security and with adequate access to essential housing resources like land, building materials, water, fuel, fodder as well as civic services and finance (Bannerjee Das, 2002)

Also in India, Aashray Adhikar Abhiyan (2001: p. xiii) defines a homeless person as

> [one] who has no place to call a home in the city. By home is meant a place which not only provides a shelter but takes care of one's health, social, cultural and economic needs. Home provides a holistic care and security [sic].

This tends to emphasise the lack of the components of a broad image of home (as expressed by Somerville, 1992) which makes it a much more inclusive definition than that used by the Indian government (Bannerjee Das, 2002).

In Bangladesh, where the official definition of homeless equates to rooflessness, the international NGO, CONCERN, takes a more holistic approach to defining homelessness. For example, it considers social issues and causes of homelessness and includes brothel workers as homeless (Ghafur, 2002).

In some countries it is left to NGOs to take account of issues of quality and condition of shelter. In Ghana, for example, the Westphalia Children's Village, at Oyoko in the Ashanti region, considers children in 'poor living environments', such as a dilapidated dwelling, as homeless. They are not considered so by the government, however, unless they live on the streets and seek shelter at night in abandoned buildings or bus shelters, or if they cannot trace their families (Department of Housing and Planning Research, 2002).

4.8 Rundown city centre *tugurios*. Occupants are considered homeless owing to the extremely poor and dangerous conditions. (Photograph by Suzanne Speak)

In Peru, where there is no official definition but the policy emphasis is on land registration, many thousands of people live in very poor conditions. They live either in inadequate shelters on registered or unregistered plots in squatter settlements or in dilapidated and hugely overcrowded *tugurios,* old inner-city tenement properties. Their plight is taken up by NGOs who, thus, widen their definition of homelessness to include poor quality and dangerous conditions, lack of facilities and infestation by vermin. For example, CEPROMU, an NGO in Lima, works exclusively with households living in the rundown city-centre *tugurios*, whom it considers homeless owing to the extremely poor and dangerous conditions in which they live (Miranda and Salazar, 2002). This is in line with the idea of including people who are 'at risk' in the definition of homelessness (McIntosh and Phillips, 2000).

Conclusions

In the definitions discussed above, an observer familiar with the homelessness literature in Europe, North America, Japan or Australia might be struck by the narrowness of the boundaries. In industrialised countries, the definition of homelessness has been widening over the years to include those in shared and transient accommodation, those with certain levels of overcrowding, in poorly serviced, inadequate or damaged dwellings, and those likely to become homeless in the near future, especially on release from institutions (UNCHS, 2000). Where definitions include measures of inadequacy in shelter, they set a much higher threshold – lack of any basic services, broken staircases, leaking roofs, etc. In developing countries, however, policymakers work within the context of a global housing shortage, concentrated within cities. In this context, inadequate housing provides shelter for billions of people.[24]

It is obvious from the above discussions that defining homelessness in developing countries is a work in progress and we have just started the process, based on experience gathered in the CARDO study. In line with our wish to ensure that 'the unique distress and urgent needs of those people who are identified by a narrow definition' (FEANTSA, 1999: 10) are not lost and neglected, we feel it is important to define homelessness quite tightly in developing countries. In the following chapter, we attempt to differentiate between those who are inadequately housed and those who are truly homeless.

5 Accommodation conditions and differentiating between homeless people and those in inadequate housing

When introducing the living conditions of households who are as much in need of work as of improved housing in a document he wrote (UNCHS and ILO, 1995: 17–18), Tipple referred to

the horrors which face many millions of people every morning when they wake from a mosquito-disturbed sleep. Their night may have been spent on a mat in a room with four, six, or up to ten others, with inadequate ventilation,[1] and an earth floor which allows the damp to rise. Their morning ablutions will comprise either a wash from tepid and cloudy water in a tin or a queue to use the only bathroom in a tenement house shared by 50 or 100 people. The toilet queue is too long, so a visit to the rubbish dump to defecate in the morning mist, or to the Augean public latrine where privacy is marginally better, is in order. The working clothes are rescued from their place over a string extended above the bed and the man sets off on the routine of queuing for crowded transport to his place of employment many miles away, often without breaking his fast.

His wife is left to feed the children on last night's left overs or some rice porridge cooked in cloudy water over a charcoal stove on the floor by the door, then to do the household chores and fetch water, before she clears a small space and begins the daily business of preparing food for city workers, or laundering clothes, or smoking fish, or sewing up garments for a manufacturer to export to Europe. At dusk she cooks the day's meal, squatting on the floor before the round of washing her children from a soapy bowl in the space outside the room. On wet days, the whole household is caked in mud, on dry days, the dust blows into the food and water, carrying cists and parasites to plague them. The earth on which they tread harbours parasites, eager to enter a human host through bare feet, the dusty air they breathe brings hepatitis A and meningitis, the fumes within it come from the sulphuric acid plant at the copper mine or the chemical works down the hill, adding coughs to malarial fever. Their water is a breeding ground for mosquito larvae, *salmonella*, *shigella*, and *E. coli*, … waiting to strike the children down with malaria or diarrhoea. Their neighbours on the steep slopes suffer added danger from land-slips in the heavy rain; down by the river, flooding is regular and brings added dangers from sewage and other pollutants. Such, and similar, are the living conditions of poor people in the cities and towns of developing countries.

In this chapter we discuss the accommodation in which many people live their lives in developing countries and tease out whether inadequate housing, such as that occupied by the hypothetical household above, constitutes homelessness. It is one of the contentions of this chapter[2] that it is important to separate the people who live in adequate but tolerable housing from those whose housing is sufficiently inadequate to cause them grave problems and have them defined as homeless.

Adequacy of housing, as we have seen in Chapter 2, is defined by the Habitat Agenda (UNCHS, 1997) in terms of a multitude of facets including security, durability, access to services and the essentials of life, and all at affordable cost. Any reader with even a passing acquaintance with cities such as Cairo, Caracas, Lagos, La Paz, Lima, Jakarta, Johannesburg, Manila, Mumbai, Mexico City or Nairobi cannot fail to realise that huge numbers of the world's households live in inadequate housing. All of them are, in some of the literature, described as homeless. However, we believe that it is important to examine just what conditions are experienced by homeless people and where the boundary between homelessness and inadequate housing might be.

In the context of accommodation conditions of homeless people, Tables 5.1 and 5.2 attempt to tease out the interrelated issues of land rights, ability to keep and store possessions and standard of shelter. Within standard of accommodation we look at the issues of privacy/security, protection from the weather, and access to shelter. They are presented as two ladders with the poorest accommodation at the bottom and the best at the top.

In Table 5.1. we identify some rungs on the property rights ladder from having no rights even to occupy a space on a pavement or other public land through to full *de jure* tenure of land. There is an evident threshold between those with *de facto* rights to use land in the medium term (months) and those who have *de facto* rights in the longer term (for more than a year).

All around the world, the most basic 'accommodation' experienced by homeless people is similar: a section of pavement or open ground on which the body can be laid down for the night and on which the person can sit when not on the move.

Table 5.1 Ladder of property rights: levels of security and standards of accommodation

	Level of rights gained by an occupant	Land		Possessions		Standard of shelter
		Legal right over land	Right to stay on land/sleeping place	Ability to keep	Ability to store safely	
6	Full *de jure* tenure	Full	Full security	Yes	Yes, in a structure, may be locked away	Shelter can be improved
5	Some property rights	None	Ability to sell/ assign/ pass on to heirs	Yes	Yes, in a structure, may be locked away	Shelter can be improved
4	*De facto* right of use of land over the long term (>1 year)	None	Able to stay; may have some fear of eviction	Yes	Yes, in a structure, may be locked away	Shelter can be improved
3	*De facto* right of use of a space over the medium term (months)	None	Has daily/nightly use of a space.	Limited possessions possible	Only through social mediation, possessions may be visible to all	Shelter can be rigged over weeks or months
2	Having the first refusal on a sleeping location	None	Has daily/nightly use of a space.	No, only what can be carried/ pushed and protected when asleep	None	Only the most rudimentary
1	Has to find a new place to sleep each night or several times a night	None	None	No, only what can be carried/ pushed and protected when asleep	None	None apart from what the environment offers

Table 5.2 Ladder of accommodation: levels of security, weatherproofing and access to services and among different standards of accommodation

	Level of accommodation enjoyed by occupant	Privacy/Security — Visual privacy	Secure from attack	Protection from the weather	Access to services
5	Has a roof, locking door in strong walls	Yes, has privacy	Yes, has personal security from all but the most determined intruder; possessions kept out of public sight and can be locked away; secure from casual attack and robbery	Mostly weatherproof, sealed against all but the most exceptional weather.	Could have any level of services from none to full formal provision
4	Has a roof, closing door in opaque walls.	Has privacy	Yes, has some personal security' limited possessions possible, out of public sight but not locked away.	Mostly weatherproof	Could have any level of services from none to full formal provision
3	Has a reasonably waterproof roof but incomplete walls/door	No, little privacy	No, little security for goods and person	Sheltered from the sun and regular levels of rainfall	Could have illegal connections or low level of formal infrastructure
2	Utilises a public roofed space (e.g. a railway station) but has no personal structure	No, only what is culturally mediated	No, only what is culturally mediated and/ or arranged by staff of the public space	Sheltered from the sun and regular levels of rainfall	Unlikely except those provided for public use
1	No structure	No, only what is culturally mediated	No, only what is culturally mediated	Only what can be arranged to protect the body	Unlikely although could have full access if on a formal plot

This is the lowest end of the ladder of property rights, spanning several rungs representing variations to this very basic 'accommodation':

1 A suitable place might have to be found each night, or even several times each night, as the person or household struggles to gain the tiniest niche in the city.
2 There may be some recognised right for a person or household to use a particular space, at least until someone 'stronger' usurps them.
3 There may be well established *de facto* rights which allow security enough even to construct a rudimentary shelter.

It is evident that the utility of a space on the pavement is influenced by the ease with which it is available and the ability to stay for many nights or even years in the same place. Thus, levels of *de facto* security of tenure are an issue for street sleepers just as they are for the housed population, only at a different level.

Rung 4 on the ladder is characterised by the all-important ability to stay over the long term, i.e., more than a year, but not necessarily with any legal (*de jure*) backing. This is likely to be off the streets but may still be on government-owned land. Occupiers may have some rights through tribal chiefs or other influential people so that they are confident they will not be evicted and they may even have full rights, especially where there has been government action to formalise informal settlements, for example, in Peru. This amount of security allows households routinely to construct a dwelling strong enough to allow it to be locked. The top two rungs on the ladder both allow considerable security of tenure, *de facto* on rung 5 and with legal backing on rung 6.

The quality of shelter ladder (Table 5.2) is complementary but not identical. On the bottom rung, the quality of shelter can be very varied but is consistently poor:

• It might be just part of the open pavement so that the homeless person's body and paraphernalia are both unsheltered and unprotected from passers-by. This might be modified by a mat, sleeping bag, cardboard sheets or boxes, etc., but it remains exposed to the weather despite the cocoon contrived around the homeless person (Figure 5.1).
• It might be set back in a doorway or other off-the-route space so that at least there is little danger of accidentally being trodden on.
• It might be covered by tarpaulin sheets stretched from a wall over pavements (Figure 5.2).
• It might be any of the above and also hidden away behind a barrier or within a disused building, giving both enclosure and privacy.
• It might be possible to leave some possessions there, protected by the reluctance of passers-by to rifle through grubby packages or because a friendly neighbour (a stall-holder, taxi-rank operator, etc.) will watch them (Figure 5.3).

Together, these variations constitute the lowest rung of the ladder of accommodation. Without a structure, all privacy and security of person are culturally mediated. In

5.1 The popular image of the homeless single male sleeping rough, in La Paz, Bolivia. (Photograph by Graham Tipple)

5.2 Tarpaulins stretched across street furniture provide rudimentary shelter in Kolkata. (Photograph by Urmi Sengupta)

5.3 A mother and her child making a life among their paraphernalia on the pavement of Kolkata.(Photograph by Urmi Sengupta)

5.4 On a cold January morning in New Delhi, homeless men buy breakfast from a stall close to their shelter. (Photograph by Tony Pietropicolo)

central Kolkata, people living on the pavement outside magnificent public buildings turn to the wall if they want privacy. There is a tap nearby for washing but no privacy other than people's averting their gaze. Their possessions hang there in sacks, suspended from magnificently carved window ledges, easily stolen but not touched as they are regarded as dirty and probably contain little of value anyway. When it rains all are soaked unless the household moves to a shelter.

There are many versions of accommodation at this level. For example, in the Indian subcontinent, it is common for a rickshaw puller or a pushcart operator to sleep on his vehicle, parked up on a street or in an open space. Similarly, a carrier in a market may sleep in a corner using his carrying basket as the basis for a bed. In India, there are so many people who sleep on the streets that an economy has grown up around them. This includes stall-holders who provide cheap food in places where homeless people gather (Figure 5.4) and those who hire out mats, blankets, etc., especially during cold weather.

At this low level of accommodation, it is obvious that the utility provided by each are intrinsically different, especially if the climate is not benign and passers-by are not sympathetic. Other benefits, such as may be provided by warm-air outlets and access to waste food from restaurants, or the option of using homeless people's shelters, could represent the difference between life and death in extreme conditions, for example, on very cold nights.

In Egypt, about one million people live on the streets. Usually, they use public toilets or bathrooms under residential blocks or within mosques and they prepare and eat their food on the pavement without any privacy (El-Sheikh, 2002). In South Africa, there are an estimated 3 million street dwellers (Mohamed, 1997). In inner-city Johannesburg, a city of about 2 million people, Olufemi (1997) estimated a total of 7,452 street homeless people in 1995 (of whom 1,103 were children); 1,300 lived in city shelters (Olufemi, 1998).

The second rung of the ladder is the use of a public roofed space which may be a busy place (a train or bus station) or a quiet place (under a flyover). It provides some protection from the weather but varying degrees of privacy, protection and security.

One of the concentrations of homeless people not in shelters in Johannesburg is in Park Station. Its concourse was home to at least 2,283 homeless people in 1995 (Olufemi, 1998), living with the constant threat of eviction. People sleep on the station platforms using salvaged sheets of plastic or cardboard and blankets for bedding and shelters. Their numbers increase at the end of each month. Most are unemployed but a few work on construction sites or do piece work; all for low wages. Many have lost any hope of being economically active. Olufemi (1998) describes Park Station as a 'disaster zone' with a very poor-quality environment and very inadequate and deteriorating provision for sanitation.

The occupation of public buildings by homeless people is not as much of a feature in developing countries as it seems to be in industrialised countries. Only a few cases occurred in the CARDO case studies. In Johannesburg, homeless people have occupied some public buildings. The Drill Hall, for example, belongs to the Department of Public Works, but it has been long-abandoned. It is an open hall where about 670 homeless people live; facilities there are totally inadequate with no electricity and no functioning showers or toilets. Occupants complain of rat infestations. The Red Cross building, at the corner of Twist and De Villiers, also houses about 800 homeless people without working facilities. The quality of the environment is very poor in such buildings. Large quantities of garbage and dirt encourage cockroaches and other insects, rats and other disease vectors. The crime rate is high and women are particularly vulnerable to mugging, robbery, rape and exploitation by other residents who call themselves 'committee members', posing as caretakers and extorting money from inmates (Olufemi, 1998).

On the third rung of the security ladder, homeless people feel that they have enough security to erect something over their heads to maintain some shelter from the sun and rain. They tend to gain no further privacy or safety except that which is afforded by having space marked out by poles in each corner. They have a reasonably waterproof roof which not only keeps off the worst of the weather but also makes a bounded space – a difference between inside and outside even though walls are probably absent. There is little protection or privacy but some general agreement that the space is not to be invaded by others unless they have malicious intent. In this doorless state, occupants are not divided off from the outside world; they are sheltered but not protected. Such households are unlikely to receive any services at all. They are unlikely to be able to protect their possessions, even when they are with them, so cannot improve the non-fixed capital of their household. They are certainly unlikely to be able to improve their shelter into anything permanent and would have no reason to expend scarce resources on doing so.

On rung four of the ladder, occupants have sufficient perceived security of tenure to invest a little in a structure and then in improving it. They do not have any rights in law but, perhaps, the authorities have not shown any propensity to move such settlements on or there are so many of them in the neighbourhood that they feel secure. The situation may change, of course, and new circumstances may cause their eviction but, for now, they can make the best of their hold on the land. Thus, through the use of second-hand materials, they can gain some privacy, with a closing door and opaque walls, though neither are likely to be strong, especially at the points where the materials are joined together. People residing on public land which is not pavement or roadway tend to have a better opportunity to consolidate some form of shelter or dwelling than those on the street. It is relatively simple for them to obtain and utilise discarded cardboard, cloth, plastic sheeting, expanded polystyrene packing materials, sticks, stones, tyres, bamboo, palm or reed matting, rope, scrap timber or plywood, and a whole host of other non-conventional building materials in constructing and anchoring a rudimentary shelter. They may then find a friendly worker who can tap into a water pipe and a power line to provide at least rudimentary servicing, and an informal settlement is born. This process is the equivalent of the first step in the classic 'bridgeheader, consolidator, status-seeker' process described long ago by John Turner (Turner, 1968; Turner and Fichter, 1972; Turner, 1976) which became informal-settlement orthodoxy despite valid criticism (e.g., Burgess, 1982; Ward, 1982) and drove international policy on informal housing for many years. However, at least some of the rudimentary settlements are established on land which is unlikely to be suitable for the consolidation phase. They may be along a railway line, on land earmarked for government development or liable to flooding or other hazards. Thus, any efforts to improve are likely to be frustrated by continuing in insecure tenure.

Shack settlements in Egyptian cities consist of dwellings built of broken wood, tin, cardboard, pressed board, broken bricks, tarpaulin, sackcloth, reeds and tree trunks. Most shacks consist of a single narrow room for sleeping, eating, bathing, receiving guests and even poultry breeding and sheltering animals. Most of them have no latrines and obtain water from neighbouring houses or buy it from tankers; there is no household equipment except for a kerosene stove, pots and plates. Paths between shacks are narrow and filled with garbage. During rainy days, when rain leaks into the shack, many residents take their children and seek shelter inside the entrances of neighbouring blocks. There are latrines inside or next to the shacks despite the narrow space available. Poultry yards are also next to the shacks. Some residents cover their shack walls with cardboard to block prying eyes from seeing women sleeping inside. Some residents of neighbouring housing feel unhappy about having these shacks nearby and sometimes they throw burning rags and cigarette butts to start fires (El-Waly, 1993; El-Sheikh, 2002).

In Greater Cairo, many households live on small open fishing boats on the Nile and use them for all domestic activities including receiving guests. In winter,

5.5 These shacks are typical of many on streets throughout the world but they are in Cairo. (Photograph by Tarek El-Sheikh)

5.6 Boats used as homes in Bangladesh. Occupants of boats are defined as homeless in many countries. (Photograph by Suzanne Speak)

the boats are covered with plastic sheets and gas lamps are used for lighting and heating. They are often harassed by the river police and so choose hidden places to moor at night (El-Sheikh, 2002). Figure 5.6 shows boats used as residences in Bangladesh in a similar way as in Egypt.

Shelters such as these serve to remove all the household members and their paraphernalia from the public gaze. Shelter from the weather usually relies on large enough sheets of material to overhang around, fixed down by piling heavy objects on top. Bricks and stones, old tyres, and household equipment such as enamel bowls serve for this. The structure remains light, however, and could easily be demolished or broken into to access its contents. The security presented by such a structure is largely illusory but most of the population is prepared to collaborate in the illusion and leave the occupants alone. Nevertheless, if villains or the police choose to destroy these makeshift dwellings the occupants can easily be rendered as vulnerable as street sleepers. Dwellings of bamboo and plastic sheets are common in peripheral areas of many cities; assemblages of expanded polystyrene and cardboard packing materials string out along the railway line out of hundreds of cities. They are unlikely to be serviced at all.

For those who are fortunate enough to build their shelters on what is officially accepted as residential land, there is some possibility of medium- to long-term security, at least *de facto* if not *de jure*, which allows the residents to embark on the consolidation phase envisaged by Turner (1976) with investment of several months income, or more, in a more durable structure. Where housing is marketable, they may be able to use their dwelling as a hedge against inflation and can assign or pass it on to their heirs. They are all likely to be able to store their goods safely, behind strong walls and doors that lock. Service providers may also be persuaded to supply water pipes, drains, sanitation services, power and access roads. Steadily and over many years, such settlements become neighbourhoods and part of the city; valid destinations for Turner's status-seekers.

The top rung of the ladder of property rights is to have full security of tenure and the right to build. On such land, accommodation is likely to have a waterproof roof, strong walls and locking door. Such a structure provides privacy and security, and protects its occupants from all but exceptional weather and law enforcers with earthmovers. Plots may be serviced or not depending on the time they have been in existence and the ability of the servicing authorities to keep up with development.

Of course, there may be occasions where levels of accommodation bear no relationship to the security of the land. Some people have relatively well-built structures but, because of their location, they are regarded as homeless in their countries. In Egypt, many households live in rooftop rooms above old buildings in the inner cities on which land tenure is completely secure. Indeed, roof extensions provide a significant proportion of the housing available to low-income households in Cairo (Harris and Wahba, 2002). Many of these rooms are constructed from temporary materials such as wood or corrugated sheets but some are well-built with concrete blocks. Such rooms may be rented, owned or gifted, few have an individual toilet or kitchen, most share the kitchen and bathroom of other residents, if there are any.

Other well-constructed but unconventional dwellings in Cairo occur in the two enormous cemeteries, the Cities of the Dead, which cover an area of 1,000 hectares. They duplicate the cities of the living in that the tombs are real houses (but often without a roof or doors), varying from a few square metres to hundreds of square metres, built in brick or stone. They may be occupied by a caretaker's household or just by anyone who chooses to take possession of them. Most occupants are migrants who have moved there from old parts of Cairo and find living conditions there better than in many neighbourhoods and squatter settlements (Nedoroscik, 1997).

Tables 5.3. and 5.4. posit ladders of rented accommodation available to individuals or households at the base of the market. The lowest rung is the nightly use of homeless shelters in which beds are let on a first-come, first-served basis and clients must leave in the morning. There is security here from those outside the institution but little security from fellow occupants who might rob or otherwise attack a sleeping resident. They do, however, provide weatherproof accommodation and access to washing and sanitation facilities. Depending on the level of care for homeless people in the local place, there may also be medical, podiatric and dental treatment available and advice on social benefits, work, training, accommodation and other issues.

In India, some shelters are provided by local authorities with pay-as-you-use toilets and washing facilities. There are drinking water supplies, lockers and dormitories. Shelters with a total of almost 19,000 beds had been constructed in eleven states by 1999 (Garg, 1999). In Delhi, there were shelters with places for about 5,000 people (calculated at 1.5 square metres each). Some are built with permanent materials but there are many in temporary materials which leak. They are not used by many street homeless people, however, as they regard them as less desirable than the streets. Garg's (1999) respondents claimed that they are expensive, crowded (people sleep very close together) and attract undesirable people who could be dangerous or have communicable diseases. Furthermore, households cannot stay together. There is little outreach work from shelters in India. For Rs.5 (£0.08) per night, occupants are provided with jute mattresses and blankets, and they can watch television. Also in Delhi, Aashray Adhikar Abhiyan provide some shelters in central locations including a large former warehouse (*godown*) close to the main railway station at the edge of the old city in which men and boys can stay, wash and eat, and a shelter for women and children in a disused school. The city authorities in New Delhi provide large tents as bunkhouse accommodation during the cold winter months.

For many years, Mother Teresa's Nirmal Hriday in Kolkata and its offshoots have provided shelters for destitute people. The Sisters of Charity focus on helping the poorest of the poor, especially providing somewhere for the homeless people who are dying to rest out their last days in relative comfort and security.

In Johannesburg, the Christian Services Foundation (CSF) manages the *usindisos,* men and women shelters which provide overnight beds, meals, showers, television and laundry services. They also provide blankets and there is a social worker to attend to the homeless people (Olufemi, 1998). Several churches in central Johannesburg provide places for Zimbabwean refugees to sleep.

On the second rung, those who occupy spaces in flop-houses or hostels have more security in that the cubicle or space is kept for them from day to day over the medium term and they can use it during the day as well as at night. As with

Table 5.3 Ladder of rented accommodation 1: tenure security and standards of accommodation among different levels of property rights/shelter

	Level of rights gained by an occupant	Land		Possessions		Standard of shelter
		Legal right over land	Right to stay on land/sleeping place	Ability to keep	Ability to store safely	
4	Medium-term tenancy of a room	None	Able to stay in the medium term	Modest quantities of possessions possible	Yes, in a structure, may be locked away	Rented room in an informal settlement
3	Medium-term tenancy of a shared room	None	Able to stay in the medium term	Limited possessions possible	Yes, in a structure, may be locked away; sharing limits security somewhat	Sharing rented room in an informal settlement
2	Short-term secure tenancy of a lockable sleeping/ storage space	None	Has daily/nightly use of a space	Limited possessions possible	Yes, but limited to a small lockable space	Space or cubicle in a flop-house or hostel
1	One night 'first-come, first-served' place to sleep	None	Renegotiated nightly, no day-time occupancy	No, only what can be carried/ pushed and protected when asleep	None	Homeless shelter

Table 5.4 Ladder of rented accommodation 2: levels of personal security, weatherproofing and access to services and among different standards of accommodation

		Privacy/Security		Protection from the weather	Access to services
		Visual privacy	Secure from attack		
4	Occupying a low rental room	Yes	Yes	Depends on structure but likely to be at least partly weatherproof	Depends on structure but likely to be at least partly serviced
3	Sharing occupation of a low rental room	Yes, except from sharers	Yes, except from sharers	Depends on structure but likely to be at least partly weatherproof	Depends on structure but likely to be at least partly serviced
2	Occupying a space or cubicle in flop house or equivalent	Has privacy from general public but low level of privacy from fellow occupants	Likely to have security from general public but not from fellow occupants	Almost certainly weatherproof	Access to services but in shared bathrooms, toilets, etc., may also have visiting medical, social and other services
1	Using homeless shelter at night	Has privacy from general public but no privacy from fellow occupants	Likely to have security from general public but not from fellow occupants	Almost certainly weatherproof	Access to services but in shared bathrooms, toilets, etc., may also have visiting medical, social and other services

homeless shelters, they tend to be private and quite safe from outsiders but have only some privacy from, and are rather vulnerable to, those with whom they share the rooms or bathrooms.

Flop-houses and other very low-cost shared accommodation have been given a bad name in the past but a new initiative by Common Ground in New York, which restores dilapidated hotels and apartment buildings for use as housing for low-income people, demonstrates that they may be a viable form of entry point into shelter once again (see Chapter 13).

Those on the third rung of the ladder, who share a rented room with another household, are likely to be able to store limited paraphernalia in reasonable security. They are more secure from attack than those in shared accommodation at rungs 1 and 2 but the standard of accommodation is only as good the building they occupy. The same can be said of access to services; if the house has them, the tenants may also have them, subject to the landlord's discretion.[3] There is only the other sharing household to create danger of attack and reduce privacy.

The top rung on this ladder is to occupy rental rooms in single household occupation in informal settlements. Privacy and security is normally very good in rented rooms and the room can be used at will for storing personal effects and, even, business equipment and stock.

The above discussion provides some insight into the accommodation available on the home to homelessness continuum (Watson and Austerberry, 1986; Neale, 1997). The question arises whether it is reasonable to regard people in these situations as homeless and, if not all, then at what stage does the transition take place?

Differentiating between homelessness and inadequate housing[4]

In the discussion on housing issues in developing countries, we feel that it is important to try to differentiate between those whose housing is inadequate, especially with respect to both land tenure and services as found among people in informal settlements, and those who are homeless. As urban planners, it is important to us to differentiate those who should be included as living in the current housing stock and those who should be seen as in need of housing. Similarly, it is important to distinguish between those processes which add viable shelter to the city's stock through household-sector activity and those which produce shelter which cannot be regarded as viable in the medium to long term. As housing shortages continue and heighten in the face of increasing urbanisation, inappropriate decisions are being made about what should be accepted and serviced, and what should be rejected, denied services and scheduled for future clearance and redevelopment. Such decisions can be very costly in the housing supply process, increase homelessness and cause inestimable damage to households who are trying hard to make their way in the city but facing eviction. Furthermore, they can divert investment away from those most in need.

Following all the experience on how seemingly inadequate housing is a staging post in the incremental improvement of households' accommodation through a long housing career,[5] we argue that to label all 'inadequate housing' together is both inappropriate for policy and insulting to its occupants. There is clearly a need for clarity; especially between those whose incrementally developing housing may be a key to their integration into urban life and those for whom accommodation is an intractable problem. We contend that the household settled in an unserviced informal settlement whose two-storey dwelling is built in brick and has some informal infrastructure (water supply by tanker, diesel generators for electricity, etc.) cannot be regarded as being in the same category as someone in a much worse structure in the same informal settlement or the man curled up in a blanket on the pavement in the city centre.

Many commentators would probably include the most-established people in informal settlements within the housed population and their dwellings in the current stock. Few would automatically class such households as homeless. They might not be so united in their appreciation of tarpaulin tents on the pavement or railway land, however. So where is the threshold for classification as homelessness? Is it a readily recognisable boundary between conditions or is it located somewhere within a broad margin? Does it vary from country to country? By what characteristics might the threshold be discerned?

FEANTSA (1999) points out that, by adopting an approach based on quality of shelter and thus including all inadequate housing as homelessness, 'the unique distress and urgent needs of those people who are identified by a narrow definition are lost and neglected'. In an attempt to follow FEANTSA, we believe that it is at least conceptually appropriate to try to differentiate between being inadequately housed and being homeless, especially street-homeless. This is, perhaps, especially difficult when differentiating between clusters of street-homeless people who have made some attempt to construct flimsy shelters and the most rudimentary informal settlements where structures may be equally flimsy and services absent, as depicted in Figures 5.7 and 5.8, or attempting to classify households living in masonry dwellings on pavements as occurs in parts of Mumbai (Figure 5.9). At the heart of this discussion is the difference between the circumstances of people who feel that they are, and are regarded as being, without a home and those with a home which is seen to be inadequate in at least one of several ways either by them or the authorities, or by both.

5.7 The occupant of this shack in Mavoko near Nairobi has lived in it for more than ten years. Is she homeless? (Photograph by Graham Tipple)

5.8 Rag-pickers have lived in these shacks for more than seven years on the edge of a middle-class neighbourhood in Bangalore. They had recently been notified of a change of status to 'slum' which might give them some *de facto* security or might increase their vulnerability to relocation. Are they homeless? (Photograph by Suzanne Speak)

5.9 Pavement dwellers in Mumbai with sufficient *de facto* security to have built a masonry 1.5-storey structure immediately adjacent to the carriageway in the foreground. Are they homeless? (Photograph by Graham Tipple)

Differences between people in informal settlements and homeless people

Three of the CARDO case studies (Egypt, India and South Africa) offered tables to demonstrate the difficulty of differentiating between informal settlements and homeless people in their countries. The three countries present quite different socio-economic and cultural contexts which could make any similarities between them more interesting. We aggregated all the characteristics mentioned in the three and, in a discussion, which can be found in full in Tipple and Speak (2006), we have assessed whether clear differences can be found and thresholds drawn between people in informal settlements and homeless people or whether all should be grouped together. In the light of that discussion, we have divided the people in informal settlements into two categories, attempting to separate inadequately housed from homeless and, temporarily, we use the term 'street-homeless' to simplify reference to those who do not live in informal settlements. It refers to those who live on pavements, in public open space, on transport interchanges, by rivers, railways and drains, under bridges and in other public places. We include all those locations when referring to living in the street.

Table 5.5 shows our attempt at differentiating based on the categorisations from Egypt, India and South Africa. Column 1 indicates the main criteria for categorising. These include issues such as access to services, citizenship, community organisation, social status and employment networks. These issues are discussed further in Chapter 7. Columns 2 and 3 disaggregate those who live in informal settlements (and would generally be classed together as 'inadequately housed') into two categories of inadequately housed (column 2) and those who we would regard as homeless (column 3). Column 4 gives the circumstances of those whose homelessness might be defined as 'street homelessness' or, in Cooper's (1995) terms, absolutely homeless.

There are several criteria which express similarities between homeless people and those 'merely' inadequately housed; the difference is based on a few key characteristics. The lack of even the most rudimentary security of tenure on the land is axiomatic and leads to a lack of consolidation on the site. Standards of accommodation which lead us to characterise people as homeless are the lack of improvement over time, the predominance of scavenged material and the consequent low durability of the dwellings and lack of personal safety. Settlements of this quality tend to be located in interstitial sites in the city centre while inadequately housed people tend to be in peripheral settlements. The residents in settlements of homeless people tend to have poorer employment prospects and fewer opportunities for self-employment than those in inadequate housing. They are unlikely to have community-based organisations (CBOs) unless their settlement is long-lasting. They are more likely to suffer summary eviction. Levels of service will be very basic or completely absent.

97

Table 5.5 Differentiating factors between inadequately housed and homeless people in informal settlements and street-homeless people

Differentiation factors	People in informal settlements		Street-homeless people
	Inadequately housed	Homeless	
Security			
Type of settlement	Spontaneous/informal	Spontaneous	Spontaneous
Access to land*	Invasion (backed by political support)	Invasion (illegal)	Invasion/illegal
Type of government land	Not assigned for other use or not likely to be used as intended	May be assigned for other use	Assigned for other use
Security of tenure*	Partial or temporary/ psychological security	None, little or misplaced psychological security	None
Permanence	Permanent	Not permanent	Not permanent/itinerant
Level of consolidation on the site	Consolidated	Not consolidated	Stable/more problematic
Type of accommodation and location			
Physical planning*	Quasi/informal planning	Quasi/informal planning	Not planned
Building quality	Improving/consolidating	Not improving/ consolidating	Stable or deteriorating
Type of building materials*	Wood, iron sheets, sometimes mud, brick or stone walls	Scavenged wood, iron sheets	Scavenged cardboard boxes/ blankets, plastic sheets
Life span of housing	More than 5 years	Under 5 years	Weeks or months
Personal safety*	Moderate safety	Minimum safety	Not safe
Type of accommodation	Renting or informally constructed owner occupation	Renting or informally constructed owner occupation	Night shelter, under flyovers, in stations, pipes, etc.

Location*	Tend to be in the urban periphery	Inner city or urban periphery	Inner-city areas
Growth	Increases/ expands in density over a limited area	Increases/ expands in density over a limited area	Expands without control
Social status and organisation			
Social status	Low but accepted for most employment	Low but accepted for most employment	Not trusted, lowest status
Recognition as citizens	Sometimes ID and ration cards can be obtained by political patronage	Sometimes ID and ration cards can be obtained by political patronage	Non-existent
Employment*	Full time in most cases, low-paid manual and domestic work' many small businesses	Lowest paid manual and domestic work, some unemployed/ very erratic; begging; few small businesses	Lowest paid manual and domestic work, some unemployed/ very erratic; begging.
Community organisation *	Organised into CBOs	May organise over time into CBOs	Not organised
Response of government	Upgrading	Resettlement/ often summary eviction	Non-recognition/ demolition and relocation
Access to services			
Access to facilities, e.g. banking	Difficult	Difficult	Impossible
Access to services	Partial, often illegally connected, likely to improve	Very basic, often illegally connected, or none; unlikely to improve	None or a few street taps and public toilets

Source: Tables compiled by El-Sheikh (2002) for Egypt, Bannerjee Das (2002) for India and Olufemi (1998) for South Africa; modified by the authors.

* indicates that the criterion was suggested by more than one of the three countries

Conclusions: the policy language of homelessness in developing countries

There is little doubt that people living on the streets, under bridges, and in structures not designed for residence are homeless. However, the margin between homeless and inadequately housed is much more vague and can be set very low, excluding people in informal settlements, or very high, including all who are not owners or renters of formally approved dwellings. The continuum approach allows some flexibility to blur the threshold of homelessness but, without a threshold, estimating the scale of policy interventions needed is difficult. Each of the criteria used above is valid but tends to generate different perspectives on homelessness.

Under the criteria used above, we lack one essential piece of information to judge whether the hypothetical household at the beginning of the chapter should be regarded as homeless rather than as inadequately housed. The crowding, lack of services and poverty would not tip the household into homelessness but would be dealt with as an issue of grossly inadequate housing. The land tenure, however, would be the crucial criterion and the pen-portrait provides no information on this. If the house is located on land over which the owner has little or no security of tenure then the household could be regarded as homeless as they are likely to have to relocate if they want to improve their circumstances from this low base.

The current sloppy use of language in homelessness generates problems for policymakers. Using 'the homeless' as an epithet for groups as diverse as street sleepers and inadequately housed people, and the grouping of all together, muddies the waters for policymaking and other interventions. Indeed, including the inadequately housed means that they, being more organised, tend to lobby more effectively than street sleepers and dominate both the argument and the benefits of interventions. Currently, empowering community organisations of inadequately housed people to improve their current housing conditions is seen to be helping homeless people. In this way, international donors and governments can tick the mental box concerned with addressing issues affecting homeless people.

We have no argument with the successful and appropriate work that is being done with many communities of very impoverished people and applaud the supporters and leaders, particularly those associated with organisations such as Homeless International and the Slum/Shack Dwellers Federation worldwide. However, we do question the loose use of the word 'homeless' by organisations and governments of all sorts in connection with people already living in established neighbourhoods of poor-quality housing. Instead, we request more honesty and clarity in nomenclature. We have attempted to differentiate between inadequate housing and homelessness, both in this chapter and in other work (Tipple and Speak, 2006), and agree that many people who live in the most inadequate housing are homeless. But the term 'inadequate' is immensely broad, including, as it does, all that is not regarded as 'adequate'. Thus, many residents of less inadequate housing neighbourhoods are routinely branded as homeless when it suits their advocates, or use the epithet themselves when it opens up resource streams. This, we feel, is unhelpful and disingenuous, co-opting the circumstances of the most deprived to the service of the less deprived.

Following the ladders in Tables 5.1 to 5.4, we believe that differentiating between groups of homeless people can now be done, even on an experimental basis, as a way to clarify the discussions of characteristics and to target interventions.

It is likely that definitional criteria will affect policies towards homeless people. Where particular criteria are seen to be 'the problem', there is a temptation to address them and expect the problem to be solved. Where criteria such as secure tenure generate a large percentage of households in homelessness, it is likely that policymakers (out of desperation at the size of the task) will simply regard existing long-term supply policies as the only way to assist households in even the greatest need. At the same time, perversely, they may come to view all housing solutions that fall short of fulfilling their criteria as invalid. Thus, informal settlements may be cleared in order to build acceptable housing on secured plots without anyone in authority noticing the paradox of clearing one sort of housing to build another sort of housing without making any material inroads into shortfalls. They might even increase shortfalls as new formal housing may be less densely developed than the informal settlement that was cleared (Kasongo and Tipple, 1990).

There seems to be a need for more agreement on who is homeless than already exists, especially if policy is to be appropriate and if lessons are to be learned between country experiences.

6 Estimating the hidden millions

This chapter discusses the efforts made to date, and in the CARDO study, in counting the homeless people of the world. As counts and the CARDO researchers' estimates generally do not reflect the caveats in the controversy over counting, we are, in a way, taking a step back in this chapter, reflecting how reported work on homelessness in most countries trails behind theoretical arguments.

Controversy over counting

There is some controversy over the counting of homeless people, not only in its practicalities but also in whether it is a useful exercise at all. Counts have most commonly been undertaken in the USA and Canada, with their frequency being so high that Hulchanski (2000) has asked whether counting homeless people represents a new Canadian pastime. Writers in the industrialised world have argued that definition is so elusive and so variable that the question of whether there is any such thing as homelessness is worth asking (Williams and Cheal, 2001). Others have argued that counting distorts the picture so badly that it can only serve the ends of the agency doing the counting rather than helping those who need housing. Thus, Hutton and Liddiard (1994) argue that statistics tell us more about the agency that collects them than the phenomenon that is measured, as the definition and categorisations of homeless people used are inseparable from ideologically constructed ideas and the political agendas of the counters. Tightly and loosely drawn boundaries to definitions of homelessness arise from the very different representations of homelessness which are in circulation, each involving a distinction between homelessness and housing need (see Chapter 5). Each may be legitimate but will lead to very different numbers and change the nature of the problem homelessness poses, the corrective measures which may be appropriate and the ability of the policymakers to argue for them (Cloke et al., 2001).

Governments may well draw the definitional boundary very tightly so that they have fewer people who can call on their assistance. Lobbying NGOs, on the other hand, have an interest in expanding the figures in order to increase the likelihood that funding will be made available or hearts will be wrung sufficiently to extract money from donors. In definition-making, there can be much room for manoeuvre and avoiding-action as people's needs can be divided between homelessness and housing issues and, therefore, the separate policy contexts (social policy and housing policy) and the separate authorities dealing with them. It is because of this that many commentators argue against counting as it concentrates on rough sleepers, separating them from the broader context (Cloke et al., 2001).

Counting tends to expose the visible and ignore the invisible. Thus, in a UK context, Cloke et al (2001: 260) argue that counts of people sleeping rough (the emergency end of the spectrum in the UK) concentrates the 'homelessness problem' into the 'sights/sites of big city locations, with a focus on visible "on-street" expressions of homelessness' and among young males. The poorly housed households, children, young adults and elderly people coping in the homes of others or in very poor accommodation, remain unenumerated, hidden and ignored. Thus, they argue, 'the focus on rough sleepers serves to distort popular appreciations of the scale, profile and location of homelessness in the UK' (Cloke et al., 2001: 260). Concentrating on rough sleepers also distorts the image people have of homeless people. Thus, the negative and anti-social images, rooted in irresponsibilities and inadequacies, predominate over those who are gallantly coping through sharing with friends and occupying the worst accommodation available (Cloke et al., 2001). As Blau (1992: 17) states, 'statistical data can become a weapon in a campaign to prove that homeless people are different from the rest of the population' (quoted in Cloke et al., 2001: 27).

The estimation of numbers of homeless people, however, is an important contribution to policy as numbers tend to drive investment and can enable lobbyists or officials to direct funding to address the problem. As Koegel et al. (1996: 379) indicate, 'estimates of the magnitude of the homeless population are a critical element in the decision-making calculus of policymakers'. Some writers in industrialised countries (e.g. Cloke et al., 2001), however, criticise the numerical approach as it privileges numeric data over other (usually more qualitative) forms.

Methods of estimation and counting

Almost by definition, and along with any other 'rare and elusive population' (Williams and Cheal, 2001: 242), the accurate estimation of the hidden millions of homeless people is a near-impossible task. Counting people who only constitute a few per thousand of the population and who are without permanent addresses, difficult to locate and even mobile, both between nights and on any particular night, is an inexact process (Chicago Coalition for the Homeless, 2006; Ohlemacher, 2007).

Methods used in counting homeless people in the USA have been reviewed in Drever (1999) and classified as:

- indirect methods, such as extrapolating shelter to street ratios from national figures to calculate total numbers from shelter registers, key person interviews and their estimates averaged;
- direct methods, such as the 'S-Night counts' used in US cities (e.g. Wright and Devine, 1999) and shelter censuses;
- mixed methods, such as medical officers' data, random telephone surveys to find who used to be homeless, windshield surveys and stratified sampling, adjusted for those hidden, welfare department data tracking, and extrapolating from 'S-Night' data.

While direct methods might seem to be the most plausible for accurate data, they come under fire from many commentators. They are subject to considerable sampling errors resulting in:

- undercounting – because it is impossible to locate all places where homeless people sleep;
- double counting – because homeless people are mobile and may be unintentionally counted at more than one location;
- temporal inaccuracy – arising from one enumeration of a very variable population

(Williams and Cheal, 2001).

Wright and Devine (1995) found in New Orleans that homeless people spend relatively few nights in locations that would make them potentially countable, even to very thorough enumerators. In the London rough sleepers count, enumerators did not attempt to count those sleeping in parks, basements and inaccessible places for reasons of personal safety (Crane, 1997, in Cloke et al, 2001). The employment of formerly homeless people as enumerators can obviate some of this as they have insider knowledge of sleeping places and are probably comfortable going to them. Nothing, however, can prevent some homeless people decanting from the area temporarily to avoid being counted by officialdom if they know it is to occur, as occurred in Taunton, UK (Cloke et al., 2000). Such undercounting is exposed when projects are set up and generate much greater demand than the counts suggested (Cloke et al., 2001). A long-term study of rough sleepers, for example, making contacts over many months with rough sleepers and asking whether they were on the streets on a particular night, will elicit much higher figures than a single-night headcount. The difference in Bristol was eight times: between 340 and 42 (Bristol City Council, 1998, in Cloke et al., 2001).

In addition, a count of people in shelters and on the street on a single night might miss a great many people who are functionally homeless but not sleeping on the streets or in facilities for homeless people. Furthermore, the numbers who are homeless during the year and those homeless on a particular night are likely to be very different but both are valid data for different purposes. For example, the yearly number accounts for episodes of homelessness that a household or individual may experience over time involving a range of temporary responses (McIntosh and Phillips, 2000). Chicago had 73,656 people who were homeless between 1 July 2005 and 30 June 2006, but on a typical night only 21,078 people were homeless (Chicago Coalition for the Homeless, 2006); fewer by a factor of 3.5. Of the latter, 4,654 were served in shelters, the remainder were living on the streets, doubling up,[1] or living in cars, abandoned buildings or other non-residential space.

A count of people using homeless shelters in Calgary, Canada, which took care to cover all agencies providing facilities and to reject duplicates, found 14,181 people was a more reasonable figure for planning than the 1,290 beds per night used in the current plans (Perras and Huyder, 2003).

Several recent studies have used the capture–recapture method (Williams and Cheal, 2001; Beata and Snijders, 2002) derived from counting elusive and rare populations in the natural world, for example, fish and animal species. At least two counts are made of the population, each of which is assumed to be independent of the other(s) and each individual is assumed to be recognisable (by name in homelessness studies). The contacts with the homeless population may be through purposive counts or may be from records at facilities dealing with homeless people. In the Budapest case, these were TB programmes and hostels (Beata and Snijders, 2002), in the case of Plymouth and Torbay, UK, accommodation used by homeless people was the sampling frame (Williams and Cheal, 2001). Following cleaning of data by checking for similar names (e.g. Bob X, Bobby X, Rob X and Robert X being assumed to be the same person in different contexts), the total of homeless people is then calculated as people 'captured' on the first count multiplied by those on the second count, divided by those on both counts. The numbers of homeless people in Torbay in the first pair of enumerations was 337 and 345 with 320 identified in both counts. The total could then be calculated as 363. Such counts rely on very good information as to who is involved in assisting homeless people, gaining their cooperation and having the manpower to conduct a detailed count. Such circumstances are unlikely to come together in our developing countries' contexts.

Probably because of the intensity of resources required, such purposive counts of homeless people are still comparatively rare in developing countries, even where homeless people appear on government policy agendas. In addition, the availability of data is likely to be influenced by the 'service statistics paradox', in that those countries with a willingness to acknowledge homelessness, and to establish services for homeless people, are more likely to be able to locate and count them and, thus, will have more accurate (and higher) figures (FEANTSA, 1999: 88).

The need for numerical estimates in developing countries

At a pragmatic level, in these early days of focus on homelessness in developing countries, there is a policymaking need to fix at least some numbers to the phenomenon of homelessness in the world. International agencies and bilateral donors, which could bring great benefit to homeless people and assist others who would otherwise join the homeless ranks, need numbers for their advocacy work and to raise money. National agencies need some figures of scale to raise political awareness and convince budget-makers to devote cash to their work. Thus, in this chapter, we attempt to conjure up some numbers for the scale of homelessness in the countries about which we have some information and, from those, to attempt an estimate for the world that is either more accurate than the 'between 100 million and one billion' (UNCHS, 1999) that is usually quoted or reinforces its accuracy in the circumstances. Our estimates do not include those made homeless by disasters or conflicts unless they register on counts made of national- or city-level homelessness. As we see when any disaster strikes, large numbers of people are made homeless at the time of the incident. Whilst many will reoccupy or rebuild their homes relatively quickly, others lose land and remain homeless for extended periods, past the point of disaster relief, and become added to the longer-term homeless population of the country.

In the European Union in the early 1990s, there were said to be 7.5 homeless people per thousand people (0.75 per cent)[2] (Daly, 1993). In Western Europe, there were said to be about 3 million homeless people (4.12 per thousand) during winter 2003 (UNEP Youth Xchange, n.d.), not including those in unsatisfactory housing. In Finland, there were said to be 7,700 homeless people in 2005 (1.48 per thousand of the national population),[3] down from 10,300 in 2002 (1.98 per thousand) (Manninen, 2006). In 1995, the European Observatory of the Homeless put the number of homeless people in Spain at around 160,000. This was derived by Avromov (1995) from the 11,000 people using hostels plus figures provided by Cáritas (Salinas, 1990–2) on 'vagrants' (between 40,000 and 45,000 per year) and the number of people with urgent housing needs (around 100,000). When a wider definition of *transeúnte* was used by Salinas, the figure arrived at was between 225,000 and 250,000 (7 per thousand of the population) if we include those living in substandard housing conditions (Daly, 1993; Munoz and Vazquez, 1999).

Munoz and Vazquez (1999: 3) point out that there are marked differences in the figures for Spain depending on the definition used.

[The] highest estimations appear when the inadequate housing criteria are included and those of social exclusion are not. The lowest estimations correspond to the single criterion of sleeping literally 'in the street', while the intermediate ones, around 45,000 to 50,000 persons [about 1.4 per thousand], are found on considering those that sleep in the street plus those that have serious problems gaining access to housing and suffer extreme social exclusion.

The official estimate for the number of people homeless in Russia was about 4.5 million around the turn of the century (17.2 per thousand) (Nochlezhka, n.d. (post 1996)). There were said to be 30,000–50,000 homeless people in St Petersburg (6.5–11 per thousand) in 1997 (Spence, 1997).[4] In Ukraine, according to the data of the Ministry of Internal Affairs, there were more than 40,000 homeless people in 2005 (0.83 per thousand). This figure only counts those people who attracted the attention of the militia officers as being on the streets without means of support and were taken to reception centres.[5]

In the United States, about 3.5 million people (10.6 per thousand) are said to be homeless, of whom about one million are children (UNEP Youth Xchange, n.d.). However, a census of homeless people in the USA in 2005 reported between 444,000 and 842,000 (1.57 and 2.97 per thousand). These are the people visible through sleeping rough or in facilities intended for homeless people. There are many more who fit into homeless definitions in those countries: those who sleep on friends' floors or in overcrowded conditions.

Figures for homelessness in Mongolia, estimated within work on HIV/AIDS, suggest 4,300 people (1.7 per thousand of the national population) in 2000 when the population and housing census was carried out (UNDP, 2006).

In 2000, the following official figures for homelessness were reported in four Asian cities studied by Mizuuchi (2004); 1,500 in Hong Kong (0.22 per thousand), 5,000 in Seoul (0.51 per thousand), 8,660 in Osaka (0.79 per thousand), and 700 in Taipei (0.196 per thousand). These turned out to be peak values which are gradually being reduced, owing to new measures against further increases in homeless people, to 700 in Hong Kong, 500–1,000 in Seoul, 6,600 in Osaka, and 500 in Taipei (Mizuuchi, 2004).

According to a homelessness census carried out in 1996, there were then 105,300 homeless people in Australia (5.5 per thousand), of whom about 20,600 (1 per thousand) were in improvised dwellings or on the streets, 23,300 were in boarding houses, 12,900 in supported accommodation and 48,500 staying with relatives or friends on the census night (McIntosh and Phillips, 2000).

As McIntosh and Phillips (2000) point out, an approach that acknowledges degrees of homelessness may allow for more carefully categorised numbers and minimise the controversy stemming from the use of disputed statistics. At this point, however, we must put these arguments to one side as data on how many homeless people there are tends to be uncategorised or divided only into a few arbitrary categories.

Numbers of homeless people in the CARDO international study

In the CARDO study, we did not stipulate how homeless people should be counted or define what we thought homelessness should be in the developing countries' context. Indeed, at the time, we had no information to allow us to make such judgements. The study asked about how many there were of whatever group or groups were called homeless people in their country. In Table 6.1, we state the figures each researcher gave as representing homelessness in their country by the local definition.[6] We make no attempt to aggregate the data as totals or means because of the inconsistencies in definition which must occur but which cannot be estimated.

Table 6.1. shows total numbers and city estimates for the nine CARDO study countries. The first noticeable feature of the data is the variability of the percentages, both between countries and cities, and between the country and city data within countries. The differences are accounted for not only by real differences in homelessness but also by the different methods used to estimate them. In the following, we review how these numbers have been derived and the utility of the numbers that result in calculating homeless

Numbers assessed by who live on the streets

Homeless people in Bangladesh have been considered in censuses as 'floating people', on the basis of the insubstantial nature of their living and livelihood, and destitute women. They are regarded as rootless, reflecting their economic deprivation manifested, in part, in their loss of homestead land. According to the 'Census of slum areas and floating population, 1997', there were 32,078 floating people in 118 cities and towns in Bangladesh (0.24 per thousand of the national population) and 14,999 people in Dhaka (BBS, 1999; Ghafur, 2002).

A survey for the 'Urban Poverty Reduction Project' estimates the number of street dwellers in Dhaka as 12,600 (1.4 per thousand). For this number, the survey defined homeless people as those who sleep on the streets, railway terminals and platforms, bus stations, parks and open spaces, religious centres, construction sites and around graveyards, and other public places without having any roof over them (ADB et al., 1996; Ghafur, 2002).

Table 6.2. shows the two most recent estimates of 'houseless' people in India. The main difference between them is the conversion from households to people. We would be more inclined to believe a lower household size than the 5.5 suggested by Government of India (1996) as so many homeless 'households' are single people.

There have also been two urban enumerations of homeless people, one in Kolkata and one in Delhi. In the Socio-Economic Survey of Pavement Dwellers in Kolkata, undertaken by the Kolkata Metropolitan Development Authority in 1997, 55,571 homeless people were found (Jagannathan and Halder, 1988), an increase of 22,367

Table 6.1 Homeless population estimates in the countries and cities in the CARDO study (July 2002)

	National estimates[a]	Per 1,000 of national population	City estimates[a]	Per 1,000 of city population
	Bangladesh		Dhaka	
Total	133.4 million		10.5million	
Homeless estimates	2.6 million[b]	1.96	15,000[c]	1.4
	China		Beijing	
Total	1.3 billion		9.3 million	
Mangliu population estimates	0.8 to 1.2 million[d]	0.62 to 0.93	1.8 million[e]	197.8
	Egypt		Cairo	
Total	70.7 million		15.3 million	
Homeless estimates	8.1 million[f]	114.8	1.4 million[f]	88.6
	Ghana		Accra	
Total	20.2 million		2.5 million	
Homeless estimates	20,000[g]	0.98	n/a	n/a
	India		Delhi	
Total	1.04 billion		13.8 million	
Homeless estimates	2 million[h]	1.92	52,765[i]	3.82
	2.9 million[j]	2.74		
	Indonesia		Jakarta	
Total	231 million		16 million	
Homeless estimates	3.5 million[k]	15.13	2.3 million[l]	143
	Peru		Lima	
	27.9 million		8 million	
Homeless estimates	480,000[m]	17.17	n/a	n/a
	700,000[n]	25.0		

continued

Table 6.1 continued

	National estimates[a]	Per 1,000 of national population	City estimates[a]	Per 1,000 of city population
	South Africa		Johannesburg	
Total	43.6 million		7.5 million	
Homeless estimates	1.5 million[o]	33.74		
	Zimbabwe		Harare	
Total	11.4 million		2.8 million	
Homeless estimates	113,000[p]	9.93	n/a	n/a

Country estimates are sourced from the CARDO country studies.

Notes
a Estimates for national and city total populations for 2002 from Brinkhoff (2003) and from <http://www.citypopulation.de/Country.html?E+World>.
b World Bank (1999) and READ (2000).
c BBS (1999) but probably an underestimate, READ (2000) estimates over 80,000 homeless sex workers.
d Chinese Floating Population Management Authority in 2001.
e Fifth Census of China, 2000.
f Census of Egypt, 1996.
g Garden City Radio of Kumasi.
h Government of India (1991).
i Aashray Adhikar Abhiyan, (AAA), (2001).
j Government of India (1996: Appendix III).
k Indonesian National Census (2000) (Badan Pusat Statistik, 2000).
l Living in poorer squatter settlements (kampung kumuh) (Yudohusodo and Salam, 1991).
m With insecure tenure (Miranda and Salazar, 2002).
n Who qualify for the Family Plots Programme (Miranda and Salazar, 2002).
o With no dwelling or in informal shacks (Olufemi, 2001).
p Without shelter, on the streets or in hostels/lodging houses (Kamete, 2001).p

Table 6.2 Houseless households and people in India, 1991

Number of houseless households	NBO Handbook of Housing Statistics	Census 1991
Rural	305,000	305,528
Urban	217,000	216,917
Total	522,000	522,445
Total National Houseless Population	2,871,000*	2,007,489
% of total population	0.34	0.23

Sources: Government of India (1991: app. III; 1996) and Bannerjee Das (2002).

Note: * assuming 5.5 people in each household

over the 1991 Census. In a headcount of homeless people in Delhi in 2000, using a similar definition to the Census, Aashray Adhikar Abhiyan (AAA) counted 52,765 homeless people, 33,000 (170 per cent) more than the 19,366 counted in Delhi in the Census of 1991. This figure is likely to be an undercount as survey limitations meant that not everyone could be included. Some of the excluded are migrants who had gone home for the harvest season and people who sleep in places that are not visible, such as on the roofs of shops and inside the structure of bridges (Bannerjee Das, 2002).

The actual figure of people living in the streets of Delhi is likely to be about 100,000 (*The Pioneer*, 2000) which is in accordance with the estimate provided by officials in the Slum and Jugghi-Jomphri Department of Delhi Development Authority. They believe that approximately 1 per cent (10 per thousand) of the total population of Delhi are homeless (Dupont, 1998; Bannerjee Das, 2002).

In other Indian cities, only rough estimates are available. SPARC estimated that there were about 100,000 pavement dwellers in Mumbai in 1985 (SPARC, 1985; Mody, 2001). However, they included those with structures on the pavement. UNEP Youth Xchange (n.d.), by contrast, estimates that there are 250,000 pavement sleepers in Mumbai early in the 21st century. The Tamil Nadu government estimates that, in urban areas of the state (particularly Chennai), there are 69,000 homeless households 'living in objectionable areas along roads and canals and places required for public purposes' (Mody, 2001).

For Peru, Miranda and Salazar (2002) provide 'best guesses' for people in different categories of homelessness. They estimate that around 15,000 people (0.54 per thousand, almost a quarter of whom may be children) live on the street. They are officially regarded by the INEI as mentally ill, indigents, drug addicts, criminals and street children (*'pirañitas'*) (INEI, 1998).

In South Africa, in 1996, 2,470 heads of households were reported as being homeless in the 1996 Census (0.3 per thousand) (Statistics South Africa, 2004: 86). This obviously low number reflects the difficulties in conducting an accurate homelessness count, especially as many of the areas occupied by street sleepers are known to be very dangerous for outsiders at night, for example, Joubert Park in Central Johannesburg. It is interesting to note that the comparable table for 2001 does not include the 'none/homeless' category (Statistics South Africa, 2004: 86).

Data in Zimbabwe are divided into several categories and not amenable to aggregation. Table 6.3 shows 'guesstimates' of the local equivalent of street homeless people at 22,000 (1.9 per thousand) and all without homes as about 113,000 (9.94 per thousand). It does not include the growing numbers, at the time of the survey, of farm workers who are roaming the 'bush' around the cities and in public places or the streets (Kamete, 2001). It was made before the major displacements of farm workers following the seizure of many white-owned farms.

Table 6.3 Homeless people in Zimbabwe

Type	Estimated numbers	Notes
Providing themselves with some sort of shelter, including tents, sheets, shelters made of vegetation	20,000	These are concentrated in large urban centres; the police have good estimates of their numbers
Living on streets, under bridges, on open land, in pipes, in deserted buildings with only the shelter provided by those places	2,000	Based on estimates that they make up 10% of the above
In shelters for the homeless	60,000	Institutionalised beneficiaries of per capita grants
In refuges, hostels, lodging houses	31,000	Almost all are refugees
Total	113,000	

Source: Kamete (2001).

Numbers assessed according to citizenship criteria

In China, it is very difficult to estimate the number of homeless people in the country and in any cities as no public sector organisations or NGOs have useful information directly on homeless people. Indeed, it is very difficult even to estimate the urban population as, in the official statistics, many urban residents are still registered in a rural area – their *hukou* (place of registration) remains rural despite their movement to the cities (Chan and Zhang, 1999).

It is widely agreed by academics that the floating population in China is somewhere between 80 million and 120 million. According to the fifth national census, a floating population of 3.87 million now lives in Shanghai, 1.84 million in Beijing and 2.68 million in Guangzhou in 2000.[7] As outlined in Chapter 4, Li (2002) felt that the people who most resemble homeless people are a subset of the floating population who are called *mangliu*, often used with a strongly pejorative mood, or *sanwurenyuan*. There were 29.7 million of them in 1995 nationwide (24 per thousand of the national population).

According to a spot check in 1993 in Shanghai, the *mangliu* accounted for about 1.07 per cent of the floating population. If we assume the national percentage is similar, then the total number of 'aimlessly flowing people' in China is between 0.8 and 1.2 million (0.62 to 0.93 per thousand). This number is very close to the more than one million people who were sent back to their native place annually by about 700 repatriation stations in the last years of the 20th century (*South Weekly*, 13 December 2001).

Numbers assessed by inadequate housing quality (including informal housing)

Much larger numbers emerge if people in inadequate housing are included in the homeless definition but estimate vary widely. According to the 2003 Global Report on Human Settlements devoted to slum housing, approximately 1.8 billion people (300 per thousand) worldwide lack access to improved water supply, and 2.3 billion (383 per thousand) lack access to improved sanitation (UN-Habitat, 2003: extrapolated from table B.4). If this process were continued for each measure of inadequacy, and all households whose accommodation could be classified as inadequate (by not fulfilling the first half of the Habitat Agenda definition of adequate housing earlier in the chapter) were included in the homelessness totals, half or more of the households in developing countries would be homeless. The second half of the same definition of adequacy acknowledges the importance of local factors and the 'prospect for gradual development', suggesting that dwellings on a potentially upward trajectory should be declared 'adequate'.

A slightly later estimate, from UN-Habitat's other flagship publication, the *State of the World's Cities Report*, has lower estimates of the population in inadequate housing. Table 6.4 shows estimates made in it for the scale of the urban population in developing regions that lack selected characteristics of adequate housing as defined by UN-Habitat (2006b).

According to UN-Habitat (2006a), there are 924 million people (about 300 per thousand in *urban* areas and 143 per thousand of total population) living in urban slums, i.e. lacking one or more of the following: access to improved water and sanitation services, sufficient living space, durable structures and secure tenure. This is close to the top of the often quoted 100 million to one billion range in the number of homeless people in world (UNCHS, 2000). However, if those lacking improved water supply (1.8 billion) or sanitation (2.3 billion) are included as inadequately housed, the numbers constitute 300 and 383 per thousand of the global population.

In Bangladesh, reports by World Bank-Bangladesh and Concern-Bangladesh, which include squatters but not slum dwellers (where land tenure is approved), estimate the total homeless population in all cities in Bangladesh to be 0.6 million households or 2.62 million people (19.6 per thousand) (World Bank, 1998; READ, 2000; Ghafur, 2002).

In China, following the end of the old housing allocation system, the government no longer collects the number of houseless people. The social welfare system, however, has some data on the scale of the poorly housed population. For example, according to a survey of those households in Shanghai who received social security in 2000, there are 11,320 households[8] whose living space is less than six square metres per capita (2.13 per thousand) and 3,183 households with less than four square metres per capita (0.6 per thousand) (Cai, 2001). Self-employed people are not eligible for social security so this estimate excludes them (Li, 2002).

Table 6.4 Housing conditions among urban populations in developing regions, 2003

	Urban population in 2003 (000s)	Having unfinished floor materials (%)	Not having sufficient living space (%)	Not having access to improved drinking water (%)	Not having access to improved sanitation (%)
Northern Africa	77,910	1.7	9.5	5.1	10.6
Sub-Saharan Africa	251,166	10.9	26.9	18.0	44.9
Latin America and the Caribbean	417,229	1.8	11.8	4.8	15.8
Eastern Asia	564,871	1.6	8.5	7.5	30.6
Southern Asia	448,738	15.2	35.0	5.7	33.0
South-Eastern Asia	228,636	1.4	26.9	9.0	20.0
Western Asia	124,370	4.6	8.9	4.9	5.1
Total population lacking (000s)		133,226	401,456	163,822	560,011
Worldwide per 1,000		21.5	64.8	26.4	90.3

Source: modified from UN-Habitat (2006b).

If we add people who live in dormitories or at their workplaces as homeless, the number of homeless people nationally will be from 33 million to 49 million (25.7 to 38.2 per thousand) (Li, 2002). Sharers are also very common in Chinese cities. According to Mak et al. (2007), about 9 per cent of urban households share a room with another. This constitutes about another 21 households per thousand nationally – a total of between 46.7 and 59.2 per thousand.

In Egypt, according to CAPMAS (1996), the number of marginal housing units and temporary accommodation amounts to 484,000 buildings; almost 5 per cent of the total stock of 9.5 million buildings. They accommodate 8,122,500 people (114 per thousand) of whom 1.7 million live in shops, shacks and kiosks and on staircases, 46,400 live in garages and 62,000 live as sharers, in single rooms, on roof tops and in cemeteries (25.6 per thousand together) (El-Sheikh, 2002).

In India, the 1991 Census (Government of India, 1991) states that, out of 152 million households in India, there were 3.89 million which share the same census house as another household (25.6 per thousand).[9] In the 2001 Census (Government of India, 2001), there are 12.7 million households in unserviceable census houses (15 per thousand), 10.6 million in dilapidated census houses (12.4 per thousand) and almost 6 million with no exclusive rooms to occupy (7.1 per thousand) (Bannerjee Das, 2002).

In Delhi, the 2001 Census shows that the number of households exceeded (occupied) housing units (3.38 million) by only 103,332 (30.6 per thousand of total usable stock) with a mean of 1.04 households per dwelling. If crowding (calculated at 48.6 per thousand) and obsolescence (at 41.4 per thousand) and all temporary housing are included, the shortage increases from 103,000 (30.6 per thousand) to 400,000 dwellings (118 per thousand) and, if the serviceable *kutcha* houses are excluded, homelessness expressed through housing shortage would reduce to 350,000 (104 per thousand). In Patna, Bihar, Fernandes (2006) counted 14,000 homeless people (11.7 per thousand) in May 2004.

In Indonesia, information regarding the number of homeless people is virtually non-existent and there is no official definition for homelessness. As we discussed in Chapter 4, the National Census divides the population of Indonesia into only two categories:

- those 'having a permanent place to stay' (*mempunyai tempat tinggal tetap*); and
- those 'not having a permanent place to stay' (*tidak mempunyai tempat tinggal tetap*).

(Badan Pusat Statistik, 2000).

Those in the second category are not just homeless people (*tunawisma),* but also include ships' crew members, people living in houseboats or floating houses, and itinerant or semi-nomadic groups of people (usually living in remote areas). According to the Census more than 3.5 million Indonesians (17.2 per thousand) do not have a permanent place to stay (Rahardjo, 2002).

In Peru, of the 5,262,000 households in 1999:

- About 150,000 households (28.5 per thousand households) may be regarded as sharing low rented accommodation (with values lower than 2,800 soles) in overcrowded conditions.
- Dwellings that are not in a condition to be occupied number about 338,000 (64.2 per thousand households). Just in Lima there are around 18,000 at risk and 5,000 at imminent risk of collapsing.
- About 320,000 of the 400,000 households occupying plots that have been invaded since 1996 cannot formalise their plots under COFOPRI.[10] Thus,

they cannot build permanent dwellings.[11] They constitute 60.8 households per thousand

(Miranda and Salazar, 2002).

In the Peruvian census, 'type of house in 1999' includes a field labelled 'others'. In it, 10.5 per cent (mainly located in urban areas) are included as improvised houses. These are built with light or waste materials, or unmortared bricks, or are shacks or huts (mainly located in rural areas) and places not planned as housing, and most have only one room (INEI, 1998; Miranda and Salazar, 2002). Thus, homelessness may amount to 105 per thousand households.

In South Africa, the production of informal housing remains an important form of shelter supply for many people. In 1995, about 11.5 per cent of dwellings were free-standing informal houses, while another 4.5 per cent were informal dwellings located on properties in formal settlements. Traditional dwellings, mostly in rural areas, accounted for 18 per cent of the national housing stock (CSIR and Department of Housing, 1999). In 1996, about 400,000 heads of households (44 per thousand) were recorded as living in backyard shacks in informal settlements while one million heads of households (110 per thousand) were living in informal dwellings. (Olufemi, 2001; Statistics South Africa, 2004: 88).

In Zimbabwe, the task of estimating the scale of homelessness is fraught with problems of classification and accuracy of data. Most groups that can be identified overlap with others so no attempts should be made to aggregate them into a total homeless group. In Table 6.5 we can see that, out of the total of 1.5 million households in urban Zimbabwe, about 67,500 households (45 per thousand) are reluctant sharers; 30,000 households (2 per thousand) are regarded as vagrants or squat in unrecognised places. The occupants of so-called shacks built on the plots of formal dwellings in formal low-cost neighbourhoods are occupied by 200 households per thousand. Even before Operation Murambatsvina, urban transit camps and other poorly serviced areas housed about 130 households per thousand and there are 320 households per thousand without any security of tenure (Kamete, 2001).

Numbers assessed by housing need

The magnitude of the homelessness problem can be expressed by the number of people for whom the government is expected to supply housing. In Peru, people or households without a registered plot or house, living below the poverty line and claiming a government plot or house, qualify to benefit by being allocated a plot under the 'Family Plots Programme'. There were about 700,000 households (25 per thousand) on the list (in 2001) and they can be regarded as the nearest thing the Peruvian government has to a count of homeless people (Miranda and Salazar, 2002).

Table 6.5 Squatters, sharers and the inadequately housed in Zimbabwe

Type	Estimate of households	Notes
In shelters for the homeless, refuges and hostels	91,000	From Table 6.3
Sharers willing to move out given the opportunity	67,500	5% of total urban households (1.5 million) are sharers (see Mubvami and Hall, 2000) with relatives and friends; 90% of these would move out given the opportunity
Unrecognised squatters and vagrants	30,000	Estimated at 0.2% of urban households
Shack-dwellers in formal settlements	300,000	Based on estimates that at least half the households are lodgers and 4 out of 10 of these live in shacks (cf. Mubvami and Hall, 2000)
Residents of inadequately serviced areas	200,000	Includes transit camps but excludes farm workers and rural residents – including these would inflate the figure to over 2,000,000
Dwellers with no security of tenure	480,000	Number combines squatters and shack dwellers and other lodgers, of whom at least 60% have no security of tenure

Source: Kamete (2001).

In Zimbabwe, the Official Housing Waiting List is the measure of homelessness. However, there are other measures of housing need not officially used to assess homelessness. Table 6.6 shows best estimates of homelessness measured by several overlapping criteria. Recalling that, in Zimbabwe, ownership of a formal dwelling is the only tenure recognised as valid by the government, the deficit of need for home-ownership housing over its supply is estimated at 200,000 or about 130 households per thousand. Estimates based on obsolescence generate 100 per thousand, on land tenure generate 200 per thousand, and on social welfare criteria about 40 per thousand. Foreign refugees numbered about 30,000 (20 per thousand) in 2001. There are obviously many overlaps in these numbers as the same households may be included under several criteria (Kamete, 2001).

Table 6.6 Homeless households by criteria in Zimbabwe

Criteria	Numbers	Notes
Housing criteria (ownership)	200,000	Annual deficit plus increase, less new construction
Housing criteria (obsolescence)	150,000	Based on 25% of stock needing replacement
Land criteria	300,000	Consists of squatters, backyard shacks, transit camps and displaced farm workers
Social welfare eligibility	60,000	Based on those who actually benefit from per capita grants in institutions such as old peoples' homes, orphanages, etc.
Residency criteria	30,000	International refugees

Source: Kamete (2001)

Conclusion: can we estimate the homeless population of the world?

Experience in the industrialised world, especially in North America, demonstrates that it is very difficult accurately to count homeless people. The exercise is either likely to be very inaccurate or to cost large amounts of resources, both in time and money. This is a consequence of lack of attention given to those who are in the lowest places in society and part of the circumstances of the 'services–statistics paradox'. While governments are unaware of the real scale of homelessness (or distrustful of poorly derived figures), few services are likely to be made available to homeless people. There is a logical bind, however, in that only when the scale of homelessness is appreciated will enough resources be available to determine the number of people to be served. However, the tenacity of those involved confirms that quantification is still an important component of the campaign to improve the lives of homeless people.

The first requirement for counting, however, is a definition that is robust enough to include all whose housing is grossly inadequate and who are cut off from rights and services because of this lack. The fuzziness of the boundary between inadequate housing and homelessness pointed out by us elsewhere (Tipple and Speak, 2006) is not helpful in this so a definition remains at the 'work in progress' stage at present.

Figure 6.1 shows that the national official estimates available to us, based on a variety of parameters, give a range of between 0.6 and 115 people per thousand; or 3.8 million to 736 million (based on a world population in 2005 of 6.4 billion), far too varied to be the basis of any useful worldwide estimate of homelessness. Even if we discount the very high figure for Egypt, the range is still between 0.6 and 33.7 people per thousand, which generates a range of between 3.8 million and 216 million.

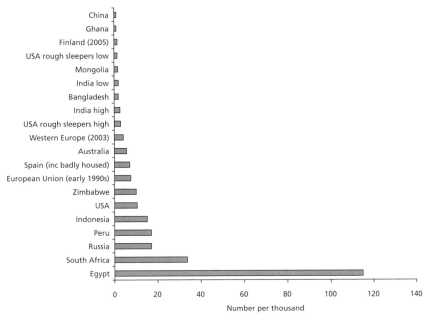

6.1 National official estimates of numbers of homeless people

If a narrow definition is used to include only those living on the street (see Figure 6.2), the number of unhoused people approximates to between about 0.3 and 3.5 people per thousand. This equals between 1.9 million and 22 million people worldwide. If only the ones based on formal counts are included, the range reduces to between 1.5 and 3.5 per thousand (9.6 million to 22.4 million people) but the discussion above shows how unreliable even such estimates are. As it has been shown that counts are very inaccurate, by a factor of 3.5 in Chicago and 8 in Taunton, the estimates for the world would increase to the range of 5.25 to 28 per thousand (33.6 to 179 million people). This is a highly unsatisfactory range as it is much too large to be useful. However, the figure used by the United Nations of 100 million people living on the street is close to (only 6 million from) the centre of this range.

Figure 6.3 shows that, if measured by numbers of people in inadequate housing, the number of unhoused people varies between about 2 and about 200 per thousand of the total population. Removing the lowest and highest from the reckoning,[12] this gives a range of 6.5 to 114 per thousand which constitutes between 41.6 million and 730 million people worldwide – lower figures than the official number of about 1 billion estimated to live in inadequate housing worldwide.

It seems that we should enumerate homeless people but currently we do not have the tools to do so with any accuracy. The estimates we can make from current data are so fraught with broad assumptions that they could constitute 'garbage

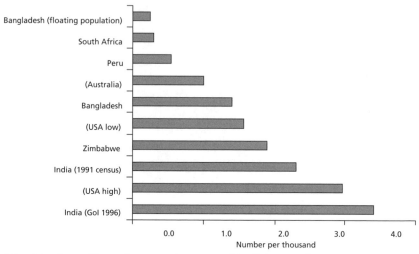

6.2 Number of homeless people assessed by living on the streets

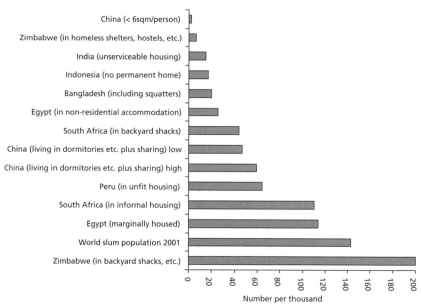

6.3 Homeless people assessed by inadequate housing quality

in, garbage out'. However, we estimate between 3.8 and 216 million by official estimates, between 33.6 and 179 million living on the streets (unhoused, see chapter 13), and between 41.6 and 730 million homeless on account of living in inadequate housing. These are probably the best we can do at present and coincide well with current 'ball-park' estimates used in international advocacy.

7 Who are the hidden millions? The characteristics of homeless people

A common characterisation, and a too frequently held public perception of a homeless person, is that of a lone, unemployed, male vagrant with substance abuse or mental health problems. It is, however, inappropriate for the majority of homeless people in developing countries and presents an increasingly unrealistic picture of homeless people in the industrialised world. It reinforces the idea that the causes of homelessness lie in personal inadequacy – what Neale termed the 'agency' explanation. However, authors such as Neale (1997: 20) and Kennet and Marsh (1999) have clearly revealed the limitations of this explanation and the broader causes of increasing homelessness (see Chapter 1) and we attempt the same for developing countries in Chapter 3 and those that follow this.

This chapter discusses the complexity and diversity of the homeless populations of developing countries in comparison with those in industrialised countries. It explores household formation, gender, age, employment (poverty, economic activity and income), health, involvement, vulnerability, and race, ethnicity and belonging to minority groups.

Any discussion of the characteristics of the world's homeless populations is conditioned by the definition used. Writers do not all define homelessness in the same way, and very few illuminate readers about their definition. As we have argued, homeless is a very broadly used category covering anyone from street-sleepers to those not adequately housed. In this chapter, we are limited by this lack of clarity in using material from the literature and, to some extent, from our case-study researchers. Where we can, we highlight differences between the characteristics of street-homeless people and those of people who are inadequately housed, as they can be very different indeed. For example, homeless people tend to have a profile that is largely lone male and adult. They might have a high level of unemployment and personal difficulties, such as mental health problems or substance abuse. However, if we include inadequately housed people then the characteristics are likely to be much more diverse and include a higher percentage of employed people and families. Table 5.5 summarises the characteristics of both homeless people and occupants of informal settlements in developing countries but we cannot necessarily place those discussed in this chapter on either side of our, admittedly fuzzy, boundary between homelessness and inadequate housing.

Household formation

If we consider homeless people in industrialised countries, most are single or at least living alone. In the UK, single people without children are most vulnerable to extremes of adult homelessness, in part, because of their weaker position in terms of statutory support from welfare services (Anderson and Christian 2003). Thus 90 per cent of homeless people in the UK, referred to as 'rough sleepers', are lone males.

To some extent, this situation is echoed in developing countries. Begum (1997) noted that 70 per cent of all homeless people interviewed for one study in Dhaka were men living alone – 55 per cent were married but with their wives living elsewhere. Similarly, our study in Ghana found that 88 per cent of homeless males in Kumasi were single (Department of Housing and Planning Research, 2002). The majority of homeless males in India are living alone, either unmarried or married with families residing in their villages (Singh and de Souza, 1980; Jagannathan and Halder, 1988; Dupont, 1998). In a UN Habitat study of 203 homeless people in Addis Ababa, Ethiopia, 69 per cent of homeless men and 25 per cent of homeless women were never married (data provided by the UN-Habitat, Global Urban Observatory, 2008).

Although it is extremely uncommon to find households with children living on the streets in industrialised countries, it is far more common in developing countries. Estimates of the percentage of street-homeless people living in household units vary widely within and between, but homeless adults with children are more likely to be found in Kolkata, Mumbai and Chennai than in Delhi, where it is unusual for family units to reside on the pavements (Singh and de Souza, 1980; Dupont, 1998). For example, in Kolkata, estimates of street-homeless people living in family groups ranged from 37 per cent in one study in the 1980s (Jagannathan and Halder, 1988) to over 74 per cent in another (CMDA, 1987; Bannerjee Das, 2002).

This household homelessness can sometimes be very long term, leading to generations of children being born and raised on the streets. However, in other cases, for example Peru and Bolivia, this is often a more temporary situation, linked with cyclical economic migration. Households migrate from the rural high Andes to live and work on the streets during summer, returning to their village homes after a few months trading.

In both industrialised and developing countries, it is more common to find households with dependent children within a broad definition of homelessness, including insecure or extremely inadequate shelter. According to the homeless charity Shelter, in the UK the number of families in temporary accommodation (the standard definition of homelessness) reached 100,000 in 2004. Each year since 1997, in the UK, between 60 and 70 per cent of those accepted as statutorily homeless have been households with dependent children or an expectant mother. In the USA, a survey of 24 cities in 2005 found that families with children accounted for 33 per cent of the homeless population (The United States Conference of Mayors, 2005b).

The study looked only at urban areas but other research indicates that households, single mothers and children make up the largest group of people who are homeless in rural areas (Vissing, 1996). In Australia, in 2005–6, over 29,000 families in were assisted by SAAP services, including 54,700 accompanying children. The number of families being assisted by SAAP has increased by about 45 per cent since 1996–7. This provides some indication of the extent of homelessness amongst families in Australia (Wright-Howie, 2007). If we look at those people in developing countries who would be classed as homeless by virtue of inadequate accommodation, we find many more households with children; indeed, probably the same proportion as in the general population.

Gender

The UN estimates that female-headed households constitute 70 per cent of the world's homeless population but this is based on those in inadequate housing.[1] The UN Habitat study of Addis Ababa noted 39 per cent of homeless people were female and 61 per cent were male. Research into more tightly defined homelessness has tended to explore gender only in relation to household formation (Watson and Austerberry, 1986; Anderson and Christian, 2003). Nevertheless, in a recent UN study (Kothari, 2005), female-headed households, particularly single mothers living in poverty, were identified as being one of the groups most vulnerable to homelessness in several countries, including Nicaragua, Argentina, Costa Rica, Australia and the United Kingdom. It is telling of degree to which women are dependent on men that the Addis Ababa study found a greater proportion of homeless women than men were either divorced (women 10 per cent, men 7 per cent), separated (women 17 per cent, men 6.5 per cent) or widowed (women 25 per cent, men 6 per cent).

In 2006, based on data on 10.3 million persons of concern in 115 countries, the UN estimated that women constituted around 46 per cent of the world's refugees and asylum seekers and 51 per cent of the world's internally displaced people, stateless people and returnees.[2] The gender breakdown of refugees and asylum seekers varies between regions, with Central and West Africa having the highest proportion of women (UNHCR, 2006).

This high proportion of women amongst some homeless populations contradicts the picture presented by most national statistics taken from censuses, which would suggest more homeless men than women. There are two reasons for the difference.

First, many enumerations of homeless people use narrow definitions, based on rough sleeping or pavement dwelling. By this definition women would be undercounted because they tend to conceal their homelessness by staying with friends and family whenever possible. If this is not the case, and they must sleep rough, they try to keep a low profile for fear of abuse or trafficking (Paul and Hasnath, 2000; Edgar, 2001). Thus, they are not readily identified in censuses.

Second, women's reluctance to use government and NGO services, as is clearly the case in the West (Edgar, 2001), leaves them out of many statistics based on service provider counts.

The cultural context greatly influences the 'visibility' of female homelessness. In some cultures women on the streets face great danger from abuse, kidnapping and trafficking (Pomodoro, 2001). In Islamic countries, the cultural unacceptability of women living on the streets means that women and girls are far less likely to be found there, either living alone or as part of homeless households. If a household becomes homeless, the women and girls may be sent to live with relatives, while the men and boys live on the streets (Shamim, 2001). In Bangladesh, for example, over 75 per cent of identified homeless people are male (BBS, 1999; Ghafur, 2002). Similarly, in Egypt, women and girls remain greatly dependent on their families for accommodation in the face of homelessness (El-Sheikh, 2002).

There is another explanation for the absence of women in counts of homeless people, particularly in Islamic countries. It has been suggested that young, single, female, rural migrants are likely to survive through prostitution. Male enumerators are reluctant to seek them out, thus they are not counted in censuses (READ, 2000).

In some countries, however, it is more common to find women living on the streets. In Ghana, for example, young women from villages go to the cities to work in order to earn money to buy household goods to make them more eligible for marriage. While they are there, they often live on the streets to save money. Both Anerfi (1996) and Korboe (1996) noted a very even gender split amongst younger homeless people in Ghana, with girls constituting about 49 per cent of the homeless population. Similarly, Olufemi (1997) estimates that, in Johannesburg, four out of ten street-homeless people are women.

If a broader definition of homelessness is used, including households in inadequate housing (see Chapter 4), women are even more likely to be identified. In the UK, male-dominated rough sleeping only accounts for a small percentage of those who might be considered as homeless. Amongst those who might be included as homeless for policy purposes in the UK there are more homeless women, generally as heads of lone-parent households, than men (Watson, 1999).

In Peru, the official definition of homelessness includes only those people, predominantly men, sleeping on the streets. However, many thousands of people live in informal settlements in housing conditions often so inadequate as to be categorised as homeless by most criteria. Amongst these people, women-headed households feature highly. In Zimbabwe, Kamete (2001) noted that (in informal settlements) women, many living as lone mothers, easily outnumber men. In Kenya, women head 70 per cent of all squatter households (Kothari, 2005).

Age

Although there has been a disproportionate focus on street children in the literature, the majority of the homeless population in both industrialised and developing countries fall within the adult age range, between 18 and 59 years old. Olufemi (1997) estimated that 73 per cent of street homeless people in Johannesburg were aged between 20 and 39 years and 87 per cent between 20 and 49 years. A study of homeless people in Delhi, in 2001, indicated that 80 per cent of homeless people were in the age group 19–58 years (Aashray Adhikar Abhiyan (AAA), 2001). However, some countries' homeless populations have notably higher proportions of children than others (see Chapter 12), whilst other countries are experiencing increased numbers of older homeless people.

Older homeless people

Poverty amongst older people is both a cause and an effect of intergenerational poverty and homelessness; when older people are poor they are unable to care for younger relatives and when younger generations are poor they may be unable to care for their older relatives. This is a growing problem in much of the developing world, especially in Africa, where many older people are left to support their grandchildren orphaned by HIV/AIDS or conflict (World Health Organisation, 2002; HelpAge International and International HIV/AIDS Alliance, 2003) rather than being cared for themselves. For example, in Tamale, Ghana, there are a significant number of young girls under 10 years of age who would otherwise live on the streets, living with their grandmothers or elderly aunts. In return, the girls glean what foodstuffs and portering work they can from the market, or trade in iced water or snack food, and help their elderly guardians to subsist (Dennis, 1997).

In industrialised countries, older people are increasing falling through welfare safety nets which once protected them from homelessness (Walker, 1996). Pannell and Palmer (2004) estimated that, in the UK, 5,000 older people were living in inappropriate hostel accommodation and a further 12,000 were living in bed and breakfast accommodation. In the USA while the proportion of older persons among the homeless population declined from the mid-1970s, their absolute number has grown. The US Department of Housing and Urban Development noted that over 10 per cent of people in homeless shelters between 1 February and 30 April 2007 were between 51 and 61 years old (National Coalition for the Homeless, 2007). The 2000 Massachusetts Housing and Shelter Alliance 'Census of Homeless Elders' identified approximately 1,228 homeless older people in the state, of which 610 were in the city of Boston (Boston Partnership for Older Adults, 2003). In Australia, 24 per cent of homeless people identified through a number of censuses and studies were over 45 years of age (MacKenzie and Chamberlain, 2003).

As populations in developing countries age, many more older people become vulnerable to homelessness. The UN defines a country as 'ageing' where the proportion of people over 60 reaches 7 per cent. Several developing countries have already reached that level. For example, India has exceeded this and is expected to reach 12.6 per cent by 2025. Many other developing countries are experiencing a growth in the older population; indeed it is estimated that by 2020 70 per cent of the world's one billion older persons will live in developing countries.

Older people who have been living and working in urban areas in developing countries might once have returned home to their villages when they could no longer work. However, increasing food insecurity and the escalating cost of living in recent years means that the extended family back home may not be willing to accept relatives returning from the city (Apt, 1993; Aboderin, 2004a). A growing number of NGOs are setting up to support older homeless people. For example, Help Age Ghana has established centres catering for the needs of the aged in some cities, such as Accra, where increasing numbers of older people are left homeless because of poverty or AIDS and the breakdown of family support systems (Department of Housing and Planning Research, 2002).

Urban systems capable of acting as a social safety net for older people are also breaking down. The family house in West Africa has traditionally been the home of the old and the young but serial inheritance in common by many family members, and the neglect which follows from the reluctance of members to pay for maintenance, has led to a decline in the state and availability of rooms in family houses for all who might need such support (Amole et al., 1993).

It is not only poverty which is pushing older people into homelessness but also a breakdown of traditional family values and a move away from multi-generational households. For example, in India, which now has the second largest aged population in the world, rapid economic development has given rise to a newly mobile and affluent middle class of younger people. As they migrate to the cities or to other countries for work they are less able or willing to care for their older relatives. The increase in women working outside the home, coupled with an increase in nuclear families, also erodes the support which once protected older people from homelessness.

Poverty, economic activity and income

Homeless people are, almost by definition, poor. In the USA, for example, single homeless people receive only 12 per cent of the median monthly income of all American households, only about half the federal poverty level (Housing and Urban Development Department (HUD), 1999). The poverty of homeless people in developing countries is undeniable, although it must be noted that not all poor people succumb to homelessness and not all homeless people are equally poor (see Chapter 8). Their abject poverty supports the persistent and, in many cases false, perception that most homeless people are economically inactive and live by crime or begging.

In the industrialised countries, the link between homelessness and unemployment or economic inactivity is self-reinforcing. For example, in the 2005 Hunger and Homelessness Survey in USA, only 15 per cent of homeless people were employed in full- or part-time jobs (The United States Conference of Mayors, 2005b). Formal employment is difficult to secure or maintain without a home and an address and without formal employment it is difficult to obtain or maintain a home. Informal economic activity, such as is commonplace in all developing countries, is difficult to undertake in most industrialised countries, with their rigidly enforced employment and taxations systems. OECD suggests that, in the high-income countries, less than 5 per cent of work is undeclared to tax authorities. Lyssiotou et al. (2004) estimate that self-employment-related black economy activities in the UK amount to 10.6 per cent of GDP.

By contrast, the majority of employment or economic activity in developing countries is within the informal sector. The World Heath Organisation reports that 45 to 95 per cent of the workforce of developing countries are in small factories and related industries (Pallen, 2001). The national proportion of jobs in the informal sector in Asian countries is mostly between 40 and 65 per cent (Sethuraman, 1997) while the informal sector accounts for 75 per cent of all new jobs in South-East Asia (Asian Development Bank, 1999; in Pallen, 2001). Particular city and country estimates show that 63 per cent of all employed people in Dhaka, Bangladesh, and 36 per cent of employment in urban areas in the Philippines are in the informal sector (ESCAP, 2001), as are 93 per cent of India's workforce, if agricultural work is included (Chen 2007). In Latin America, the informal sector varies among countries with up to 58 per cent in Bolivia in 1989 (Sethuraman, 1997) and between 60 and 75 per cent in Guatemala, El Salvador, Honduras, Costa Rica and Nicaragua (Funkhouser, 1996). In 1998, the informal sector accounted for 85 per cent of all new jobs in Latin America (Brown and Lloyd-Jones, 2002).

In Africa, 60 per cent of the urban labour force (and about 78 per cent of non-agricultural employment in Sub-Saharan Africa) are in the informal sector (ESCAP, 2001). About 22 per cent of the adult population are in micro- and small-scale enterprises (MSEs)[3] in five Sub-Saharan countries,[4] compared to only 15 per cent in the formal sector (Daniels, 1999). In South Africa, one quarter of the labour force is in the informal sector (Mayrhofer and Hendriks, 2003). In Kenya, 16 per cent of the labour force (about two million people) work in almost one million micro and small enterprises (Frijns and Van Vliet, 1999). The proportion of GDP earned by the informal sector is difficult to quantify. However, Sethuraman (1997) estimates that it contributes between a quarter and a half of urban regional incomes.

Whilst work in the informal sector is often temporary, insecure, unskilled and low paid, it does not require the rigid framework of a formal residence, address or bank account which is frequently required for employment in industrialised

7.1   A homeless shoe seller sleeps amongst his stock under a motorway flyover in Cairo. (Photograph by Suzanne Speak)

countries. It is relatively easy to obtain informal work on a daily basis but this imposes daily uncertainty over both employment and income. As Dupont (2000) points out, construction workers, loaders/unloaders, cart pushers/pullers and many workers in the catering industry have to be recruited daily; they have no certainty of demand for their services from one day to the next. In many cities, there is a place at which people looking for daily labouring work assemble, waiting to be hired. Even skilled workers with specialist tools may gather there awaiting daily work.[5] This is the context within which most homeless people find their livelihoods.

Homeless people in the CARDO study countries do not share the very high levels of unemployment experienced by their peers in industrialised countries. Most are involved in at least some economic activity. In China, the sixth spot check on the 'floating population' in Shanghai, in 1997, found that the most common occupation was in construction work for state-owned construction companies (Wang and Shen, 2001). A study of a settlement in Karang Anyar, Jakarta, by the Urban Poor Consortium (UPC), shows that most of the residents make a living as *pemulung* (sidewalk vendors) or *becak* (auto-rickshaw) drivers and bearers/ porters in the market (Rahardjo, 2002). Those who cannot find employment often engage in self-employment, generally trading what goods they can afford to buy or can find. Figure 7.1 shows a homeless man in Cairo who runs a business selling second-hand shoes.

Studies of homeless people in Delhi found that the majority in urban centres are employed, mainly engaged in occupations such as handcart or cycle-rickshaw pulling, driving, waiting on tables, cooking and construction work (SPARC, 1985; Jagannathan and Halder, 1990; Dupont, 1998; AAA, 2001). Dupont (1998) noted that many homeless people in India have more than one job. In Chile, Bernasconi and Puentes (2006) note that many street-homeless people rely on 'street jobs' collecting and processing waste materials, selling goods on the street, guarding parked cars, washing windscreens of cars at intersections and, only if nothing else is available, begging.

In Table 7.1, the higher figure for cooks, waiters and related workers in the main occupation than in all occupations shows the importance of this sector in providing supplementary employment for homeless people. Of Dupont's sample 56 per cent benefit from such work when it arises. The demand for construction and catering is seasonal. In catering, many private parties and public celebrations are concentrated around the festivals and at auspicious times for marriages. Many of these are in the cooler months from October to January during which many homeless people supplement their incomes with a second job (Dupont, 1998). In construction, working hours are long and the work may be dangerous, with few safety precautions in place. It is also seasonal.

Unexpectedly, Table 7.1. shows that only 2.1 per cent of homeless people are rag pickers and 1.2 per cent are beggars; the occupations most associated with the poorest in urban society. Both Tables 7.1 and 7.2 demonstrate the importance of transport in providing work for homeless people and also the importance of homeless people in the transport sector, in occupations such as rickshaw-pulling (Jagannathan and Halder, 1988; AAA, 2001) into which entry is easy as it does not require any financial capital. A rural migrant can hire a rickshaw within hours of reaching the city and start earning money instantly. It might be suggested that, without the willingness of rickshaw-pullers to eschew a fixed dwelling and locate near their vehicles, the transport systems of cities such as Delhi would grind to a halt.

Table 7.1 Occupations of 'houseless' people in Delhi (% frequencies)

	Main occupation n=243	All occupations n=325
Handcart pushers or pullers	23.9	20.0
Cooks, waiters and related workers	22.2	30.8
Cycle rickshaw drivers	19.8	16.6
Construction workers	9.1	8.9
Loaders, unloaders and porters	8.6	9.5
Sales workers (vendors, shop assistants)	4.1	3.4
Others (clerical, service and production workers, drivers, beggars, rag-pickers, etc.)	12.3	10.8

Source: Modified from Dupont (2000: 104)

Table 7.2 Occupations of 'houseless' people in Old Delhi in 1996 by industrial category (% frequencies)

	Houseless people	Male population
Transport, communication	51.9	7.9
Trade, commerce, restaurants, hotels	28.4	38.3
Construction	9.0	2.8
Manufacturing, processing, repairs	6.2	32.0
Community, social and personal services	4.5	18.3
Agriculture, livestock, mining, quarrying	0.0	0.6
Total	100.0	100.0

Source: Modified from Dupont (2000: 105)

Table 7.3 shows that similar employment opportunities exist for homeless people in Bangladesh. Such jobs bring in so little money that their holders have no choice but to occupy the cheapest accommodation available. In his *magnum opus* on rickshaws in Bangladesh, Gallagher (1992) tells of rickshaw-pullers in Dhaka living in ramshackle *messes* varying from 15 to 100 occupants in which they have the part-time use of a bedspace on the floor, a place to hang their few belongings and someone to cook their meals for a few taka per day.

In South Africa, where the formal sector was dominant until recently, there is a poorly developed informal sector and homeless people have fewer choices of occupation. They commonly work as parking guards, porters or cleaners, or as hawkers trading low-value goods (Olufemi, 2001).

It is clear that, whilst homeless people in developing countries do work, their employment tends to be only low-skilled and poorly paid. The employment homeless people can obtain is conditioned by their education and skills, which are limited. For example, in India, homeless people are more likely to be illiterate than others. While the national illiteracy rate is 35 per cent (Government of India, 2001), the majority of urban homeless people are illiterate. Over 50 per cent of homeless people never attended school and most of those that did only studied up to primary level (AAA, 2001; PUCL, 2000).

Moreover, this lack of skills leads to insecurity even for those who have employment. For example, in Delhi, only 44 per cent of homeless people manage to secure work every day (PUCL, 2000). Although such casual employment may look irregular and unorganised, there are often informal leaders who organise the working individuals or groups of people, taking a percentage fee in return for their protection and organisation of work (El-Waly, 1993; El-Sheikh, 2002).

On one level, large-scale informal employment is problematic for governments and workers alike. It circumvents taxation systems and employment regulations,

Table 7.3 Economic activities of 'floating' people and those living in slums in Bangladesh

Main activities	Dhaka megacity (%)		Total urban (%)	
	Floating pop. (14,999)	Slums (533,788)	Floating pop. (32,078)	Slums (971,719)
Begging	33.73	0.60	26.94	0.71
Daily labour: construction	27.34	6.12	17.40	4.98
Porter	12.03	1.62	16.02	2.05
Business	6.70	9.18	4.91	9.26
Hawker	4.07	1.94	4.13	1.74
Maid servant	1.60	5.13	5.50	4.88
Rickshaw-puller	1.59	10.27	4.08	9.03
Tokai (child waste-picker)	1.03	–	1.62	–
Daily labour: agriculture	0.68	0.78	2.80	1.23
Daily labour: industry	0.68	10.46	3.96	8.31
Van puller	0.68	–	1.41	–
Service	0.23	6.54	0.20	6.41
Student	–	7.37	–	8.60
Not working	5.61	4.86	7.10	4.70
Others	4.03	35.13	3.93	38.10
Total	100.0	100.0	100.0	100.0

Source: Calculated from BBS (1999)

diminishes a government's revenue and places workers at risk of exploitation. Nevertheless, it is clear that the informality of employment in many developing countries provides a degree of flexibility which allows even the most destitute to earn a living, however meagre. Moreover, in being homeless, the informal worker who is at risk of exploitation might find a degree of empowerment, in that he or she is not trapped or limited to one location and one set of employers. In addition, the homeless person's low living costs allow him/her to undercut wage levels with those who pay rent. Such self-exploitation is quite common in the informal sector (Tipple, 2006). It might be argued, indeed, that homelessness and informal economic activity are mutually supportive.

A contentious form of economic activity amongst homeless people is prostitution. Campaigners against both adult and child prostitution object to the idea that it should be called 'work'. They argue that the term 'work' suggests a degree of choice and oversimplifies what is a complex issue, dehumanising the struggles that the vast majority of male and female sex workers go through just to survive (Khan, 1999: 196). Nevertheless, it must be mentioned here because it is the only means of survival available to some homeless people and has bearing on their health and their ability to return to their family homes.

A survey of 'disadvantaged women' in eight cities and towns in Bangladesh noted that homeless (young and single) women migrants, without any peer support, prior information about the area of destination, education or skills, are most likely to turn to prostitution for survival (READ, 2000).[6] However, their numbers are unclear. This is in part because they are hidden and in part because of the reluctance of enumerators to count them. Mamun (2001), for example, deliberately avoided interviewing prostitutes and beggars. When they are counted, estimates vary widely. For example, Begum (1997) found only four cases of prostitution within a sample of 505 females, while a recent studies prepared for Concern-Bangladesh (READ, 2000) estimated the numbers of sex workers amongst the 'floating' population of Dhaka at between 83,000 and 171,000.[7]

Income

Different categories of homeless people exhibit different poverty and income characteristics. Street-homeless people are the poorest and women the poorest amongst them. In Bangladesh, those in slums and squatter settlements tend to be better employed, and earn more, than street-homeless people and the better or more 'formal' the settlement, the higher the income level tends to be. According to a study by Begum (1997), average income per day of pavement dwellers in Dhaka was Tk. 43 (about £0.5); but men earned considerably more than women (at Tk. 47 and Tk. 18 respectively. Even among homeless women there are great variations. For example, the average daily incomes of sex workers is Tk. 120 (about £1.50) while other women make only Tk. 40 (about £0.50) (READ, 2000: 26).

According to studies in India, (Centre for Media Studies (CMS), 2000), the majority of homeless people earn below the minimum wage of Rs.96 (£1.20) per day for unskilled labour and Rs.100 per day for skilled labour. While they contribute to the growth of cities and subsidise mainstream costs of living (by providing cheap labour), they receive little in return, except insults and indignities. Using the official India poverty line of Rs.362.68 (rural) and Rs.505.45 (urban) per capita per month,[8] very few homeless people in Delhi would fall below the line.[9] Approximately 60 per cent of Indian urban homeless people are able to save money which they send back to their families in their villages.

It has been argued that, because the majority of homeless people in India earn above the poverty line and are able to save money and make remittances to their families, their economic marginality is an exaggeration (Kundu, 1993) nor are they necessarily the poorest of the urban poor (Dupont, 2000). They are able to save money, however, because they make conscious sacrifices, the most obvious being not routinely paying for accommodation and accepting homelessness.

In Indonesia, households in informal settlements in Jakarta, earn about Rp 10,000–15,000 (£0.80–£1.25) per day, with between Rp 4,000 to Rp 9,000 spent on water, sanitation and electricity. Income data for street sleepers is not available.

In Zimbabwe, Kamete (2001) noted that those in formal settlements were generally better off than those in informal settlements, with 16 per cent of homeless people in informal areas earning less than Z$500 (£50) per month against only 6 per cent in formal areas. In Ghana, about 79 per cent of the homeless people in Kumasi earn less than C10,000 (£1) per day or about C250,000 (£25) per month (Department of Housing and Planning Research, 2002).

Health

Ill health is strongly correlated with homelessness. To live in the conditions endured on the street or in the most inadequate housing is to confront pathogens and physical dangers daily (see the introduction to Chapter 5). Studies into different categories of homeless people in several countries have found a significantly higher mortality rate than for non-homeless people. Male rough-sleepers have the have the highest mortality rate of homeless people in UK at twenty-five times higher than the housed population and an average age of death of 42, lower than most Sub-Saharan African countries. At the same time, hostel residents had a life expectancy of 63 and those placed in bed and breakfast accommodation 67 (Shaw et al., 1999). For a review of literature on mortality of homeless people, see O'Connell (2005).

Our current understanding is that this increase is based largely on issues such as lack of medical facilities or health problems associated with poor living conditions. As Guirguis-Younger et al. (2004) note, we have little understanding of the social determinants of high mortality amongst homeless people. This is equally true in industrialised and developing countries.

UNCHS (2000) reports that about one-third of homeless people in Italy and Spain and 11 per cent in Norway have serious physical health problems. If the health of homeless people in industrialised countries is so poor, it is no surprise that the health of homeless people in developing countries is even worse.

Both street-homeless people and those living in slum and squatter settlements suffer from a range of physical and mental health problems associated with poverty, poor nutrition and damp, overcrowded, unsanitary living conditions. In Peru, the CARDO study reported high prevalence of acute respiratory infections (28 per cent); followed by the genito-urinary diseases (9 per cent), dysentery and gastroenteritis (8 per cent), and skin diseases (6 per cent) (Miranda and Salazar, 2002). An unpublished report on a study of the health of over 2,000 homeless people in Delhi noted a predominance of respiratory tract disorders, including asthma and bronchitis. Other health problems included gastroenteritis, dysentery, worms, skin problems such as boils and scabies, infected wounds and sexually transmitted diseases (STDs) (AAA, 2001).

Sleeping outside also means that homeless people are especially susceptible to mosquito bites and diseases such as malaria and dengue fever. Stray, rabid dogs are a major problem in cities and many homeless people suffer from dog bites or cuts and scratches that become infected. In South Africa, Olufemi (1999) notes that infections are associated with poor living or housing conditions because bacteria flourish under certain climatic or environmental conditions.

The weather affects the health of homeless people in many countries. For example, in Delhi, summer temperatures reach over 40 degrees centigrade, causing severe dehydration but, in winter, the temperature can drop to freezing and homeless people, especially the old, can suffer from hypothermia. Indeed, the city authorities erect emergency tent shelters to save lives during the winter (Figure 7.2). In 2001, 76 of the 96 unclaimed dead bodies picked up by the local authorities were destitute beggars (*Times of India*, 2001b). In winter 2007, snow fell in Johannesburg and at least one homeless person died on the street (*Africa News*, 2007).

Homelessness and HIV/AIDS have a mutually reinforcing relationship. As discussed in Chapter 8, HIV/AIDS can make people more vulnerable to homelessness by increasing vulnerability to unemployment, poverty and to relationship breakdown. More importantly for this discussion, homeless people are more vulnerable to HIV than the housed population and homelessness speeds the progression of HIV into AIDS as it is closely associated with poverty, malnutrition,

7.2 Winter shelters erected by Delhi Development Authority to protect homeless people from freezing to death. (Photograph by Tony Pietropicolo)

polluted environments and lack of access to clean water or decent sanitation (Patel and Kleinman, 2003).

Some homeless people engage in risk-taking behaviour, such as selling sex or drug taking, as a survival strategy or a means of relief. In the USA it has been noted that homeless youths are more likely to be HIV positive than others of the same age (Centre for Disease Control, 2004). In a study of street youth in South Africa, Swart-Kruger and Richter (1997) found that the street youths and children regularly sold sex for money, goods or protection. They were also sexually active with homeless women and girls who, themselves, sold sex.

Homeless girls, women and young boys are also at risk of rape, increasing their risk of HIV infection (Fisher et al., 1995). This is notable in many African countries including South Africa (Olufemi, 2000) and Kenya (Amuyunzu-Nyamongo, 2006). Widows or abandoned women are at risk of HIV as they may need to remarry unsuitable, infected, partners for security in order to avoid homelessness.

The inheritance systems in some societies increase the chances of women becoming homeless as a result of the death of a husband, an occurrence which is ever more frequent as AIDS takes its toll. The husband's matrilineal family will turn her out of the marital home, with her children, regardless of whether she has anywhere else to live. She is then highly vulnerable and likely to live with another man as soon as possible, even though she is likely to be HIV positive herself.

Mental health disorders are also common amongst homeless people, although it should not be assumed that they are necessarily the cause of homelessness (see Chapter 8). In the UK, the Department for Communities and Local Government (2008) estimated that around 35 per cent of people sleeping rough suffer from mental health problems

In a study of 83 Brazilian street-homeless people of 18 years of age or more, who had been living outdoors for at least twelve months, Heckert et al. (1999) noted that all but one had at least one form of mental health disorder. The most frequent diagnoses were alcohol abuse/dependence (82 per cent), mood disorders (32.5 per cent), drug abuse/dependence (31.3 per cent) and varying forms of schizophrenia (9.6 per cent). One investigation into homeless women in Delhi found that almost all were mentally ill (AAA, 2001: 33).

Homeless women face particular health problems. In Bangladesh, more than half of the members of the 'floating' female population reported having diseases in a 2000 study, with the sex workers among them having very high prevalence of STDs (READ, 2000, reported by Ghafur, 2002). A study of reproductive health and fertility of homeless women in Kolkata found they suffered from conditions such as leucorrhoea (28.5 per cent), menstrual irregularities (12.3 per cent), infertility (2.5 per cent) and STDs (1.3 per cent). Most of these illnesses were untreated (Ray et al., 2001).

The reproductive behaviour of street-dwelling women is characterised by early marriage, teenage pregnancies and scarce use of contraceptives as well as frequent abortions. Very few pregnant women receive adequate antenatal care. Coverage of tetanus immunisation and the uptake of iron and folic acid supplementation are also poor. The delivery of babies on the street is not uncommon amongst homeless women in some countries and these are mainly conducted by untrained birth attendants (Ray et al., 2001). Table 7.4 shows the causes and intensities of diseases suffered by homeless women in South Africa (Olufemi, 1999). It is evident that homeless women suffer from the same ailments as the housed population but the problems are less likely to be treated early and are exacerbated by the problems of homelessness: malnutrition, unhygienic living environment, lack of clean drinking water, violence, and exposure to the elements. Olufemi (1999) also points out that, among the homeless women, there is a total lack of control and awareness of their health predicament.

Not only do homeless people suffer from poorer health than those who are adequately housed but they also face greater difficulty in accessing treatment. In countries where health insurance is routine, street-homeless people fall out of the

Table 7.4 Causes and intensity of ill health among homeless street women in South Africa

Causes	Ill health	Intensity
Infection	Coughs, flu, dysentery and diarrhoea, skin diseases, skin rash, sexually transmitted diseases (STDs), tuberculosis, conjunctivitis	Very high
Stress and strain	Headache, depression, frustration, despair	Very high
Poverty and neglect	Tuberculosis, cold, arthritis, malnutrition, poor diet	Very high
Environmental factors/ climate	Cold, flu, tonsillitis, pneumonia, headache, asthma, birth abnormalities	Very high
Trauma from rape, mugging or accident	Wound sustained from stabbing, assault or violence	Very high
Promiscuity	Sexually transmitted diseases (STDs), thrush, gynaecological problems, use of contraceptives	Very high
Childbearing/ menopausal stages	Headache, dysmenorrhoea, obstetric problem, uterine infection, ovarian cyst, fibroid	High
Ageing	Gynaecological problems, arthritis, menopausal syndrome, cancer, stomach problems, asthma	Low

Source: Modified from Olufemi (1999: 490).

system and have to make the best of life without health care. Addiction, accidents and violence all take their toll (Bernasconi and Puentes, 2006: 48).

In India, Direct Observation Treatment System (DOTS) Centres have been set up to help the two million people who develop TB every year (Bannerjee Das, 2002). The treatment requires that the infected person attends a clinic each day to receive TB medicine. If the person does not come for treatment, DOTS staff are obliged to go to their home. For this reason, the DOTS centres refuse to treat homeless people because they cannot supply an address where staff can follow up on treatment.

Difficulties in accessing what should be freely available health care were noted in South Africa, as the following quotation from one homeless man indicates.

> Most of the government clinics in town is free and there is access but the attitude in the clinic is bad. They ask you why are [you] dirty? Why don't you go home? Some of the homeless people stay with the ailment and when their condition deteriorates, we call the ambulance. The ambulance people will tell you we can only come if it is gunshot, hit by car and maybe they come after 3 hours.
>
> (Olufemi, 2001)

Involvement in and vulnerability to crime

In some countries homeless people do not actively need to commit crimes in order to be 'criminals', as states construct various laws, such as the Bombay Prevention of Begging Act (1959) in India, which make vagrancy or begging illegal. Thus, simply being on the streets, and presumed to be begging, is cause for arrest. In a statement concerning *Olga Tellis* v. *Bombay Municipal Corporation* (1985), regarding the eviction of pavement dwellers in Mumbai, the Indian Supreme Court said, 'The boys beg. Men folk without occupation, snatch [gold] chains with the connivance of the defenders of law and order, when caught, if at all, they say: who doesn't commit crime in this city?' (Bannerjee Das, 2002)

Whilst crime does form part of the survival strategies for some homeless people, it would be wrong to assume that all, or even most, are criminals or that the crimes they commit are of a serious nature. Indeed, the CARDO study highlights that homeless people are more likely to be victims than perpetrators of crime. In almost all countries, the researchers report that it is uncommon for adult street homeless people to commit crimes, especially violent crimes. Homeless people interviewed in Chile were keen to distance themselves from any criminal perception of homeless people and all reported that they had been victims of crime. In contrast to expectations, the homeless people living in small groups (*caletas*) probably reduce crime as they act as guardians of neighbourhoods because they are eyes on the street at all hours (Bernasconi and Puentes, 2006)

Drawing on the views of magistrates, crime reporters, criminal lawyers, police, jailers and selected households, Siddiqui et al. (1990) compiled perceptions of crimes and criminals in Dhaka City. The consensus of opinion was that homeless people were mainly involved in petty crime such as theft, drug addiction or prostitution, but were less often involved in serious crimes.

Large informal or squatter settlements can be associated with criminal activity. However, they can also be 'self-policing'. The researcher in Zimbabwe for the CARDO study noted the case of Killarney settlement in Bulawayo which operates strict vetting criteria when a new entrant comes in. There are checks of background and track record. References are required from residents of good standing. It is difficult for anyone who does not have a 'recommender' to gain residency (Kamete, 2001).

Regardless of their involvement in crime, homeless people's insecurity, living on the streets or in makeshift and insecure shelters, means they are extremely vulnerable to it. Street-homeless people are the victims of theft and abuse, both verbal and physical; frequently perpetrated by police or other authoritarian figures such as security guards. Many struggle to keep their few belongings or meagre earnings safe. Many street-homeless people in South Africa lose their identity cards through theft and so lose their citizenship rights as the state will not give them the benefit of the doubt over whether they are from South Africa rather than one its neighbours (Plaatjies, 1999). In India, Bangladesh and South Africa this was perceived to be a major problem (Banerjee and Sengupta, 2000; Olufemi, 2001; Ghafur, 2002). They are also vulnerable to violent crimes such as beatings and rape; assault and sexual abuse are particularly common against the most vulnerable: women, young boys and girls. In many countries the risk to women is so great that it acts to conceal real levels of homelessness among women and girls as they stay with relatives or hide from enumerators. Olufemi (1998) noted that, in South Africa, homeless people were at risk of mugging, beating and rape even in shelters, where self-appointed 'wardens' extort money from residents against promises of protection accompanied by threats of violence. It is common for homeless people to gather together in groups for protection and company. In Chile, such groups are known as 'caletas' (Bernasconi and Puentes, 2006).

Some police forces seem to target homeless people for brutal treatment. The police in São Paulo, Brazil, killed around 1,500 people in 1992. Their victims were mainly poor men, homeless beggars and black people, as well as young and adolescent street children. Street children are perhaps most affected, because of their age and vulnerability. Human Rights Watch/America estimated that 5,000 children were murdered in Brazil between 1988 and 1991 (Lalor, 1999). The Brazilian Centre for Childhood and Adolescence (CBIA) revealed that 202 children and adolescents were murdered in São Paulo in the first quarter of 1993.

Possessions are an important part of 'who you are' and have important symbolic values (Csikszentmihalyi and Rochberg-Halton, 1981) but the security of possessions for shelterless people is an issue which has received little attention. Writing about unhoused people in the USA, Hill and Stamey (1990) highlight how difficult they find keeping possessions safe. They tend to resort to keeping their possessions on or close to their person, including pushing them around in shopping trolleys (known there as 'ships of the ghetto'). Hill and Stamey's (1990) sample possess tools, but only those which assist in their daily survival (wrenches to loosen water hydrants; hammers, etc., to assist in scavenging and recycling activities). They did not tend to have business paraphernalia that some of the unhoused people in India, Bangladesh and elsewhere do.

Race, ethnicity and belonging to minority groups

People of ethnic minorities are over-represented within homeless populations. For example, Australian Aborigines comprise just 2 per cent of the population but 12 per cent of the homeless population.

The approximately 30,000 *zabaleen* (garbage collecters) of Cairo are numbered among the homeless population. Members of the Christian minority, they live in seven peripheral settlements around Cairo, the largest of which, the 'Garbage City' of Muqattam, has many substantial dwellings. Others live in less salubrious homes built of salvaged wood, plastic and cloth. They all remain subject to eviction as the city spreads to engulf them. As Christians in a Muslim country, their livelihood opportunities are restricted and they have specialised in collecting domestic solid waste each night under licence. Going out in pairs with a donkey cart, the collectors bring the garbage from approximately 350 households per day to their dwelling very early in the morning and dump it inside where all members of the household cooperate in sorting it to extract the recyclable materials such as paper, cardboard, plastic, metals, etc. Organic and food wastes are fed to their pigs. The dwellings lack water and sewage connections or legal connection to electricity; nor do they have schools or health centres. Even when improvements have been made to the housing, the garbage is still brought into the living space for sorting (El-Sheikh, 2002; Fahmi, 2005).

In South Africa, the large number of homeless black Africans is a manifestation of the racially segregated accommodation policies of the apartheid period, when blacks were restricted to townships or other specific locations and where there was no room for expansion. Many ended up squatting, living in backyard shacks (Crankshaw et al., 2000) or, as a last resort, on the streets. The very small number of homeless Indians in South Africa can be explained by the very strong cultural support system within the Indian communities.

It appears that not all minority ethnic groups are more vulnerable to homelessness than the majority groups. For example, until recently the minority ethnic groups in Zimbabwe tended to be landlords of properties in the old suburbs, having been the first to obtain urban housing when it was still taboo among the locals who regarded the urban area as a workplace not home (Kamete, 2001).[10] However, the more recent disturbances on farms are now introducing people from Malawi, Mozambique and Zambia to the ranks of the homeless in Zimbabwe (Kamete, 2001).

Conclusions

This chapter has tried to show the broad profile of homeless people in developing countries. Moreover, it has attempted to dispel some of the myths about homeless people, especially the visibly homeless, and to highlight how different they are from the perceived profile of their industrialised world counterparts.

Contrary to common perception homeless people in developing countries are largely not workless or beggars but working and productive members of society, without whom much of the current rapid urban development would not be possible. While undoubtedly poor, they are not always poorer than some poorly housed people in the same country. Despite the illegality of their homelessness in many countries, homeless people are more often the victims of crime than the perpetrators.

They are by no means all male or single but include amongst their ranks women, children, older people and, indeed, entire multi-generational families. They are frequently not as isolated or socially excluded as homeless people in industrialised countries might seem. They can and do form small, supportive and tight-knit social networks.

Their 'homelessness' manifests in a range of living and accommodation situations from them being completely or absolutely homeless (i.e. unsheltered) to having significantly inadequate shelter, lacking many of the basic requirements of security and services, to having adequate shelter which does not provide the safety and security which is associated with home. Each situation requires a different approach or intervention. Nevertheless, they are all subject to similar vulnerability to ill health, crime and attack, low income and exploitation. They are all also generally undervalued and poorly perceived by the general public and the authorities. Until these poor and largely false perceptions are overturned, policymakers and NGOs will struggle to improve their situation.

8 Economic, social and cultural causes

Introduction

The earlier part of this book focused on the role of housing shortages in creating and perpetuating homelessness. However, homelessness is, for many people, caused by a far more complex set of circumstances and issues than can be addressed by improving the housing supply system alone. While it is true that poverty underpins much homelessness in both industrialised and developing countries, not all poor people become homeless and not all homeless people are equally poor. Nor are they automatically poorer than adequately housed people in the same society. As Bernasconi and Puentes (2006: 6) note: 'Homelessness may be precipitated by a housing problem, but there are other factors that define it and perpetuate it, such as the lack of income, insecurity, stigmatisation, vulnerability, lack of choices and the inability to plan ahead.' Thus, for many, homelessness is the result of a complex combination of social, economic, political and cultural constraints or problems

Cooper (1995) argues that an economic dimension to homelessness suggests that it occurs where the core economic institutions of the housing market, the labour market and the financial markets fail to produce and distribute housing resources in an effective, efficient and equitable manner. These core institutions are all markets which create and reinforce inequality, especially for those in the lowest income groups.

A social dimension to homelessness is seen 'when core social relations have undergone radical change or ruptures that make it impossible for traditional households to function adequately' (Cooper, 1995, quoted in UNCHS, 2000: 53). Rapid changes and disruptions in social relations can contribute to the stress of housing insecurity. Supportive family life is axiomatic in preventing homelessness while ineffective parenting tends to increase the chances of homelessness among children and adults (Cooper, 1995).

Cooper also highlights the political dimension to homelessness, suggesting that homelessness arises from the government's inability to achieve or maintain its social justice policy:

> A political dimension suggests that homelessness is a state in which political institutions are unresponsive to the needs of the most vulnerable in the community and cannot intervene effectively to achieve an equitable distribution of housing costs and benefits.
>
> (Cooper, 1995, quoted in UNCHS, 2000: 53)

This chapter unpicks a range of social, economic, political and cultural issues which make people move vulnerable to homelessness

Economic issues

Global economic change

Along with shortfalls in the housing supply system (Chapter 3), a fundamental cause of homelessness in most developing countries is poverty, especially rural poverty which drives large numbers of people to seek employment in cities (e.g. Rahman, 1993, on Bangladesh). Clearly, the extent of poverty in industrialised countries is not as extreme, or as widespread, as that in developing countries. Nevertheless, Okongwu and Mencher (2000) note that, in both, the inequality which leads to extreme poverty frequently results from similar macro-level policy decisions.

Recent decades have witnessed a major economic change in both industrialised and developing countries. The economies of industrialised countries have been undermined by the globalisation of production and investment. This has had major implications for government revenues, for welfare states and, ultimately, for housing security (Forrest, 1999; Avi-Yonah, 2000).

In industrialised countries, the need for governments to reduce their welfare spending has been addressed through privatisation and the contracting out of service delivery to both private and non-governmental sectors (Foster and Plowden, 1996). Kennett and Marsh (1999) argue that the result is an increased risk of poverty and homelessness for the mass of the population.

Dehavenon (1996) relates the increase in homelessness in the USA closely to the reconfiguring of welfare programmes. For example, the USA introduced a programme of welfare reform called Temporary Assistance for Needy Families (TANF) in 1996 which, by limiting support to those working for a minimum period each week, excluded many more people than previous programmes had. One effect of this was a greater number of people seeking support from homeless shelters and food kitchens (Schleiter and Statham, 2002).

Developing countries have also experienced fiscal crises in recent decades. In the early 1980s, Argentina, Chile and Uruguay all suffered from the financial deregulation that had taken place in the previous decade. Throughout the 1990s there was a tightening of large-scale lending, causing fiscal crisis in the emerging markets of Mexico, Venezuela and, more recently, in the East Asian countries of Indonesia, Korea and Thailand. The causes of these crises are well covered in literature (see e.g. Pilbeam, 2001). Following the 1997 economic crisis in East Asian countries, a significant increase in homelessness was noted in a number of them, including Japan (Kakita, n.d.), Korea (Douglass, 2000) and Indonesia (Rahardjo, 2002). The Metropolitan City Office of Seoul reported the number of homeless people to have increased in 1998 from 2,550 in September to over 6,000 in December.

Perhaps one of the most far-reaching economic changes in developing countries has been that brought about by the Structural Adjustment Programmes (SAP) in the 1980s and 1990s which resulted in major tightening of public spending and the shedding of many government jobs, with resultant increases in unemployment and homelessness. There is little argument about the need for some form of tightening of government spending and greater efficiency in fiscal management in many developing countries. Nevertheless, the economic impacts of structural adjustment, especially on specific subgroups including women, remain unclear (Schatz, 1994; Elson, 1995). While the long-term effects may not have been as negative as some early predictions suggested (see Chapter 2), nor were they particularly beneficial. Moreover, the effects have differed between regions. In some cases, increased poverty has not been as great or as long-lived as predicted, however, there may be other mitigating circumstances.

More recently, the collapse of communism in the Soviet Union brought an end to state institutions and the virtual collapse of the state-based economy. The state system had provided employment and housing for many people and a social security net for more vulnerable groups (Deacon, 2000). Increasing numbers of homeless people, often referred to as *bomzhies* ('persons without a definite place of residence or employment') began living in disused or derelict buildings. Many of the 'new homeless' were abandoned children, with an estimated 300,000 homeless children in Russia in August 1995. Adding to the ranks of homeless people were the thousands of Red Army soldiers returning from postings in Eastern or Central Europe and finding it difficult to obtain housing.

In both the Soviet Union and China, people with disabilities were traditionally employed in special state enterprises to ensure their economic security. The collapse of the Soviet socialist system and the recent introduction of neo-liberal financial structures in China have undermined state welfare provision which protected these vulnerable people from homelessness. Prior to reforms in China, state enterprises provided strong welfare and pensions schemes for the elderly, sick or disabled. The adoption of new reforms has been hampered by several factors including old and inappropriate financial systems and vested interests.

Around the world, financial insecurity is exacerbated, particularly in rural areas, by decreasing security of food from household production. Changing farming practices, loss of land through subdivision at inheritance and declining civil security in rural areas have contributed to increasing rural poverty (Ellis, 2000).

Recently, India has actively founded its role in the global economy upon the information technology sector. From early focuses on software development and information management, India has more recently engaged in providing call centre support for some of the world's largest companies. The city of Bangalore, in southern Karnataka, is at the epicentre of an explosion of IT companies which have brought increased employment and wealth to a growing middle class. This move has demanded considerable development, with major IT parks springing up on low-value land on the city's periphery, bringing a booming housing market for a new wave of middle-class households (Madon, 2004). Land is somewhat cheaper in Bangalore than in many Indian cities.[1] This has, no doubt, helped Bangalore develop this industry but land formerly of little commercial value is often the very land on which informal settlements form and remain uncontested for years. Rising land prices mean that informal settlements, in cities and at their peripheries, become obstacles in the way of development (Berner, 1997, 2000). Those living in such settlements are increasingly at risk of eviction, especially tenants and subtenants, who are the least well protected (Durand-Lasserve and Royston, 2002).

Although Bangalore has had a somewhat lower proportion of people living in slum areas than other major cities (De Wit, 1992), the proportion has been growing rapidly since the early 1990s. While this has been occurring, the urban poor and the original middle classes have been edged further and further out of the city by rising land prices, increasing rents and, sometimes, by evictions (Madon, 2004).

During the CARDO study, one of the authors (Speak) visited Bangalore, where she was shown some of the peripheral development under way. People had been evicted not only to make way for the construction of an IT park but also to clear the way for a major road to service it and link it to the city. Moreover, land adjacent to the new road, previously too remote to be of interest to developers, was suddenly subject to speculation and clearance ready for further development.

This construction itself provides valuable jobs for people who will never be employed in the high-technology industry. Nevertheless, there was no system for providing compensation or support for those who lost their (albeit poor) homes because of it. Moreover, the construction workers, and their families who accompany them, are themselves homeless, living in the poorest of straw or tarpaulin dwellings at the side of the construction site. Indeed, it could be argued that new economic development is, to a degree, dependent on the willingness of a labour force to live in the poorest conditions. In this respect new economic development not only stimulates homelessness but is dependent upon it.

Clearly India's meteoric rise in the global information technology market is a major achievement for a country with a literacy rate of only 52 per cent (National

Literacy Mission – India, n.d.). It presents the opportunity to achieve incomes and a standard of living for many which would have been unthinkable two decades ago. However, this new affluence is not only limited to a very small elite of well-educated middle-class Indians, it also has little impact on the wider state economy. For example, over 75 per cent of Karnataka's population still live in rural villages. Whilst high-technology companies are offering a salary of $395 per month, 90 per cent of the rural population lives on little more than $100 per year (Madon, 2004). Moreover, achieved as it is in a context of deregulation and privatisation of urban services and the housing sector, this new economic development seems doomed to leave many in a worse position than they were before it, especially the poorest and most vulnerable.

Much of Indonesia's urban growth during the 1980s and after (at rates in excess of 5 per cent per year) was fuelled by declining agriculture in the outer islands and high levels of foreign investment in export-oriented manufacturing, especially along the northern coast of Java (World Resources Institute, 1999). During recent decades, many people have been evicted from the land they had been occupying for generations, because it was needed for development. Eviction did not just take place in urban areas and in the surrounding rural areas but also in remote places. In Kalimantan and Irian Jaya, indigenous tribes were 'resettled' to allow for the exploitation of their rich natural resources. Even after the fall of the Suharto regime, eviction of people from their land has continued (Rahardjo, 2002).

In testimony to the fragility of such military-controlled economic development, General Suharto's kleptocracy was ousted in May, 1998, amid severe recession, lack of confidence in the economy and steep falls in the value of the rupiah. In August 1998, the rupiah stood at 13,000–15,000 per dollar whereas it had been 2,500 per dollar only one year before (*The Economist*, 1998b). The GDP per capita fell to below $500 in 1998 (*The Economist*, 2000). Despite initial optimism arising from the change of government and a rallying of the rupiah, the economy continues to be extremely troubled (Rahardjo, 2002).

The price of rice, a popular barometer of well-being in Java, more than tripled in 1998 so that government estimated that 17 million households (89 million people) could only afford one meal a day (*The Economist*, 1998a; Rahardjo, 2002). The situation was further exacerbated by civil unrest and a consequent down-turn in tourism, even ahead of the events of 11 September and the Bali bombing, both of which occurred after the CARDO study period. As a result of the prolonged crisis, more than 100 million Indonesians (or nearly half of its population) were living close to or below the poverty line in 1999 (Jellinek and Rustanto, 1999).

We have no details of whether the economic collapse at the end of the century drove many middle-income households into homelessness. However, evidence from Thailand (Yasmeen, 2001) suggests that many formerly relatively prosperous households will have had to make major adjustments to their lifestyle. The more fortunate or entrepreneurial will have managed to survive through establishing small enterprises but some of the less fortunate may well have joined the ranks of the homeless.

It is clear that economic decline can lead to homelessness but so, too, can economic success. Despite many governments seeing migration as problematic (de Haan, 1999), the booming economies of countries such as India and China are heavily dependent on a rapidly swelling urban labour force. However, new low-skilled migrants to urban areas are poorly catered for in terms of housing and many live on the streets, in workplaces and makeshift shelters or in very poor dwellings in informal settlements.

Unemployment

In industrialised countries in Europe, the USA and Japan, homelessness is strongly linked to unemployment (Fitzpatrick and Kennedy, 2001). That is to say that homeless people are more likely to be economically inactive and that unemployment, or loss of employment, is a precursor to homelessness. The majority of homeless people in Japan, cite unemployment as the main reason for their homelessness. This is exacerbated by a failure to receive severance payments or unemployment benefit (Ezawa, 2002). Aoki (2003) noted that the majority of homeless people in Osaka had become homeless after losing their jobs following the decline of the Japanese economy during the early 1990s. This relationship between homelessness and unemployment in industrialised countries is further witnessed by the increasing concern about the apparent growth in begging associated with homelessness (Adler, 1999).

In most developing countries, however, homelessness does not necessarily have such a strong association with either unemployment or economic inactivity. There are a number of reasons for this. Although the welfare networks of industrialised countries are increasingly insecure, they remain strong enough to protect all but the most vulnerable or troubled from homelessness. Therefore, those few who fall through the net into rough sleeping and begging are often those with the greatest personal difficulties, such as disability, mental health difficulties or substance abuse problems, which may make them less easily employable than other people. Thus, the welfare environment means that homeless people in industrialised countries are a concentration of the most vulnerable with least ability and greatest problems. In the absence of welfare networks in developing countries, however, the profile of homeless people, especially street sleepers, contains a greater mix and diversity of individuals, with a broader range of backgrounds and abilities than in industrialised countries.

Olufemi (1997) noted that, in South Africa, 96 per cent of homeless people were unemployed prior to becoming homeless and 79 per cent were unemployed after becoming homeless. It is obvious that unemployment increases poverty and the link between poverty and homelessness has been well documented (from as far back as Lewis, 1969).

Poverty and homelessness

We need only look at the incomes of those in developing countries to understand the difficulty they face in achieving adequate accommodation. Land and construction prices for new formal sector housing are extremely high relative to incomes, particularly in metropolitan areas where land prices have often been pushed up by large increases in population (Kamruzzaman and Ogura, 2006).

In metropolitan Dhaka, with a minimum plot area of 195 square metres, a building plot in the lowest income area exceeded Tk. 3 million (£37,500) in 1998, which even the upper middle-class could barely afford (Hoek-Smit, 1998). The construction costs for a small 30 square metres dwelling, excluding land, would be Tk.135,000 (£1,700). Such a structure on its own would be quite affordable to the median household by income but the inclusion of the costs of developed land take it out of what even households well above the median could afford (Kamruzzaman and Ogura, 2006). It has been estimated that the median household in Dhaka would have to pay its whole monthly income on a housing loan to afford the lowest-cost formal two-roomed dwelling. Only 25 per cent of the capital's households could afford such a dwelling. Indeed, even though the ratio of the median free-market price of dwelling unit to the median annual household income decreased between 1993 and 1996, it still remained a very high 12.5:1 in 1996 (Ghafur, 2002).

Measurement of poverty in Bangladesh focuses on a daily minimum per capita calorie intake, even though its limitations are well known. The poverty thresholds are a minimum intake of 2,122 calories per person per day for 'absolute poverty' and 1,805 calories per person per day for 'hardcore poverty'.[2] In 1995–6, there were 9.6 million urban dwellers in absolute poverty (50 per cent of urban residents), of whom 5.2 million (27 per cent of urban residents) were in hardcore poverty (BBS, 2000: 389). It would be reasonable to assume that any housing cost imposed on such households is likely to be paid at the expense of another commodity such as transport to work, health care or food. Thus, the universal affordability percentage so beloved of policymakers (say, 25 per cent of income on housing) is dramatically inappropriate to those close to the poverty line. For a landless labourer, average monthly household expenditure on food and clothing constitutes more than 70 per cent of income, with little more than 7 per cent to be spent on housing and house rent, so that an adequate shelter is beyond their affordability (Ghafur, 2002).

In Egypt, the Household Income Expenditure and Consumption Survey (HIECS) conducted in 1999/2000 noted that 20 per cent of households (around 12 million people) could not then satisfy their basic food and non-food needs. The poverty gap index was 3.8 per cent, implying an average deficit of L.E.206 (£33) for those living in poverty. Using a poverty line based on all the needs of a low-income household, 52 per cent or almost 32 million people would qualify as living in poverty in Egypt (El-Sheikh, 2002).

In Ghana, the percentage of the population defined as poor according to the upper poverty line, of what is needed to afford essential food and non-food consumption, fell from almost 52 per cent in 1991–2 to just under 40 per cent in 1998–9. This was highly variable by region, however, with most reductions concentrated in Accra and the forest area. In the north, the proportion of the urban population defined as poor increased during the period 1991 to 1999 and poverty is more common in rural areas, especially in the northern regions which have benefited very little from the national poverty reduction programmes (Ghana Statistical Service, 2000; Department of Housing and Planning Research, 2002). These regions are traditional sources of migrants to the southern cities where they tend to live in their own overcrowded neighbourhoods known as *zongos* (Schildkrout, 1978).

Poverty arising at least partly from the political order of the last 20 years is likely to be the main cause of homelessness in Indonesia (Rahardjo, 2002). In order to maintain political stability, former-President Suharto's New Order regime allowed the military to become very powerful at the expense of political parties, the press and labour organisations. The economic success which the country enjoyed during the 1980s and early 1990s was dependent on foreign loans, until it became one of the most indebted countries in the world.[3] The rights of workers were suppressed for the sake of attracting investment and Indonesian workers became the most low-paid in the region (Budiman, 1993). Strikes were outlawed and those who dared to question the government's labour policy were dealt with severely (Rahardjo, 2002).[4] The priority given to big business (most of which were rent-seeking companies well connected to the ruling elite), seen as key to economic growth, resulted in the impoverishment of ordinary people. Many were evicted from the land they had been occupying for generations because it was needed for a new toll-road, an office block or a factory (Rahardjo, 2002). When it came, it was estimated that the collapse of the formal economy cost the jobs of 20 million people while unemployment was estimated at 17 per cent in 2000 (INFID, 2000; Wirakartakusumah and Hasan, n.d.).[5] As a consequence, there were more than 100 million people in Indonesia (or nearly half of its population) living below the poverty line (Jellinek and Rustanto, 1999; quoted in Rahardjo, 2002).[6]

In Peru, the social and economic situation is very fragile and the country has one of the highest poverty rates in Latin America. More than half of the population remains below the poverty line and half of the labour force is poorly paid for long working days and lacks any social or employment protection. The minimum wage is just less than US$80.00 per month.

The Peruvian National Statistics Institute (INEI, 2001) shows that poverty increased between 1997 and 2000 by 5.7 per cent, while extreme poverty decreased by 3.2 per cent.[7] Over a longer period, 1994 to 2000, the population in poverty was reasonably constant at just over 50 per cent, while extreme poverty decreased from 19.0 per cent to 14.8 per cent (Miranda and Salazar, 2002).

During the regime of President Fujimori, a number of basic labour benefits, particularly for women, were withdrawn, but the government of President Toledo restored many of them. In a low-wage and high-unemployment economy, young couples have only two housing options: to 'lodge' in their parents' house or to invade poor land at the edge of the city and claim a plot. At a conservative estimate, 50 per cent of the 700,000 individuals and households registered in PROFAM for a plot were younger than 25 years old (Miranda and Salazar, 2002).

Poverty is also institutional; 2,162 municipalities together receive less than 4 per cent of the national budget from the central government.[8] A considerable amount of national resources goes to the payment of the external debt and to the military, leaving little for social investment and even that has been managed very inefficiently (Miranda and Salazar, 2002).

In South Africa, 58 per cent of the population and 67 per cent of ethnic Africans lived below the lower poverty line of R322 per capita per month in 1995 (Hoogeveen and Özler, 2005). This means that the majority of South Africans are eligible for a full housing subsidy of R36,000 (£2,500) so could only afford housing costing up to R45,000 (about £3,000) (Rust, 2007).

At the end of last century, about 75 per cent of Zimbabweans were classified as poor, with 47.2 per cent being very poor[9] (Zimbabwe Congress of Trade Unions, 1999). The former is a 43 per cent increase from 1991 (Central Statistical Office, 1998) and an increase of over 25 per cent from 1995 (Nyakazeya, 2001).

The median house cost-to-income ratio for Zimbabwe increased from 3.1 in 1980[10] to about 5.1 in 1995 (Ministry of Public Construction and National Housing, 1991, 1995) and to more than 7.1 for Harare and above 5.1 for other centres by the year 2000 as wages remained static.[11] On average rent was above 50 per cent of income in 2001 for Harare and about 40 per cent for large other centres. The rural picture is different as there are no rentals in commercial farming areas. In mining settlements, estates and plantations only a nominal rent is paid (less than 1 per cent of income for the lowest paid worker). Tied government houses in urban areas are also rented or very little (Kamete, 2001).

There is no doubt that rents and housing costs are increasing. In 2000, in Harare, dwellings could be bought for less than Z$100,000 (c.£1,000) but only one year later the lowest priced house in the high-density areas (HDAs) was Z$300,000 (c.£3,000). The rise was exacerbated by the sudden availability of mortgage finance after a five-year hiatus. The same picture was repeated but to a lesser degree in other urban areas (Kamete, 2001). In 1981, rents were about 10 per cent of income (Ministry of Public Construction and National Housing, 1991) and remained fairly stable in the 1990s, However, they rose dramatically at the turn of the century. From less than Z$400 (c.£4) a room in the HDAs in 2000, rents increased to Z$1,500 (c.£15) per room in one year. In other urban centres rents have on average doubled or trebled. Wages and salaries have not kept pace with the escalating housing costs, indicating that the affordability gap is widening (Kamete, 2001). More recent hyper-inflation has caused unsustainable stresses to all parts of households' expenditure, with dwellings in low-income neighbourhoods selling for billions of the devalued Zimbabwe dollars.

This picture of poverty is similar for many millions of people in developing countries. For some 75 per cent of the world's women, however, their vulnerability to homelessness is exacerbated by the fact that they cannot get formal bank loans because they lack permanent employment and do not have title deeds to land or housing that they can offer as security. In many cases the laws of their countries classify them as minors, not eligible to make legal transactions.

Rural to urban migration

Poverty in rural areas is driving rural to urban migration in developing countries, in some cases on a massive scale. Industrialised countries last experienced mass rural to urban migration during the industrial revolution and, since the 1970s, most have experienced something of a reversal, with people increasingly seeking to return to rural areas (Moore and Begg, 2001).

The literature on migration is interlinked with the literature on livelihood diversification. Both identify a distinction between involuntary, distress or survival factors leading to migration and diversification on the one hand and voluntary, choice or accumulation factors on the other (de Haan, 1999). It is important to note this distinction because homelessness resulting from migration needs to be understood differently depending on the degree of choice involved (Speak, 2004).

Extreme poverty, natural disaster, loss of traditional lands and homestead, or loss of labouring work through mechanisation or intensification of farming are amongst the factors leading to much rural to urban migration (de Haan, 1999; Ellis, 2000). Choice or accumulation factors include taking advantage of increased unskilled labouring or semi-skilled manufacturing jobs to earn money to educate children, pay for a family wedding or funeral, or extend a dwelling (Taylor, 1999). Bangladesh is a prime example of this. Rural livelihoods in Bangladesh are predominantly agricultural in nature and land remains the main asset for income-generation. However, according to the 1995/6 Household Expenditure Survey (HES), 5.5 per cent of rural households are landless while 49.5 per cent of households are 'functionally landless' (i.e. owning up to half an acre). The total number of these two categories is a staggering 10 million (55 per cent of households in Bangladesh) leading, inevitably, to a high incidence of rural poverty (Ghafur, 2002).

Whatever the cause, the implication of this rural to urban migration for homelessness is manifested most conspicuously in the proliferation and expansion of slums, informal settlements and people living without shelter on the streets in urban areas of developing countries.[12] As well as the push of poverty, however, rural people also respond to the pull of perceived wealth and increased opportunity in the city, which is not necessarily based on truth. For example, while rural to urban migration in Peru has swollen the populations of cities such as Lima, from 5 million in 1985 to 7.4 million in 2000 (UNCHS, 2001a), it has taken place at a time of economic stagnation. Thus, those arriving in the city are competing for very limited jobs and money. The urban pull probably exists in all developing countries but is arguably stronger in those countries where urbanisation is driven by a rapid rise in economic activity, such as in South-East Asia. Rural to urban migrants here have arrived at a time of great economic expansion based on developing new technology and industries. While they might not be directly involved in the new industries themselves, they can benefit indirectly by finding a niche in the informal economy, such as retail or informal building and development, serving those more directly involved.

Such migration is frequently the route by which lone men find themselves living on the streets in developing countries. Most often a single man will move to the city to work and send money back to the family home. As he will usually have little to offer the urban economy but his strength, he will only find a low-paid job such as day labouring, market portering or rickshaw-pulling. Once earning, he will often choose to sleep on the city streets or in a public space rather than spending any of the little money earned on accommodation and transport to work. If the weather is bad, he might pay to stay in a hostel, if places are available, but the rest of the time he will save money by sleeping rough. In some cases, other family members will follow him to the city as his earnings are insufficient to improve their rural lives. Figure 8.1 shows one such man who sleeps on his basket, the tool of his

8.1   This market porter in Dhaka sleeps on his basket on the street close to the market. (Photograph by Nasir Ali Mamun. (Courtesy of Shayer Ghafur)

trade as a porter. The role for homelessness as part of a housing career or pathway is particularly common in India and Bangladesh, where one more frequently encounters families living in the streets than in other countries in the CARDO study, such as Peru or Egypt (Speak, 2004).

In India, rural to urban migration increased throughout the 1980s and 1990s and is continuing to increase, swelling the ranks of homelessness. In Delhi, approximately 95 per cent of homeless people are from outside Delhi, mainly from Uttar Pradesh and Bihar and most of them come from rural areas (Chan and Zhang, 1999). Less than 14 per cent of homeless people in Mumbai are from the city, with the majority of homeless people there coming from Maharashtra, Uttar Pradesh, Bihar and Tamil Nadu (SPARC, 1985). Similar situations exist in other countries especially Bangladesh and those in Latin America (see e.g. de Janvry and Sadoulet, 2000, on Latin America; Kuhn, 2003, on Bangladesh).

In China, movement is controlled through the *hukou* or household registration system, which links employment, education and provision of welfare services to the locality of registration (Chan and Zhang, 1999) (see Chapter 4). Nevertheless, internal migration has increased since economic reforms brought a relaxation of restrictions on movement to satisfy the demand for unskilled labour in booming cities and towns. In recent years, there has been a wave of rural–urban migrants seeking labouring jobs in China's growing cities. Having only temporary permits for unskilled jobs and not being registered in the city, they do not have access to state provision of services and housing (Wang and Zuo, 1999; Liang, 2001). The high price of commercial housing means that most migrants are lone males who must leave their families behind and live in collective dormitories or worksite shelters, or even in the workshops themselves (Ma, 2001).

Korboe (1996) notes that, in Kumasi, Ghana, about 46 per cent of the homeless people have migrated from the distant Northern and Upper East Regions of the country. About 26 per cent are natives of Kumasi, whilst the remaining 28 per cent are migrants from the nearby rural areas of Ashanti Region (Korboe, 1996).

In many countries, the process of rural to urban migration begins with temporary, seasonal migration. The migrant's intention is to send money home for a few months and then return. For some this may be a forced response to failed rural livelihoods. For others it provides an opportunity to accumulate capital (Mosse et al., 2002). Temporary economic migrants are often homeless while in the cities. Many such migrants choose not to spend money on shelter, particularly if the weather is not too harsh, preferring to save even the limited cost of night shelters. In Delhi, a place in a night shelter run by an NGO costs only a few rupees per night but these might be better saved or spent on food. For a temporarily shelterless able-bodied lone male, sleeping on the street may be uncomfortable and insecure but not enough of a problem to spend the few rupees for a shelter place.

Rural to urban migration resulting in homelessness can involve entire households, including women, children and older people. Women's weaker position in the urban labour market makes them more vulnerable to homelessness. Olufemi (2000) suggests that, in South Africa, women's homelessness is increased by the limited skills and discrimination which make women's entrance to, and engagement in, the labour market far more difficult and less rewarding than it is for men.

One reason for couples and households to migrate together might be that it is generally the most destitute and vulnerable rural households who send migrants to the cities (Ruthven and David, 1995; Hampshire, 2002). So great is their need for financial help that one person alone may not be able to provide enough. Mosse et al. (2002) noted that, in western India, the poorer the family, the greater the number of people from it who migrated. Rogaly (2003) notes that migrant couples in West Bengal (India) often leave behind their younger children until they are old enough to work, when they will migrate to join their parents.

Some studies note the benefits accruing to the rural home from cash remittances from the members who may be homeless in the city (Hampshire, 2002; Rogaly and Coppard, 2003). Others, however, suggest that the migration of productive adults contributes to rural decline and diminishes rural livelihoods. The cash returns are often insufficient, or lost in the process of return, and the loss of labour and diminished social networks compound the rural poverty (Cleveland, 1991; Croll and Ping, 1997). This is particularly problematic when it leaves the rural livelihood dependent on women's labour. Waddington (2003) notes that the experience of those remaining in the rural area may be one of increased vulnerability. In such cases, it soon becomes more economically viable for the household to concentrate on cash employment in the city rather than continually failing subsistence in the village.

Household migration is not always the result of destitution, however, as it can form part of traditional, long-standing livelihood strategies. In some parts of Latin America, seasonal economic migration of entire households has been practised for many generations. The indigenous people of the Andes move down from the Alto Plano each year to trade on the streets of cities such as Lima, La Paz or Cochabamba during the summer tourist months. Their rural migration, and resulting lack of shelter, differs from that of the Indian or Bangladeshi lone male migrants in that it is more a planned cyclical event as part of an ongoing economic strategy than a reaction to permanent unmanageable rural poverty. Some observers might not consider these migrants as homeless as they have homes and families in their villages. Nevertheless, while some are in short-term cyclical migration within their control, other migrants stay on without shelter in the city, for protracted periods, during which time the rural home may become increasingly inaccessible or valueless.

It is clear that rural to urban migration can be seen as a cause of urban homelessness. Conversely, rural homelessness or insecurity of tenure and lack of access to land can be a cause of rural to urban migration. For example, Mosse et al. (2002) note the failings of land rights leading to migration in western India, as does Rogaly (2003) in West Bengal.[13] Some rural households lose their land altogether when river courses change during periods of flooding. This is common in Bangladesh (Rahman, 1993) (see Chapter 10).

It appears, then, that rural to urban migration has a multi-faceted relationship with homelessness. First, there is the direct homelessness of the initial migrant worker. Second, there is the increased vulnerability to poverty and subsequently homelessness, of those remaining in the rural area. This dualism is significant for intervention policy because cities are dependent on migrant labour but cannot adequately house and support the labourers' dependants. Third, there are the implications of limited land rights for the rural poor, which may serve to push them from rural insecurity into urban homelessness.

Social and cultural issue

The globalisation of economies, ideas and cultures inevitably leads to social change. In both industrialised and developing countries, one form of social change which has major implications for homelessness is the breakdown of traditional family and household structures and the diminution of the support those structures provided.

The causes and experiences of both men's and women's homelessness are similar in many respects. However, it would be naïve to overlook the specific impact of gender in relation to homelessness. Women are more vulnerable to homelessness because their security is based upon their ability to form and maintain autonomous households, independent of male breadwinners or other financial support (Jejeebhoy, 1995; Chant, 1996). Thus, it can be argued that social change, which impacts so directly on family and relationships, has a greater effect on the housing security of women than of men and, as Buvinic and Gupta (1997) note, they should be targeted for poverty alleviation policy. The gendering of homelessness has been well documented in the Western context (see e.g. Novac et al., 1996; Edgar, 2001).

Relationships and family breakdown

In industrialised countries, relationship breakdown, divorce and separation are well-documented causes of homelessness (Hutson and Clapham, 1999; Kennett and Marsh, 1999; Watson, 1999; Edgar and Doherty, 2001). This reflects the socio-demographic and economic changes affecting European and, indeed, most industrialised societies. For example, in the UK in 2006, 20 per cent of homeless households were homeless owing to the breakdown of a relationship. For 13 per cent, this was related to domestic violence (Department of Communities and Local Government, 2006). Studies routinely show that around half of homeless people ascribe their homelessness to relationship breakdown (Anderson and Christian, 2003). In one survey the homeless NGO Crisis noted that around one in four hostel residents left their last permanent home because of family or relationship breakdown (Randall and Brown, 2001). In Australia, in 2000–1, 23 per cent of clients of the Supported Accommodation

Assistance Program (SAAP) cited domestic violence and 10 per cent cited relationship or family breakdown as the main reason for seeking assistance (Wright-Howie, 2007). In a study of 777 homeless parents in ten cities in the US (the majority of whom were mothers), 22 per cent said that they had left their last place of residence because of domestic violence (Wright-Howie, 2007).

Female-headed households are increasing in frequency in developing countries also but they appear to be more common in Latin American, Caribbean and Sub-Saharan African countries than in Asia or the Middle East (Buvinic and Gupta, 1997). Such households are formed through divorce, abandonment, bereavement or separation following domestic violence. Heise (1994) and García-Moreno et al. (2005) detail an alarming picture of violence against women from a range of industrialised and developing countries. In Peru, over 52 per cent of women in one survey reported having been abused by their husbands and over 40 per cent by their cohabiting partner (Pomodoro, 2001). In Tanzania around 80 per cent of women have experience of domestic violence and, in Kenya, one study identified 42 per cent of women being beaten regularly (Heise, 1994). Bernasconi and Puentes (2006) found that several women in their Chilean study had left home because of sexual and other abuse in what they regard as a decisive action in proof of their autonomy.

Regardless of how lone women-headed households are formed, most women in the West are in a considerably better position to support themselves and their children. They also tend to remain adequately housed upon the break-up of their relationship more often than many of their counterparts in developing countries. In the West, the traditional route to a home for women, through marriage and a male breadwinner, has changed significantly in recent decades (Gonzalez Lopez and Solsona, 2000; Doherty, 2001). In industrialised countries, it is now increasingly socially acceptable and financially possible for women to maintain their own homes, and raise children alone. However, most women in developing countries still rely on marriage as their only route to a home independent from their birth families. Thus, when marriage or cohabiting relationships break down, women there are at greater risk of homelessness for several reasons.

1 Many countries still operate gender-based discrimination and do not recognise women's rights to own land or property, thus, even if they can afford to, they are not able to buy land to build their own homes.

2 Even where land rights for women do exist, they may be partial and may not include a presumption of spousal co-ownership. Thus, if a marriage ends, the wife might not be entitled to any part of the home. Despite the adoption of the African Charter on Human and People's Rights (ACHPR) by 35 African states, many African countries have very poor records on women's rights to land, housing and property. For example, in Kenya, where women head 70 per cent of all squatter households, over 25 per cent of women slum dwellers migrated from their rural homes because of land dispossession (Benschop,

155

2004). Similarly, in Tanzania, whilst gender-based discrimination is ostensibly illegal, women do not have equal rights to land or housing upon the dissolution of marriage (Benschop, 2002). Thus, those women who find themselves without a male partner almost certainly face extreme poverty and homelessness, as do the children who live with them. In many matrilineal societies, property rights may be passed down through the matrikin. Thus, land and housing belonging to a husband might well pass, on death, to his brothers and his sisters' children rather than to his wife and children (Tipple and Willis, 1992).

3   The existing property rights are not always upheld, as custom preventing women's ownership often remains alongside the changes to the law. In Kenya, for example, whilst there is a Married Women's Property Act and Registered Land Act, there is no presumption that women have equal rights to property on break-up of marriage, and customary law, which favours men, is not prohibited (Benschop, 2002).

4   Women in many countries face unequal inheritance laws, for example, in many Muslim countries. This might also occur in non-Muslim countries where different inheritance laws apply to those married there under Islamic law. Under Islamic law (*Sharia*), a daughter, married or unmarried, inherits half of the amount given to a son. Unfortunately, in many male-dominated societies, it is common for daughters not to receive even this and few can afford to resort to the courts. A Muslim widow only inherits one-quarter of the husband's estate, in the absence of a child, and one-eighth in the presence of a child. Where there are two or more wives, as is common in Africa, this prescribed share is divided equally between them (Benschop, 2002; El-Sheikh, 2002).

5   The likelihood of homelessness resulting from loss of a partner or relationship break-up appears to depend also on societal acceptance of women-headed households and of working women. Few developing countries have any form of social welfare benefit for lone-parent households. Thus a lone mother needs to work. In Latin America there is considerably more social acceptance of lone women-headed households and women going out to work than in, for example, Bangladesh.

In theory, Muslim women around the world are provided security in the event of abandonment or divorce, in the form of *mehr* – an amount of money allocated to them at the time of marriage. In reality, many women do not receive this and are, therefore, unable to leave an abusive relationship. Moreover, in most developing countries, they have little recourse to the law to demand support if their husbands abandon them. It is difficult for women to work in many Muslim countries, or certainly to earn adequately to support a family independently. In some situations, particularly in cultures where lone working women are often perceived as immoral, the woman and her children may be ostracised to the point that they must leave their home and the area. Thus, leaving an abusive husband, or being abandoned, almost certainly results in the woman falling into extreme poverty and homelessness. This is more clearly the case in Muslim countries than in non-Muslim ones (Speak, 2005).

Weakening of extended family support

In a context of diminishing or non-existent welfare support networks, extended family, kinship and social networks are vitally important to protect people from homelessness. However, these too are weakening. In 2005 in England, 38 per cent of homeless households were homeless because relatives or friends were no longer willing to provide accommodation and this percentage is on the rise. It also suggests that effective intervention such as family support, child protection, family mediation and the prevention of domestic violence can be important in addressing homelessness (Cooper, 1995; UNCHS, 2000).

Nuclear family households have increasingly been the norm in industrialised societies since the industrial revolution. However, most developing countries have long traditions of extended family support and kinship responsibilities, which have acted as safety nets in societies without formal welfare systems. Extended family responsibilities are so strong in some cultures that they impact on the very concepts of home and of homelessness. However, Foster (2000) presents evidence that these family support networks are beginning to change and, in some cases, fracture, affecting the housing security of more vulnerable people. These changes are not sudden but have been developing over several generations. In Bangladesh, for example, the duties and responsibilities of a solvent person toward a destitute one were seen as their *dharma*, meaning whatever is right and righteous for the individual. Duties were performed, reciprocated and perpetuated in a context of abundance and indulgence (Maloney, 1991). However, these traditional roles and obligations recognised and performed by kinship units (*bangsa* and *gushti)* toward their vulnerable members have gradually become extinct in the recent past (Ghafur, 2002).

As in many other developing countries, the main suppliers of housing in Ghana have been house-owners in the upper echelons of low income who build compounds and large rooming houses. These are partly for their own and family occupation and partly rented out room by room (Tipple and Korboe, 1998; Tipple et al., 1999; Andreasen et al., 2005). In this system, the familial obligations to provide accommodation to the poorest members of the extended family, and the inheritance system in which most houses become family-owned in common, have traditionally provided an important social safety net. Those who would otherwise be homeless are accommodated by their kin rent-free. When the 700,000 Ghanaian migrants arrived from the mass expulsion from Nigeria in January 1983 (Afolayan, 1988), they simply went home; there were no refugee camps required. Whether this could be repeated so effectively 25 years later is open to question; many would now probably become homeless in Accra or Kumasi.

Ghana provides an interesting case in which a very strong traditional system is breaking down gradually under the pressure of global influences and contributing to homelessness in the country. Of course, increased contact with the outside world alerts people to different ways of life and reduces the hold tradition has. Ghanaians are great travellers, both within their country and abroad, and they assimilate values along the way. Thus, while tradition and ties to the home village remain strong among the diaspora, change towards individualisation and nuclear family loyalties increase and weaken the social safety net both for the dependent migrant and the receiving relative in Ghana and for the contributing migrant abroad. Migrants are likely to remit less of their income to relatives back home both as attitudes change and as they do not make as much money as they expected to (Department of Housing and Planning Research, 2002). Education alerts young people to the chances they may find in the cities but then they find they are less equipped than they expected and can only do menial jobs or petty trading or portering work, sleeping in their workplace or in the market.

There is also an economic breakdown occurring between successful households and those who would have been their dependants in the past. As Apt (1999) describes with respect to elderly people, the strains of supporting relatives on low urban incomes are cutting many off from their former social safety nets and they might fall into homelessness. Indeed, the definition of homelessness in Ghana includes being cut off from the assistance of family (Department of Housing and Planning Research, 2002). In the context of urban poverty, support groups grow up which are not family-based and some people inevitably miss out.

One of the main expressions of the familial support structure in Ghana is the family house: a place where any member of an extended family has the right to live. Many still survive and provide a hugely important safety-net role for those who are most vulnerable: the unemployed, young people on low incomes, the elderly and the infirm (Amole et al., 1993). However, the commodification of housing, which threatens to engulf even the very traditional Ghanaian system, will inevitably lead to the disappearance of family housing unless it is actively encouraged.

There have also been some fundamental changes in the social system in Zimbabwe over the last two decades. The monetisation of the economy and the continual rise in the cost of living have both been eroding the basis of the extended family that offered mutual security and interdependence especially in urban areas. The difficulties of survival have forced people to withdraw into tighter family units and only interact with outsiders when reciprocity is assured (Kamete, 2001).[14] Adults infected with HIV/AIDS and AIDS orphans are particularly becoming victims of the disintegration of the traditional social safety nets (see below).

This explains why it is not uncommon now for those who come into urban centres to stay with relatives while they look for work to be given set periods to find jobs and leave. In the unlikely event of the visitor finding a job, they are allowed to

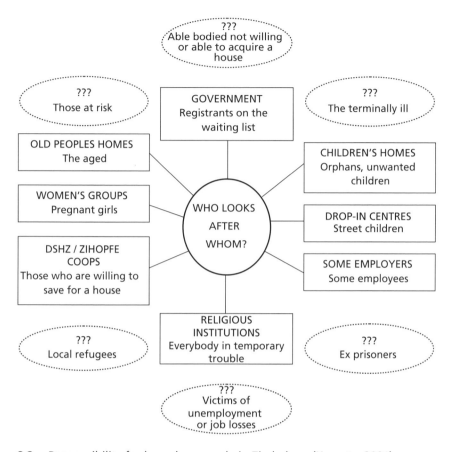

8.2 Responsibility for homeless people in Zimbabwe (Kamete, 2001)

stay and contribute towards household expenses but, in most cases, they stay with friends in rented rooms which are usually backyard shacks in the low-income formal neighbourhoods, squatter settlements or transit camps (Kamete, 2001). Even rural safety nets are being adversely affected; many rural dwellers have retired from the cities with altered views of their role in social safety nets (see Kamete et al., 2000, 2001). Figure 8.2 shows how institutions have grown up to fill vacuums in social care left as the traditional systems decline.

One measure of the strength or weakness of traditional family support roles is the propensity for inheritance of widows and orphans, a practice common in many cultures until recently (Foster, 2000). Drew et al. (1996) note that, in Zambia, widow inheritance by a brother of the deceased husband is no longer common. This may be, in part, because of the spread of HIV/AIDS in Africa and a man's fear of bringing an infected woman into the household (see below).

Economic, social and cultural causes

It is clear that, in many countries, widows are at an extreme risk of homelessness. It is all too common for a man's kin to evict his widow, and her children, from the marital home upon the husband's death. The position of a widowed second wife is even more tenuous (Sossou, 2002). Where the inheritance of widows is in decline, so too is the inheritance of orphans by surviving family members. As children's land and property rights are even more tenuous than women's, this can leave orphans, particularly older ones, to live alone and on the streets (Drimie, 2003; Foster et al., 1997). This lack of rights leads to difficulties for children when they lose both parents, as have many millions of children orphaned through HIV/AIDS (see below). There may be no formal system for them to take over ownership of the traditional family homesteads and land, thus they may become homeless as older relatives who can inherit squeeze them out (Drimie, 2003).

Ageing societies

One group particularly at risk of homelessness, by virtue of weakening family support networks, is older people, who form the fastest growing demographic group. As with many subgroups of the homeless populations, the number of older homeless people is difficult to estimate. Nevertheless, it is reasonable to assume that, as populations age and the percentage of older people increases, the number of older people at risk of homelessness will also rise. Studies in the USA identified a disproportionate growth in the number of older homeless people during the 1990s. In Boston, the older homeless population grew by 20 per cent in the three years between 1994 and 1997 (Kisor and Kendal-Wilson, 2002).[15]

The greater representation of older people amongst the homeless population in developing countries has several causes. The first is that developing countries' populations are ageing more quickly than industrialised populations. Currently 60 per cent of older people live in developing regions. This is set to rise to 80 per cent by 2050. Moreover, many developing countries are experiencing an 'older old' population, above the age of 80, for the first time. It is predicted that the population over 80 years of age will increase from 32 million to 265 million by 2050, again most of these older old people will live in less developed countries (United Nations, 2004).

The second reason behind an increased older homeless population is extensive rural to urban migration and, in some countries, international migration of younger people. There were predictions in the 1980s about the 'abandonment' of older people in developing countries (see e.g. Neysmith and Edward, 1984), based on the idea that their societies would evolve in the same way as industrial societies. These predictions were largely overstated (Lee et al., 1994; Aboderin, 2004a, 2004b). Hashimoto (1991), in a study of seven countries, noted support generally remains strong. Data showed that the elderly continue to live with children despite changing socio-economic and demographic conditions. It appears that socio-economic and individual characteristics are more likely to have an adverse effect on an older person's vulnerability to homelessness than changes to family formation. Nevertheless, older people are facing greater insecurity as social norms change and family support diminishes. In Bangladesh, for example, daughters are usually given in marriage in their early teens to men much older than themselves. Traditional society has a large number of widowed mothers as a result of this age difference. Widowed or divorced mothers expect to be supported by an older son in their old age (Ghafur, 2002) but, as younger people migrate to the cities in search of work, they leave their ageing relatives unsupported (Kabir et al., 2002).

In some cases older people find themselves victims of the dual challenge of social change and fiscal crisis. For example, in Indonesia, there were 14,800 elderly people in 157 institutions in 2002, many of which were being forced to close as the introduction of decentralisation left many local governments with less money to allocate. About 10 per cent of care institutions had been forced to close down by 2002 and it was feared that others would have to follow (Rahardjo, 2002).

The social changes discussed above, unsupplemented by formalised welfare networks, are increasing vulnerability to homelessness around the world. However, in some areas they are exacerbated by additional factors which we discuss below.

Ill health, infirmity and HIV/AIDS

It is clear that homeless people suffer considerably poorer health than adequately housed people, and their health characteristics have been discussed in Chapter 7. However, poor health can act as the tipping point which finally pushes vulnerable people into homelessness. While ill health and infirmity in all its forms increases vulnerability to homelessness by reducing people's ability to work, probably the greatest health threat to housing security is HIV/AIDS. The HIV/AIDS pandemic sweeping the world is undermining families and society leaving millions of people ill, dying and unsupported. In 2007, the UN reported an estimated number of people living with HIV to be around 33.2 million (30.6–36.1 million). In the same year around 2.1 million (1.9–2.4 million) people died of the disease. Sub-Saharan Africa remains the most seriously affected region, with AIDS remaining the leading cause of death there (UNAIDS/WHO, 2006).

HIV can be seen as a precursor, either directly or indirectly, to homelessness in a number of ways. At a structural level, as Arndt and Lewis (2001) show, the AIDS pandemic has reduced economic growth in affected African countries with a resultant reduction in employment in low-skilled sectors, which provide work for those most at risk of homelessness. At an individual level, illness is likely to render people incapable of maintaining a job. At a household level, already scant incomes are stretched further by the expense of medical treatment, where it is available, followed by years of reduced or no earnings, and funerals.

Economic, social and cultural causes

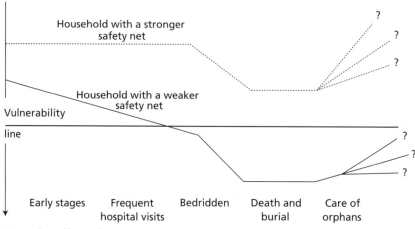

8.3 The effect of HIV/AIDS on households' livelihood strategies (from Drimie, 2003)

Figure 8.3 shows how HIV/AIDS sets in train the economic degradation of households by consuming resources until the death of the patient. However, the impact of this is not equal, those who have a strong safety net and wide range of resources are likely to survive better than their less well-off counterparts. If the household was sufficiently well protected by savings and several sources of income, for example, they might survive the episode, absorbing the economic shocks, without dipping below the vulnerability line into real poverty. Mutenje et al. (2008) note how much the sale of livestock, particularly small animals such as chickens and goats, helped in smoothing the economic shocks caused by HIV/AIDS in rural Zimbabwe. Where the safety net is weak, as soon as expenses for treatment begin to accrue, however, households will suffer and sink below the vulnerability line where they might stay over the medium to long term. Such fragile incomes and increased poverty increase vulnerability to homelessness and an inability or unwillingness to uphold traditional extended family support roles. Children can be particularly badly affected (see Chapter 12).

Persecution of those associated with HIV/AIDS can lead quite directly to homelessness. Sex workers, so acutely vulnerable to HIV infection, and whose housing tenure is generally fragile to begin with, are one example. This can be seen in the case of the Baina red light district in Goa. The site of a decade of HIV prevention programmes with local prostitutes, the area was demolished under a High Court order, ostensibly to rehabilitate commercial sex workers. No rehabilitation or rehousing was offered and thousands of vulnerable women and children were made homeless (Shahmanesh and Wayal, 2004).

As we have discussed above, for many widows, remarriage offers the only security on the death of their husbands. However, there is evidence that some widows may now be rejected by other men who fear being infected by them if their husband died of AIDS. As noted by Gregson et al. (2001; cited in Bracher et al., 2003), incidence of HIV is higher among the widowed in some African countries than among any other group.

Just as frail bodies contribute to vulnerability, so too do mental health problems. Poor mental health can make it impossible for people to function well enough to earn a living to pay for housing. In some countries mental health problems evoke great stigma. People released from mental hospital can only take to the streets as their relatives will not take them in and they cannot secure tenancy of a room. For example, mental health service reforms in Japan brought fears of increased homelessness as people with mental health problems were no longer cared for in institutions and were not easily accepted by their families or wider society (Ito and Sederer, 1999).

In the CARDO study, several countries had an implied link between homelessness and poor mental health. In both Indonesia and Ghana, people with mental illness can be found wandering the streets naked. In Indonesia, the government is legally obliged to care for the *gelandangan psikotis* (psychotic wanderers), but the resources are often inadequate (Rahardjo, 2002).

Conclusions

It is clear from earlier chapters that the failure of the housing supply system underlies homelessness in developing countries. However, it is equally clear that poverty makes accessing any available housing impossible for vast numbers of people. Poverty also makes improving inadequate housing and consolidating informal dwellings more difficult. Nevertheless, it is too simplistic to suggest that insufficient housing or poverty are solely responsible for homelessness. As noted earlier, not all poor people succumb to homelessness and not all homeless people are necessarily poorer than housed people. Without social and cultural change no amount of additional housing or reduction in poverty will be completely effective.

Inequality and social change are also important drivers of homelessness. A failure to uphold land and property rights means that women and minority ethnic groups do not have equal opportunities to housing and independence. A lack of welfare support systems and social attitudes to lone women-headed households in some countries means that many homeless women would not be in a position to access housing even if it was available.

Ageing societies and social change, including the breakdown of traditional family support, means that vulnerable older people, children or those with disabilities are increasingly at risk of homelessness. The spread of HIV/AIDS is producing a generation of children and older people who need support as well as housing. Improving housing supply alone would not help them.

The diminution of rural livelihoods and the continuing growth of urban areas, with all the earnings opportunities they offer, set up push and pull forces for migrants. Many do not need, or necessarily want, housing in urban areas and for many, merely to address their lack of shelter, through the provision of housing, would be futile. Other assistance would be more important and some non-housing interventions are featured in Chapter 13.

9 Political and legal issues

Homelessness is a highly political, and politically contentious issue. It could be considered as a state in which political institutions are unresponsive to the needs of the most vulnerable in the community and cannot intervene effectively to achieve an equitable distribution of housing costs and benefits (Cooper, 1995). This argument suggests that homelessness arises from a government's inability to achieve or maintain a policy of social justice.

Another argument might suggest that homelessness is maintained by some governments as a means of controlling political opposition. This has been demonstrated recently in Zimbabwe, where acknowledging as homeless sections of the population who were politically opposed to the ruling Zanu-PF party provided the justification for their subsequent eviction and dispersal. Bracking (2005: 343) notes that, following some of the evictions:

> Some displaced persons, an estimated 10,000, live on the roadside toward Dombashawa, others with Zimbabwean ID cards were returned in army lorries to their province of origin as stated on the card. They were taken to the Sabhuku (subchief), where they were more often than not asked for their ZANU-PF party card, and without it denied land and expelled again into the wilderness.

Thus, the institutional and regulatory frameworks established by governments to control access to land and to provide housing can help or hinder the urban poor in their quest for secure housing.

At another level, homelessness represents an issue about which governments should 'do something'. Acknowledging its existence in this way establishes in the public mind a responsibility for action. This is at the heart of the services–statistics paradox (Chapter 6 and FEANTSA, 1999).

This chapter explores the political and legal issues associated with homelessness at several levels. It begins by discussing issues of tenure insecurity, evictions and the way in which tenure can be used as a political tool. It explores the relationship between homelessness and citizenship in a number of countries including Indonesia, India and China. The chapter goes on to highlight the impact of major political and civil unrest, such as that currently ongoing in Zimbabwe and Iraq, and, as the work was being written, Kenya, in 2008.

Access to land

In cities around the world, the poor have an unequal access to land for housing. In Mumbai, for example, the slum dwellers account for over 50 per cent of the population but live on only 8 per cent of the land (Lall, 2001). In Nairobi, informal settlements provide homes for over 60 per cent of the population but take up only 5 per cent of the total residential land (Payne and Majale, 2004).

The origins of unequal access to land and tenure insecurity for the poor in developing countries often lie in colonialism. Colonialism and apartheid, in much of Africa and South Africa respectively, set the basis for post-colonial and post-apartheid class-based access to land. In much of colonial Africa, governments categorised much of the local populations as unskilled labour, only to be allowed into the urban areas as temporary labour in extractive and other heavy industries. Both the colonial and post-colonial governments deliberately constrained housing provision and land ownership for these groups to deter them from settling in the cities and towns.[1] In South Africa, unequal access to land was held over and reinforced, after all the independent governments to the north had abandoned it, to become the residential segregation policy of apartheid. This led to the dislocation and removal of the Africans, to peripheral townships and the pseudo-independent Bantustans.

Current neo-liberal policies in land use have perpetuated segregated access to land. Racial and class patterns remain intact in Nairobi and Johannesburg (Omenya, 2006). For example, in Kenya a draconian legislative framework, inherited from the colonial government, merely transferred power over land from the Crown of Great Britain to the President of Kenya, without much transformation. This is reflected in the Government Lands Act (Cap. 280) and explained by Syagga et al. (2001a).

Despite considerable post-apartheid legislation in South Africa (see below) access to land and security of tenure remains weak for the poor. Indeed, in many cases, legislation, regulation and programmes appear to make tenure even more insecure (Beresford, 1998). In Kenya, recent land reform has focused rather narrowly on land regularisation but has paid little attention to broader issues such as equity in access to land (Republic of Kenya, 2002).

In addition to the political constraints on land ownership, the high cost of urban land and low incomes have become major barriers to legal housing for many households living in poverty (Payne and Majale, 2004). In the 1990s, the World Bank promoted tenure security based on land ownership. This was intended to provide the urban poor with the benefits of solid legal rights, and physical capital upon which to raise mortgage finance. However, it underestimated the problems of lack of land registration systems, poor or non-existent legal and regulatory frameworks and lack of mortgage finance systems (Durand-Lasserve and Royston, 2002).

Because of the difficulties poor people in developing countries experience in acquiring land through legitimate channels, they must step outside the law in order to house themselves, committing the misdemeanour of trespass. In many cities in rapidly urbanising developing countries, especially in Africa, over 70 per cent of the population lives in informal settlements on land over which the residents have no ownership recognised in law.

Illegality and informality

The term 'informal housing' is now generally used to describe housing developed by the poor outside a country's legal and regulatory development frameworks. However, the legitimacy of the terms 'illegal' and 'informal' are complex and hide a multitude of degrees of ownership and legality. Indeed, Fernandes and Varley (1998) call into question the legitimacy of laws which act against the vast majority of poor people in a country. It is important to consider the difference between the two terms, not least because policy responses to the insecurity and problems they pose may be different. This is explained to some extent in Chapter 4 on differentiating between homeless people and squatters but warrants further consideration here.

In Indonesia, Act 4/1992 on Housing and Settlement treats the issue of housing more in terms of adequacy by defining two aspects of adequacy: physical and legal. The Act acknowledges the right of all citizens 'to live and/or to have the use and/or to own an adequate house located in a healthy, safe, harmonious and orderly environment'. Furthermore, the Act defines adequate housing as 'a house structure that, at least, meets building safety, minimum floor area and health requirements'. A healthy, safe, harmonious and orderly environment is defined as an environment which 'meets spatial planning, land-use, ownership and service provision requirements'.

Poorly serviced settlements can fall into either or both categories of informal and illegal. In Indonesia, illegal settlements are called *kampung liar* or *permukiman liar*. Others, called *kampung kumuh* or *permukiman kumuh*, are informal but not always illegal (Yudohusodo and Salam, 1991). The 'illegality' of *kampung liar* and *permukiman liar* does not refer to the status of their makeshift shelters but to the fact that the plots of land are being occupied without the consent of the owner (which in many cases is the government). The occupied plots on vacant land are usually located in economically strategic areas, where informal income-generating opportunities are available (Sriyuningsih, 2001). Their strategic position, whilst beneficial to the occupants, makes them prime for formal economic development, placing the settlements at risk of demolition.

However, some *kampung kumuh* or *permukiman kumuh* settlements are classed as informal, owing to the inadequate nature of the dwellings and the lack of regard for planning and building regulations, but the occupants may own the land.

In many cases, the informality of housing puts the occupants at risk of homelessness, either directly through eviction or indirectly through its physical inadequacy and lack of services. It is easy to see that someone who builds a home on land which they do not own, and which they have no formal legal rights to occupy, is at risk of eviction and subsequent homelessness. Such a household would lose not only their home but the land on which it was built and be left with nothing.

However, the position of someone who has land to which they have some form of legal title but builds on it informally, in that they do not adhere to planning or building regulations, is completely different. Whilst the authorities might demolish their home if it breaks planning and construction regulations, the occupants may still retain title to the land and may be able to rebuild.

In Bangladesh, in the absence of well-established formal land and housing markets, the informal sector has been playing the major role in providing housing for the vast majority of the low income urban population. Around 92 per cent of urban land and 96.5 per cent of dwellings are provided through the informal sector (GOB and ADB, 1993). However, not all are illegal and many properties built informally, and not complying with land and planning regulations, are on land legally owned by the householder.

Both illegal and informal housing could be considered equally insecure, but for different reasons. For example, most regulatory frameworks dictate building standards and materials specifications which are too high or too complex for people living in poverty to fulfil. Many act to limit incremental development of housing, for example, by limiting the amount of time taken to complete development. In the absence of housing finance, low-income people build incrementally as and when they can afford to (UN-Habitat, 2005). In adding rooms as and when they can, owners may be able to generate some income, through letting rooms or running a small enterprise in the home, but regulatory frameworks often also prevent a household from running income-generating activities from their home (Tipple, 2005b).

The minimum plot size regulations set in many countries indirectly increase the risk of homelessness because they impose high threshold costs on any prospective home-owner and so increase housing cost per unit area. For example, in Southern Africa, 250 square metre plots are a common minimum in new development. In the subsidised housing programme in South Africa, the plot and its services[2] absorb so much of the subsidy that the dwelling itself is now referred to as a 'top structure' and is of minimal size and standard. This is particularly acute in hilly areas where plots are substantially more expensive to lay out and service (Napier et al., 2003). If plots were much smaller, they could be considerably cheaper, allowing lower housing costs.

There is a counter-argument, however. If regulations were more hospitable to the incremental extension of housing to accommodate several households per plot, there are advantages in planning large plots. Where plots are designed for extension activity, i.e. relatively square and with the original dwelling to one side or on one corner, and regulations encourage them, large amounts of investment should follow from household budgets to provide rental rooms, extra dwellings, etc. Research has shown that such extensions are likely to be very good value for money and to provide large numbers of rooms at the very bottom of the market where households are at risk of homelessness (Tipple, 2000).[3]

Housing which is illegal because the owners have no legal right of occupation on the land tends to be more vulnerable to removal than that which is merely breaching regulations. The means of defence against this vulnerability has tended to follow the herding behaviour of prey animals: safety in numbers. The most-publicised occurrence of this is in the invasions of Latin America.

In Peru, a large part of the urban development has been implemented by people who have invaded land *en masse* and set up informal, illegal settlements. More than six million people in Peru are living under such conditions on over one million plots. In 1996, Fujimori's government established the COFOPRI programme under which the central government has financed the basic service infrastructure (water, sanitation and energy) and the municipalities paved the main roads and provided land titles to 100,000 households, legalising the ownership of their plots. Estimates in 2003 suggested that there were around 400,000 plots still to be granted land title (Miranda and Salazar, 2002). This included those who settled in invasions since 1996 who are not included under the COFOPRI programme which only provides legal security of tenure; it fails to address housing conditions, which remain very poor for the majority of properties. Another difficulty of this approach is that, in the absence of redistributive policies that could have balanced urban development, it failed to control the rapid urban expansion, particularly of Lima (Miranda and Salazar, 2002).

Tenure and land allocation as a political tool

The importance of access to land and legal tenure in providing security makes them powerful political tools. So powerful, indeed, that the leading advocate of secure land tenure as the key to eliminating poverty, Hernando de Soto (2000), has gained huge power in his native Peru and around the world to sway governments and influence international agencies. That many feel that his ideas are heavily flawed (see e.g. Gilbert, 2002), appears not to have made much difference to the political acclaim that his popular capitalism attracts.

The political systems of developing countries are often based upon 'clientelism'[4] and patronage. Those with the power to allocate land and tenure can use it to sway political allegiance, to reward loyalty or to control those who are not favoured by the political regime of the time. There is, therefore, scope for the use of land allocation or tenure security by politicians to secure votes at both national and local elections. Further, both the affluent and those in poverty are implicated in the manipulation of the political system in exchange for land, although not in quite the same way.

Corruption and land grabbing by upper-income groups, enabled through political linkages and patronage, are widely reported (see e.g. Syagga et al., 2001b; Majale, 2002; Republic of Kenya, 2002). Omenya (2006) notes that 'Corruption and inadequate land legislation are the two main issues that come through with regard to land in Nairobi'. Whilst more affluent people knowingly and wilfully manipulate the political system to acquire land, the political bargaining power of the poor is manipulated by the system. At the local level, rather than improvements for the poor being delivered based upon their rights and politicians' responsibilities, they are frequently delivered as a form of favour in return for votes (Chabal and Daloz, 1999; Hyden, 1999) in a clientelist relationship. Benjamin (2000) noted the aggregation of votes of poor people in Bangalore into 'vote banks', by which entire communities would vote for a given candidate in return for agreed improvements to their settlements. This results in far higher levels of voter turn-out in poor areas than in more affluent areas.

While homeless people and illegal or informal settlers form a potential political constituency, they are often deprived of voting rights. Their security and housing needs can be overlooked for years until a local election becomes imminent. In some cases, particularly in India, the incumbent politicians can confer voting rights on illegal settlers by formalising illegal and informal settlements,[5] thus giving the residents a greater level of security, implying future improvements and securing votes. While this would seem to suggest a level of empowerment of the poor, many promises of help are not fulfilled once the politicians are in power.

At a macro level, national land and housing policy can be used to control or reward entire populations or section of populations. In Iraq, prior to 2003, special interest groups (especially the army and Ba'ath party officials) were favoured in land allocation decisions. The government controlled land centrally, allocating rights of use to political allies and denying it to those regarded as hostile (UN-Habitat, 2007b).

Until 1994, the majority black population of South Africa had great difficulty gaining secure tenure to land through apartheid legislation such as the Group Areas Act of 1966. During the transition to the post-apartheid policy environment, the government undertook very detailed land legislation to redress past inequalities. In spite of this, however, urban land problems in South Africa remain almost intact (Beresford, 1998). There is very little redistribution of urban land but rural-related legislation has generally been more effective in securing tenure for farm workers. Furthermore, white landowners are being joined by members of the new black elite who are more concerned about property values than social justice (Beresford, 1998)

Evictions

Just as rooms, land and security of tenure can be given by powerful groups, they can also be taken away through officially sanctioned acts of eviction. Eviction is an essential tool in the control of relationships between the owners of land or housing and the occupants so that troublesome occupants can be removed, use can be changed or redevelopment can take place. Without the power of eviction, very few owners would rent out their land or housing. Furthermore, other measures would be taken to persuade occupants to leave, ranging from neglect of the fabric so that it becomes uninhabitable to assaults and arson.

In Peru, in the centres of Lima and Rimac, 18,000 old traditional houses (many of them historic) are intensively subdivided and very heavily occupied. Five thousand of them are estimated to be in imminent danger of collapse but eviction of tenants, so that they can be restored and reused sustainably, was impossible at the time of the CARDO survey. Thus, occupants suffered appalling conditions but owners would do nothing to ameliorate their plight (Miranda, 2002). In other countries, eviction is quite easy. In Ghana, any tenant can be evicted if the room is required for a family member of the owner. Oddly enough, however, the length of stay of renters in their rooms has been found to be very long, so the easy eviction has not resulted in insecurity for renters (Malpezzi et al., 1989). Similarly, in Zimbabwe, eviction at this individual level is not difficult legally but is very difficult socially as it is regarded as impolite except in the most dire of circumstances (Kamete, 2001). Elsewhere, it can be much more difficult to remove tenants. At the same time, eviction often creates homelessness, either in the very short term, before other properties are found, or longer term if too little is available at an affordable price.

Forced mass evictions, on the other hand, are less evidently necessary and are usually very disturbing events. They are officially sanctioned acts, with many harmful consequences for the affected people, carried out by an institution (usually the local authority) which should protect vulnerable people and their interests. States usually justify evictions as being for some greater good. They are, however, are generally violent and discriminatory in nature, usually affecting people who have neither the money nor the powers to defend themselves. They are often used to allow commercial developments to make 'productive use' of the spaces that informal settlements occupy. Ironically, sometimes dwellings are demolished to make way for others of higher quality (and price) in an effort to improve housing quality.

In Chile, Bernasconi and Puentes (2006: 18) discuss the vulnerability to eviction of Nino who, despite his good behaviour in the neighbourhood where he lives as a homeless person, notes the fear that 'some day a council lorry will come and take away all my stuff'. Filipe the 12-year-old son in a homeless household comments: 'sometimes they come with those huge bulldozers, and they take our little *ruco*, demolish it, and we have to build it up again'. Evictions can be viewed as a type of urban violence (Agbola and Jinadu, 1997) with lasting physical, economic and psychological effects. In some respects, they might be considered a form of revanchist activity, whereby the authorities set out to reverse territorial losses to migrants and reclaim land for their own use, at the same time as using the migrant armies to build the city.

A resolution of the 49th session of the United Nations Commission on Human Rights in 1993 recognised forced evictions as a 'gross violation of human rights, in particular the right to adequate housing', and urged 'all governments to undertake immediate measures, at all levels, aimed at eliminating the practice of forced evictions'. In its 14th session the following month, UNCHS (Habitat), in a resolution on the 'Promotion of the Human Right to Housing', joined in the commitment towards the promotion of housing as a fundamental human right. It urged

> all States to cease any practices which could or do result in infringements of the human right to adequate housing, in particular the practice of forced mass evictions and any form of racial or other discrimination in the housing sphere.
> (Audefroy, 1994: 9–10)

Tenants are vulnerable to eviction when the property of their landlord is threatened. Although they do not lose their investment in a dwelling as their landlord does, tenants can be badly affected as they must compete with an increasing demand for the diminished stock in the area and may well filter down into poorer housing or have to sleep on the street. During the eviction event, tenant households' paraphernalia is even more vulnerable than that of the owners as eviction usually happens during working hours and tenants in many societies have fewer household members than owners and, therefore, are less likely to have anyone in to rescue their household effects when the bulldozers arrive. Evictions are a sure way to move at least some people from inadequately housed to homeless.

In some cases evictions are driven by political motives, to control or disperse political opposition. In extreme cases, regimes use evictions extensively, even to the extent of depopulating large areas of the country – to the extent of ethnic cleansing. The government of Saddam Hussein in Iraq used eviction and the destruction of villages, particularly in Kurdistan, to ensure the survival of the regime or punish dissenting groups.

In 2000, the Zimbabwean government embarked on its Fast Track Land Redistribution Programme (FTLRP). The intention was to resettle 100,000 landless peasant households on farms formerly owned predominantly by white farmers, especially those of suspected supporters of the main opposition party. The 250,000 workers on such farms, who were mainly immigrants with Zimbabwean residency, were assumed to be supporters also. They, and their dependants, totalling 2 million, or more than 10 per cent of Zimbabwe's population, were evicted, often violently (Zvauya, 2001).

In 2005, 'Operation Murambatsvina' (referred to in Chapter 4) resulted in the major destruction of homes and businesses in which an estimated 700,000 people in cities across the country were made homeless, lost their livelihoods or both. The UN suggests that around 2.4 million people have been affected in some way (Tibaijuka, 2005).

Evictions and economic development

In other cases, evictions are driven by economic imperatives when land, once of little economic value, becomes prime development land or where the overt presence of poverty offends a growing elite, worried about property values. There is a close link between political and economic motives for slum clearance and evictions. However, even where political opposition to slums does not directly result in eviction, it can act to prevent in-situ improvement.

For example, in Dhaka, where about one-third of the city's residents live in unauthorised settlements (*bastees*) across the city, the provision of basic urban services is directed towards the better-off. Elitist attitudes toward rapidly spreading slums and squatter settlements (Shakur and Khan, 1986; Firozuddin, 1999; Ghafur, 1999), and unrest about increases in income disparity between the rich and poor, led the government to introduce a programme of evictions from increasingly valuable urban land. The programme was eventually abandoned (Ghafur, 2002) but the government refused to release necessary land for upgrading. This effectively jeopardised the implementation of the Asian Development Bank-assisted in-situ upgrading of slums (with education and health components) in Dhaka. An unresponsive attitude toward this project is evident in the following words of a senior policymaker of the Planning Commission, 'any attempt to improve the condition of the urban poor would accelerate migration' (Afsar, 2001: 12, cited in Ghafur, 2002).

The eviction of people from slums and squatter settlements, often accompanied by burning of the dwellings, has become the major cause of homelessness within the city. At the beginning of 1975, 173,000 squatters were evicted from different parts of Dhaka and dumped in resettlement camps in three different locations outside the city. This was the first of many similar actions which became known as the Squatter Rehabilitation Programme. It used a number of resettlement camps located far to the periphery of the city and away from economic opportunities, in conflict with both earlier ideals and policies and the lessons which were being learned internationally (Choguill, 1993: 330, cited in Ghafur, 2002). From 1990 to 1992, an estimated 200,000 people in Dhaka had been affected by evictions and US$2.5 million worth of property was destroyed in 30 major forced evictions (Sinha, 1994; as cited in Rahman, 2001). According to a local pressure group, between May and August 1999, residents of 42 settlements were evicted; in 34 of them 22,000 households were affected (Ghafur, 2002). At the same time, the

National Housing Policy (NHP) was being formulated to assist the less fortunate sections of society – homeless, destitute and landless people and those in slums and squatter settlements (Ghafur, 2002). Thus far is the reality from the rhetoric!

When the Constitutional Hill retail and commercial project was constructed in Hillbrow, Johannesburg, unhoused people living there were forced to move to the other end of Kotze Street. Even the Osindisweni home for elderly unhoused people was removed. Hillbrow now celebrates international consumption while still being a focal point for homeless people (Sihlongonyane, 2006). On the one hand, police and security guards keep away unwanted people whose class and cultural positions diverge from the developers' target markets. On the other hand, the unwanted are exposed to violence and neglect in the world that is, by exclusion from the new interdicted spaces, 'other' (Sihlongonyane, 2006); bronze sculptures replace the slumbering poor in the financial district's avenues.

The Delhi Development Authority (DDA) has a land protection branch whose duty it is to detect all squatter settlements and remove them. The branch's concern is not homeless people but the integrity of government land. When the evictees move on to the pavement, they remain within the jurisdiction of the Municipal Corporation who then deprive them of its use (Bannerjee Das, 2002).

Burning is another way used in Bangladesh to evict people from unwanted settlements to secure the valuable land for commercial or political vested interests. Although many fires occur through faulty wiring and untended earthen ovens, they are also started intentionally using hired arsonists. In six incidents reported in the media between March 1998 and March 2000, around 10,300 makeshift dwellings were gutted and approximately 50,000 people were made homeless by the fires. High shelter density, highly inflammable construction materials and delayed and non-effective fire fighting are all factors that maximised the destruction (Ghafur, 2002).

Summary eviction is illegal in Bangladesh. To evict illegal occupants requires 30 days notice to be given by the District Commissioner. A court of law can also grant an order of eviction but usually stipulates a longer notice period. In reality, however, government and other authorities usually give less than 48 hours notice to the people to evacuate their illegally occupied premises (Rahman, 2001). To make matters worse, during the melee of eviction, looters come and snatch away the few remaining valuables and there is risk of beatings by the police (Ghafur, 2002).

In Bangladesh, the authorities usually give one or more of the following 'good reasons' for evictions:

- an improvement in the overall crime rate;
- ending the illegal consumption of public utilities;
- the recovery of prime *khas* urban land for publicly beneficial uses;
- an improvement in the hygiene and aesthetic qualities of the city; and
- boosting the already booming (housing) construction sector (Ghafur, 2002).

Similar reasons are given in other countries. These reasons are, of course, only partly valid and can be refuted as easily as they can be supported. What is undeniable is that, although many hundreds of thousands of households are made homeless annually through evictions which are meant to improve conditions in the city, the promised rehabilitation or improvements rarely benefit the poorest in society and many evicted households never fully recover. In Peru, low-income households have been involved in a settlement and eviction cycle with the authorities an almost normal housing experience. In the last few years of the 20th century, eleven huge invasions of desert land took place, mostly in Lima, from which residents were violently evicted by the police. The last was in January 2000, when more than 10,000 people took possession of plots in the district of Villa El Salvador, to the south of Lima. After two weeks, they were evicted and transferred to an undeveloped area to the north of Lima. All the evidence shows that the invasion and its subsequent relocation was promoted by the government for electoral purposes; the households received strong support from the governmental authorities in creating the new settlement called 'Pachacutec' (Miranda and Salazar, 2002).

Major international events can be used as an excuse to expel poor inhabitants from central areas of cities and send them to the periphery. In the colonial period, an area of Lagos, Nigeria, was cleared to improve the city's appearance for Queen Elizabeth's visit (Agbola and Jinadu, 1997). Other examples include preparations for the Olympic Games (720,000 evictions for the 1988 Games in Seoul – Asian Coalition for Housing Rights, 1989) and the '500 Years' Commemorations in Santo Domingo in 1992 (Schutz, 1989). Currently, the 2010 Commonwealth Games are generating city beautification programmes in New Delhi which are resulting in the removal of centrally located squatter settlements to peripheral resettlement areas. Such acts are justified on the grounds of safety for participants or the international image of the city but, after the event, private development not directed to the poor often takes place on the cleared land (Audefroy, 1994).

In Nigeria, the notorious evictions from Maroko, Lagos, were even being planned at the same time as the government representatives were taking part in the International Year of Shelter for the Homeless! The 300,000 residents of Maroko were squatters on government land, 1.5 metres above sea level. The government claimed that Maroko's environment was dangerous so it was cleared in the public interest and to make life better for those evicted. More likely reasons, however, were the need for land for high-value uses and the pressure from nearby high-income areas of Ikoyi and Victoria Island over fear of epidemics, crime and threats to their property values (Agbola and Jinadu, 1997).

Of the estimated 41,776 house-owning households displaced from Maroko, only 2,933 were considered for relocation to small flats in government housing estates many of which were not ready for occupation; some were even waterlogged. Most of the relocated residents were very dissatisfied with their new accommodation.

Many evicted households settled near the beach in newer squatter housing built from materials taken from the ruins of Maroko (Agbola and Jinadu, 1997).

Citizenship and the illegality of homelessness

The link between citizenship and homelessness is complex and multi-dimensional. However, it can be understood most starkly at two levels. First, the citizenship, or otherwise, of the homeless person should be considered. Second, the way in which homelessness or, more accurately, homeless people can be perceived to interfere with the citizenship rights of others must be understood.

The work of Marshall (1950) gives us the basis of our current understanding of citizenship. He considered citizenship to be built upon a set of civil, political and social rights, embedded within national constitutions and delivered through the workings of social and political institutions. It is not difficult to see, then, how homelessness is both a political challenge and an embarrassment to national governments. Where housing is seen as a basic right of citizenship, homelessness represents a failure of government to uphold its citizens' rights. As Jacobs et al. (1999) note, this may be one reason why many governments are so reluctant to undertake adequate enumerations of homelessness. To do so would be to highlight and acknowledge the problems and their own failings in providing for the basic rights of their citizens.

The physical and residential segregation of blacks in South Africa could be seen as a direct act of excluding them from citizenship by the apartheid government. Although it seems ridiculous in hindsight that such a law could last into the final few years of the 20th century, the Native (Urban Areas) Act of 1923 defined an African's legal ability to be in urban areas as contingent upon employment and empowered the white authorities to control non-whites' access to such areas. An African who was not needed to work for whites had no right to urban residency and those with permission to be in town lived in segregated areas.

During apartheid, the Group Areas Act (GAA) empowered white authorities to demarcate urban neighbourhoods for specific races, and to remove people living in the 'wrong' areas. Pass Laws enabled white authorities to control Africans in urban areas, and thousands without the correct documents were arrested annually (Lanegran and Lanegran, 2001: 673).

Where these laws proved insufficient to fully exclude black people from the city, people were removed physically and their shelters destroyed (Posel, 1991). Parnell (1997: 901) argues that '[the] colonial discourse excluded concentrations of African settlements from the definition "urban" and thus perpetrated the myth of Africans' inherently rural, traditional, and uncivilised position'. This exclusion of some citizens from rights to freely occupy the physical space of the city and to gain access to its services continues today in other countries. It is often exacerbated by homeless people's inability to comply with the requirement to obtain or carry identity cards, as in the case of India and Indonesia, or for formal household registration, as in the case of China.

In Indonesia, all people above the age of 17 should possess an identity card called the *Kartu Tanda Penduduk* (KTP) issued by their respective local authority. A KTP is the sole defining element for citizenship in Indonesia – without it, a person is excluded and has no official identity. For the homeless person, however, the KTP, which literally translates to 'card indicating domicile', presents a significant barrier to citizenship; non-possession of KTP is a serious offence for which a person can to go to prison and be expelled from the city. In order to acquire a KTP a person has to have an officially recognised address.[6] Homeless people in Indonesia do not have any official address and so they are not eligible for KTPs. Not having a KTP means that a person is not officially registered as a resident of the city where they live, does not appear in any official statistics, cannot carry out many legal processes such as marriage and birth registration (without which school entry is impossible) and cannot obtain formal housing. They are, in effect, caught in a vicious circle: having no officially recognised address they cannot obtain a KTP; having no KTP, they cannot gain access to formal housing and, therefore, have no formal address (Rahardjo, 2006).

The effects of not having a KTP can come from many directions. In October 2005, the Indonesian government stopped subsidising fuel as the cost was posing too a heavy burden on the state budget. This caused the cost of fuel (petrol, diesel, kerosene) to rise by 87.5 per cent virtually immediately. To assist poor families in coping with the rise of living costs the government devised the so-called *bantuan tunai langsung* (literally 'direct cash assistance') scheme in the form of cash amounting to Rp.100,000 (a little over £8) per household per month. This is seen as being more fair and effective than indiscriminate fuel subsidies which are seen as benefiting rich and poor alike (Rahardjo, 2006). The registration of poor families and the distribution of the financial assistance, however, have not proceeded smoothly. Well-connected households are included alongside those who qualify on income while many who qualify have been overlooked. Those who do not have KTPs are automatically excluded. The excuse given for this by Jakarta's Governor Sutiyoso was that those without a Jakarta KTP are not residents of the city and are probably registered in other places. Therefore, to avoid duplications they are automatically not listed (Rahardjo, 2006).

Homeless people are not organised into the official community and neighbourhood units (*rukun warga* and *rukun tetangga*)[7] of which every household (at least theoretically) should be a member. Thus, they are not able to gain access to urban services such as education and health care. Even though the Indonesian government has launched many housing programmes for the urban poor, especially its world-renowned Kampung Improvement Project (KIP), people without KTP cannot be included. As in many countries, there is a reluctance to implement the KIP measures in non-legal settlements because there is a fear that improving them could be seen as *de facto* recognition by the government. Thus, the most poorly housed miss out as usual (Rahardjo, 2006).

A similar situation exists in Russia where rural to urban migration is restricted through the registration system known as *propiska*. This resulted in uncontrolled growth of unofficial cities (Gang and Stuart, 1999). The *propiska* is still needed to access a range of benefits such as welfare support, childcare, schools and healthcare. Although, legally, all applicants should be granted registration in their new location, there is evidence that the authorities deny it to some people in some areas, effectively rendering them non-citizens and making them more vulnerable to homelessness (Andrienko and Guriev, 2004)

We have discussed in Chapter 4 the plight of China's internal migrants who, having left their place of household registration or *hukou*, have not been reregistered elsewhere and, thus, are effectively non-citizens (Chan and Zhang, 1999). Despite their essential contribution to China's economic boom and physical development, they are denied the most basic rights afforded to their fellow citizens (Mackenzie, 2002).

Vagrancy, street sleeping and the law

Homeless people experience this disconnection from full citizenship most harshly in relation to the illegality of street sleeping and pavement dwelling in many countries. For example, in India, the Bombay Prevention of Begging Act and its clones across India, make vagrancy and begging illegal. Section 2(i)d of the Act defines begging very widely. It includes much more than soliciting alms; indeed, being shabbily dressed, having no visible means of subsistence, wandering about in a public place, singing, dancing, fortune telling, performing, or offering articles for sale can all be regarded as a pretence for soliciting or receiving alms, at the discretion of the police. In addition, the Police Acts give the police power to act against people living on the street. Under the Delhi Police Act, 1978, urinating in the streets, bathing and washing in places not set apart for those purposes, and being found on the street between sunset and sunrise and not being able to give a satisfactory account of oneself, are all offences (Aashray Adhikar Abhiyan, 2001).

A conversation with a resident of a winter shelter in Delhi in 2006 exposed a way in which homelessness laws exacerbate illnesses and illness can exacerbate the potential to fall foul of the law. A homeless man had broken his leg at work and had it in a plaster-cast. Thus, he could not work. Normally he would go to places where food is distributed each day as well as to work. While his leg was broken, he could not show that he had any means of livelihood and was, therefore, liable to arrest under the Bombay Prevention of Begging Act. Thus, not only had he no income because of the injury but his access to food, and the efficiency of the healing process, were even more compromised than it would be for a housed person. He was reliant on friends in the night shelter to provide for him.

The penalty for being found 'vagrant' is incarceration in an institution for between one and three years for a first offence and ten years for subsequent offences. Once confined in this way, a homeless person can languish for long periods because they are too poor and illiterate to secure bail or gain legal representation, except through NGOs such as Aashray Adhikar Abhiyan. Many prefer not to inform their families because of the stigma attached to being labelled a beggar or because of the sheer futility of trying to obtain release (Bannerjee Das, 2002).

Under vagrancy provisions, the police routinely round up large numbers of homeless people to fulfil targets of 'preventive detention' under sections 109 and 151 of the Criminal Procedure Code, to prove to their superiors that they are being proactive in maintaining civic peace. The magistrates routinely concur with the police for the sake of maintaining harmonious relations. Thus, in India, simply being on the streets is cause for arrest and confinement at any time (Bannerjee Das, 2002).

In Zimbabwe, anyone regarded as a vagrant can be detained and 'repatriated' to their rural home (Mafico, 1991). This colonial law, drafted in times when Africans without formal employment were unwelcome in cities, has never been repealed. In an even more extreme circumstance, there have been well-publicised cases where street children have been shot by police in Brazil (Rizzini and Lusk, 1995) and in Davao City, the Philippines, by motorcycle-riding 'death squads' (PREDA, 1999).

Homeless people may gain some respite from police harassment by paying a bribe, as this homeless boy in Delhi notes:

> The police are always after us, we do not know when we will be in jail. They beat us and take away whatever money we have. It is always those who work to earn their living that are caught, the boys who pick pockets are not troubled as they pay *hafta* (a bribe paid on a weekly basis) to the police. If we do not pay they can level a number of false charges and put us inside.
>
> (Rajkumar, 2000)

In Chile, police routinely harass homeless people within a general policy of containment and displacement (Bernasconi and Puentes, 2006). Containment measures include patrolling areas occupied by homeless people and checking identity cars. Displacement measures include demolishing their shacks (*rucos*), arresting and fining homeless people for public order offences and selling on the streets without authorisation, and confiscating sale goods. Bernasconi and Puentes (2006) noted that some homeless people demolish their own *ruco*, before the authority does it, in order to regain control of the situation.

Conclusions

Clearly, the relationships between politics and homelessness is strong and homeless people are frequently used as pawns in political moves for power and control. What we see above is a situation where, rather than housing being a right of citizens, citizenship has become a right of the housed.

In many countries, a series of legal frameworks around land and property rights, planning and building regulations, inheritance and women's rights act to victimise the most vulnerable, the very people they should be protecting. Some legal obstacles to adequate housing, for example, unnecessarily large plot sizes, or complicated and costly transaction costs for development, are unintentional 'by-products' of a country's move to develop a series of standards and regulations aimed at progressing development in a manageable way. Others, such as the criminalisation of vagrancy or unnecessary forced evictions might be seen as more intentional activities aimed at social engineering and 'cleansing' the city of homeless people perceived to be undesirable. Thus, homelessness tends to be exacerbated by the way the law hinders or prevents homeless people gaining greater security so that they can maximise the benefits of their labour and their efforts to provide their own housing.

This chapter raises four specific issues in relation to the political and legal position of homelessness. First, homeless people and their advocates should attempt to influence the political process, often in opposition to such powerful groups as home-owners and the housing industry. Second, homelessness is a sign of the inequitable distribution of housing costs and benefits in the community. Third, effective intervention in the realm of social policy and programmes cannot be ignored (Cooper, 1995; UNCHS, 2000). Finally, citizenship is inextricably entwined with homelessness as long as rights are seen as belonging to the housed.

10 Disaster and conflict

> Like economic crises, natural disasters can cause sharp increases in poverty and slow the pace of human development. And like economic crises, they hurt people in the short run and diminish their chances of escaping poverty in the longer run.
>
> (World Bank, 2001: 170)

Times of disaster and conflict bring homelessness into the headline news. One of the figures quoted by the press for any disaster is how many people have been made homeless. In the context of this book, this is an imprecise conceptualisation of homelessness as it includes both rich households temporarily decamped from their mansions for fear of aftershocks and destitute households who have lost everything and may have seen even their farmland washed away as a mighty river changes course during a flood event. For a time, all are accommodated in transit accommodation, reduced to camping in serried ranks of tents on a barren hillside or in a sports stadium. But their chances of recovery and being housed in the short term could not be more different. Thus, disaster-related homelessness figures hide almost as much as they reveal.

However, many of the more catastrophic natural disasters, for example the 2004 tsunami or the Chinese earthquake of 2008, hit countries where a high percentage of the population was already living in poverty and where many had only a tenuous hold on adequate accommodation in the first place. Estimates in Table 10.1 show that about 165 million people have been rendered homeless by the main types of natural disaster since the turn of the 20th century. It also shows how dominant are flooding and windstorms (cyclones, hurricanes, typhoons) and how Asia is by far the hardest hit continent. Indeed, 87 per cent of all people rendered homeless by natural disasters have been in Asia (which has 59 per cent of the world's population).

It is also evident, however, that there was a major increase in people affected over the second half of the 20th century. Most of this is undoubtedly caused by the worldwide improvement in reporting the number of people affected by disasters;

Table 10.1 Number of people rendered homeless by the main types of natural disasters worldwide 1900–2007, by continent

	Flooding	Windstorms	Earthquakes	Landslides and avalanches	Waves, cyclonic surges	Volcanic eruptions	Total
Asia	77,595,091	46,457,967	14,101,406	3,825,311	1,079,844	97,900	143,157,519
Americas	3,380,422	2,449,811	3,693,353	186,752	1,850	31,180	9,743,368
Africa	5,540,470	1,448,339	894,874	7,936	70	180,710	8,072,399
Europe	1,906,576	37,017	1,280,017	8,625	0	14,000	3,246,235
Oceania	107,400	284,525	19,820	18,000	0	46,000	475,745
Total	88,529,959	50,677,659	19,989,470	4,046,624	1,081,764	369,790	164,695,266

Source: EM-DAT (2008)

the data for 1980 to 2000 contain almost 90 per cent of the people reportedly made homeless in disasters in the whole of the century.

Using EM-DAT data, Gilbert (2001) estimates that 141 million people have been made homeless through 3,559 disasters between 1980 and 2000. Ninety-seven per cent (138 million people made homeless) occurred in developing countries and more than half in just two countries, China and Bangladesh. This figure, if correct, highlights the potential underestimate of the OFDA/CRED figure of 165 million.

According to Gilbert (2001; cited by Freeman, 2004: 428), 'since 1980, 141 million people have lost their homes in 3,559 natural hazard event. Of those who lost housing, 97.7 per cent lived in developing countries.' There appears to be an increase in disaster effects year on year as more people are in locations where disasters strike and humankind's presence in the world makes a greater impact on the causal and contributory factors in disasters. According to UN-Habitat (2007a), natural disasters are increasing in frequency with a fourfold increase since 1975 and each of the three years with the most disasters all having occurred in the 21st century. There has also been a tenfold increase in human-made disasters from 1976 to 2005 and the greatest increases seen in Africa and Asia (UN-Habitat, 2007a).

Disasters have an effect on homelessness by destroying existing housing and livelihoods which enable people to pay for housing or to construct their own. They reduce the housing stock that can be occupied, forcing unexpected spending on reconstruction and putting improvement efforts back many years. They also undermine economic progress both by diverting expenditure to housing reconstruction and by reducing people's ability to earn incomes, especially in the months following the disaster event (Gilbert, 2001).

It is clear that vulnerability is exacerbated by disaster events; where persons or groups are vulnerable in ordinary life, they are likely to be particularly seriously affected by the disaster. Figure 8.2 shows vulnerability as affected by the disaster of AIDS. Similar trends could be posited for a natural disaster but with different markers along the time co-ordinate. Any process which increases vulnerability among low-income households is likely to exacerbate the effects of a disaster event just as it does with AIDS.

The lack of housing insurance is one obvious issue which makes low-income households particularly vulnerable. Few low-income households have insurance on their homes partly out of a lack of affordability but also because many regard the government as having a moral responsibility to cover their risks, many have no legal documents proving ownership, and there may be cultural factors present such as fatalism. A situation in which there is an accepted wisdom that 'the government will help', which reduces the incentive of owners to insure their private property, is known as the 'Samaritan's dilemma' (Freeman, 2004). On the supply side, insurance companies are not attracted to the business offered by innumerable small-value policies, difficulty in assessing actuarial risks of large aggregate claims, and market

Table 10.2 Countries with most people made homeless by disaster, 1980–2000

Total made homeless by disasters		Disaster homeless per 1,000 of total population[a]	
PR China	45,150,654	Bangladesh	299
Bangladesh	37,609,000	Samoa	166
India	12,271,585	Sri Lanka	138
Pakistan	10,136,069	Philippines	123
Philippines	9,271,951	Mozambique	111
Sri Lanka	2,598,291	Comoros	95
Vietnam	1,970,133	Maldives	91
Mozambique	1,880,800	Vanuatu	85
Sudan	1,166,700	Chad	80
Brazil	1,030,367	Pakistan	77
Chile	783,876	Chile	53
Turkey	747,600	Nicaragua	52
Madagascar	717,000	Madagascar	49
Colombia	698,334	Benin	48
Nigeria	627,750	El Salvador	43

Source: (Gilbert, 2001: 1).

Note:
a This is different from the figures of homeless per 1,000 in Chapter 6 because it is over a 20-year period and not how many are homeless at one time.

distortions because of the way local insurance markets are often organised through quasi-government institutions (Gilbert, 2001).

Freeman (2004) points out the problem which arises from the devotion of recovery programme funds to housing projects, which tend to benefit only those who owned housing before the disaster, rather than to infrastructure projects, which are vital to the economy's recovery and assist everyone. A major part of the reason for this is the political benefit accruing from being seen to provide replacement housing.[1] While this may be possible in a rich country where rehousing costs may be a small part of the national GDP, the strain on a poorer country could be crippling.

Housing and its occupants are very likely to be vulnerable to the effects of natural and human-made hazards in the developing world because of the context in which urbanisation takes place. Low wage levels through competing for work in global markets, or expansion of peripheral neighbourhoods, of flimsy constructions on hazardous land, or reduction in free medical care, could all be translated into increased homelessness following a disaster. In the 'urbanisation of poverty', much informal housing is erected on land which is unsuitable for formal settlement; steep and unstable slopes, flood plains, low-lying coastal land, land close to sources of pollution, and other hazardous sites. Indeed, so closely are disadvantaged people associated with difficult environments that Susman et al. (1983) proposed a general geographical law that marginal people are allocated to marginal places (cited in Wisner, 1998). In this way, urban vulnerability to hazards has increased so disasters are more likely to follow (Tipple, 2005a). This is one of main reasons why, although the number of people killed by natural disasters per decade has reduced from 2 million in the 1970s to 800,000 people at the turn of the century, the number affected by injury, losing their housing and hunger has tripled (Walter, 2003). Indeed, the global imbalance in the effect of disasters is worsening. According to Berke (1995: 3–4):

> The mean annual death tolls [owing] to natural hazards declined by 75 percent or more in developed countries [such as] Japan and the United States during the 1960s through the 1980s, but increased by over 400 percent in developing countries [such as] India and Kenya over the same period.

Within particular disasters, the majority of victims are likely to be the poor (El-Masri and Tipple, 2002). Even after the so-called 'class-quake' or 'poor-quake' in Guatemala in 1976, when nearly all of the victims lived in slum neighbourhoods, little has been done to ensure that the urban poor are not still most at risk from disasters. Twenty years later, a study around Guatemala City identified about 200 precarious settlements with a total of almost 600,000 inhabitants, of which 76 sites were considered highly susceptible to earthquakes, floods and landslides (IDNDR, 1996). In the floods and landslides in Venezuela of December 1999, many of the victims were living in informal settlements in the mountain ravines and beside rivers in Caracas and in towns along the coast (Sancio, 2000). These examples, and many others that could be cited, are the results of urbanisation that is both rapid and carried out in a context of poverty. Similarly, many of the victims of the 2004 Indian Ocean tsunami were the poorest inhabitants who lived close to the high-water mark. Most of the people at risk in this way have too few resources to prevent their extreme vulnerability to any sort of crisis in their lives.

While many different types of disaster might lead to homelessness for poor people, the way in which they do this, and the longevity of their effects, differs. For example, while prolonged drought might not destroy houses, it makes people more vulnerable to homelessness by reducing livelihoods. Floods, earthquakes and wind storms also erode livelihoods but add more immediate problem by destroying dwellings and even land. Carter et al. (2007) highlighted the difference in long-term effects of drought and hurricane on poor households, noting that the sudden impact of the latter led to a longer recovery period.

Poverty is, in itself, a polluter and despoiler of the environment. While poor people create less waste and throw less away than affluent people, what garbage they do produce is generally not collected by authorities (Satterthwaite, 2003). Thus it is dumped on local empty land, adding pollution to their environment. In the absence of electricity or gas, they strip woodland to burn under their cooking pots and so poor people can contribute to the causal factors of disasters such as landslides. With no sanitary waste disposal system, they dump faeces into streams and lakes, polluting ground water and destroying marine life. Thus, in failing to provide basic services to people living in poverty, authorities can cause or worsen what seem to be natural disasters, such as river floods, for example, by allowing watercourses to become blocked with garbage, or loss of food sources through pollution of rivers.

Millions of people are extremely vulnerable to natural hazards because of the land on which they have had to settle.

- They live in squatter and other informal settlements clinging to steep slopes, whose mineral structure may also be very unstable, prey to heavy rain and water runoff.
- They live on low land liable to flooding from rivers swollen by forest clearing upstream, from the sea at high tides and through tidal surges.
- Their housing is usually poorly built and, regardless of its site, is more vulnerable to even minor natural events than that of the rich

(Tipple, 2005a).

It is important that people have somewhere to settle which does not expose them to increased vulnerability. In turn, this is a function of the supply of adequate land, especially at appropriate prices for low-income households and of appropriate regulations for construction which they can afford to fulfil (Payne and Majale, 2004).

Thus, a well-functioning land allocation system, in which there is good information, clarity of title and an appropriate regulatory environment, is a prerequisite for housing development which reduces vulnerability.

The social geography of vulnerability

It is intuitively obvious that age, gender and disability will affect the ability of people to withstand the trauma of a disaster. In addition, however, characteristics such as poverty and homelessness are also influential. Indeed, those who have the least resources are most likely to suffer injury and death, and the most long-lasting damage. Those who have precarious livelihoods are most likely to suffer financial loss, those who are inadequately housed will probably suffer catastrophic damage to their dwellings; those who are living on the streets are likely to be missed out of disaster-preparedness work altogether (Wisner, 1998). Similarly, women are less likely to be helped in post-disaster reconstruction efforts (UN-Habitat, 2007a) and in disaster-preparedness projects.

Housing technology and vulnerability

The link between construction technologies and the reduction or increase in effect of hazards is well known. Despite papers over many years on, for example, the construction modes available to prevent the collapse of roofs on adobe buildings (Razani, 1978), blanket dismissal of traditional construction and imposition of reinforced-concrete-based technologies are still common in response to disasters. The reaction to the Maharashtra earthquake is typical here (Salazar, 1999; Schilderman, 2004).

Salazar (1994) shows how modernity prepared the ground for disaster in Maharashtra. The traditional 'Wada' form of housing, developed in its full form, is earthquake resistant. With the growth of modernity, however, the traditional building system and division of labour had begun to break down and poor construction was becoming the rule. Thus, the seeds of the disaster were sown through policy changes and the regard the people had for the more 'modern' concrete technology.

When the earthquake struck, many recently built traditional houses fell down but the mason's houses remained standing! Poor quality was more influential in the damage suffered than the traditional technology. The government's relief teams concentrated on concrete and steel construction after the earthquake, despite advice on how effective local traditional construction could be if well built. This further destroyed the traditions of building, imposed alien expensive built forms and damaged the social structure of villages – increasing residents' vulnerability because of the higher technology (Salazar, 1999).

Current thinking, however, is much less bound up in the physical environment and much more aware of social and political influences and the importance of recognising the local resources. Schilderman (2004) argues that developing more rigorous planning and building standards from the industrialised countries to try to build more strongly is inappropriate and damaging because such standards:

- turn out to be even less affordable than the previous set;
- force even more households to build illegally because they cannot fulfil them;
- require enforcement rather than carry public opinion with them; and
- may require scarce specialised professionals to oversee them.

Thus, they are not widely practised, especially by the informal sector and self-builders[2] who do most of the building in developing countries and may require a higher level of expertise than is usually held by the contractors and building inspectors (Ruskilis, 2002, cited by Schilderman, 2004). Even in the formal sector housing for those who can afford to fulfil the regulations, there is both a lack of capacity to enforce regulations and corruption among the staff who inspect construction. Coupled with the informal sector's exclusion from control, these lead to what UN-Habitat (2007a: 188) calls a 'deadly cocktail of human vulnerability, unsafe dwellings and high hazard'. This was evident in the building collapses following from the Marmara earthquake in Turkey in 1999 and in Spitak, Armenia, in 1988 and will, no doubt, be repeated many times in future disasters.[3] More recently, the 2008 earthquake in China has highlighted the importance of governments having the capacity to enforce building regulations. The rapid urban expansion has seen huge increase in development. However, it is notable that despite building regulations many of the newer properties, especially schools, collapsed, while buildings only a decade older survived. In an attempt to maximise profits, regulations were either ignored entirely or scarcely adhered to.

Some country experiences of homelessness and disasters

Bangladesh is one of the most disaster-prone countries in the world; it is downstream of some of the largest rivers in South Asia and at the apex of the triangular Bay of Bengal. Thus, disasters such as flooding, cyclonic surges, tidal-bores, and river erosion occur frequently, causing immense loss of life and property. Bangladesh was struck by at least 63 different natural disasters of various intensities during the period 1960–81. Flooding is the most frequent and damaging disaster event, with between 25,000 km^2 to 40,000 km^2 affected annually and causing extensive temporary and permanent loss of housing, especially among the poor (BIDS, 2001; Ghafur, 2002).

Floods in Bangladesh cause major changes in the course of the great rivers eroding away tracts of land along the banks. It is estimated that annual riverbank erosion in Bangladesh causes some dislocation to one million people, many of whom are permanently displaced (BIDS, 2001). The demographic and socio-economic consequences are twofold: a direct loss of arable and homestead land and a sudden onset of poverty, both of which lead to migration away from the ancestral village.

Tropical cyclones originating in the Bay of Bengal cause havoc in coastal areas of Bangladesh. During the April–May and October–November periods, Bangladesh is particularly vulnerable to cyclone events which severely damage lives, livestock, crops and shelters. The cyclone is accompanied by a surge of seawater 3–5 metres high which leaves behind a landscape stripped of any shelter, trees, living things and infrastructure. A cyclone in 1970 killed an estimated 300,000 people and another in 1985 killed 19,000. Advances in early warning systems, construction of stilted, concrete cyclone shelters, and a well-coordinated disaster mitigation system have significantly reduced the loss of life over the years. However, inexpensive land and chances of eking out a living encourage households living in poverty to resettle the vulnerable coastal areas (Ghafur, 2002).

The events of 2008 have shown how neighbouring low-lying areas are also vulnerable to cyclonic surges. When Cyclone Nargis hit the Irrawaddy Delta of Myanmar on 6 May 2008, a 4-metre storm surge destroyed most dwellings in the Delta area and severely damaged the former capital, Yangon. Between two and three million people are thought to have been made homeless in this disaster (*Times Online*, 2008).

In Egypt, earthquakes are a cause of homelessness. Indeed, El-Sheikh (2002) regards the sudden collapse of deteriorated buildings as the main disaster which causes homelessness. According to the 1996 census, there were 3,139 residential buildings listed for demolition. Most are old and decrepit, having been neglected owing to rent control. When a collapse or demolition occurs, households are often left without replacement homes, despite municipal promises of rehousing. The 12 October 1992 earthquake killed over 560 people, injured 4,000, and left thousands more homeless as it destroyed more than 1,343 houses. The homeless households moved in with relatives or stayed on the streets in tents provided by the government and charities until a rehousing programme was started (El-Sheikh, 2002).

China's food supply is quite vulnerable to climatic variation, especially because of the unequal distribution of natural resources. Increasing drought in the north and flooding in the south have destroyed the income of many farmers, causing them to leave for the big city (Li, 2002). Flooding disasters have increased in frequency from one per decade in the mid-20th century to four per decade in the 1990s (Yin and Li, 2001). The effect on housing has been very severe. For example, there were eighteen major floods in the Yangtze River basin in the 20th century. Of these, the one in 1954 destroyed 4.3 million dwellings and the most recent, in 1998, destroyed 4.9 million dwellings with a total direct economic loss of RMB166 billion (Zong and Chen, 2000).

In India, two major disasters have occurred in recent years, the super-cyclone in Orissa and devastating earthquake in Gujarat, to show how vulnerable are the country's millions of people living in poverty. Seven per cent of the respondents of a survey by SPARC (1985) stated that droughts, floods, cyclones, communal and caste riots were the reason they migrated to the city. Nearly 1 per cent of the housing stock in the country (about 1.5 million dwellings) are destroyed every year owing to natural hazards (NHHP, 1998).

Among all the natural disasters that India faces, floods are the most frequent and often most devastating, mainly because about 80 per cent of the total annual rainfall falls during the short monsoon season (June–September). In addition, about 50 million people are seriously affected by drought in India annually. In 2002, states such as Uttar Pradesh, Madhya Pradesh, Rajasthan, Gujarat and Delhi were declared 'drought-hit', owing to poor rainfall for the fifth consecutive year. Drought is often a reason for migration to Mumbai as the surrounding state of Maharashtra is drought-prone. Pushed off their small landholdings and unable to find work on other farms, many people's only alternative to starvation is to move to towns and cities, put up a tent of rags on a pavement and look for ways to earn something to eat (D'Monte, 1989; Bannerjee Das, 2002).

In the ten years before the CARDO study, India faced five earthquakes: Uttarkashi (1991), Latur (1993), Jabalpore (1997), Chamoli (1999) and, the most devastating one, in Gujarat (2001). In Anjar, one of the towns devastated in the Gujarat 2001 earthquake, a total of 17,205 buildings were damaged, out of which 15,222 were residential (Mamladar Office, Anjar). About 33,000 homeless households stayed in tents for months after the earthquake in January 2001 and most of the people living in the remaining 9,650 buildings also had to leave until safety inspections had been carried out. Therefore, the actual number of people made homeless for at least nine months was much higher than the 33,000. In the surrounding area, 10 villages collapsed completely and 52 villages suffered more than 70 per cent destruction (Bannerjee Das, 2002).

In the decade before the CARDO study, India faced severe cyclonic storms in Andhra Pradesh, Gujarat and the super-cyclone in Orissa of October 1999. In this, a wind speed of over 250 km per hour and unprecedented flash floods completely destroyed all dwellings in twelve districts of Orissa. Twenty-three thousand houses were washed away, 820,000 totally collapsed and 1.2 million partly collapsed. Millions of people were affected, the infrastructure was uprooted and there was serious habitat and environmental damage. The government of Orissa planned to rehouse 250,000 homeless people from the group below the poverty line under the Indira Awas Yojana (IAY) programme; a huge effort but not enough for all those affected by any means (Bannerjee Das, 2002).

Indonesia is a nation which benefits hugely from the fertility brought to it by tectonic activity, but it has to suffer the tragic effects of earthquakes and volcanic eruptions on a regular basis. Two earthquake belts cross Indonesia, the Circum-Pacific and the Trans-Asiatic, so that tectonic earthquakes are frequent. The earthquake in Bengkulu on 4 June 2000, for instance, killed 30 people and injured hundreds more; 43,000 houses were destroyed (Rahardjo, 2002).

Though usually not as disastrous as earthquakes, floods happen more frequently and, every year during the rainy season, many parts of Indonesia suffer from flooding. On 24 October 2001, torrential rain in Tasikmalaya, West Java, caused flooding followed by landslides which inflicted heavy material damage. About 550 houses were badly inundated and at least 600 people had to be evacuated (*Pikiran Rakyat*, 25 Oct. 2001). On the same day in Kebumen, in the southern part of Central Java, landslides following heavy rain damaged hundreds of homes, many beyond repair (Rahardjo, 2002).

The Indian Ocean tsunami of 26 December 2004, which devastated Aceh, is reported to have left a varying quantity of people homeless, ranging from 800,000 soon after (Aspinall, 2005) to 190,000 with 67,000 living in tents one year after (Hestyanti, 2006). Many citizens lost their KTP identity cards during the tsunami. Part of the aid effort of GTZ has been to set up mobile offices to restore citizen rights by reissuing a KTP to people affected (GTZ, 2006).

When the region south of Mount Merapi was struck by a magnitude 6.4 earthquake, the city of Yogyakarta and its suburbs were severe damaged, leaving an estimated 6,000 people dead, 50,000 injured, and between 500,000 and 1 million homeless. Over 155,000 dwellings were totally destroyed and 200,000 damaged (Walter, 2007). The earthquake which devastated the small Nias islands, Northern Sumatra (on 28 March 2005), left over 150,000 people homeless *(Anthropology Today*, 2005).

Human-made disasters are also an issue in Indonesia. Between 440,000 and 1.3 million people have been internally displaced within Indonesia owing to the separatist and ethnic conflicts in the last few years in Timor, Aceh, Papua, Maluku, Central Kalimantan and Central Sulawesi (Rahardjo, 2002). The plight of the refugees from Ambon on Buton Island provides a telling example of the problems their presence impose. The local authority, with an indigenous population of less than half a million, is finding its resources stretched to the limit trying to look after the tens of thousands of refugees. Little help has reached them from the government, from the local people or from humanitarian relief organisations. In the absence of adequate assistance, most of the refugees live in tents and makeshift shelters. Many refugees have tried to improve their situation by doing labouring work or finding other means of self-employment – an admirable effort that, unfortunately, further stretched the already limited sustaining capability of the local authority's resources (Rahardjo, 2002).

In Peru, in less than five years before the CARDO study, four serious natural disasters affected different parts of the country, one owing to the 'El Niño phenomenon' that affected most of the country, and the other three owing to earthquakes in San Martín, Nazca and the south region of Peru. Natural disasters in Peru affect the poor more than richer groups. A total of 70,888 houses in critical condition, sheltering 352,571 inhabitants, were identified in fifteen affected cities (Miranda and Salazar, 2002).

In 1997, after the earthquake in Nazca, in which 3,868 dwellings were destroyed and 9,691 damaged (Laquian, 1983; UNCHS/ILO, 1995; EERI, 1997), 4,305 credits were granted through the Construction Material Bank for a total amount of US$14 million. The loans over five years attracted interest rates of 7 per cent, with a maximum loan amount of US$1,885 (Miranda and Salazar, 2002). More recently, in July 2001, more than 25,000 households lost their dwellings after the earthquake in the south of the country that affected Arequipa, Moquegua and Tacna. Of them, only 17,000 were assisted with loans from the Construction Material Bank, of 6,000 to 10,000 soles (£1,200 to £2,000), with preferential interest rates and a two-year grace period (Miranda and Salazar, 2002).

Between 1990 and 2001, three major natural disasters hit rural Zimbabwe. First, there was the worst drought in living memory in 1992. This dislocated people as they moved to urban areas to seek survival. No documents are available but it is known that sometimes whole villages moved. It is difficult to assess the impact of this on homelessness. It is known, however, that, in the absence of government shelter, the migrants stayed with relatives and sometimes friends. Government intervened for future mitigation through the introduction of a mandatory drought levy that was set at 3 per cent of payable tax[4] (Kamete, 2001).

In the 1999/2000 and 2000/1 rainy seasons, cyclone-induced floods hit the country, affecting the eastern and southern parts of Zimbabwe. Rural areas fared the worst; homes were destroyed and over a quarter of a million people were affected (IFRC, 2000; Chinaka, 2000). After an immense fundraising effort, government and NGOs, led by the Zimbabwe Red Cross Society, embarked on major relief and reconstruction work. In addition to mounting rescue operations, providing temporary shelter and food, and repairing damaged infrastructure, the relief efforts also rebuilt homes for affected people (Kamete, 2001).

In 2000, a new human-made disaster cropped up following the rejection of the new constitution. Farms were invaded and rural folk harassed under the FTLRP (see Chapter 9) with two million more made homeless.

Emergency assistance with accommodation

Unlike the main homeless population, people made homeless by disaster are often the subject of emergency assistance. While this is by no means universal or totally effective, many of the 141 million people made homeless by disaster since 1980 will have been rehoused quite quickly either by relief efforts or by their repairing their damaged dwellings.

The nature of disaster is very varied. Within types of disasters, effects on homes vary. In Bangladesh, the flooding of the main rivers can change their course so that someone's land disappears altogether and there is nowhere to rebuild. This is a double jeopardy – both dwelling and land destroyed. In contrast, a dwelling at the edge of the Zambezi flood plain in Mozambique might be inundated by gently rising water and its occupants have to flee until it recedes. It could be damaged but is likely to remain intact and could be habitable within days even if major repairs to mud plaster are needed to restore it to the pre-disaster state.

Disaster types differ in their effects on housing and livelihoods also. Cyclonic surges in Bangladesh sweep everything away before them over large areas of delta land so that not only does the dwelling completely disappear but also the materials from which a replacement might be made (timber, reeds, bamboo) are stripped from the ground and washed many kilometres away. In addition, the legal documents to the dwelling may be washed away, leaving the occupants liable to lose their home if someone contests their rights. In contrast, an earthquake may destroy a dwelling but the materials are still on the site and might be reused to rebuild. This is not as easy with so-called modern materials, especially reinforced concrete, as they lose integrity and cannot be reused except crushed as aggregate. Materials in smaller units, however, including bricks, blocks, stones, tiles, roof sheets, etc., may be reused. It is clear that a household whose homestead and dwelling have both disappeared for ever into the Brahmaputra River is homeless in a different way from one camping close to their collapsed stone traditional dwelling in northern Pakistan.

Conflict

Warfare and other conflicts are major contributors to homelessness. At one end of the scale, war veterans are over-represented in homeless populations. Among homeless people in the USA, for example, 32–42 per cent have been found to be war veterans and they have significant problems with physical injury, mental health, alcohol abuse and medical conditions (O'Toole et al., 2003). They also tend to be homeless for longer than non-veterans (Tessler, 2003).

According to Summerfield (1997), there had been 160 recent wars in developing countries by 1997 and there were at least 50 being waged at that time, making at least 12 million people homeless and 18 million refugees across international boundaries. Many of these wars are 'low-intensity' with little differentiation between soldiers and civilians, and with terror and mutilation of non-combatants being used to quell or drive away local populations. Cheap hand-held weapons mean that anyone can take part and thus trust is destroyed among neighbours. Women and children are routinely involved either as combatants or as victims of rape and abuse which then scars their lives and reputations, leaving them even more vulnerable to homelessness and other crises than before. Many women raped by soldiers during offensives in Philippines have become prostitutes in Manila (Summerfield, 1997).

War has always rendered victims homeless, sometimes in huge numbers. The Second World War resulted in many millions having their homes destroyed, but it was ever thus with war, though, perhaps, in smaller quantities. The early anthropologist, Malinowski (1920), tells of how warfare in the Trobriand Islands resulted in the vanquished people's village being destroyed and the survivors remained homeless until atonement could be made for the incident which caused the war in the first place. In modern days, wherever war is spoken of, large numbers of homeless people appear as a statistic in the narrative. The war between Serbia, Croatia and Bosnia-Herzegovina is said to have created 2 million homeless people, a staggering numbert considering the population of the countries involved (Ramet, 1992). During the long civil war in Sudan, people have fled rural areas in large numbers. Known as *shamasa* (literally, having no roof but the sun), the assetless and homeless poor number about 6 million. They have been displaced internally or to neighbouring countries (Suliman, n.d. (*c.*1992)). During the Sri Lankan civil war it was reported that there were 100,000 Tamils homeless in Colombo and 175,000 elsewhere in the country (Rotberg, 1999). During the five-day war between El Salvador and Honduras in 1969, at least 100,000 Salvadorans were made homeless (Sack and Suster, 2000). Children are also badly affected by war (see Chapter 12).

After the invasion of Iraq in 2003, and especially after the bombing at the Samara mosque, many thousands of people were displaced every month. This follows the experience of Iraqi Kurdistan to which displaced persons had been moving for well over a decade before 2003; Leus et al. (2001) report more than one million there in 1999. Zanger (n.d.) reports that, week after week, dozens of minority families were forcibly expelled from Iraqi government-held areas and fled, destitute, to the Kurdish self-rule region. A government source says that, in northern Iraq, there are an estimated 800,000 internally displaced persons (IDPs), many of whom had their land in the south taken over by the pre-2003 regime in its Arabisation policy (Ministry of Municipalities and Public Works et al., 2005).

It is well established that refugees and internally displaced populations have crude death rates (CDRs) from 12 to 25 times higher than the non-displaced. Death rates among children less than 5 years of age are also far higher than among older children and adults, usually from preventable conditions such as diarrhoeal disease, measles and acute respiratory infections (Toole and Waldman, 1993; UN-Habitat, 2007b).

Conclusions

Disasters and conflicts render many thousands of people homeless every year, some for a short period but others for a more protracted time. Asia is the most heavily affected continent with the great majority of all people rendered homeless by disaster events. Disasters have a two-way relationship with vulnerabilities such as being homeless. They create and increase vulnerability by destroying homes and livelihoods but their effects are exacerbated by underlying vulnerability. Efforts to improve the resilience of housing and livelihoods can be very effective in limiting the disastrous effects of a natural or human-made hazard.

11 Exclusion, perceptions and isolation

This chapter explores the perception and treatment of homeless people in developing countries as 'others' and somehow isolated or excluded from mainstream society. It begins by discussing homelessness in relation to concepts of social exclusion and exclusion from welfare entitlements, then continues by focusing on the perceptions and persecution of homeless people. Some of this chapter draws on Speak and Tipple (2006).

Homelessness and social exclusion

It is not uncommon for public opinion to be hostile to homeless people. Even local authorities, charged with looking after the people in their jurisdictions, are frequently hostile to homeless people. DeVerteuil (2006) points out how the authorities in many cities in the USA have antagonistic responses to homeless people, especially those on the streets and those involved in aggressive begging ('panhandling') and the 'squeegee men' who clean windscreens at traffic lights whether the motorists want them to or not. In addition, space used by homeless people is increasingly the focus of policies and police actions to remove them in the name of improving quality of life. Homeless people occupying these spaces are criminalised by the policies. Law (2001) demonstrates how city authorities within Los Angeles metropolis regard homeless people as not appropriate in some locations and use their mobility to dodge any responsibility for helping them. The authorities in Tucson even proposed privatising the city centre pavements to ensure that homeless people were controlled more effectively than the public authorities could do (Snow and Mulcahy, 2001).

Homelessness represents an extreme form of social exclusion. There is, however, much discussion about the definition of the term 'social exclusion'. In the UK, certainly in its early evolution, the term referred more accurately to exclusion from economic activity and the market-oriented benefits, such as access to services and housing which adequate income provide. However, in other European countries, for example, France, the term is more closely associated with lack of social integration and cohesion (Pleace 1998). The interpretation that is more appropriate for discussing the isolation and exclusion of homeless people in developing countries is open to argument and dependent on the country.

Nevertheless, it is important to understand how social exclusion is perceived to relate to homelessness in different countries because it conditions public and government responses. For example, early understanding of homelessness and rough sleeping, especially of young people, in the UK was treated purely as a housing issue. Thus, responses to it focused on providing housing and training to manage housing. Only since the late 1990s have those working on homelessness and rough sleeping treated it as a form of social exclusion (Jordan, 1996). Given the emphasis on social inclusion through economic inclusion, however, interventions now tend to emphasise skills training for employment as Pleace (1998) explains.

An economically based interpretation of social exclusion may be less appropriate as a context of homelessness in developing countries because the poverty levels of homeless people in such countries may not differ from their housed peers as much as hearsay might suggest. In his empirical work in Mumbai, Swaminathan (1995) compared pavement dwellers with people living in low-quality tenements in Dharavi slum. He comments that all live in conditions characterised by terrible poverty, squalor and deprivation which are not captured adequately by measures of income poverty. Among homeless households living on the pavements of Dimtimkar Road in 1995, 69 per cent had incomes below the official income poverty line. More of the homeless women were in the workforce than women from the 'slums' (49 per cent and 17 per cent respectively), even though the former sample was from the Muslim minority and the latter from the Hindu majority. Only one of Dupont's (2000) sample of homeless people from Old Delhi had a monthly income below the poverty line of Rs.310 per capita in 1995–6 prices, even after taking account of their loss of income through remittances to family back in the rural area.

An interpretation of social exclusion based on isolation and lack of cohesion or belonging is also problematic for understanding homelessness in developing countries. While it is clear that many are excluded from the social and material benefits of economic development, it is difficult to suggest that homeless people are isolated from mainstream society if that equates to the majority or the mass of the population. Indeed, as we will see later in this chapter, the perception of homeless people as lone, isolated and helpless is, in many cases, completely false.

Exclusion from welfare entitlement

In some countries, the state of homelessness, as locally defined, removes people from benefiting from rights that others enjoy and these are, arguably, some of the people most in need of those rights. Those living quite literally on the streets are the very ones least likely to have their housing needs addressed and the most likely to be considered illegal. In UK, for example, many adults without accompanying dependants (pregnant women excepted) sleeping on the streets are excluded from direct provision of housing.

In the People's Republic of China, the state has, for decades, prided itself on its strong socialist welfare system with no unemployment and no homelessness. A strong national housing registration system, tight links between employment and housing, and rigid constraints over movement of people, meant that few households would ever be without a dwelling of their own or, at least, one shared with family members.[1] All were supported under the welfare system unless they moved illegally away from their place of registration. Until recently, the term 'urban poor' did not feature in official documents in China. Only recently have documents referred to the low-income group or 'weak social and economic groups' (*ruoshi qunti*) and 'poor urban residents' (*chengshi pingkun jumin*) (Wang, 2004). In this context, homeless people in China are not only the most poorly accommodated people but also excluded from many of the benefits available to others.

In India, pavement dwellers and many in informal, illegal settlements not formally designated as 'slums' do not possess ration cards (UNCHS, 2000). Thus they are not entitled to receive food supplements available to other poor people. As they are rarely on the voters' list they are usually not entitled to receive housing plots either. Hindu *sadhus* (wandering ascetics), who travel around India dressed only in loincloths and giving up all worldly attachments in order to obtain enlightenment, are not included in the category of homeless people. *Banjaras* (Gypsies) and *Loharas* (a nomadic tribe involved in the blacksmith trade) have also been excluded (Bannerjee Das, 2002). Thus, they will never receive any assistance that the government attempts to offer in addressing homelessness.

In Indonesia, people without a 'permanent place to stay' are also, generally, without an identity card (*kartu tanda penduduk,* KTP) issued by the local authority. Thus, they are not entitled to education or other welfare services. Children born to such people cannot be officially registered and receive a birth certificate. Thus they are not recognised as official citizens.

People in illegal settlements are not organised into community and neighbourhood units (*rukun warga* and *rukun tetangga*[2]) in which every household (at least theoretically) should be a member. As a consequence, they do not benefit from development projects and their dwellings, regardless of standard or quality, cannot be fitted with any electricity or piped water connections (Rahardjo, 2002).

While the government of Peru addresses homelessness through its land allocation programme, it does not include those living on the streets, arguably the most in need.

Perceptions of homeless people

A series of self-reinforcing perceptions serve to keep homeless people as 'others' in society. This increases the difficulty they face, not only in surviving on a daily basis but also in achieving a degree of legitimacy, through being housed and employed, even where both housing and jobs are relatively plentiful. Perceptions of homeless people differ according to the type of accommodation, the reason for it and between countries. For example, an NGO in India considers that people made homeless by disasters are thought of as 'unfortunate' but those considered destitute are thought to be a 'burden on society' and are often harassed and abused (Aashray Adhikar Abhiyan, 2001).

There is a marked difference in perceptions of the homeless among different countries because of what they are perceived to represent within any given society. For example, Mitra (1988, 2008) notes that homelessness in Japan reflects a downward social mobility, but such an association is not as strong in India. Indeed, Speak (2004) considers that homelessness can play a part in an upward trajectory of livelihoods (see Chapter 5).

Nevertheless, despite some culturally conditioned views on homelessness, general perceptions of homeless people can be seen to fall into eight categories. We discuss these here and attempt to dissolve some of the myths about homeless people in developing countries.

The 'villain'

The perception of homeless people as criminals is common throughout the world. In Bangladesh, street children are referred to with words meaning 'thief', 'illegitimate' or 'son of a beggar'. Similarly, in Peru, street children are referred to as '*pirañitas*' – little piranhas – implying that they are dangerous. However, while children do commit petty crimes out of need to feed themselves, this image and the degree to which they are incarcerated exaggerates the seriousness of their alleged offences (El Baz, 1996; Bartlett et al., 1999).

Some homeless people earn their living in jobs which the majority population regard as on the edge of legality or acceptability. Windscreen washers in cities such as Santiago, Chile, as in many other countries, provide a service but often an unwanted one for which they expect payment, often against an implicit (even if unmeant) threat of violence. Such self-reliance inspires negative perceptions almost as much as if they were stealing from passers-by (Bernasconi and Puentes, 2006).

The 'beggar'

One of the most common public perceptions of homeless people is that they are all beggars. However, Chapter 7 shows that the majority of homeless people are working in some way. Those in India are mostly casual labourers who often travel long distances across the city every day to reach work, although in Delhi only 44 per cent of homeless people manage to find work daily (PUCL, 2000). Similarly, in Ghana, whilst popular imagery and perception again portray homeless people as beggars, our study found only around 3 per cent actually engage in begging. The vast majority of homeless people undertake some form of work to earn their livelihoods.

Ironically, it is poor perceptions of homeless people which limit their ability to work. For example, In Chile, Bernasconi and Puentes (2006) noted that occupying a shelter brings a stigma which generates problems for employment.

The 'mentally Ill'

In some countries, the common perception of people on the streets is of their being mentally ill or personally defective. For example, in Peru, those who live on the streets, in parks or in abandoned buildings are officially referred to as 'mentally ill people on the streets' regardless of their actual mental health.

In Ghana, homelessness, as defined by charitable institutions and non-governmental organisations, refers to beggars, and destitute and mentally ill people who are not under the care of relatives or the extended family and do not have a home. An official at Oxfam's office in Tamale described homeless people in Ghana as 'the mentally ill people whose movement cannot be easily controlled' (Department of Housing and Planning Research, 2002).

Not only can mental illness be a contributory factor in some people's homelessness but homelessness can be a contributory factor in some people's mental illness. However, what we see here is an automatic association between homelessness, especially street sleeping, and mental illness. The CARDO study found no evidence to uphold this association; the vast majority of even the most destitute of street dwellers must be emotionally robust in order to construct the complex strategies by which they survive.

The 'immoral'

There is a strongly perceived association between the possession of an adequate home and upholding adequate moral values. Thus, those who are seen to be without a home are assumed to be without morals. This is more strongly seen in relation to homeless women. The negative labelling found in the Indonesian *tuna* terms (see below), especially *tunasusila* used for 'women having no morals', is repeated in Bangladesh, where a young homeless divorcee or widowed mother is publicly called a whore, especially if she is homeless, regardless of her sexual activity

The stigma of immorality leads many homeless households to split up. In the strongly Islamic moral culture of Bangladesh, for example, it is uncommon to find women or girl children living on the streets. When a family becomes homeless, the women will most often be sent to live with relatives whilst the man sleeps rough on the streets. This produces a self-fulfilling prophecy, in which any women or girls who are living on the streets are perceived not to care, or be cared about, and may be abused, even raped.

However, many women, either widowed or abandoned have no choice but to live on the streets (Speak, 2005) where the stigma of perceived immorality then attaches to the children. Discussing the plight of homeless women and children in Durban, Gray and Bernstein (1994) note that children left with relatives are less stigmatised while their mother is away living on the city streets than when she briefly returns to the village to check on them.

The 'transient'

There is a perception, common in many countries, that homeless people are largely transient individuals moving from place to place, sleeping where they can with no longer term association with a location or the people in it. For example, a term often used in Indonesia to describe homelessness (though not in official documents) is *gelandangan*, meaning 'tramp', derived from *gelandang* meaning to wander. In South Africa, the use of labels such as *malunda* (those who sleep away from home) reinforces this. One ex-homeless man interviewed there recounted:

> In the olden days people used to tie their stuff on a stick and put it around their shoulders and they look like a bull hump and they trek from Eastern Cape to Johannesburg. Because they sleep in different places, they used to call them 'Umanlunda', or 'Malunda'…

In China, as well as being known as *mangliu,* which means the 'aimlessly flowing people', homeless people are also called *liulanghan*, meaning 'people who are floating or vagrant'. These terms reinforce the perception of homeless people as being alone and without permanence. In reality, many of them are relatively stable, living in *chengzhongcun,* villages which have been subsumed into the expanding cities, often as tenants in housing developed by local villagers on their communally owned land (Zhang et al., 2003). Strict policing of Chinese cities means that transient, itinerant street sleepers or informal squatters would not be tolerated.

Whilst street-homeless people do suffer extreme insecurity of place and are frequently moved on, the perception that they are all transient, constantly wandering, with their few possessions on their backs, is generally misleading. Even if we only consider pavement dwellers, we can see that they often remain in the same place for extended periods of time, living together in stable clusters. Pavement dwellers in India, for example, often collect in small groups and form semi-permanent settlements on the edge of the road or on vacant land plots. Although their dwellings are poor and they do not have access to services, they build social networks and may become an accepted part of the local community.

In the same way, street-homeless people in Santiago, Chile, collect in small groups (*caletas*), which give them some stability, often erecting makeshift shelters known as *rucos* in which some level of domesticity and neighbourly reciprocation is possible (Bernasconi and Puentes, 2006).

Although street-homeless people generally keep on the move, either as a means of protection or as part of a daily or periodic round to garner opportunities for work, food, support and other necessities, their ambit may be quite small. Some even confine their movements to the neighbourhood in which they were born and brought up, making sure they can be contacted through a local shop or a housed family member nearby in case of work or other opportunities arising. One homeless young man in Chile noted 'even if I do not have an address they know where to find me'. Describing his routinised movements ('his circuit') in some detail, Bernasconi and Puentes (2006: 32) show how he lives centrally to places he needs to access. He moves between the shop which supplies his alcohol, where he meets his drinking pals and keeps his most precious belongings, the factory, where he collects electrical wire to strip, the chair on which he sits to strip the wire (his 'office'), the place he uses as a bathroom and the market at which he sells the stripped copper wire. His transience is very local.

The 'loner'

Cartoons in popular media particularly perpetuate the common perception of a homeless person being alone, indeed, generally a lone male. Glasser (1994) quotes a definition of homelessness as suggested by (Caplow et al., 1968: 494): 'Homelessness is a condition of detachment from society characterised by the absence or attenuation of the affiliative bonds that link settled persons to a network of interconnected social structures.' One Spanish term used to refer to homeless people is *desamparado* (without protection or comfort from other people), which implies loss of family (Juliá and Hartnett, 1999).

However, in developing countries, the nature of homelessness means that this may not be the case for the majority of homeless people. Affiliative bonds with the home, either in the village or at the periphery of the city, remain strong for many homeless people who send money home and visit to keep up the family connection. Migrants from the same village, who follow brothers, cousins and friends on a well-travelled migration route to the city, may stay in a group on the pavement. For example, many of the handcart-pullers in the Khari Baoli wholesale market in Old Delhi group together at night, cook food collectively and sleep on their handcarts in the security of the group (Dupont, 1998).

Moreover, in many countries, household migration has led to a rapid increase in the number of children living on the street with their parent(s). In India, households are more likely to be found in Kolkata, Mumbai and Chennai than in Delhi, where it is less usual for households to reside on the pavements (Singh and de Souza, 1980; Dupont, 1998). In Kolkata, 37 per cent of homeless people were found to be living in households (Jagannathan and Halder, 1990). Moreover, in the 1980s, the percentage of families among the homeless people increased from 39 per cent in 1976 to 74 per cent in 1987. While to the Western eye the presence of women, children and older people living on the streets seems unacceptable, the Indian government sees the increase in homeless families as a good indication of social stability.

In Peru, many households have no option other than to settle on poor desert land, under makeshift shelters of straw mats and without any form of services. They are likely to remain there for many years with very poor shelter and living conditions. However, like others in comparable circumstances in many countries, they often form tight and supportive social networks as they band together to gain secure title. In some cases, they form community groups to campaign and to improve their environment (Miranda and Salazar, 2002).

Even on the streets, some homeless people rely on other homeless people for protection from personal attack and from the authorities moving them on. These networks often also include the local population, especially tradespeople who deal with street-homeless people on a daily basis and may provide services such as a place to leave valuable possessions and a postbox for messages (Bernasconi and Puentes, 2006). Some of Bernasconi and Puentes's (2006) respondents were living on the streets of their home neighbourhood to keep up with contacts while not being able to afford accommodation. Thus, the reference to a 'lack of affiliative bonds' presented by Caplow et al. (1968) would not hold for homeless people in developing countries.

The 'anti-citizen'

The perceptions discussed so far, when brought together to form a characterisation of homeless people, present a picture of extreme exclusion and deviant behaviour. So strongly is this perceived in some cases as to present homeless people as 'anti-citizens'. They are seen not only as excluded from society but a danger to it.

In industrialised countries, there has been a growing negative association between homelessness and 'poor citizenship' since the 1990s. In the UK, Prime Minister Tony Blair, and his predecessor, John Major, made the association between homeless people and what might be termed 'anti-citizenship'. In speeches and in the media both associated homeless people, especially rough sleepers, with anti-social activities which are perceived to run counter to the rights of citizenship or to make them undeserving of these rights (Hartley, 1999: 13). Hunter (1985) recalls the days of growing homelessness in the USA when homeless people became symbols of incivility (cited in Snow and Mulcahy, 2001).

This loss of citizenship manifests itself in a lack of even the most basic rights in some countries. As discussed earlier, the residents of *permukiman liar* (illegal settlements) in Indonesia are not registered as citizens of the city (which must be verified with the possession of an identity card (KTP) issued by the respective local authority). Likewise in India, street-homeless people do not have ration cards allowing them access to important nutritional supplements, the right to vote and access a range of services. A similar situation also exists in China where the *mangliu/ sanwurenyuan* are virtually invisible to the authorities; they have no identity cards, no temporary residence cards and no work approval cards (Chapter 4).

As a reaction to this perception, some street-homeless people in Chile try to make their small clusters of shacks (*caletas*) into havens of cleanliness and respect, not only for the residents but also for passers-by and domiciled neighbours (Bernasconi and Puentes, 2006).

The 'helpless'

Through their terminology, advocacy or support, organisations can inadvertently portray homeless people as helpless. Emotive pictures used by NGOs to gain sympathy for their cause undermine the strength, resilience and capacity of homeless people to work and support themselves. Such practices confuse vulnerability with helplessness and overlook the contribution homeless people make to society and economy. They do a disservice to homeless client groups. This is particularly relevant to children of and on the streets, who, especially to the Western eye, are the personification of helplessness. However, for many, life on the streets represents a degree of empowerment and freedom from abuse and hunger (see Chapter 12).

In Chile, Bernasconi and Puentes (2006: 18) tell of a homeless man who regards himself not only as a leader in his small cluster of homeless people but as a mediator and spokesperson for the 'humiliated of the streets'. Filipe, a young homeless boy of 12 in their sample, sees homeless people as resilient and strong, noting that the way to survive is to be like 'stubborn dolls: they throw us down and we stand up again'.

Language and labelling

These largely false and negative perceptions of homeless people are reinforced and perpetuated by negative and exclusionary language and images used to describe and discuss them. As Daly (1996) notes:

> Language used to describe homeless people in the literature is broadly construed. It includes media images, sound bites and defamatory rhetoric, as well as policies and programmes that convey mainstream society's message of power, influence and authority. The messages that raise a number of dilemmas can become tools of manipulation. Homeless individuals may be silenced by such power relationships, control mechanisms and by messages contained in popular media.

> (Daly, 1996: 6)

Names and images help to construct homeless people as 'other' and institutionalise their stigmatisation, keeping them dissociated and disconnected from society (Olufemi, 2002). For example, in Finland, in the 1980s, homelessness had become so closely associated with a growing alcohol problem that there was an active movement to 'delabel' homeless people in order to distance them from this negative stereotyping. The result is a coded language in which homeless people are referred to as those having 'certain individual needs and inclinations' (Glasser, 1994: 29)

A review of cartoons in publications, and particularly in daily papers, shows how negatively homeless people are portrayed. Broadly, cartoons represent all homeless people as street vagrants falling into two categories of deserving and undeserving. The first category shows Neale's (1997) 'agency' approach to homelessness by portraying homeless people as rough-sleeping, alcoholic beggars. More recently, a second category presents the structural understanding of homelessness by showing the homeless businessman or redundant executive falling on hard times. Often the humour hinges on some business language used in beggars' petitions for alms. It is valuable to explore some of the web-based cartoon-supply companies to see how homeless people are presented (see e.g. http://www.cartoonistgroup.com/ or http://www.cartoonstock.com/).

A range of negative and judgmental terms are used to portray homeless people around the world. For example, in Chile, homeless people are thought of as having 'the value of a mushroom' (*valen callampa*) (Bernasconi and Puentes, 2006). Sometimes terms are light-hearted or jocular, such as the terms *mukomana [musikana] wekuseri* (meaning boy [or girl] from the back), used in South Africa, to describe adult lodgers who live in backyard shacks.[3] More often there is a broad range of terminology which labels homeless people as personally inadequate, belonging to an underclass. For example, in the Indonesian language the term *tunawisma*, meaning 'no (*tuna*) house (*wisma*)' is in the same vein as the words for unemployed people, *tunakarya* ('no work'); blind people, *tunanetra* ('no eyes') and sex workers, *tunasusila* ('no morals'). The Suharto New Order government often used such labels during its three decades of rule (Rahardjo, 2002).

In Bangladesh, labels emphasise what the homeless person lacks and links the lack of shelter to destitution. One term used in Bangladesh is *sharbohara*. Broadly meaning 'utterly destitute', it comes from *sharbo* meaning 'all' and *hara* meaning 'the state of not having'. Thus the inference is that a homeless person has nothing, which is not necessarily the case. This labelling is particularly pertinent to Bengali society, where individual or group identities, based around home and family reputation, are hugely important in locating a person within a social hierarchy. Thus a woman is the wife or a boy the son of a certain 'home' (Ghafur, 2002).

Sometimes, terms used are serious and derogatory labels, which serve to condition and reinforce the public perception of homeless people as drunks, mentally ill, unemployed, thieves and beggars. In China, for example, the term *jiaohuazi,* meaning beggar, is often used to refer to homeless people. The word *mangliu* is a reverse homophone for *liumang* meaning hooligan. This establishes a negative attitude towards rural migrants (Cheng and Selden, 1994).

Justification for negative perceptions

The justification given for the negative perceptions of homeless people falls into four categories.

- Worth or desert: governments and their agencies tend to use language indicative of worthiness for help. Moral or financial pressures demand pseudo-logical rationing of help. Thus, some potential clients are labelled as less deserving of help and, therefore, rightly excluded (Neale, 1997).
- Competitiveness: economic and business interests, with homeless people on the streets outside their premises, adopt unsympathetic language and attitudes towards them as they are seen to reduce competitiveness with other businesses not so affected (Daly, 1996).
- Appearance: cities, conscious of their image, especially in an international economic market, justify street-clearing operations as important to the city's image. Thus they remove 'unsightly' homeless people.
- Pity, charity and compassion: while adopting more sympathetic and positive language, religious and philanthropic institutions can undermine the potential of many homeless people, by labelling them as victims, helpless and in need of charity.

These reasons underpinning the common perceptions and labelling of homeless people are important because, as we will argue in Chapter 13, they condition interventions and responses to homelessness.

Self-perception

Public perceptions affect the self-perception homeless people have. Indeed, many homeless people make positive efforts to present themselves in such a manner as to actively refute negative perceptions, by keeping their environment and themselves clean, by always being polite and showing respect to others. In a study of homeless people in London which involved their taking and then describing photographs which depicted their lives, Radley et al. (2005) found that they felt an equivalence between social worth and moral acceptability both in their own minds and in how other people treated them. Thus, if possible, the homeless people interviewed made the best of their appearance to maintain as much social acceptability as possible.

Bernasconi and Puentes's (2006) Chilean study highlighted the range of perceptions homeless people hold about themselves and other homeless people.

Discussing a couple they interviewed, they noted a feeling that the street is 'a place that does not belong to them and which they don't feel a part of'. Another interviewee, an alcoholic male, however, accepted that he belonged to what he called 'the big family of the street' (Bernasconi and Puentes (2006: 14). Thus, there are differences in perception between living on the streets, being from the streets and participating in the culture of the streets.

A homeless person's perceptions of his or her situation is affected by a number of factors, including the reasons for the homelessness, their level of control over it and how they view it in relation to the rest of their lives. In industrialised countries, Hertzberg's (1992) typology is helpful as a means of expressing this. However, as discussed in Chapter 4, it is less valuable in developing countries. Speak's (2004) typology may be more helpful, as it is based on the degree of choice and control the homeless person has and their perception of the role the homeless period plays in their life.

Empirical evidence from developing countries suggests that, for many, homelessness is actually a form of empowerment. Women or children who become homeless when fleeing familial violence are not only protecting themselves physically but taking control over their situation.

Conclusions

Clearly there is a relationship between social exclusion and homelessness. However, the degree to which this is true in developing countries depends on the particular interpretation of social exclusion. In the UK, for example, despite government rhetoric, the interpretation of social exclusion is based largely on income and its impact on access to services, facilities and goods enjoyed by the mainstream. In France, however, social exclusion is more strongly associated with a sense of belonging and inclusion. Thus, to view homelessness as a form of social exclusion in developing countries, with very broad and diverse societies, might be simplistic. This is particularly true where the line between adequately housed and homeless is blurred.

Nevertheless, public and institutional perceptions do serve to exclude and distance some homeless people from the rights of other citizens. Moreover, they serve to keep homeless people from improving their own lives and perpetuate their homelessness.

Labels for homeless people may reinforce the 'individual pathology' approach to homelessness (Jacobs et al., 1999), presenting the causes as inadequacies (mentally ill, evictees, refugees) or behaviour (immoral and criminal), but both are unhelpful. The image presented of homeless people, as criminals, prostitutes and beggars is unfounded and unhelpful to the homeless people themselves but serves to justify inappropriate and unjust treatment by the authorities. Perpetuating the image of homeless people as solitary and transient limits public sympathy for them when settlements are cleared in the name of development.

Language which confuses vulnerability with helplessness, to extract sympathy for homeless people, may serve to disempower them further. Moreover, it does not recognise their contribution to society. Indeed, the representation of homeless people as helpless suggests that they are unproductive which, in turn, reinforces their image as undeserving of the benefits designed for other poor people (rations, land allocations, etc.). We have seen that most homeless people work and, therefore, contribute positively to the economy. Through spending their incomes, they are also part of the tax base. Thus, exclusionary language implying non-citizenship is unjust and very damaging.

12 Children and homelessness

In planning this work, the decision was taken, after some consideration, to deal with the specific situation relating to children within a dedicated chapter, which largely mirrors the structure of the book. This not only allows for a fuller discussion but also provides an easy reference for those specifically interested in the subject of homeless children. Any discussion of children's homelessness in developing countries automatically suggests to the reader the emotive and visible subject of 'street children'. However, despite what Rizzini (1996: 226) calls a 'prodigious outpouring of texts' on the phenomenon of street children, there is need for clarification when writing about children in the context of homelessness.

UNICEF's definition of street children offers us two categories: 'children *of* the street' who are perceived to live without the shelter and support of a family or household and 'children *on* the street' who spend much time working or playing on the streets but generally can and do return home at night. As Ennew and Swart-Kruger (2003) note, the categories are frequently misunderstood or misused. Certainly, in the context of homelessness they can be misleading, in that they imply that children *of* the street are without family support or worse, that they have run away or been abandoned, and that those *on* the street are not homeless but have a home to which they may return. Neither is necessarily true. In India, for example, it is not uncommon to find entire, multi-generational households living on the streets or in public places, such as parks. The children of these households may roam the streets playing or working during the day but return to their collective 'sleeping place' at night for support and protection. In which category do they belong? Categorising children into these two subgroups also disregards the fluidity of children's lives, guardianship and housing situations in developing countries. The assumption that children are in either one or the other is seldom true. Perhaps a more valuable description is that offered by Thomas de Benitez (2003) of 'street-living children' as this could include those living on the street alone or within a household. However, here 'street' needs not to be taken too literally and should include all unacceptable levels of accommodation in all locations. Regardless of where they sit within UNICEF's categorisation, homeless children fall into two main categories: children within homeless households and children who are homeless outside of or estranged from a household. Their needs are, however, very similar at most levels.

The very great academic and policy focus on children *of* the street overshadows the plight of the potentially greater number of children living in homeless households (Speak, 2005). For example, India is one of the countries where it is more common to find homeless households living on the streets or in public places. The children of these units may return to the collective family 'sleeping' place each night, or they may not.

In this chapter the line between the children *on* the streets, children *of* the streets and children within homeless households is deliberately not defined because the states are fluid and children move between them. However, much of the data has been drawn from literature on street children, of which there is so much, rather than children in homeless households as such literature is virtually non-existent in the developing countries context.

As we have discussed elsewhere in this work, the language of homelessness is weighed down with emotive terms and subjective meaning. The use of the word 'street' when discussing children who might not live permanently with their family unit is also confusing as it emphasises the obvious, visible, publicly owned road and pavement. However, the locations where homeless children live out their lives are many and diverse. Lucchini (1996) opens up children's worlds, from the duality of 'home and street' or 'home *v.* street', noting that they are constructed of a series of 'domains'. Domains include the family home, whatever that may be, NGOs, public places, hiding places, meeting places and a range of locations, institutions and people amongst which they circulate.

Children, in industrialised or developing countries, whether homeless or not, construct their own worlds to include all those domains that bring them advantages and facilities which 'home' does not. The difference is that in developing countries poverty, larger households and poor housing may mean that more is required from outside the 'home'. This may mean leaving home temporarily or permanently. It also means that more of the domains are constructed at an informal, individual level (learning a skill from a friendly craftsman) rather than an institutional one (school education).

Social science now accepts that childhood is largely socially rather than biologically constructed and that children are active, productive agents in their own right (Aries, 1962; James et al., 1998; Holloway and Valentine, 2000). This, therefore, requires us to recognise that childhood must also, therefore, be diverse amongst different social and cultural contexts. Thus, while the drivers which make children vulnerable to homelessness might be similar in many developing countries, the way in which children respond to them will be different. Similarly, the way in which society responds to homeless children, will depend on how people perceive the meaning of home and of what a child is expected to receive and experience within the home. In industrialised cultures, home is perceived as a relatively small, geographically located unit, centred on parents and siblings. It is expected to provide for the physical and emotional needs of children until such time as they are deemed able to provide for themselves. Even then, there is increasingly a 'nursery' period of practised independence, through university.

In developing countries, however, home is associated with the broader concept of kin. Families are extended and the skills and abilities a child needs to provide for itself physically and emotionally can be learned much earlier. Thus, far from being 'throw aways or runaways' (Ennew and Swart-Kruger, 2003) some children might simply 'out-grow' home earlier than Western expectations allow. However, others do not and, despite children's agency and the many differences in context, it must be accepted that many millions of children around the world do find themselves without all that home should provide before they are ready. For example, Young and Ansell (2003) discuss the plight of children in AIDS-torn Africa, many of whom find themselves orphaned, sent out of the home to care for themselves or sent to live with relatives who may not want or be able to care for them.

Numbers of homeless children

If it is difficult to come to any robust estimate for the number of homeless people in the world (Chapter 6), it is even more difficult to disaggregate that estimate by age or gender. One reason for this is the difficulty in counting children *of* or *on* the street, who may be suspicious of adults and figures of authority and are adept at hiding. Their lack of permanent address, wandering lifestyles and changing workplaces make them a particularly difficult group to locate (Patel, 1990). Another reason is that homeless households tend to be even less visible and more 'hidden' than homeless single people. In many countries, when a household becomes homeless, the women and children are sent to live with relatives in overcrowded and inadequate conditions, or kept hidden for safety, rather than being visibly homeless or unsheltered. The World Health Organisation (WHO) and UNICEF in the mid-1990s estimated the number of homeless children to be 100 million.

Estimates of homeless children have focused, like most other work on 'homeless' children, on children of the street. While these children are labelled as 'homeless' numerous studies have not identified significant numbers of such children who are totally without connection to their homes and families. Some might suggest that they are, therefore, not homeless (Ennew and Swart-Kruger, 2003). However, as discussed earlier, frequently the families to which they may return are themselves homeless.

It is in this context of ambiguity that we attempt a broad picture of the scale of child homelessness pieced together from data on homeless children and street children for individual countries, although these refer to several different time periods. As with our previous attempt to estimate homelessness, we do not suggest it is robust. Nevertheless, it helps the reader develop an understanding of scale.

In industrialised countries the vast majority of homeless children are part of a homeless household. In England, the number of statutorily homeless families with children in bed and breakfast accommodation at December 2002 was 5,620, a reduction of more than than 1,000 since the end of September that year. Of the 96,000 homeless households in temporary accommodation at 31 March 2007, 75 per cent had dependent children (Department of Communities and Local Government, 2003).

In Australia, 10 per cent of officially homeless people are under the age of 12 and 36 per cent are aged between 12 and 24 years. In the United States, about 3.5 million people (10.6 per thousand) are said to be homeless, of whom about one million are children (UNEP Youth Xchange, n.d.). A survey of 24 US cities in 2005 found that families with children accounted for 33 per cent of the homeless population (The United States Conference of Mayors, 2005a).

In developing countries, variations between numbers within one country, over a relatively short period of time, show the difficulty in estimating number of street children. South Africa is a good example of this. The National Programme of Action (1994: 34) indicates 10,000 street children in South Africa. UNICEF and the National Children's Rights Commission (NCRC) estimated a similar number (9,390), of these about 90 per cent were boys between the ages of 7 and 14 years, found mostly in the metropolitan areas (Department of Welfare and Population Development, 1998). However, only a few years later, the South African White Paper on Welfare (Government of South Africa, 1997) estimated approximately one million street children in the country by 1997.

Through a headcount, Olufemi (1997) established there were 1,107 street children in Johannesburg inner city alone in 1997. She also estimated that about 40 per cent of homeless women have their children living with them. Headcounts in 1999 revealed 1,500 street children in North West, 244 in Northern Province and 2,000 in Gauteng. In the Free State 225 children were recorded as living in the streets (*of* the street) and about 675 as being *on* the streets. In 1999 more than 90 NGOs catered for over 6,000 street children in shelters alone (Office on the Rights of the Child, 2001). More recently, in Johannesburg and Cape Town alone the Green Paper (Department of Social Services and Population Development, 2000: 41) stated the number of street children, based on best-guess estimates, to be approximately 9,000 between the ages of 7 and 18 years, with the majority aged 13–16. Of these one-third are '*of*' the street while the rest are '*on*' the street, working but not living there. A small proportion of these children are orphans but many are functionally homeless because of family abuse, poverty, alcoholism or eviction.

According to UNICEF, there were about 25 million street children in Asia and an estimated 10 million in Africa in the late 1990s. Other estimates for individual cities suggest similarly high numbers. The Consortium for Street Children estimates there to be between 100,000 and 125,000 street children each in Mumbai, Kolkata and Delhi, with 45,000 in Bangalore (Consortium for Street Children, 2001). In India, estimates of the percentage of street-homeless households with children vary widely but they are more likely to be found in Kolkata, Mumbai and Chennai than in Delhi, where it is unusual for households to reside on the pavements (Singh and de Souza, 1980; Dupont, 1998). For example, in Kolkata, estimates of shelterless people living in family groups ranged from 37 per cent in one study in the 1980s (Jagannathan and Halder, 1988) to over 74 per cent in another study (CMDA, 1987; Bannerjee Das, 2002). In India the Tamil Nadu Government estimates that, in urban areas of the state (particularly Chennai), there are 69,000 homeless families 'living in objectionable areas along roads and canals and places required for public purposes' (Mody, 2001). The majority of these families will include children (Bannerjee Das, 2002).

Following the collapse of the Soviet Union and the subsequent economic crisis sweeping Eastern Europe, homelessness increased dramatically. Many of the 'new homeless' were abandoned children, with the estimated number of street children in Russia ranging from 100,000 to 150,000 (ILO, 2001b). Statistics show that in one region of Russia, Primorskii Krai, 'one out of every ten youths becomes homeless' (Stoecker, 2001: 322).

A term used for homeless youth in Russian is *besprizornyi*. The legal definition is *beznadzornyi* – one who is without a place of residence. Some live in institutions. A recent survey of almost 90 shelters for street children in the Ukraine recorded more than 120,000 children are registered with them (Kabachenco, 2006). Some street children remain with their parents and a survey of Moscow street children by the ILO in 2001 showed that only 8.9 per cent of them defined themselves as homeless (ILO, 2001a). Nevertheless, this still equates to a considerable number.

In Indonesia, estimates of homeless children vary widely according to definition used but studies suggest around 50,760 street children nationwide. (Consortium for Street Children, 2001). PKPM Atmajaya and the Department of Social Affairs suggest that, by 1998, the number of street children in Indonesia was somewhere between 50,000 and 170,000 (Rahardjo, 2002). However, it is believed that about 60 per cent of all 'new' street children are children *on* the street, in that they live with their families, work some of the time on the streets and go to school some of the time. With school dropout rates rising, many children are being forced onto the streets to work and live (Rahardjo, 2002)

There has been a sharp increase in the number of street children in Zimbabwe in recent years. From a figure of less than 1,000 in 1990 the number of street children rose to over 5,000 in less than ten years (MPSLSW, 1999; Searfoss, 2000). This figure includes both children *of* the streets and children *on* the streets. Data from MPSLSW (2000) suggests that the number of children *of* the street rose from 742 in 1995 to about 3,000 in 2000, no doubt as a result of the worsening economic climate and increasing violence in the country. We have no data on what has happened in the increasingly difficult years since 2000.

Like India, Latin America has become well known for street children. Estimates of the number of street children throughout Central and South America, again, vary widely, but the United Nations Children's Fund figure of 40 million is the most generally accepted (UNICEF, 1996).

In Bolivia, UNICEF (2003) estimates there to be over 3,700 children and adolescents living on the streets in the cities of La Paz, El Alto, Santa Cruz, Cochabamba, Tarija and Sucre. A further 9,200 children and adolescents live in homes for orphans, abandoned and disabled children.

Miranda and Salazar (2002) provide a best-guess estimate that almost 25 per cent of the 15,000 people who live on the street in Peru are children. The vast majority of street children in Peru are believed to be 'children *on* the street', who return at night to their families, many of whom are squatters and as such can be classed as inadequately housed or, in many cases, live in such poor conditions as to be classed as homeless by our criteria (see Chapter 5). Of these, Alarcón (1998) estimates there to be around 1,300,000 nationally. Children '*of* the street' are fewer in number but estimates vary considerably. CEDRO (Information and Education Centre to Prevent Drug Abuse) estimated in 1997 that there were around 1,000 in the country whilst a more official statistic by INABIF (National Institute of Family Welfare) put the figure higher, at 2,000 (Miranda and Salazar, 2002).

In Brazil, using the 'capture–recapture' method, in an attempt to develop a more robust enumeration, researchers estimated there to be 1,456 homeless children in Aracaju, roughly halfway between the previously wide-ranging estimates of 200 to 3,000 (Gurgel et al., 2004).

Street children are also common in Africa. In Ghana, Korboe (1996) estimated that there are about 1,000 to 1,500 active street children in Kumasi, whilst Beauchemin (1999) estimated that Accra alone had over 15,000 street children in 1999. A survey conducted by the Department of Housing and Planning Research (2002) in October 2001 found that over 70 per cent of homeless people were below the age of 20 and approximately 53 per cent were below the age of 18. The majority of the younger homeless people are migrants to the cities.

In Egypt, multiple definitions of street and homeless children complicate estimating their numbers, thus there are no official or reliable statistics. The high mobility of street children also complicates the validity of any survey. One indicator used by CSC is the number of children arrested. Of the 42,505 children arrested in 2001, 10,958 of them were charged with being 'vulnerable to delinquency' an indication of having no family home (Consortium for Street Children, 2004a).

Causes and precursors of child homelessness

While acknowledging that children are active agents in their own and adult worlds, as Holloway and Valentine (2000: 6) note, 'Recognition of children's agency does not necessarily lead to a rejection of an appreciation of the ways in which their lives are shaped by forces beyond the control of individual children.' Thus, it is important to understand the issues which might make children vulnerable to homelessness. Discussing street children, Ennew and Swart-Kruger (2003) cite three levels of cause of children's leaving home – immediate, underlying and structural. Their analysis is equally appropriate for understanding the causes of children's experiencing homelessness as part of a household. At the 'immediate' level, reasons might include withdrawal of adult support, through death or abandonment or a reduction in household income. Underlying causes include cultural perceptions of a child's role, chronic poverty or the desire to experience the city and independence. Finally, at the structural level, causes might include economic downturns, structural adjustment programmes, the impact of globalisation or the impact of physical development. Here we try to highlight the key, interrelated factors which lead to the large number of children living either homeless or in inadequate housing, alone or with their families.

Socio-economic factors

There are many socio-economic reasons behind the increase in the number of homeless children including children on the streets. For those children living within a homeless household, issues raised in Chapter 8 apply. A number of studies have identified household poverty to be the major 'push' factor. UNICEF (2008a) concludes that over 50 per cent of children in developing countries (more than 1 billion) suffer from at least one form of severe deprivation; around 700 million children suffer two or more deprivations. In many cases the situation is worsening. For example, current indications are that, in Sub-Saharan Africa, the percentage of people living on less than a dollar a day will reach almost 40 per cent in 2015.

Poverty plays a major part in children's having to satisfy basic needs from sources other than the household or family. In Ghana, Korboe (1996) indicated that a majority of Kumasi's street children are independent but originate from poverty-stricken homes. They are, therefore, working on the street as a survival strategy. Out of his sample of 74 children, only one of them did not cite financial need as a fundamental reason for being on the street. Beauchemin (1999: 9) noted that many parents do not feel obliged to take care of their children because, they believe, 'God will feed them'. Not all children leave home to provide only for themselves, however. In Zimbabwe, over 35 per cent of street children in one study left home to earn income for their families (MPSLSW, 2000). In this context, the view of homeless children as separated or estranged from their families is clearly false as they are actively contributing to the maintenance of the nuclear family and other family members.

Of the 3.8 million people living in extreme poverty in Peru, 2.1 million are children. Of the total of 10.2 million under-18 population, more than 6.5 million live below the poverty line (UNICEF, 2008b). They reside in informal peripheral neighbourhoods. The poverty of their dwellings, in many cases, is such that we would class them as homeless (see Chapter 5).

This extreme poverty underpins inadequate or lack of housing for many and leads some to leave home in search of better conditions. Matchinda (1999) noted a direct correlation between household income and the likelihood of children leaving home in Cameroon. The lower the family income level, the more likely it was that children would seek to fulfil their basic needs on the streets.

In India, 23 per cent of children in the Association for Development's (2002) sample gave 'search for employment' as the main reason for leaving home and 30 per cent cited 'looking for a better life'. The Department of Education in India estimates that Delhi has 100,000 street children who arrive in the metropolis from neighbouring states, generally in search of work. Most commonly they work as helpers in roadside restaurants and tea shops but another large number work as vendors. Many small industrial units depend heavily on child labour, despite anti-child labour laws and enforcement officers (Bannerjee Das, 2002).

Women's economic dependence on their husbands in developing countries, and lack of support for those who leave has a direct impact on both street children and other forms of child homelessness. For example, mothers are frequently unable to protect their children by taking them away from abusive situations. Thus, in some cases, children must leave alone, becoming children *of* the streets. Those mothers and children who do leave, or who are abandoned, are at greatest risk of extreme poverty and homelessness.

However, for some young people, homelessness is a planned and temporary situation. For example, in Ghana it is not uncommon for young girls to go to the cities to work for a while in order to earn money to buy household goods which will make them more eligible for marriage. While they are there, they often live in the street, bus station or lorry park to save money (Korboe, 1996)

The economic implications of major structural factors such as high birth rates, poverty and changing rural economies were once cited as the primary reasons for an increase in street living children (Lusk, 1989; Carrizosa and Poertner, 1992; Peralta, 1992). However, as noted in Chapter 8, not all poor people are homeless and not all homeless people are necessarily poorer than housed people; the same is true for homeless children. As Hecht (1998) notes, there are many complex reasons for children being homeless, especially in the case of those estranged from their families.

Abuse and family breakdown

There is a tendency, particularly in the media, to picture homeless children as either 'throwaways' or 'runaways' (Ennew and Swart-Kruger, 2003). Moreover, a focus on family dysfunction or breakdown presumes the existence of a single, preferred or most effective family type, which in a global, multicultural context is unlikely. Studies have shown street children to come from a wide range of family backgrounds (Espínola, 1988; Swart, 1988; Abdelgalil et al., 2004). Nevertheless, there is evidence that the stresses of poverty, and the erosion of traditional support networks, lead to increased family and relationship breakdown. Families under pressure of extreme poverty are more likely to be harsh on their children than those with adequate income (Moser, 1993; Bartlett et al., 1999).

In some countries, particularly in Africa, poverty is compounded by rapid social change affecting family formation and traditional kin-based support systems (Suda, 1997). In Ghana, some believe the growing exodus of children from the rural areas to the urban centres is linked to the breakdown of the nuclear family. There is also a perceived problem of parental neglect, irresponsibility and indifference (Beauchemin, 1999).

Family breakdown and abuse are frequently reasons given by street children for running away from home. Many researchers working with street children have noted that a high percentage have fled a violent or neglectful home and interviews with children suggest a higher rate of violence and abuse than some statistics might suggest (Newell, 1997; Bartlett et al., 1999; Ebigbo, 2003). This is true in industrialised countries as well as in developing countries. In a study of 120 runaway adolescents and their parents in USA, both groups reported high levels of family violence and sexual abuse (Whitbeck et al., 1997).

In a survey in Zimbabwe, while economic factors were a leading cause of children leaving home, family abuse also ranked highly, with 25 per cent of street children saying they had fled abuse or were 'fugitives from home' (MPSLSW, 2000). In Brazil, both Rafaelli (1997) and Ribeiro et al. (2001) noted abuse as the main reason for children leaving home. Ribeiro et al. (2001) also noted the significance of a mother's absence and family disintegration. They also pointed out that those who were returned to their families by the authorities, without support, quickly fled to the streets again. In Peru, research suggests that family violence and child mistreatment are the precipitating factors in 73 per cent of cases of children leaving home for the streets (Bustamante, 1999).

In a study of 201 street children in Cameroon, Matchinda (1999) found that abuse by parents or step-parents accounted for the running away of 23 per cent and 16 per cent of the sample respectively. In India, 47 per cent of children in the Association for Development's (2002) sample cited abuse by a parent as their reason for leaving home. In one study of street children in Kolkata, 7 per cent of the girls had been raped by their fathers, uncles or brothers (Banerjee and Sengupta, 2000).

In Indonesia, violence and neglect are mentioned in one study as main reasons for leaving home by 23 per cent of street children (Consortium for Street Children, 2004b).

A study of households in the very poor informal Sharabya area of Cairo found poor relationships between children and parents to be a main reason for children leaving home. In Sharabya, 45 per cent of fathers beat their children and 20 per cent of surveyed children stated that they had deserted the family or only return late at night to sleep (El-Sheikh, 2002). The study showed that 60 per cent of children have daily fights with their brothers because of overcrowding or violence from siblings.

The absence of a mother or father, by death, abandonment or parental separation, has been noted as a cause of many children leaving home. In the Cameroon study above, the death of a father or parental divorce both accounted for around 5 per cent of home leavers (Matchinda, 1999). Such a loss can be especially problematic when the parent is replaced by a step-parent. This quote from a South African street child is typical of the stories they tell: 'My mother's boyfriend used to abuse me when I was 6 years old because my mother is always sick and she is unemployed' (Olufemi, 2001: 104).

HIV/AIDS

In addition to the 5 million children who have been infected with the HIV virus, around 15 million children under 18 worldwide have lost at least one parent to AIDS. The impact of HIV/AIDS, coupled with a breakdown of extended families and a weakening of the bond between families, in the face of decreasing levels of reciprocity, has increased the number of 'homeless children' in many countries. Increasing numbers of relatives are shying away from taking care of orphaned children, leaving a child with nowhere to go other than the streets. In addition, in some places the traditional carers are already so overburdened with orphans that they cannot cope with any more, however accommodating they might wish to be.

In Sub-Saharan Africa, the worst-affected region, it is currently estimated that 9 per cent of all children have lost at least one parent to AIDS (UNAIDS et al., 2004). In Malawi and Lesotho, 17.5 per cent of children aged under14 are orphans, around 50 per cent of these having lost parents to AIDS. In Lesotho, where the epidemic is more recent but spreading rapidly, the number of AIDS orphans has been rising dramatically. Hunter and Williams (2000) estimated numbers of AIDS orphans in Lesotho to be 76,000 in 2000. By 2008 there was an estimated 100,000 AIDS orphans in the country (SOS Children's Villages 2009). In Zambia, there are estimated to be 1.7 million orphans, of whom 750,000 have lost both parents and 910,000 have lost their father. About 7 per cent of households have no adult member (Kelly, n.d.). Not all AIDS orphans are homeless and it is widely recognised that most Southern African orphans are cared for by their extended families (Barnett and

Whiteside, 1999). Nevertheless, in July 2006, Zambia's Health Minister estimated that 6 per cent of the country's AIDS orphans were homeless, with less than 1 per cent living in orphanages.

Conflict and disaster

An estimated 20 million children are currently 'displaced' by armed conflict or human rights violations alone (UNICEF, n.d.). UNHCR (2006) has age data on 7.8 million people who are classed by it as 'persons of concern'. Of these 45 per cent were children under the age of 18, with 11 per cent being under the age of 5 and 19 per cent between 5 and 11 years. The regional distribution shows that children and adolescents represent 54 per cent of persons of concern in East, Central and Southern Africa. The lowest proportion of children as persons of concern, at 26 per cent, is currently in the Americas.

Albertyn et al. (2003) report that modern wars have made 12 million children homeless in Africa alone. War and political violence are linked to the increase in children on the streets in northern Ethiopia and in Angola (Veale et al., 1993; Moberly, 1999). These, and the others surviving but affected, are sufficiently vulnerable and traumatised to have a greater chance of being homeless at some time in their lives than children not affected by war. Escalating conflicts in parts of the Middle East and Africa have contributed to the child homeless population. In Iraq, orphanages are being confronted with increasing numbers of abandoned or homeless children (Millar, 2006).

Political conflict brings with it increased poverty and rapid social change, especially to family life. As men go to war, are killed or incarcerated, women take on their roles, changing the family dynamic and the amount of time they can spend caring for children. This has been suggested as one of the causes of increased presence of children on the street in Nairobi during the Mau Mau uprising and the struggle for independence (Aptekar, 1994). In Zimbabwe, more than 150,000 children have been made homeless by the Government's 'Operation Murambatsvina'. Conservative estimates of the effects of the Maoist uprising in Nepal suggest that 2,000 children have been orphaned and 3,000 have become homeless (Singh et al., 2005).

Children's and women's rights

The United Nations Convention on the Rights of the Child (UNCRC) has become the most widely accepted legal instrument in the world. It details how children should be treated in relation to their protection, survival, development and participation in matters affecting them. Children's rights relating to housing and a home are embedded in a number of articles within the Convention. Article 23 on health, for example, emphasises the right to a living environment that promotes the highest attainable level of health. Whilst dealing broadly with standards of living, articles 18 and 26 stipulate that children have the right not only to shelter but to housing which can support physical and mental development. Moreover, this part of the convention also makes clear that, whilst parents have prime responsibility, the state is obliged to ensure that responsibility is met, providing support where necessary. In this respect alone, many millions of children around the world, living alone or with their families, on the streets or in inadequate dwellings, are failed by their government's inability to execute its commitment to the Convention through adequate housing supply systems.

Children's rights cannot be separated from women's rights. As Speak (2005) notes, children's homelessness can frequently be attributed to the failure of women's rights to ensure women's access to land and property and thus protect them from homelessness. As mothers, women's rights to housing are also enshrined within UNCRC and upheld by the 1990 World Declaration on the Survival, Protection and Development of Children in its Plan of Action. A particularly valuable and concise explanation of the Convention is given in Bartlett et al. (1999).

Despite the international recognition of children's needs for protection, they remain dependent on their parents for security. Many become homeless because not only children's property rights but also women's property rights are either not recognised or not upheld. Thus orphans and widows, or abandoned women and children, can find themselves with no rights to the family home and no rights, or economic ability, to buy land and establish a new home.

Land rights for women are only just being established in many countries. In Uganda, for example, women and children are made more vulnerable by the fact that women's equal rights to inherit are not yet recognised within legislation. Many of the more recent Land Acts, in Ghana, Tanzania and Uganda, for example, are couched in gender-sensitive terms, with clauses specifically relating to the equal access of women. However, in practice there is still considerable discrimination, and the complexity of customary, Islamic and constitutional laws which prevails places women at a disadvantage, meaning that, realistically, only women rich enough to buy land in their own right are protected (Benschop, 2002). Even where legal rights to land and property ownership for women have been enshrined within a county's legal system or constitution, enforcement is limited and cultural attitudes slow to change. The breakdown of relationships or widowhood can render women and their children homeless or trapped in dangerous situations.

Inheritance laws vary widely around the world, influencing the vulnerability of girls. For example, in Bangladesh, as in other Islamic countries, family law, based on religious law or *Sharia*, does not give women and girls a share of inheritance equal to men. A daughter only inherits half of the amount left to a son. This discriminatory practice is based on the assumption that a wife is maintained by her husband, and an unmarried daughter is maintained by her father. Regarding a Muslim wife's legal situation, Shamim and Salahuddin (1995: 43) observe, 'she is not obliged to give anything of her wealth, whatever she possesses to her husband, but he is obliged to maintain her even if she is rich and he is poor'. Unfortunately, in reality, the male-dominated society means that daughters very rarely receive their rightful share and wives and widows can seldom afford to resort to the courts (El-Sheikh, 2002). In Egypt, it has been noted that houses in informal neighbourhoods are often only 'owned' in the name of the male head of the household and disputes, where brothers try to exclude their sisters from their rightful share, are common (Benschop, 2002; El-Sheikh, 2002).

In some African matrilineal societies, it is common for a man's relatives to congregate near his home at the first signs of his impending death. They will settle the division of the property between them, according to their relationship with him, even before he dies. In some cases, close relatives will move into his house to protect their share. The widow is low down on the list of beneficiaries, and may be evicted, along with the children, to live on the street.

In many countries, children have no rights to inherit or own their family homestead. This is problematic for the many millions of African children whose parents have died from AIDS. There may be no formal system for them to take over ownership of the traditional family homesteads and land, so they may become homeless.

Children, crime and authority

Street children are often portrayed as petty criminals. In Zimbabwe, for example, one study noted that 63 per cent of respondents believed the majority of street children are engaged in criminal activities (MSPLSW, 1999). The types of crime most often associated with street children include harassment of motorists and pedestrians, food grabbing, stealing cell phones, bag-snatching and vandalism. In Peru, street children are commonly called *pirañitas* – little piranhas.

In South Africa, Cape Town Police blame the 150–250 children on the street for the majority of crime in the city centre, so they have borne much of the brunt of the recent 'zero tolerance' campaign. Cape Town youth workers are increasingly reporting that children are being harassed and beaten as a way to teach them to stay away from the downtown area. Street children are also being arrested, often without cause, and shipped off to Pollsmoor Prison, recently called the worst prison in South Africa by the South African Law Society (Samara, 2003). In Kenya, Kilbride et al. (2000) also noted police abuse of homeless children.

Certainly, homeless children are extremely vulnerable to being recruited into criminal gangs and illegal schemes. The Main Directorate of Internal Affairs (GUVD) in Moscow notes many homeless children being drawn into criminal activity (Stoecker, 2001). However, children are also adept at hiding and in Peru it is estimated that, while theft is a relatively regular way for street children to make a living, only 25 per cent of them are arrested by the police (Vasquez, 1997).

Nevertheless, there are, no doubt, hundreds of thousands of children incarcerated around the world, despite article 40 of the UN Convention on the Rights of the Child (UNCRC), which affords children the same legal protection as adults.[1] Many are held without legal representation or trial and sometimes in the most desperate of conditions. Accounts of torture and murder are commonplace (Bibars, 1998).

The exact number of children in conflict with the law worldwide over a given period is unknown. However, in September 1999, in South Africa alone, there were 2,026 children awaiting trial and 1,375 serving sentences (Government of South Africa, 2001). Not all of those arrested are homeless. In India in 1998, only 987 of the 18,923 juveniles under 18 arrested were homeless (Banerjee and Sengupta, 2000)

Many children suffer abuse at the hands of the police. In Bangladesh, violence against street children by police has been noted to take place in the three different settings: in the street, in a police station under 'safe custody' and in 'state custody' in juvenile correctional facilities and homes for vagrants (Khair and Khan, 2000). In Chittagong, 66 per cent of 246 children surveyed complained that they are mentally and physically abused by the police, railway police and the general public (Aparajeyo-Bangladesh, 2000). Of these, 79 children (68 boys and 11 girls) accused the police of abusing them. Participatory research conducted with these street children identified and prioritised eleven problems they face but the brutal treatment by law-enforcing agencies was their main problem (Khair and Khan, 2000).

> 'As we don't have any relatives in Dhaka City, we have to live under the open sky at night, after working hard for the whole day. We never get involved in any "bad" activities. Actually, we do not have enough time to do anything else, but work. The police pick us up every now and then without any specific reason.' According to our research, police caught 20 children out of 30 without having any specific case against them. These children were accused of 'sleeping on the street'. If children have no other option but to sleep on the street, is it their fault?
> (Khair and Khan, 2000: 27)

Ribeiro et al. (2001) noted that incarcerated Brazilian children complained about the aggressive treatment by guards, teachers and other children, as well as the poor conditions of their detention and of the time taken to reach judicial decisions. There have been well-publicised cases where street children have been shot by police in Brazil (Rizzini and Lusk, 1995) and in Davao City, the Philippines, by motorcycle-riding 'death squads' (PREDA, 1999). Human Rights Watch/America estimated that 5,000 children were murdered in Brazil between 1988 and 1991 (Lalor, 1999).

The Association for Development (2002) noted that almost 80 per cent of the Indian railway-platform children complained that the government railway police or the railway protection force beat them while they slept at night. Fifty-six per cent stated that the police demanded or snatched money from them.

Assaults or rape are rarely reported as girls complain that the police just make fun of them and do not provide any assistance or else take money from the accused boys and then let them go. In one Indian study, 64 per cent of those who were raped said the police refused to file a report. The police themselves are also accused of sexual abuse. The same study maintains that children in detention or remand homes are exposed to violence, abuse and unwanted sex there (Bhaumik and Srivastava, 2002). Similar stories of police abuse and refusal to help street children can be found in virtually all other developing countries.

Lifestyles, behaviour, survival and coping strategies

> . . . street children who have broken off from their families and fend for themselves have the greatest space to construct a world of their own. Many of them describe the freedom of the street as an intoxicating experience, and once a child has known it, he or she cannot go back to the constraints of family life. These children live in a heroic world where the ability to survive is attributed to their own wits and nobody else's. They care little as to whether they are considered children or adults.
>
> (Blanchet, 1996: 17)

Homeless children, whether *of* the street, *on* the street or part of homeless households, are a broad and diverse group. Many do, clearly, fit the image of vulnerable and victimised which the very term brings to the Western mind. Others, however, are strong, capable and independent. Some are even empowered by the act of leaving their families.

Some children are *on* the streets temporarily, returning to their families. Others, *of* the streets, are estranged from their families and remain living alone or in groups for many years. A study of 100 'railway children' in India noted that 64 per cent had no contact with their families. Of the 36 visiting their families, 8 per cent went once a week and 16 per cent once a month. The rest visited their families once a year (Association for Development, 2002). In Peru, Miranda and Salazar (2002) noted a third of children remained on the street for less than three months; a fifth between three months and one year; another third had been living on the streets for five years, and 11 per cent had been living on the streets for more than five years.

Education

There is some evidence in developing countries that household size influences the likelihood of poor children attending school, with larger numbers of siblings possibly being beneficial in this respect (Patrinos and Psacharopoulos, 1997).

Levinson (1991: 202) suggests that, in some cases, poor families prioritise the schooling of only one child, preferring to let others work to support the family.

Nevertheless, poverty appears to be one of the main causes of children dropping out of school, which is itself a precursor to homelessness for some children. The lack of education for all homeless children, and their low-skilled, poorly paid work is important – as Overwien (2000) notes, it is extremely difficult for children without education ever to make the transition from informal to formal employment.

In Egypt, Bibars (1998) notes that a high proportion of children on and of the streets have dropped out of school, either to work to help support their families or because of abuse from teachers. Indian statistics reveal that almost 100 million children in the age group of 5–14 years are out of school. These children are what Chaudhuri (1997) calls 'nowhere' children (Banerjee, 2000: 795). They are generally found in unorganised slums, at railway stations, beneath flyovers, etc. In Mumbai, D'Lima and Gosalia (1992) found that 30 per cent of school-aged street children had dropped out of school and 54 per cent had never enrolled.

Making an income

In Bangladesh, Rahman (1997) reports that, although there are about 16,000 working children in four metropolitan cities (including Dhaka), most of their activities require technical skills which few street children have. They must concentrate on unskilled work: hawking, portering and waste picking. Begging, as a last resort, is also prevalent. Korboe (1996) noted very similar types and levels of employment amongst street children in Ghana. Indeed the picture seems to be similar in most countries.

In India, many inexpensive eating places, both registered and unregistered, illegally employ children known as 'hotel boys'. Often employers choose homeless children from outside the city as they are less likely to know their legal rights and are amenable to taking orders. It is estimated that some 50,000 are employed in 11,750 hotels, restaurants, canteens and teashops in Mumbai (Patel, 1990). Most railway children in India worked as rag-pickers. Out of 100 respondents in a survey, 60 per cent are involved in rag-picking, 13 per cent sell various products and the remainder do any work that comes their way (Association for Development, 2002). The monsoon is a particularly difficult time for child rag-pickers as garbage is wet, heavy and cumbersome (Aashray Adhikar Abhiyan, 2001).

In Java and Sumatra up to an estimated 19,000 homeless children work daily on the *jermals*, or fishing platforms, surrounding the islands. Lured there by contractors promising high earnings, the children are exploited and receive around $1–$2.50 per week (Parker, 2002).

The types of work and amount of money children earn usually vary according to age and sex; older children and boys earn more than younger ones and girls. In Bangladesh, READ (2000) noted daily earnings then of Tk.10–20 per day. Although

Table 12.1 Monthly incomes and percentage of incomes saved by street
children in Ghana

Subpopulation	Income per month	Share of income saved (%)
Males	71,900	34
Females	61,600	43
Migrants	67,800	39
Non-migrants	64,800	33
'On the street'	73,150	34
'Of the street'	61,550	41
All	67,100	38

Source: Korboe (1996: 7)

there were cases where daily income exceeded Tk.100 per day, they were very few in number. The mean daily income found among 626 children in eight cities was Tk. 35 per day (just less than £0.50) of which mean saving per day was Tk.10. Similarly, in Ghana, Korboe (1996) noted that street children could earn enough to survive and even save (Table 12.1).

Homeless children generally earn less than non-homeless working children. A key difference between the two is the latter's access to capital, however small, to establish an enterprise and become self-employed. This self-employment makes a big difference to their income. From his study on working children in Bangladesh, Rahman (1997) reports that the average monthly income of the self-employed children was Tk.797 (£10) and the average monthly income of the child worker employed by others was Tk.369 (£5).

Sexual activity

In a study of 120 street children in Kolkata, 76 per cent (aged 8–16) reported penetrative sexual activity while 61 per cent reported sexual abuse (Banerjee and Sengupta, 2000). A Delhi study, which explored the sexual behaviour of street children living in railway stations, found that 'to them forced sex is just a way of life' (Rajkumar, 2000). One of the elder boys said in an interview, 'when I was growing up here the older boys had sex with me, now I have sex with the younger boys'.

Studies of street youth in South Africa have found that the street youths and children regularly sell sex for money, goods or protection (Swart-Kruger and Richter, 1997; Olufemi, 2000; Nkomo and Olufemi, 2001). An extensive study in eight cities in Bangladesh estimated that 12,000–15,000 street children are involved in prostitution, three-quarters of whom are girls (READ, 2000). Another countrywide survey of street children in Bangladesh found that girls generally enter prostitution between the ages of 12 and17 years and that around 50 per cent of these 'floating child prostitutes' were in this age range at any time (Rahman, 1997). In Kolkata, 19 per cent of girls in Banerjee and Sengupta's (2000) study supplemented their income through prostitution

Substance abuse

Life for street children is hard, with few pleasures. It would be surprising if drug use was not a feature of their lives. In many countries, both female and male street children use alcohol and other drugs to block out adverse physical conditions such as cold weather, hunger and physical pain (Olufemi, 1997, 1999; Seth et al., 2005).

A study conducted by the Association for Development (2002) at the railway stations of Delhi found that over 67 per cent of the children on the railway platform smoked cigarettes and 78 per cent regularly took drugs (48 daily, 10 often, 20 occasionally). The commonly used substances are correction fluid, cannabis, smack, and alcohol. Those using correction fluid said that they procured it from stationery shops while the drugs came from dealers inside the railway station or through friends. Considering their meagre incomes from rag-picking and other odd jobs, the amount they spend on drugs is high; over one-third spend more than Rs.50 per week and 10 per cent spend more than Rs.150 per week (Association for Development, 2002).

In Indonesia, a survey in 1999 found that more than 60 per cent of girls of the street are involved in substance and alcohol abuse. No figures are available for boys. Drugs are readily available in Semarang and dealers often target places where street children hang out. Locally produced alcoholic drinks can be bought by anyone at many roadside stalls and are relatively cheap (Rahardjo, 2002).

In Kampala, Young and Barrett (2001: 148) had to adapt their action research because they could not meet with street children at night as they were 'high on drugs'. Researching a group of mixed children of and on the streets in Brazil, Forster et al. (1996) found drug use to be a regular activity. Tobacco was the most frequently used drug but alcohol was also used. There was a higher prevalence of use of both among children *of* the street. Inhalants and cannabis were also used, mainly by children of the street. Sometimes these were used only experimentally. However, inhalants were used regularly by 42 per cent of the sample and cannabis was used regularly by 26 per cent. In some countries there has been a marked increase in the use of synthetic drugs such as amphetamines amongst the general drug-taking population and amongst street children. For example, Kulsudjarit (2004) noted that the abuse of amphetamines among street children has significantly increased in Cambodia.

West (2003) notes an even more sinister drug-related activity for street children, in that they are sometimes used as drug couriers by professional gangs in Asia and the Pacific.

225

Health and healthcare

Street children are highly susceptible to many adverse health outcomes related to their living style of extreme and high-risk personal behaviour (Ribeiro et al., 2001). Poverty, poor diet and the environment in which they live are the major drivers of poor health amongst street children. The urban environment in which homeless children live and sleep can be harsh for small and less than robust young bodies. Inhalation and ingestion of pollution can be particularly harmful to children sleeping amongst traffic or in unclean environments.

Lack of access to a balanced diet causes malnutrition that, in turn, has negative impacts on their normal physical growth and mental development. Lifestyles, sexual activity and poor hygiene also take their toll. A study of adolescents in Delhi found that 30 per cent of the boys had sex-related health complaints; 10 per cent had signs of syphilis. Infections in the urinary tract and around the genitals were common for girls (Rajkumar, 2000).

The popular image of street children begging or stealing to feed themselves is not necessarily true. Indeed, many, perhaps most, work and earn enough to buy food, although, as will be discussed below, their diets are meagre. In Zimbabwe, one study highlighted that 62 per cent of street children bought their food, 18 per cent gathered leftovers from restaurants and shops, 8 per cent relied on charities and drop-in centres and 9 per cent received food from their home (MPSLSW, 2000). Nevertheless, in general, both the quality and quantity of homeless children's food is very poor. In India, about 78 per cent of the street children are malnourished and 42 per cent severely malnourished (Kaur, 1997). This level is similar to that among other 'urban poor' children such as slum dwellers. About 70 per cent of street-dweller children suffered some form of growth stunting (Roy and Ray, 2000). Very few can afford breakfast and a large number of children have their first meal at midday.

In Bangladesh, available studies suggest that 65 per cent of the street children are able to eat at least twice a day (Aparajeyo-Bangladesh and Terre des hommes, 2000) but the quality of their diet is questionable. In a study conducted in Khulna, Barisal and Jessor, over 70 per cent of street children reported not being able to eat properly (DSS, 1999a). Street children usually buy their food from cheap pavement restaurants – *eetalian* hotels in popular vocabulary.[2] Those who eat prepared meals do so on the streets.

When they cannot afford to buy food, street children are known to beg or survive by scavenging rotten food from the dustbins and waste thrown away by restaurants. In Bangladesh DSS (1999a) reports that 23 per cent of the respondents used to meet their food requirements through door-to-door begging; in another study, 32 per cent survive on residual or waste food (DSS, 1999b). Similar tactics are adopted in other countries, as these two street children in South Africa explain.

I get food from the hawkers down the street and sometimes go to the Spar supermarket to beg for food. I also push trolleys in the evenings because I wake up late in the mornings. I get R2.50c for each trolley I push. I get my clothing from a shelter called INTUTUKO .

I push trolleys and park cars for survival and I get up to R20. There is a corner shop that gives us food at 2 p.m. daily so I don't have to go the soup kitchens. We also get help and clothes from the Central Methodist Mission

Access to toilets and washing facilities is problematic for homeless children, whether alone or within homeless households. For example, in Bangladesh, DSS (1999a) found that 78 per cent homeless children lived in an insanitary manner owing to the lack of facilities near their places of living and working. This is slightly less problematic in Dhaka where many public buildings (e.g. transport stations, vegetable markets) provide public toilets. There are also pay-to-use facilities specifically made available by different NGOs for the street children. This highlights the importance of small-scale provision of services to support unsheltered people to live with dignity. Much more could be done to improve this in cities around the world.

In Ghana, only 53 per cent of street children have access to bathrooms which are part of a house; 30 per cent pay to use commercial bathing places; the remainder bathe in the open and under cover of darkness. The fees per bathing are ¢50.00 for a bucket service and ¢150.00 for use of a shower. Table 12.2 shows the number of baths per month per person amongst categories of street children.

Homeless children have limited access to healthcare and, where it is available, several factors limit their use of it. Thus, they do not consult medical advice early enough and complications develop (Sherman, 1992; Pande, 1993). Ali and Muynck (2005) noted that street children in Pakistan preferred to self-medicate. The reasons for their reluctance to seek medical help included low perceptions of the severity of their medical condition, the cost of services, the waiting times, the negative attitudes of healthcare workers and mistrust of adult authority figures.

In South Africa mobile clinics are available to care for the medical needs of street and homeless children free of charge. However, where these do not exist, most hospitals or clinics do not attend to street children, leaving a gap in service provision (Ritchie, 1999). Hospitals often contact the South African Police Services (SAPS) and the Department of Welfare to investigate the identification of the child. This consultation with the police may deter some children from seeking medical attention.

In Mumbai, Patel (1990) asked street children about their strategy for coping with illness. Just under 30 per cent were looked after by friends, nearly 15 per cent simply fended for themselves. Over 40 per cent said they had gone to municipal or government hospital and clinics for treatment, indicating a wide knowledge

Table 12.2 Personal hygiene in Ghana measured by mean number of baths[a] per month

(Sub-) Population	Baths per Month
Males	21
Females	27
Migrants	23
Non-migrants	37
'On the street'	32
'Off the street'	16
All	24

Source: Korboe (1996: 9)

Note:
a In Ghana, a shower or all-over wash are referred to as a bath. Many houses only have a bathing enclosure either inside or just outside the house in public space into which a user carries a bucket of water, soap and towel.

of these services. Only 7 per cent sought private medical care, mostly when it was paid for by an employer who wanted to reduce the time a boy was away from his work (Patel, 1990).

Perceptions and characterisations

There is an ambivalence to public perceptions of homeless children. On the one hand, and particularly from a Western perspective, they are perceived as the most vulnerable of all homeless people to be pitied and cared for. On the other hand, they are seen by the public in many developing countries as scarcely human, criminals and social pariahs. Beazley (1999, 2000, 2002) notes that street-living children are either demonised by press and authorities or romanticised by charity groups. Broadly, however, public perceptions of street-living children are not favourable (Le Roux and Smith, 1998). For example, in Zimbabwe, a study found little sympathy for street children. About 35 per cent of the general public dislike them, 28 per cent are convinced that they are hooligans and about a quarter of the population want them removed from the streets (MPSLSW, 2000). Public perception changes as the 'child' grows older. For example, in Colombia, Aptekar (1988) noted that age was a child's enemy: younger children are pitied, helped and perceived as 'victims' while older ones are portrayed as 'villains'.

Antagonism towards homeless children results in stereotypical characterisations and labelling. In Peru, street children are commonly called '*pirañitas*', referring to small, aggressive piranha fish. In Semarang, Indonesia, they are ridiculed and called '*ionthe*', the insulting Javanese word for a prostitute.

There is some literature on how street children perceive themselves and their lives. According to Rahardjo (2002), Adidananta, an activist working with street children in Yogyakarta, notes that the homeless children there never use *gelandangan* or *tunawisma,* the accepted terms for homeless people, which they consider demeaning. Instead they call themselves *tikyan,* short for *sethithik ning lumayan,* a Javanese sentence which roughly translated means: 'just a little but quite adequate'.

Children's perceptions of their lives also differ from those of adults. Despite hunger, discomfort and danger, many younger children see their lives on the streets as lives of freedom and safety away from poor experiences of family, where they construct new 'families' and friendships (Ennew, 1994; Ribeiro et al., 2001). Others are less comfortable with their new lives and take longer to adapt or return home if they can.

Ghafur (2002) features a typology of street-based children, developed by Stoecklin (2000) in Chittagong, Bangladesh, which is based largely on their perceptions of themselves but also includes some references to the characteristics they epitomise. He develops six profiles as follows:

- *The hero*: this child is characterised by a strong sense of being virtuous against all odds. He/she does not stand injustice, fights to defend others, feels responsible for family members, generally has a good self-image and wants to be recognised as an honest street worker.
- *The hardworker*: he/she has strong willpower; sees him/herself as an honest and loyal contributor to family income and would just like to live a normal life as a street worker. Like the 'heroes' these children like to be in a peer group because it gives them opportunity to work in an organised way. They have a mixed image of themselves: as good and honest boys, but helpless, deprived and stigmatised as 'street children'.
- *The survivor*: these children are either orphans and engaged in work for their own and siblings' survival, or they are used for begging to benefit abusive step-parents. Facing violence on a daily basis (from adults and elder boys) their self-image is ambivalent: they have a negative self-image linked to their social position, while remembering love and affection of their family which helps them maintain some kind of positive personal identity.
- *The ambivalent*: any child in a street situation is somewhat ambivalent but these children have quite contrasting motivation, the heroes and the hard workers on the one hand are somewhat positive and show self-confidence. The survivors, the isolated and the dependent-abused on the other hand are rather negative and desperate. The ambivalent stands somewhere in between these two.
- *The isolated*: isolated children in the street have absolutely no group insertion. Some even refuse the group's lifestyle. They are usually newcomers and have no or quite weak work skills. Abandoned by parents or tortured and exploited by in-laws or older siblings, these isolated children are often abused and assaulted

by the mafia, the police and the general public. They feel apart from society: socially excluded, rejected, neglected, 'nobody'. Nevertheless, they tend to have a mixed image of self, mainly because they are not engaged in criminal activities.

- *The dependent-abused*: these children are in the street under close and abusive family supervision (mother, stepmother, stepfather). They have no independence, and all they can do alone is roam around and play for a few moments when they are not compelled to beg or work. Cautiousness and fear, and absence of group insertion and protection, prevent these children from acquiring work skills and the capacity for negotiation.

As children grow up, and public perceptions of them change, so too do the perceptions they hold of themselves and their street-based lives. They begin to resent the limitations of their existence and the stigma society places on them. The 'cute urchin' or 'victim' identity children can assume when they are young, and which can help them survive on the sympathy of adults, becomes inappropriate and unhelpful, indeed, unbelievable. It is at this point that some begin to miss the support of home and may decide to return (Aptekar, 1988; Boyden and Holden, 1991).

The 'careers' concept, discussed in Chapter 1, is valuable to understand the changes which street-living children undergo and how they adapt to them. It provides a framework for understanding how their changing experiences and perceptions over time might shape their behaviour and desire to escape homelessness as they get older. In Peru, Invernizzi (2003) explored how self-perceptions and social experiences over a child's years on the streets influenced a homeless career and dictate whether or not they chose to return home, if this was possible. Baker and Panter-Brick (2000) noted similar findings in Nepal.

Interventions

All the interventions discussed in Chapter 13 will ultimately help reduce homelessness amongst children. However, other, more specifically focused interventions are needed to address the needs of many currently homeless children, especially those living largely apart from their families.

Many governments do not see the issue of child homelessness or street children as their specific responsibility. For example, the Provincial Department of Housing in Johannesburg does not deal directly with homeless children. Policies, programmes and legislation on housing are made out of the assumption that there is a functional household with an adult at the head. Children are thus assumed to belong to a particular household that has the responsibility of caring for its children and meeting their housing needs.

At another level, however, it can be argued that no other form of homelessness has provoked as many interventions as child homelessness, particularly as it manifests in children *of* the street. Categorising children *of* and *on* the street as homeless (and homeless children as *of* the street) assumes they are equally without access to family. Moreover, it prioritises a socially constructed concept of the family which may be false in many contexts, regardless of housing situations, and which underestimates the value and importance of a range of extended kin and non-familial relationships.

Interventions can be broadly based or more tightly targeted. Broadly based interventions aim to improve opportunities and living standards for all poor children and, in so doing, work to prevent children slipping into homelessness. They are often operated by supranational agencies (e.g. UNICEF) or NGOs (e.g. Save the Children, Plan International) and are based on a set of broad themes. For example, between 2002 and 2005, UNICEF focused on five priorities: primary school education, early childhood development, prevention of disease and disability, stopping the spread of HIV/AIDS, and reduction in violence, exploitation, abuse and discrimination (UNICEF, 2002).

Such interventions are critical to improving the lives of children living in poverty and generate many more targeted interventions. Ultimately, they may well reduce the vulnerability to homelessness of future generations of children by limiting, or mitigating, the effects of poverty, violence and disease in destabilising households. However, even when policies translate into direct services for poor children, they do not necessarily specifically target, or are not accessible to, homeless children (Thomas de Benitez, 2003). Under pressure from output targets and 'success stories', practitioners may find it easier to contact and work with poor children within encouraging and supportive households. For example, it is easier to immunise or educate children in identifiable poor households in a settlement than it is to locate and treat the children of homeless households or children alone on the street. Moreover, such broadly based approaches often overlook the very specific needs of homeless children.

Targeted interventions seek to direct their attention specifically at street children. For example, street children were given priority in UNICEF's regional programme in Latin America and the Caribbean, developed in 1988 (Boyden and Holden, 1991). More recently, UNICEF has sought to target work with street children through local NGOs. However, targeted projects are more often associated with national or local governments, generally in association with NGOs.

By targeting projects directly at street children, it is easier to address their very specific needs which are, in some cases, more basic and extreme than those of housed urban children living in poverty, who have a greater chance of support from their families. However, one of the issues here is the criteria for accessing such services. Projects which seek to identify and engage street children, by working on the streets and focusing on the locations street children collect, hide and sleep, may unintentionally exclude the children of homeless households.

Within the two main approaches discussed above, specific interventions are developed which adopt, or are premised upon, different and contrasting attitudes to homeless children, especially to street children. Thomas de Benitez (2003) presents a threefold typology of interventions: *reactive, protective and rights-based.* Noting that the only appropriate approach is a rights-based one, she highlights that many governments develop or sanction reactive or protective interventions, both of which are unhelpful and ineffective in different ways. This section turns now to present some suggestions for interventions based on these three categories.

Rights-based approaches

Adopt and enforce women's and children's rights

Land rights for women are only just being established in many countries. Even where they exist, as discussed in Chapter 9, they may not be enforced. It is vital that governments adopt women's right to own land and actively ensure that this has priority over customary law, which is often gendered towards maintaining male hegemony. Governments should presume spousal co-ownership of property, ensuring women's rights to a fair share of property on the dissolution of marriage.

Likewise, inheritance laws vary widely around the world. The inequity iniquity in inheritance rights between boys and girls should be addressed. Particularly in the context of HIV/AIDS, many African countries could support children and prevent homelessness by rethinking a child's right to own property and land at an early age. For very young children this may require innovative interim tenure systems until the child is older.

Two ways of reducing the danger of 'property grabbing' for both widows and orphans is to promote knowledge of women's and children's inheritance rights and to encourage the writing of will, a practice not common in many developing countries. A study in Uganda, where property grabbing is common, highlighted that only 76.5 per cent of parents interviewed knew that children have a right to inherit property in the absence of a will. Even fewer (63.1 per cent) were aware that widows could inherit property in the absence of the will (Gilborn et al., 2000)

Empowering children

Implicit in children's rights is the idea that children, like everyone else, should be consulted and, indeed, participate in decisions about their lives. Informing and involving children can help them to understand changes to their lives which might otherwise lead them to feel rejected. For example, in Sub-Saharan Africa, many children are sent to live with relatives long before their AIDS-infected parents die but are not told why or involved in the decisions. The result is a feeling of rejection and children running away from their new carers to live on the streets. Informing them and involving them in the decisions may help them understand the reasons for their being sent away. Agencies working with HIV/AIDS families should adopt policies of open dialogue with children where possible. Such policies which seek to empower children, and inform them of their rights, might reduce disenfranchisement (Young and Ansell, 2003).

Reactive approaches

Reactive approaches are largely negative and see homeless children as at best a nuisance and at worst a threat to respectable society. They are based on the construction of homeless children as 'other' or villain, displaying deviant behaviour, outside socially acceptable norms (Holland, 1992; Aptekar and Heinonen, 2003). This view presents a moral platform for developing interventions which prioritise the higher values of society and good citizens over the actual needs of homeless children. Such ideas lead to arrests, beatings and murder.

As discussed in Chapter 13, begging and vagrancy should be decriminalised. This is even more important for children. Government should actively discourage harassment or beating of children by the police and other authority figures, introducing heavy penalties for those found guilty.

In countries where media are heavily state-controlled, perceptions can be manipulated such that the public do the work of controlling or removing street children themselves and there is little sympathy for those NGOs working to support homeless children. Where they are allowed to operate, reactive approaches also influence the ability of NGOs and others to perform appropriately for homeless children. For example, drop-in centres can be closed down or moved to the periphery of cities, out of easy reach of children, in an attempt to clear children away from city centres (Bartlett et al., 1999). Such tendencies should be avoided. Governments should actively support NGOs and other agencies supporting homeless children. This may mean resourcing them or it may mean simply allowing them to function in the most appropriate location, where they can be most effective.

Protective approaches

Many protective interventions are generally well meaning. However, they tend to seek to normalise children, integrating them into mainstream society, as much as they seek to provide what children actually need or want. They attempt to change behaviour and lifestyles to make homeless children conform to society's expectations. To this end, some interventions hold accommodation or food as a ransom, offering it as a condition of other 'services', such as education. Children are, however, adept at extracting what they need from projects and, to an extent, manipulating project workers to their own ends.

Project funding for many protective interventions, particularly those of international NGOs, such as Save the Children or Plan International, can be insecure, either for purely financial reasons or because of political constraints (Cooley and

Ron, 2002). This not only limits their effectiveness in the long term but damages their efforts to empower and support children in the short term, reinforcing children's suspicion and distrust of adult agencies. All efforts should be made to ensure sustainability of programmes and project work and to recognise that projects take time to develop and embed into children's communities and to become trusted and respected by them.

Although literature on street children highlights their agency and that many are empowered by their own independence, clearly some are apart from their families against their will through disaster or conflict. One approach to addressing the problem is 'repatriation', back to home villages, which under some circumstances might seem an honourable one. Nevertheless, there is evidence that it can be not only individually traumatic but also collectively lead to an increase in homeless children. For example, Veale and Dona (2003) question the relationship between socio-political and demographic change in Rwanda following the violence there and the creation of street children. They highlight that, following the 'repatriation' of children looked after in centres for unaccompanied children, the number of street children escalated. There is a suggestion that the previously existing kin-based support system had eroded to such a degree that it could not cope with the influx of children needing to be accepted into extended families. China, used a policy of repatriating children with their families wherever possible but abandoned it in 2003 (Li, 2002). To send children and adults to a 'home' rural area without addressing the underlying reason for their leaving in the first place is folly and likely to be unsustainable. Forced repatriation of children and family, against the express desire of either party, must end.

Globally, there is a wealth of both good and bad practice on homeless children available. This chapter has not sought to discuss it in detail because the very individual contexts of each country, culture, city, NGO, policy framework and child make replication difficult. However, there are some broad lessons to learn.

Interventions in relation to homeless children cannot be prescriptive. They must recognise the enormous diversity of homeless children from those within homeless households, to those on the margins of the household and family unit, to those willingly or unwillingly estranged and separated. What they must not do is seek to use the provision of services as a means to force children to conform to a socially accepted norm. Nor should they seek to prescribe parental or child behaviour based on idealised notions of the family.

Interventions should, first and foremost, seek to provide for homeless children's basic needs, as dictated by children themselves, without compromise or qualification. Second, they should seek to protect children from unjust interventions by police or other authority figures. Third, interventions should recognise the very great capabilities and strengths homeless children develop in their fight for survival. Finally, they should empower children to engage in mainstream society as they see fit themselves and at a pace dictated by them.

13 Towards strategic interventions for homeless people

This chapter discusses current and proposed policy interventions for people who are homeless. These can be seen at a number of different levels. At one level, they include interventions to improve the housing market in order to address the housing shortage underpinning much of the problem in developing countries. At other levels, they include policy addressing welfare support and the legal context of the homeless population and those facing, or who are already victims of, major trauma such as eviction and disaster.

Intervention in homelessness is probably as old as the recognition that there were homeless people in society; the major religious creeds enjoin assisting those who are destitute and without a home. In the modern era, early accommodation-led responses to destitution and homelessness, such as workhouses in the UK (Driver, 2004), tended to be punitive. They emphasised the need for homeless people to mend their ways and adopt conventionally respectable lifestyles. As these harsh institutions were phased out in the post-Second World War welfare state, the emphasis of policy turned away from housing. Assistance for homeless people through the 1950s and 1960s tended to be through the welfare ministries or departments of local authorities rather than housing departments. The film *Cathy Come Home*,[1] screened in the UK in 1966, led to a change in public opinion and policy back towards housing. The UK Housing (Homeless Persons) Act of 1977 shifted responsibility away from welfare services and onto housing departments. However, the idea that some households were more deserving than others was enshrined in the legislation (Neale, 1997). The impact of this for current UK legislation is discussed in Chapter 4.

Much of the discussion of interventions in homelessness in the industrialised world concentrates on aspects of the accommodation–services mix offered to homeless people and the way people can be enabled to access existing housing (see e.g. Edgar et al., 1999: 56). In the developing countries context, however, where a lack of housing is both obvious and of major proportions, we feel it is worth concentrating some of our attention on accommodation-led policy to mitigate homelessness.

Current practices in addressing the needs of homeless people

Traditional means of helping the most vulnerable

In many developing countries, traditional social systems have catered for anyone who became destitute or lost their home. As discussed in Chapter 8, family values, neighbourly relations, obligations under Islamic social structures, etc., have all been important to ensure that no one was left without assistance. Many of these were confined to rural communities but others persisted in urban areas also, especially where there has been a long history of urban living. In West Africa, for example, the family house provided a place where any family member could go to live at minimal or no cost and with others around to support them (Amole et al., 1993).

Kamete (2001) provides a useful review of traditional systems in Zimbabwe which are reproduced, in many variants, around Africa and elsewhere. As can be seen from Table 13.1, the traditional system in Zimbabwe was well able to care for those who fell on hard times or could not cope with ordinary life. In 2001, however, it was already beginning to break down even before the more recent catastrophic economic times.[2] Where once help was given as an expected obligation of stronger members of extended families, now assistance is often expected to be reciprocated with rewards at least in the medium term.

While it is difficult (and may be unacceptable) to tinker directly with social networks, it is possible to restore the physical and fiscal contexts in which they thrived. Government and NGO interventions that can reinforce surviving traditional safety nets and, if possible, reintroduce those that have recently disappeared, could help vulnerable people to survive without other help. For example, the family house culture can be encouraged by banking practices which enabling joint-owners and owners-in-common[3] to raise capital together for maintenance, by planning regulations that allow incremental building of large structures, and by inheritance laws which protect family loyalties. Similarly, the family itself can be protected and enhanced by laws governing taxation, marriage and divorce, and assistance with children's health, education and subsistence.[4]

There is a danger, however, that traditional safety nets might act negatively for some actors. For example, the marriage of a widow to her brother-in-law may be welcomed by her or cause her much distress. It may prevent her from becoming homeless or it may drive her to leave the home and live on the street in order to protect herself and her children. Interventions must, therefore, be sensitive and be constantly subject to monitoring.

Table 13.1 Traditional responses and assistance to the potentially homeless in Zimbabwe

	What happened traditionally	The status of the traditional system
Inability to afford shelter	If temporary, informal loans from friends and relatives; if permanent invited to share or provided with lodging with friends, relatives or tribes-people.	Still intact in terms of informal lending and organising accommodation elsewhere. Sharing is only acceptable in the form of temporary lodging.
Infirmity	The sick one is take in if the illness is not prolonged. Relatives (sometimes friends, employers and workmates) are obliged to contribute to help the caregiver.	Still working for short periods of serious illness. If illness is prolonged, the contributions are used to send the patient to their rural home or to hospital.
People in crisis[a]	Ready help for short periods; relatives chip in and may distribute members of a large household among themselves (those who have houses or are allowed to have lodgers by the landlord/lady).	Still being practised but for very short periods as the affected people recover. If it is prolonged, contributions are made to send them to the rural home. Relatives may continue to take care of school children until the end of term or year.
Orphans	Extended family members are obliged to help take care of all orphans. Immediate family (uncles, aunts, and siblings) have the prime responsibility. Cousins and others assist if these are not able or willing. The load is shared.	This is still practised but is disintegrating among an increasing number, especially with HIV/AIDS. If there is an inheritance, relatives will offer to take care of the orphans who may later be thrown out. Older girls fare better.
Young people leaving home	If they have relatives in the new location, they take the person in. If not, it is the duty of immediate family adequately to prepare the individual.	This is still practised for job-seeking, education and medical care. At times, if the stay is prolonged without benefits, or the expectation of such, the young person is no longer welcome.

Source: After Kamete (2001).

Note a This covers economic, social and political crises.

Housing supply

As we have argued, housing supply is at the core of homelessness in developing countries. If countries can keep pace with population growth and make up the backlog of appropriately priced housing supply, many homeless people can find accommodation. In addition, many who currently become homeless because they cannot find independent housing at a price they can afford will be able to find what they need. In the struggle to keep pace with the need for housing for the lowest-income households, countries have performed very differently and with a variety of emphases. In Peru, for example, the tolerance of invasions of peripheral land, with subsequent formalisation, service provision and loans, has allowed many thousands of homeless and potentially homeless households to develop their own secure dwelling, even if it has taken many years to build (Miranda and Salazar, 2002).

Other countries have used direct supply both for low-income housing generally and for the very poorest households. China, South Africa and some Indian states have been directly involved (with private-sector partners) in supply for low-income households generally. China has been particularly successful in scale and in keeping the supply of low-income housing ahead of the growth in population (Wang, 2004).

South Africa is an important case as it made a substantial break with the policies of the past and devoted relatively large efforts to catching up on low-income housing supply. Most housing policies there, after 1994, have been guided by the basic needs approach of the ANC's Reconstruction and Development Programme (RDP, 1994) which has, as its main feature, subsidised low-income housing provision. The subsidy is a one-off grant in the form of a plot and dwelling, or other housing improvements, available to households living on less than R1,500 per month.

The subsidy amount has changed several times; in 2002, around the time of the CARDO survey, it was increased from R16,000 to R20,300, with a specially high subsidy for people with very low income, disabled people and elderly people of R22,800 (Napier et al., 2003). In 2007, the subsidy for households on R1,500 or less was about R34,000 (c.£2,500) (Rust, 2007). Above this income, the subsidy amount reduces until it disappears altogether at a monthly household income of more than R3,500.[5] More than 80 per cent of the subsidies were project-linked, in which an NGO implemented a project using future residents' subsidies to repay its capital investment and often including several years of community training followed by participatory construction to maximise recipients' benefits from the process (Napier et al., 2003).

The bulk of subsidies have been delivered to households in the lowest income band but there has been substantial post-project raiding of subsidy housing by higher income groups offering cash or gifts for the dwellings, often not to their real value. However, many households moving from informal settlements, where they pay no service charges, find the new dwellings too far from their workplace and the new compulsory payments too high. Thus, they sell out and move back

13.1 In South Africa, subsidy houses (the three at the top of the picture) are built for people living in informal settlements (in the foreground). Even where no locational disadvantages occur from the move (as here), many feel that the increase in costs involved in moving to the new and formal dwellings are neither affordable nor worth the improvement in housing conditions.

into informal neighbourhoods. There are waivers and reductions available for the poorest ('indigent') households but these do not seem to be preventing the very poorly paid from being excluded by their own reluctance or inability to take on the overhead costs of 'going formal' (Napier et al., 2003). Figure 13.1 illustrates the difference between subsidy dwellings and those in informal neighbourhoods, but the move may not be worth the increased cost for many households.

Many national programmes aimed specifically at the lowest-income population have run into the problem of targeting a benefit to the poorest that others higher up the income scale lack. Thus, Bangladesh's *bastuhara* (homeless) housing was taken over by middle-income households (Tipple and Ameen, 1999; Ghafur, 2002). In the same way, anecdotal evidence from India in 2008 suggests that many of the plots intended for squatters cleared from central locations around Old Delhi have been bought up by middle-income households for development as rental housing for lower-income households, despite their distant location and lack of servicing.

Improving the conditions of inadequate housing reduces the number of people whose accommodation is so poor that they can be regarded as homeless. It also makes good use of the existing stock, in some cases transferring it into the category of 'formal housing stock' and prevents it from entering the 'to be replaced' column in the housing supply calculation. The in-situ upgrading of informal settlements through the provision of water and sanitation services, power supplies and access routes is important in reducing homelessness. In most of the CARDO study countries, in-situ upgrading is done, at least in some types of neighbourhoods. By carrying out such work, governments are signalling to the residents that they can stay and implies increased security of tenure. Thus, households begin to invest in their homes whether they actually have improved security of tenure or not.

Some NGOs are involved in upgrading, also. In Egypt, the Coptic Evangelical Organisations for Social Services (CEOSS) and Plan International have both carried out several upgrading programmes in very poor neighbourhoods (El-Sheikh, 2002).

Night shelters

UNCHS (2000) features interventions in North America in which people are protected from freezing to death in winter. Shelters specifically designed for homeless people have been considered in only a few of the countries in the CARDO survey, and developed only in Bangladesh,[6] India and South Africa. In India, local authorities or HUDCO have provided night shelters in major cities, such as New Delhi, but they have not been very popular. The main concerns seem to be about personal security, location, lack of storage, sharing with other castes, having to separate household members by gender and poor hygiene standards (Garg, 1999). In winter, local authorities in New Delhi provide large tents as emergency night shelters to prevent people dying from hypothermia and cold-related illnesses.

Shelters are provided by NGOs and faith-based organisations in many cities in the developing world. In some cases these seem more popular, partly because they are clean and occupants have a stake in how they are run. For example, Aashray Adhikar Abhiyan run several shelters near Old Delhi (Figure 13.2) in which rules and modes of operation are agreed with the clientele. In Kolkata, the Lutheran World Service and the Ramakrishna Mission have shelters, and Mother Teresa's Nirmal Hriday provides shelter for the destitute (Bannerjee Das, 2002). In Santiago, Chile, Hogar de Cristo have shelters but theft is a concern within them (Bernasconi and Puentes, 2006).

In South Africa, shelters exist but are provided by less clearly defined organisations and controlled by the strongest of their residents. For example, Petanenge House in Johannesburg accommodates 185 homeless people in a building that was abandoned by its owners after a serious fire. Similarly, Glue House in Johannesburg accommodates 1,500 homeless people in a former barracks (Olufemi, 2001).

Assisted returns to rural areas

There have been several institutionalised attempts to encourage or force homeless people to return to the rural areas from whence they migrated. Repatriation

13.2 An NGO-run hostel for men, women and children in a former school in central Delhi. Several services such as advocacy, schooling, health, etc., are provided on site and residents can stay for many days at a time. (Photograph by Tony Pietropicolo)

stations were used in China to send *mangliu/sanwurenyuan* back to their places of registration before August 2003 and many millions of people passed through them (Li, 2002). Their conversion into places where people can be helped, rather than sent back to a rural life they have opted to leave, is an improvement.

In Bangladesh, there have been several programmes aimed at resettling homeless people back in their rural home areas and enabling them to establish livelihoods there.

- The Ghare Phera (Return Home) Programme was launched by the Bangladesh Krishi (Agricultural) Bank on 20 May 1999, at a time when the state was evicting people from slums and squatter settlements. Micro-credit is available at a flat rate of 10 per cent per annum. In the first two years, 2,372 slum dwellers and squatter households (or 14,220 people) received Tk.42.2 million as loans and allegedly went back to 31 rural districts (Ghafur, 2002).
- The Adarsha Gram (Ideal Village) Project establishes cluster villages on state-owned *khas* land or on *char*[7] land, to help households who have lost their land through river erosion. Recipients are involved in establishing homesteads and community facilities, including latrines, kitchens, tubewells and community centres. The target is to establish 1,104 Adarsha Grams for 45,647 homeless households (Ghafur, 2002).
- The similar Asrayan (Shelter) Programme promotes shelter and socio-economic development for homeless households. Housing is provided in barracks, each

accommodating ten dwellings of 21 square metres, with only basic servicing. It is intended that 50,000 homeless households will receive 0.8 acres of *khas* homestead land, in the joint ownership of wife and husband, and micro-credit for income-generation activities (Ghafur, 2002).

While these programmes have had differing levels of success across the country, they are part of the evidence that the Bangladeshi government has been concerned with poverty alleviation as its stated policy priority. In this way, it is addressing, with varying success, landlessness and destitution, the long-term causes of homelessness.

Food distribution

Some interventions with homeless people are survivalist in intent. They endeavour to keep people alive and well rather than move them out of homelessness. Like some night shelters discussed above, food distribution is in this vein. It has long been conducted by religious groups and other NGOs – so much so that the 'soup-kitchen' or 'soup-run' is a regular part of the popular conception of homeless people's lives. The Sikh community provides a unique service to homeless people in India. Every *gurudwara* (Sikh place of worship) provides simple food to all-comers. In addition, Sikh business people carry van-loads of hot food out to street dwellers in the major cities to regular places and at regular times. In New Delhi, street dwellers can be found, early in the morning, lining the pavement edge on a highway near the Red Fort awaiting the food distribution (Figure 13.3). In addition, the injunction to give alms in many religions allows many homeless people to survive on food hand-outs.

13.3 On a Delhi morning, as the rush-hour traffic builds, homeless men await a regular charitable food distribution by the Sikh community. (Photograph by Graham Tipple)

Proposals for interventions to help homeless people

Improve the context of homelessness

Honour housing rights

According to UNCHS (n.d.: para. 48) few states devote the 'maximum of available resources' towards the full realisation of the right to adequate housing as they are required to by housing right declarations. In this context, the guidelines laid out by UNCHS, as the international body responsible, suggest that states should give enforceable rights to homeless individuals, couples or families to 'the provision by public authorities of adequate, self-contained affordable land or housing space, of a public, private or cooperative nature, and which is consistent with human rights standards (para. 44).

Additionally states should give 'a measure of priority' to the housing rights of the most poorly housed in housing law and policy (UNCHS, n.d.). However, we demur from the 'self-contained' nature of the housing recommended for reasons of high cost. As explained above, many millions of households can only afford shared services and multi-habited accommodation.

It is important to recognise, however, that upholding someone's rights to housing by moving them off the street and into a resettlement area may actually worsen their situation. Issues such as less central location and new duties to pay property taxes and service charges may remove any advantage gained from the improved tenure and turn the relocation to secure tenure into a harmful development. A similar point was made by Turner (1976) over 30 years ago in the context of relocating squatters to peripheral formal housing estates.

UNCHS (n.d.) also calls for progressive improvement in the laws of states, with respect to housing issues, in line with international law. Thus, laws on evictions, security of tenure, landlord–tenant relations, equitable access to land, housing credit, subsidies, etc., and emergency housing for the poorest, should be improved in line with human rights declarations.

Recognise the contribution of homeless people to the economy

In industrialised countries, people classed as homeless are mostly perceived as a drain on the economy, requiring welfare assistance to keep going but creating little wealth through whatever work they may do. In developing countries, however, the situation is very different. The great majority of homeless people there appear to be in work and not just in marginal, street-based economic activities such as guarding cars and begging. Unless the differences between homeless people in the mainly industrialised country literature and those in the reality of developing countries is recognised, it is unlikely that positive views of homeless people, and their contributions, will be held by policymakers.

When homeless people are evicted and moved away, the economic repercussions are felt by many city-centre businesses and households. The security guards, cleaners, market porters, transport workers, garbage collectors, house maids, nannies and many others will not turn up for work the next day. The working mother who runs a department in a bank will have to take the day off work to find a new nanny for her children. The delivery of food will not be made because the driver cannot report for duty. The ice will melt awaiting the porter to take it to the butcher's shop from the market. The streets will remain strewn with litter because the sweeper does not live close by any more. These and thousands of other crises will disrupt the smooth flow of commerce and production in the city because a group of homeless people have been evicted from their open space and resettled 40 kilometres away.

Moreover, rapid physical development in many developing cities is completely dependent on the labour of migrant workers, prepared to live either homeless or in grossly inadequate housing and work for minimal wages. Municipalities and developers alike should be encouraged to provide at least basic shelter and services for the workforce which is so vital to the massive building projects under way in the developing world. For example, Figure 13.4 shows the makeshift shelters of a group of migrant labourers who worked on the building of a major road in Bangalore. The men, and their households including young children, had lived in these conditions

13.4 Staying close to their work-site (in the background), these construction workers' dwellings in Bangalore have been moved and assembled many times as the road progresses. By recruiting men off the street or in the rural areas, who are then joined by their families, construction companies are major actors in homelessness in India. (Photograph by Suzanne Speak)

for several years, following the road as it progressed. The construction company had agreed to provide adequate shelter for its workforce, but the agreement was not enforced.

Adopting a more positive attitude to the contribution of homeless people to both local and national economic activity might promote more appropriate policy measures to assist homeless people to continue with their livelihoods while benefiting from some improvement in their shelter conditions and general welfare.

Count using most effective methods

Counting is a first stage in understanding the need for assistance for homeless people in developing countries (Bernasconi and Puentes, 2006). This is recognised by the SDI initiatives in which inadequately housed people under threat of eviction carry out self-enumeration. In developing countries, information is power. When a group who have been ignored can go to the City Hall and confront policymakers with a line such as 'there are 20,000 of us and what are you going to do about it', they have much more chance of leveraging benefits than if they remain hidden and easy to ignore.

It is important, therefore, that countries take steps to include homeless people in their statistics. Spot checks are notoriously inadequate for accurate enumeration but, in many countries, they would be a great improvement over no counting at all. The inclusion of homeless people in censuses at least recognises that they are part of society with rights and making contributions to society, just as the housed population does.

Use terms other than 'homelessness'

We suggest that the term 'homelessness' has been used too widely and in too all-encompassing a manner to be helpful in developing solutions to the problem of lack of adequate accommodation or those things which 'home' is supposed to provide. In choosing what might be more helpful terms, we would suggest beginning by avoiding the problem term 'home' which includes many implications of comfort, belonging, safety, etc. It is evident from our own empirical work that some people living in the most inadequate housing do feel a sense of home, while some people in good-quality accommodation but, for example, experiencing family violence, are not at home in their dwelling. There is, therefore, a need to develop a new language which helps to identify and prioritise those in need of improved accommodation.

We also suggest moving away from the word form '—lessness' as a means of removing the clumsiness which this seems to impose. We suggest the form 'un—ed' instead. We recommend the term 'unsheltered' for those without any form of tenure rights or shelter; those on rungs 1 and 2 of the ladders in Tables 5.1 and 5.2. The term unsheltered implies only what is the reality of their accommodation; they lack shelter. Those within publicly roofed places, such as stations, may not feel the rain but they are likely to be vulnerable to the other vagaries of the weather (cold, wind, etc.) and to arbitrary attack and being moved on. 'Unroofed' would probably serve as well but it sounds more appropriate for a building than a household or person. Unsheltered is equivalent to rooflessness, i.e. sleeping rough, as suggested by Daly (1994), UNCHS (1996) and Edgar et al. (1999) and close to the Spanish term *sin techo* (without a roof).

If we include those who have only brief rights to remain on land and a reasonably waterproof roof, such as tarpaulins, or plastic sheets, but incomplete walls/doors, people on all the first three rungs of Tables 5.1 and 5.2 could be termed 'unhoused' – those who are not housed. Unhoused seems especially relevant as, in engineering, 'housing' refers to a fully enclosed case and support for a mechanism. Similarly, 'to house' in nautical language[8] means to stow securely (of cargo or the anchor) or to make secure an upper mast alongside a lower one. If mechanisms, stored goods or masts come adrift, no longer where they should be, they may be said to be unhoused. They are still there, probably undamaged and capable of resuming their task, but out of their intended location and place of security. There seems to be some resonance with this in the situation of those coping under the most rudimentary of structures or making do with shelter from cover which is available to the general public. They are adrift, vulnerable, but still whole and capable of functioning given the opportunity.[9]

The floating populations of China and Bangladesh bring to mind the term 'rootlessness' which, to follow our syntax, might be 'unrooted' or, better perhaps, 'uprooted', but this does not imply any shelter conditions.

The differentiation used in India between street dwellers, those who have no home in the city but the street, and street sleepers, those who have a home nearby but relieve crowding in it by sleeping on the street outside (Bannerjee Das, 2002), seems helpful where this occurs. In this context, it may also be relevant to adopt terms such as 'people *of* the street' and 'people *on* the street', echoing the terms used for children *of* and *on* the street, to differentiate between those who have no dwelling and those who have a home somewhere near but find it more convenient to use street space at night. We are unsure whether it would be helpful to use these terms for those who live unhoused lives in the city while having dwellings in the rural home area available to them but too far from their employment to be of any use as their accommodation. We do not, however, feel the need to use these terms in the arguments presented in this book.

On rung 4 and above, in Tables 5.1 and 5.2, all households could be regarded as inadequately housed, not unhoused or homeless. The major characteristic which sets these apart from the unhoused is the ability of people living in such housing to improve their accommodation and other circumstances. People in informal settlements are more likely than unhoused people to see themselves on an upwards housing trajectory, on which their shelters and the services provided are likely to improve over time. [10] This is, perhaps, the key difference between people who are in particular need of assistance and those who are not. In most cases, unhoused people do not perceive themselves to be on an upwards trajectory. In particular, as they live in almost constant fear of being moved on, they are most unlikely to invest in their dwellings. This is probably one of the most important points coming out of our case studies to differentiate people in informal settlements from street dwellers who have shelters. If the circumstances of a settlement enable its denizens to improve their lives, we would argue that they should not be regarded as homeless and the housing should be included in the housing stock calculation, albeit with caveats on the need to improve it substantially.

For households who rent rooms or spaces, we would classify those on rungs 1 and 2 in Tables 5.3 and 5.4 as unhoused but no one as unsheltered. In some countries, where sharing is unacceptable to the majority of the population (e.g. where privacy norms are very strict), rung 3 might be included but this would not be so in any of the CARDO study countries.

The task of differentiating linguistically among varying degrees of inadequate housing is still to be resolved and may be a study in itself. We have pointed out the importance of some security of tenure and a lockable door, and the disadvantages that not having them impose. We hesitate to continue the syntax of naming with 'unlocked', neither do we suggest 'locklessness' in the old syntax with any conviction, but there does seem to be a need for a term for those whose housing does not protect person or goods. 'Unlockable' may be suitable or, harking back to Oscar Neumann (1972), 'Undefensible'.

We are aware, however, that using language which emphasises the accommodation situation at the expense of the concept of 'home' brings its own problems. First, as identified above, it does not include many millions of people who are adequately housed but whose accommodation lacks the attributes of home to do with feeling comfortable and safety. In particular, this would include people experiencing family violence and who might be trapped in this circumstance by the home. This is particularly relevant as much of the discussions of homelessness is based at household level and does not differentiate between the situation of different members within it (women, children, older people) or their security.

Second, in emphasising the inadequacy of accommodation, we run the danger of overlooking the very great degree of emotional investment and social capital which is evident in even the most abjectly inadequate settlements. The results can be relocation which, even though it might improve accommodation, destroys communities and social networks and exacerbates poverty. An alternative view, which does not privilege physical attributes, might result in upgrading which tends to keep social and emotional capital largely intact and encourages their in situ reinforcement.

The terms suggested are intended to start off a process of discussion and refinement rather than being put forward with confidence that they are likely to be universally acceptable. We will use them, where appropriate, in this chapter.

Proposals for housing interventions

Addressing the unhoused – inadequate housing duality

The coexistence of different levels of inadequate housing and no-housing-at-all calls for a more moderated approach to housing supply at the bottom of the range and below the reach of the market. As we have argued elsewhere, simply calling all those in inadequate housing 'homeless', as is the current habit, is not helpful for housing supply policy or for developing other specific interventions aimed at the most vulnerable. It is neither affirming to those who have succeeded in providing themselves with some shelter and feeling of belonging (albeit in 'inadequate housing') nor does it empathise with those whose lack of shelter and detachment from mainstream society require special measures. Two examples might help to illustrate the differences between those who are currently inadequately housed and those who are unhoused.

First, imagine a household whose head earns a daily living as an auto-rickshaw (*bejak*) driver in Jakarta and who have erected a small wood and corrugated iron shelter in an informal and unserviced settlement on a river bank from which the woman of the house sells snacks to neighbours and passers-by. The needs of such a household may best be met, in the short to medium term, by flood control measures (a public good paid for by the city) and clean water and sanitation services (for which they would pay economic charges). In the longer term, an increase in the low-cost housing supply, so that it is no longer so difficult to obtain, is likely to help them secure affordable formal housing.

Second, and in contrast, imagine a household of a market porter in the Old City of Delhi whose work is intermittent and depends on his being at the market before the city wakes up. His wife picks up small labouring jobs on construction sites around Connaught Place. They sleep under a tarpaulin shelter outside the Jamaa Masjid (the largest mosque in Delhi). Their needs are unlikely to be met by the neo-liberal enabling of increased housing supply through freeing up the supply chain. Even more certainly, the current Delhi Development Authority allocation of resettlement plots in peripheral neighbourhoods is both beyond their means and completely unsuitably located. Their acute need may best be met through the provision of public taps and toilets and almost cost-free (and, therefore, subsidised) rooming accommodation close to the central employment concentrations.

Both households would benefit from improved servicing (water and sanitation at different levels for the inadequately housed) and accommodation improvements (one in improving the physical safety of the shelter, the other in providing some centrally located accommodation the unhoused households can afford). The first, however, can be implemented without subsidy with some hope that the beneficiaries can meet all of the cost. It deals with the household as a private unit living an independent existence in its own dwelling or room. Moreover, it can be replicated to huge numbers of households because there is no long-term charge to the state or city.

In contrast, however, the second must be subsidised so that it can be provided, and there is no hope of full reimbursement by the users. It accepts that less-than-private accommodation might be suitable as a welfare measure for people with little medium-term hope of an independent dwelling where they need it to be. However, it would provide for a few in society who need help at the most basic level, at least for a short time.

It is evident from research on people living in the most extreme poverty, in this volume and by others (e.g. Rust, 2007), that some households cannot be reached effectively by the market. This is particularly the case when interventions improve standards and impose a transaction cost in the formalisation process. An example of this is when squatters in South Africa receive the free (subsidy) house but have to start paying for services which they either coped without or did not pay for in their previous location. Further assistance is given to the poorest to help pay for this but those who do not qualify have to increase greatly their housing and related payments (Napier et al., 2003).

If we are to reduce the number of inadequately housed people, some in-situ raising of standards is necessary and may price many households out of the market. The lessons of the Making Markets Work for the Poor (MMW4P) programmes developed by SIDA and DFID (DFID, 2005) are useful here; markets should be utilised to house the poorest but in ways in which they work on their behalf. Thus, measures to increase the reach of markets down the income range, for example, through demand-side subsidies, and means of redistributing market benefits, through cross-subsidies from better-off households, could be employed in the housing sector. However, though these can be very helpful in extending the number of households within the ambit of the market, there will always be some who fall into the supra-market zone who need to be helped directly through non-market mechanisms such as direct welfare.

In the following, we address how special arrangements need to be made for the unhoused while the enabling approach may be appropriate for inadequately housed households.

Treating the unhoused as special cases: a framework for approaching interventions on shelter among unhoused people

Once the limits of the enabled market are recognised, there is a strong case for treating the unhoused differently. The major difference would be in resuming subsidised housing, or a form of housing subsidy to assist with access to the housing market, for the proportion of households and individuals in each country who fall within this category. This argument is in line with the Grootboom judgment and with recent developments in the Making Markets Work for the Poor (MMW4P) programmes.

The heart of this programme is not allowing policymaking for the poor to ignore markets nor markets to ignore the needs of the poor. In our context, there ought to be ways for the market to operate effectively for people who normally cannot find housing to suit them through it. In addition, those who may normally be harmed by market forces, for example, by being evicted to make way for commercial uses, should be included in its benefits. The usual methods of stretching the market, by reducing prices, by ironing-out lumpiness and lowering thresholds, or by using economies of scale are unlikely to bring home-ownership or formal renting within the reach of unhoused people.

There is a need to adopt standards and regulations that are much more in tune with the needs of the poorest in society, even if these are confined to particular areas or tenure categories in the short term. In general, policy insists on a minimum standard of construction and a minimum size of unit. With respect to physical standards, prices of dwellings are unlikely to reduce when they are constructed using materials that are marketed internationally (cement, steel, glass, fossil fuels) and whose prices are not conducive to much local discounting. However, restoring local materials, especially those based on earth and vegetation, to the list of materials with which it is legal to build in urban areas could reduce the price of construction significantly. For example, Hogar de Cristo, a charity in Latin America, provides very low-cost dwellings of bamboo panels and wood, which are prefabricated very cheaply in a factory in Guayaquil and assembled by the new owners. Only 23.5 square metres, these dwellings are targeted at households living in precarious settlements, households living in the streets, young couples wishing to start their own families, and abandoned mothers or female heads of households with an average of three children and an income of $100 per month (Inter-American Development Bank, n.d.). In Ecuador, alone, Hogar de Cristo has provided the materials for 118,000 dwellings to households in extreme poverty. Interest-free loans are given for three years to pay for the materials (Hogar de Cristo, n.d.).

With respect to minimum size of units, policy is almost always directed towards a self-contained dwelling for each household. One of the most effective interventions in reducing housing cost could be made by officially accepting that a self-contained dwelling is not the necessary requirement of every household and many would be content with a room or rooms in shared accommodation. Occupying rooms in a multi-occupied house is the reality for most low-income households in many countries, and is probably completely acceptable to the unhoused. Thus, it should be made a focus of housing supply policies and be seen as of equal value to self-contained dwellings for those who can afford them. If policies were directed to increasing the supply of rented rooms, for example, by allowing or encouraging home-owners to add extra rooms to their homes, the supply at the bottom of the market is likely to increase and many more households would be able to find adequate accommodation that they could afford. Tipple (2000) found that, where owners extend their homes, the new rooms for rent tend to be much lower in the market than the original dwelling, indeed they are close to the bottom of the market. Interventions to encourage extension activity, such as regulatory frameworks to allow extension activity, removal of rent controls and helpful housing designs can all assist relatively low-income households to build extra housing accessible to the poorest households.

Readers used to industrialised countries' practice may object to our proposing the provision of special approaches and most basic accommodation commensurate with human dignity for unsheltered and unhoused people. In some industrialised countries, where special supply systems, for example, social housing, are in place for particularly needy groups, there is a strong argument against them on the grounds that they become the stigmatised last choice for households with particularly acute problems. This has become increasingly the case in UK since the introduction of the 'Right to Buy' policy in 1980.

However, given the scale of the problem in most developing countries, to propose anything greater would be naïve, and interventions would, probably, be unachievable. Moreover we must remember that people living on the street are already in the most stigmatised and poorly equipped and undignified accommodation available so any improvement will probably be welcomed. We are encouraged in this by the Grootboom judgment's recommendation that a bare minimum of tents, portable latrines and regular supply of water (in this case by tanker) should be supplied for the critical time until people could obtain some housing (Huchzermeyer, 2003).

In addition to lowering threshold costs through reducing the standards required, housing activity at the bottom of the market might also be encouraged through appropriate loans and other finance available to low-income households. These are on the increase through the extension of micro-finance from the business sector into housing, such as through Mibanco in Peru, Banco Sol in Bolivia, and the Utshani Fund in South Africa, and through innovations such as the Community-led Infrastructure Financing Facility (CLIFF) (UN-Habitat, 2005). Through them, communities, groups, households and individuals who are much too poor to raise mortgage finance, and whose requirements are not appropriate for the long-term, largish loan secured on marketable property which a mortgage represents, can borrow small amounts of money, usually against group securities, to improve or extend their homes. Such initiatives should be extended and encouraged through policy.

An interesting method is used by the Kuyasa Fund in South Africa, modelling itself on the hire-purchase arrangements used by millions of low-income South Africans to buy furniture. Thus, collection of repayments is local, frequent and uses moral and community pressure if default occurs. Small amounts, similar to those used for furniture purchases, can be borrowed for the incremental building process required by low-income owners, and qualification is based on membership of a community savings scheme.

In the Philippines, the HPFP financial model, introduced in 1995, mobilises the savings of its members. Within its first year, the programme had 2,000 enrolled savers but, by 2001, there were nearly 28,000 individuals belonging to the federation of savings groups nationwide, with an accumulated savings of P35 million.[11] HPFP's financial model offers a range of financial programmes and savings aimed at helping members realise their aspirations of acquiring land with secure tenure, achieving decent living conditions, and rising out of poverty (HPFP, n.d.).

Such finance schemes, although generally very popular, operate high interest rates. For example, the Kuyasa Fund operates an interest rate of 38 per cent per annum (Mills, 2007). HPFP's Urban Poor Development Fund's interest is lower but still considerable at 9 per cent per annum. The scheme's group Compulsory Savings operates at 18 per cent per annum. While high interest rates are arguably necessary, given the risks associated with lending to very poor people, the lack of alternative sources of funding and the very low incomes of the savers and borrowers limits the value of such schemes for many, especially in the poorest echelons.

Progressive improvement in accommodation

The progressive improvement in accommodation is intrinsic to the American concept of the continuum of care (USA, 1994) and the European 'staircase of transition' model for the reintegration of unhoused people (FEANTSA, 1999). Both have been criticised, on the grounds that stalling on any level becomes stigmatising and the transition steps in each can be used for 'demoting' as well as 'promoting'.[12] The idea of different levels of provision as temporary (or even permanent) goals, however, is potentially fruitful in our context. Just as Payne (2002a) argues that land tenure is a bundle of rights that are not all necessary to gain sufficient confidence against eviction and to invest in better housing, so accommodation for unhoused people need not be everything that housing policy desires for it to be an appreciated improvement on the *status quo ante*.

The industrialised country approaches rely on moving the unhoused person between different types of accommodation – off the street into a hostel, then into a halfway house, then into an independent dwelling. For unhoused people who cannot improve where they find themselves, this is probably as good an arrangement as is available. However, many of the unhoused households in developing countries regard their current location as home and just need better accommodation or opportunities there. Thus, the household living under a tarpaulin on the streets of Delhi or Dhaka would welcome improved access to services (which are being provided in some cases), more security of tenure and the ability to improve their shelter without being afraid that it will be torn down. As much of the improvement will not involve moving amongst different properties or institutions and will be focused on the physical stock, the revolving door effects may be less likely.

This is a major change from industrialised country policy. It accepts that the unhoused household should receive assistance in situ, to improve the standard of their accommodation on the street or in the most marginal settlements, rather than moving them away from these locales into currently better-quality accommodation in less advantageous places.

We recognise that improvement of street dwelling may be politically difficult in many places, especially in cities such as Johannesburg where the city centre is being reclaimed as a globally important financial and commercial centre through corporate-led regeneration. In this process, unhoused people on the streets are seen as symptomatic of the old problems, danger and neglect, and an anathema to the new middle-class ambience associated with international consumption (Sihlongonyane, 2006).

The improvement of conditions in the most marginal settlements, however, is probably less politically sensitive and should be high on the policy agenda of any city sympathetic to the plight of unhoused people. Not only would it assist those who already live in such settlements but it would provide affordable and, sometimes well-located, alternatives to street-sleeping.[13]

The relatively sophisticated process of incremental improvement in industrialised countries is probably too resource-rich for most developing countries to contemplate on the required scale. Instead, the best that can be expected in the medium term is some basic shared accommodation offering improvements in between the street and a rented room in an informal neighbourhood. This would offer a more permanent base for some and an intermediate step between street and rented room for others, making the transition easier than it is currently.

In some situations, there is value in moving unhoused people off the street and into formal shelter in many developing countries, as long as it is voluntary for those who are moved. When targeting interventions, unhoused people and their advocates should be recognised as stakeholders to be involved through participatory decision-making processes in which they can have a real say in what happens and in executing the strategies to assist them. The SPARC/NSDF/Mahila Milan federation demonstrated the value of grass-roots planning in the way it supported 60,000 low-income people in a voluntary move from their settlements beside the railway tracks of Mumbai to make way for improvements to the infrastructure (Patel et al., 2002). Such initiatives from NGOs and CBOs are likely to be vital in making a difference for unhoused people.

We would expect participation at least at Choguill's (1996) 'partnership' level, and at the level of 'empowerment' whenever it is possible. Unhoused people and their advocates should always be involved when city-centre issues are to be decided as they are users of the spaces there. It is inequitable to continue to regard unhoused people as non-entities and worthless individuals. There is a valid argument for moving unhoused people off the street and into formal shelter in many developing countries, as long as it is voluntary for those who are moved. There is a risk, however, that participation might use scarce resources, especially in emergencies or conditions of acute need (Hamdi and Majale, 2004).

Provide and improve shelters

There is an important role for shelters and other very low-cost or no-cost accommodation in city centres. Jain (2006) recommends a wider choice of shelter in Delhi near large places of work, particularly a network of night shelters, transit accommodation, dormitories and *dharamshalas*,[14] These require a mixture of local authority, NGO and charitable activity in which faith-based organisations probably have a major role.

There has been some discussion of whether shelters for homeless people provided in industrialised countries are punitive/revanchist. De Verteuil (2006) found that, although revanchist activity against unhoused people is common in USA, the shelters provided in Los Angeles did not represented such a perspective. They increased and institutionalised homeless space within the city and, as the local authorities withdrew from responsibility and left the NGOs and churches to implement shelter provision, they reflected none of the revanchist idea of greater state control. However, homeless shelters are embedded in a larger effort to manage homelessness and poverty, especially in relieving prime urban areas of the troublesome presence of unhoused people.

The reality remains that, for many unhoused people, their only relief from the danger and climatic challenge of sleeping on the streets is to enter a shelter for a night or two. However, shelters are frequently provided with little consideration for how accessible and useful they are to the already struggling homeless person. They are generally located on the periphery of cities, rather than in the centre where homeless people can find work. We would suggest they should be no more than 20 minutes walking distance from ample opportunities for work.

Cleanliness and freedom from parasites and other disease vectors are vitally important for buildings, furniture and bedding. Experience from India and Africa shows that many people consider the street to be cleaner, safer and more private than some shelters, where overcrowding and poor conditions lead to disease and crime. Shelters must provide safe drinking water, washing and toilet facilities. There must be processes in place to keep them clean and in good repair and residents could be expected to help with the cleaning before they leave and submit to cleansing if they are carrying parasites.

They should have reasonable levels of space for multi-habitation, offering accommodation for lone men, lone women and households with and without children with acceptable levels of privacy. Accommodation may be anything from large dormitories to single-person cubicles with secure doors. A mixture might be feasible.

Safety and cultural integrity considerations are paramount. Thus, administration must ensure freedom from violent attack or intimidation and be sensitive to ethnic, caste and gender separation traditions. This will probably lead to issues concerning whether to ban the use of drugs and alcohol in the buildings. Experience in India highlights that involving unhoused and unsheltered people in the development and management of their own shelters can produce very good results, including improving security.

Legal, personal and employment advice, counselling, medical, dental and chiropody/podiatry treatment, hairdressing and other facilities should be available in or close to the accommodation. Maintenance of buildings and, where appropriate, services for clients, should be provided by homeless people as a form of paid employment.

Many homeless people do have meagre possessions, often associated with their trade or labour. Thus, shelters should provide space for safe storage of personal effects. Some larger storage units are also important so that those with business paraphernalia, especially stock items and cycles, carts, barrows, etc., can be accommodated, but it would be reasonable to charge something for such storage.

Such shelter need not be costly either to develop or run. Most cities in developing countries have ample appropriate, very low-cost, centrally located accommodation which could be adapted for use as night shelters. Disused warehouses and other spacious redundant buildings, upper storeys of city-centre commercial and government buildings could all play a part. The overnight use of sports halls and other spaces with a daytime use should also be considered. The cost of such accommodation should be payable by the night (or 24 hours). It would be reasonable for charges to equate pro-rata to the market cost of a rented room in peripheral informal neighbourhoods.

Think the unthinkable: reintroduce the flop-house

An extension of the night shelters idea, and a step to more permanent housing, is to provide longer term, but still temporary and very basic accommodation. For several generations, flop-houses provided a low-cost entry-point into accommodation for very poor individuals (usually men). The 'Skid Row' areas of hostels and flop-houses in American cities, in which a highly transient, powerless male population operated within a disaffiliated subculture outside of the matrix of social relationships that bind the rest of society (Lee, 1978), has branded flop-houses with a very poor image. The recent experience of Common Ground in reintroducing a revised form of flop-house in New York may be helpful in developing countries.

Common Ground is a non-profit organisation which restores dilapidated hotels and apartment buildings for use as housing for low-income people. Working on the theory propounded by Jencks (1994) that being unhoused was, *inter alia*, a result of the removal of the cheap rooming house and cubicle hotel accommodation in cities, the founder of Common Ground, Rosanne Haggerty, decided to reintroduce and update flop-houses as supportive accommodation for the poorest in society. Common Ground uses four ingredients to make supportive housing successful. They are:

1 good design so that they are attractive and function well;
2 provision of attentive but not-compulsory on-site services which include mental health and addiction counselling, job training and placements, and life-skills help with cooking, cleaning and money management;
3 demographically and economically mixed tenants so that there is a different atmosphere from places that only deal with unhoused people;
4 strong, hands-on management presence in the buildings to keep them clean and secure.

Through the application of the 'four ingredients', Common Ground hopes to escape from the repugnant, filthy and stigmatised image of the flop-house. In line with the need to prevent raiding by higher income groups that we have recognised, Common Ground aims to provide something not comfortable enough that people would want to stay forever but something that would provide a starting point to reintegration into mainstream society.

When designing the new flop-house environment, Common Ground interviewed unhoused people locally and found their priorities to be safety (34 per cent), low-cost (23 per cent) and cleanliness (22 per cent). They also wanted to avoid institutional colour schemes and bolted-down furniture, and appreciated ventilation, lighting, privacy, storage space, leisure activities and the ability to interact with their environment.

In the Andrews Hotel redevelopment in New York's Bowery area, cubicles are 2.4 metres by 2 metres, more than twice as large as before the redevelopment. They will be rented for $7 per day[15] for a maximum of 21 days to individuals coming directly from city shelters or referred by outreach teams. Design innovations include partitions which do not reach the ceiling, for good ventilation and lighting, but with strong ceiling netting for security without impeding the operation of fire-fighting sprinklers. The modular units come flat-packed so that they can be quickly assembled in any large room (McGray, 2002; Haggerty, 2006).[16]

The flop-house provides accommodation midway between the shelter and the market in low-rental rooms. It allows some privacy, permanence and access to services at less cost than renting a room. Under the improved management regime proposed by Common Ground, it is worth experimenting with the flop-house in developing country cities.

Making life on the street more bearable

Regardless of night shelters or longer term very basic accommodation, many people will continue to have no alternative but to sleep on the streets and in public places. For these people security from attack is a constant preoccupation. Anyone sleeping in a public space is extremely vulnerable to attack from passers-by or police. Flimsy structures hardly reduce the vulnerability of the occupant. Indeed, street sleepers may be safer without such shelters as the structure may draw attention to their presence without giving them much protection from attack. Obviously, assistance with improving the strength of a structure can increase security. Wherever it is feasible to build a structure, at least some rights of tenure and some assistance in cash or kind can enable it to be as strong as possible. This is particularly important when the occupants run a business as they might store cash or valuable stock. In research on home-based enterprises in a squatter settlement and the adjacent formal housing area in Pretoria, South Africa, it was clear that the formal brick housing generated higher value enterprises as burglary was more difficult (Gough et al., 2003).

Within hostels and other shared accommodation for unhoused people, security is a major issue (Olufemi (2001). Where this occurs in a building, occupants are extremely vulnerable. The solution to this issue may lie as much in good management as in improving conditions so that each resident has a cubicle, rather than a bed in a dormitory, and somewhere lockable to store possessions. Lessons can be learned from NGOs, such as Aashray Adhikar Abhiyan in Delhi, which involve unhoused and unsheltered people in the management and running of the hostels.

For many unhoused people in developing countries, the safe storage of possessions is important. The security of their possessions could be improved by lockable facilities similar to left-luggage offices, even if leaving possessions there costs small amounts of money per day/night. They should include cubicles and boxes ranging in size from some large enough to store a hand cart to others to hold small valuables, money and documents. For households and individuals with rudimentary shelter, an important improvement in the issue of keeping possessions would be to reduce the permeability of the structures they occupy, both through lockable doors and opaque (and preferably solid) walls. This is what we would regard as most representing the threshold between being unhoused and being inadequately housed. Access to recycled materials at very low cost, and the permission to use less-than-perfect materials in construction, can be very helpful in improving the security of the physical shelter. It demands, however, a less precious attitude to building standards than most governments are prepared to take (Payne and Majale, 2004).

Lack of privacy is a mark of inadequacy and an issue for unhoused people (Table 5.2). Indeed, the Habitat Agenda states that adequate shelter means, *inter alia*, adequate privacy (UNCHS, 1997). Interventions to improve privacy should generally hinge on more solid structures, to prevent inward views, and multiple rooms to divide households and household members from each other when necessary. This can be enabled by improving both security of tenure and ability to afford to upgrade the structure. The latter can be achieved either by demand-side subsidies (such as housing allowances) or measures such as minimum wages and economic progress to boost low incomes.

The privacy issue takes on a different guise in hostels and other low-rental accommodation. In dormitory accommodation with shared bathing facilities, it is likely that privacy will be low within the confines of the rooms but high with respect to the outside world. Improvements in privacy within the building can be made through providing cubicles and single bathrooms (both with locks) but these also need careful maintenance through high-quality management practices. The discussion on flop-houses broaches this question more fully.

The current wisdom for the inadequately housed: the enabling approach

Currently the inadequately housed population (on rungs 4 and 5 on Tables 5.1 and 5.2) are probably the most vulnerable to becoming unhoused; they are the future unhoused population without some intervention in the way housing is provided. Their settlements or rooms can be subject to eviction or fall into such dilapidation that they are unsuitable for occupation. The current 'solution' to the housing problem of the inadequately housed population is couched in the enabling approach by which states provide the fiscal and policy context for all actors in the housing process to supply dwellings as efficiently as possible in a neo-liberal, market-led context.

By differentiating between inadequately housed and unhoused people, we signal our concern that the enabling approach is only of use in addressing the needs of the poorest in society by ensuring that those who are currently inadequately housed (rungs 4 and above on the ladders) do not slip down into the unhoused and unsheltered categories. Thus, working the enabling approach for those for whom it is relevant has an important role but it is unlikely directly to help the unhoused.

The World Bank (1993) provides a useful list of 'do's and 'don't's for formulating policies within the enabling approach and some are directly or indirectly relevant to policy concerned with preventing inadequately housed people from becoming unhoused. Table 13.2 shows the policy recommendations for enabling housing which can be helpful in this. While not discussing the contents of Table 13.2. in detail, we feel it worthwhile to highlight the last point, organising the building industry, as very important, as it is at the root of the shelter problem in many developing countries.

Under the enabling approach, governments should involve all actors in the housing process at the level at which they are most effective. In most developing countries, the most effective provider of housing for inadequately housed people is the informal sector. This comprises millions of lone contractors and very small

Table 13.2 The 'do's and 'don't's of enabling housing markets to work which are relevant to inadequately housed people

	What to do	*What not to do*
Developing property rights	DO regularise land tenure DO expand land registration	DON'T engage in mass evictions
Rationalising subsidies	DO target subsidies to the poor DO subsidise people, not houses	DON'T build subsidised public housing DON'T allow for hidden subsidies DON'T let subsidies distort prices DON'T use rent control as subsidy
Providing infrastructure for residential land development	DO improve slum infrastructure	DON'T allow bias against infrastructure improvements DON'T use environmental concerns as reasons for slum clearance
Regulating land and housing development		DON'T impose unaffordable standards DON'T maintain unenforceable rules
Developing a policy and institutional framework		DON'T neglect local government's role
Organising the building industry	DO encourage small firm entry	

Source: World Bank (1993: 46-7)

businesses constructing housing for households in millions of tiny contracts (usually between US$5,000 and US$20,000). This process usually receives no assistance from government business-promotion activities or from infrastructure or financial providers. Indeed, it is often dealt with by being persecuted and harassed instead.

The poorest people are the client groups most affected by this, either through the lack of housing suitable to them or the poor quality of the provision. The key to improving housing supply for the poor, therefore, lies in reversing this trend and assisting the supply of housing by the informal sector, both through the businesses that construct and through the needs of the customers. Many years ago, Tipple (1994) argued that the interfaces in which governments should intervene are those between the contractor and the house, and the household and the contractor.

The contractor–house interface refers to measures which can ease the construction of housing by small contractors. It includes assisting them in market information, business management and, particularly, finance so that they can improve equipment and be able to finance the construction of at least part of each contract before receiving money from the customer.

The household–contractor interface involves helping ordinary people to know when the contractor is doing good work and/or providing means of redress when things go wrong. One of the great advantages of the former is that it could be done very cheaply through media input on housing issues. In most developing countries, everyone knows how much cement costs;[17] they should also know, for example, how many blocks should be made from one bag and how to tell whether the material has been contaminated. Information such as this could be included in soap opera story lines (e.g. a character who is given poor service by her builder) or in newspaper supplements on practical housing issues. The household–contractor interface requires a consumer protection law which includes housing issues.

When both of these interfaces are addressed, housing can be supplied much more efficiently in the informal sector. Meanwhile, regulatory frameworks that allow the informal sector to supply fully legitimate housing must be put in place (Payne and Majale, 2004).

Address lumpiness in supply

One of the major issues in obtaining housing for the poorest in society is the size of the threshold: the cost of the cheapest accommodation available. This is the most serious element in lumpiness for people in danger of being unhoused. The supply of improved shelters, opening up of public buildings for hostel accommodation, and provision of flop-houses would smooth out lumpiness in the housing supply below the level of independent living in rooms.

Many countries have laws which discourage home-owners from building extra rooms to rent or from adding other buildings within their, often quite large, plots. Such laws are not helpful to housing supply at the bottom of the market and should be reviewed with the problems of the unhoused population in mind. In other work, we have found that rooms within extensions are often very much cheaper per square metre than established dwellings in the same area. The tolerance or encouragement of extension activity can also serve to reduce lumpiness in supply so that virtually any size and price of accommodation can be found (Tipple, 2000).

Improve access to land

This is not the place to argue for or against particular approaches to making some measure of secure land tenure more accessible to the lowest-income households. Nor is it a time to stipulate whether *de facto* tenure is enough in all cases. Even the most cursory examination of volumes on land tenure around the developing world (Payne, 1999, 2002b; Durand-Lasserve and Royston, 2002) demonstrate how varied are the circumstances in different countries. Some solutions can really improve the access of low-income households to land in one place but have little positive effect in another. Even seeming universals, such as the need for smaller, narrower plots so that land is cheaper, might not be as helpful as it seems. Tipple (2000) argues that, in a context of extension activity providing rooms for low-income households, larger plots can be more efficient than smaller, and wider better than narrower. This allows owners to extend more efficiently and it transfers the cost, effort and benefits from rental income of housing the poorest households from states (who do it inefficiently) to households (who are very efficient and often make a small profit out of it).

The important thing about land tenure for the poorest households is to provide enough security so that they need not fear eviction and so that the authorities can legitimately provide water, sanitation, waste disposal, drainage, access and power services. Where ability to sell is important, tenure should reflect this in the bankability of residential land. Where inheritance is more important, long-term right of use may be more important. Where there are likely to be aggressive attempts at raiding by higher-income households, bankability may be a hindrance. Households on different rungs of the property rights and accommodation ladders may need different land tenure solutions to provide the desired improvement in their housing and livelihoods. These variations are legion but each case should be treated in a locally sensitive context and in consultation with homeless people and the NGOs that work for their benefit.

Improve formalisation processes

While arbitrary regulations more suited to wealthy property developers in industrialised countries continue to rule development for the lowest-income households in developing countries, they will deprive large proportions of the population of the right to occupy housing they can afford. Furthermore, they will drive such people into unregulated housing which is likely to be of even poorer standard than it would be if regulations set the formalisation threshold much lower.

In line with Payne and Majale (2004), the needs of unhoused and inadequately housed households for improvement in the formalisation process points towards:

- recognising the reality of how people live;
- focusing regulation on only the key issues;
- involving residents in the process of regulation in their neighbourhood; and
- using regulation as a process favouring incremental building of the housing stock and gradual improvement in the standards it fulfils.

The idea of fulfilling standards as a goal rather than a minimum is helpful for planning interventions in neighbourhoods of inadequate housing. It is a helpful context within which authorities can assist residents to work up to a standard incrementally rather than having to fulfil a standard before they can be assisted.

Improve access to services

Access to services is often a daily preoccupation for homeless people. For unhoused people with no structure, well-located public taps, bathing places and toilets are likely to be important in improving their lives. In the very low standard of shelter occupied by many unhoused people, services are usually absent or provided on a shared or public basis for monetary return. India is particularly well provided with public wash places and toilets and many are in good condition and relatively clean. A joint action of SPARC, NSDF and Mahila Milan has shown great ingenuity in providing toilet blocks for very low-income neighbourhoods. Their capital cost and the cost of maintenance and cleaning can be covered by incorporating a community hall or meeting space in the upper floor from which small charges for use provide money to fund the cleaner's wages and maintenance (Burra et al., 2003). This combination of uses also overcomes obstacles to the use of public toilets as it allows people to use the building without any stigma attached to being seen to be approaching and leaving it.

In areas where mains servicing is feasible, well-targeted urban upgrading is undoubtedly a great contribution to the living conditions of people in inadequate housing. Slum upgrading is likely to be the only way MDG-directed activity will include the most inadequately-housed people. Other MDGs will be much easier to fulfil by excluding the poorest in the population, for example, reducing by half the number of people living on less than a dollar a day and those suffering from hunger (MDG 1, Targets 1 and 2), reducing by three-quarters the maternal mortality ratio (MDG 5, Target 6), halting and reversing the spread of HIV/AIDS and the incidence of malaria and other major diseases (MDG 6, Targets 7 and 8). Slum upgrading, however, addresses MDG 7 (Targets 10 and 11), aimed at reducing by half the proportion of people without sustainable access to safe drinking water and achieving significant improvements in the lives of at least 100 million slum dwellers by 2020.

Work towards both of these will only improve the poorest neighbourhoods if positively directed that way; that tends to be the political reality. However, the cost of improving the life of dwellers in the poorest slums may be lower than those in better ones as even small investments may generate significant improvements. Cotton and Franceys (1991) argue that improvements from a 'zero baseline' of no services can result in substantial health benefits even though they cost little per household. Thus, to provide a single source of safe drinking water can reduce diarrhoeal disease for as many consumers as can manage to use it, save many lives and improve more. Improvements elsewhere over a higher level of current service would be more expensive per household and might have little noticeable benefit. Thus, it is in governments' interests to target unhoused households in fulfilling their MDG targets on slum improvements and water supply.

However, service provision for the unsheltered is more problematic. As noted earlier, we must recognise the value of unsheltered and unhoused people to the physical and economic development of cities. As part of this, municipalities might begin by providing mobile basic services units, which could be located where needed in relation to new development and the resting places of migrant workers. Such units should provide basic sanitation and bathing facilities, in the form of toilets and showers, safe drinking water and a venue for the delivery of basic health and advocacy services by NGOs. This resembles a mobile version of both the Area Resource Centre provided by SPARC and the toilet blocks provided by the SPARC/ Mahila Milan/NSDF Federation in India (Patel et al., 2001).

Reduce vulnerability to being made homeless by a disaster

Most countries also supply housing for people made homeless by disasters, conflict and other upheavals. There are cases, however, where this is of very poor quality and, after several years of occupation without any chance of replacement, conditions become very poor.

Knowledge of hazard risk is important as a first step to reducing vulnerability; GIS and other digital modelling can be most useful for this. Its dissemination, through visual material in public buildings and in newspapers and other media, could assist in avoiding dangerous settlement patterns which inevitably lead to displacement and being homeless in the medium to long term.

Alternative sites, designated, planned, and provided with at least some infrastructure, onto which prospective informal settlers can be directed, can minimise the need to settle in dangerous places. If such alternatives exist, it would then be reasonable to ban settlement in designated hazard areas, to keep such areas under frequent surveillance and to implement eviction measures against those who break the ban (Tipple, 2005).

Top-down approaches to disaster mitigation are unlikely to be embraced by local people. Schilderman (2004) argues that local artisan-based technologies are often effective in building a disaster-resistant housing stock and have the added advantage of empowering local people rather than turning them into clients of the state. The work of Intermediate Technology Development Group (ITDG) in Peru showed that working with local builders to understand and modify traditional or commonly used technologies and practices to resist the live forces generated in a disaster reduced vulnerability more than new technologies which might be imposed from above (Schilderman, 2004).

Simple processes can make the difference in building survival. For example, in the Philippines, annual checks are made on the tightness of wedged joints in wooden buildings. In Andra Pradesh, India, people throw fishing nets over thatched roofs when high winds are expected. Timber beams are built into masonry walls at intervals for added strength in Turkey and many other places. In areas prone to flooding, for example, Indore, India, lofts, high storage shelves and watertight grain storage containers are built into dwellings (Schilderman, 2004).

Routine maintenance can greatly improve the chances of dwellings remaining intact in disasters (Schilderman, 2004) but many countries have no maintenance culture for housing; costing of construction projects rarely takes account of maintenance expenses and few owners have the skills to recognise small faults as they arise. Thus, media-led knowledge-boosting campaigns and other methods to improve maintenance could greatly reduce housing vulnerability to disasters and reduce the numbers of people made homeless when they strike (Tipple, 2005). As Ellis and Barakat (1996) argue, relief programmes put so much effort into saving lives but not nearly enough into saving livelihoods.

When disaster strikes, the housing recovery effort tends to interrupt general housing supply programmes but should only be allowed to do so for a few years at most. Then normal supply should dominate as many will still be needy who were unaffected by the disaster or its recovery effort (Gilbert, 2001). In the recovery process, great efforts should be made not to disrupt good housing sector policies and to use the best from current policies in the recovery. Housing and other relief interventions should benefit development. They should be upon the 'relief-to-development continuum' (Ellis and Barakat, 1996; Demusz, 2003), rather than only having the quick-relief orientation. Thus, Sorrill's (1998) 'permatent' which provides a strong shelter which can become a self-supporting roof is a better long-term intervention than tents or plastic sheets as it provides both relief and development effects. The concentration of funds on rebuilding housing after disasters has come in for serious criticism on the grounds that only those rich enough to afford some sort of dwelling benefit at the expense of infrastructure which would benefit all. Comerio (1997: 177) offers lessons learned from disasters in USA, Japan and Mexico, to focus on the importance of insurers in the division of responsibilities for financing recovery and so the reduction of vulnerability to disastrous loss. Gilbert (2001) agrees that this is eminently sensible for developed nations' cities where most owners can probably afford house and contents insurance and where insurers are willing to cover the dwellings. In developing countries, on the other hand, where very few households indeed have any insurance even when they can afford it, and where insurers are reluctant to extend their reach down the market, private insurance may only be a small part of the picture.

More important, perhaps, will be the attention on improving livelihoods before the disaster strikes to reduce vulnerability so that people can recover more quickly from a disaster event. In this vein, Holzmann and Jorgensen (2001) recognise that social capital, the networks and community solidarity built up among people in low-income neighbourhoods, provides them with immediate post-disaster care. Those whose homes survive take in those whose homes are destroyed and know that such help would be reciprocated if required. The growing community savings activity, through which people in low-income neighbourhoods join savings clubs and meet regularly, builds up both social capital and financial assets which both reduce vulnerability.[18] Attention to building up these links can reduce vulnerability. While it would be easy for homeless people to be excluded, efforts should be made to include them in disaster mitigation as well as post-disaster recovery.

Proposals for non-housing interventions

All the interventions discussed thus far are, largely, accommodation-focused. They are directed towards either providing immediate, temporary shelter, such as flop-houses and night shelters, facilitating the development of housing and helping people to access it or assisting people to maintain their home so that they do not lose it. However, we recognise that there will be a great many people for whom these interventions can do little other than provide the most basic shelter. They may, at least, move people from being unsheltered to being unhoused but, for some, these accommodation-focused interventions will not move people from being unsheltered or unhoused to being housed. These will include people without land on which to build and whose income is too low, even with subsidy, and people who are unhoused or unsheltered and have neither the time nor the desire to put down roots, such as migrant workers. It will probably also include lone-woman-headed households who are prevented from owning land or building independent homes either by law or by social pressure.

From experience of working in Delhi for several decades, Jain (2006) reports that the problems of people without shelter are quite different from those in very poor shelter; their priority is not shelter but security and being integrated into the wider social network. Conventional programmes, such as ready-built housing and resettlement, have not touched their lives. He believes that, in the Indian context, strategies should focus on job security and improvement of labour laws and their enforcement in the informal sector. The services required for people without shelter should include literacy, education, health, nutrition, sanitation and toilet facilities, recreational and cultural development, and skills development.

This assessment of what is needed in India holds true for much of the developing world. What is most needed by many people is major socio-cultural and economic change which includes themselves. This calls for the development of some form of welfare-driven framework which redistributes the benefits of the current economic development taking place in some developing countries and recognises the role the worst off in society play in that development.

Improve the role and capacity of local government

Just as it is in crisis and disaster management (Tipple, 2005), the role of local government is important if the needs of local people in the poorest neighbourhoods, and on the streets, are to be addressed. Local governments should not only be sympathetic to the plight of the poorest but also recognise their contribution to urban development. In developing countries, most local government only engage with people in poor neighbourhoods at the point when they are seeking to upgrade or resettle them. Thus, their residents are perceived merely as problems – disfiguring modernising cities and occupying commercially valuable land – and a drain on resources. Thus, they make little attempt to understand the situation of the poor or to engage in any meaningful way. Instead, local government should recognise the value which such neighbourhoods represent, in terms of labour, production and knowledge, so that they can address the needs of unhoused and inadequately housed people. Work in Mumbai by the NGO SPARC highlights the way in which residents of informal settlements can act as a knowledge resource, undertaking surveys and mapping for local authorities, and become empowered by the process (Patel et al., 2002).

One of the barriers to better engagement between local authorities and poor neighbourhoods is a lack of capacity for the types of participatory governance and urban planning which are becoming increasingly common in industrialised countries. This is particularly true of civil servants, such as municipal planners, many of whom see themselves as the professional 'experts' and are reluctant to relinquish any level of power or expertise to residents of poor settlements. There is a need, therefore, to encourage capacity-building in areas of participatory planning and community engagement through all professional development and education.

Legal issues

Decriminalise being unhoused and unsheltered

The illegality of street sleeping is a major issue for unhoused (and, especially, unsheltered) people and should be abolished everywhere. There are several ways in which being unhoused has been made illegal, often by criminalising some of the basic human activities if carried out in public places. Thus, it may be illegal to sleep, sit, loiter or store personal belongings in public places. The laws may be selectively enforced, making it illegal to sit in one place but not another. Laws against begging, either passively or more aggressively,[19] or both, have the effect of punishing unhoused people more than others. Furthermore, it has been found that jailing unhoused people[20] can be more expensive than placing them in supportive housing (National Coalition for the Homeless and National Law Center on Homelessness and Poverty, 2006). Once a person has a criminal record, they can find it a great burden in ordinary life. It seems to be an unfair thing to do to someone who has problems enough already and, out of humanity, it should stop.

Thus, laws which incarcerate unhoused people just for being on the street without any means to find accommodation, such as the Bombay Prevention of Begging Act, should be repealed. Instead, more constructive approaches should be adopted working with unsheltered and unhoused people to assist them in improving their livelihoods so that they can move into more secure accommodation.

Improve legal and other rights to land

The Habitat Agenda calls for innovative tenural arrangements and land titling techniques to allow poorer households to gain as much security of tenure as they need to feel sure that they will not be evicted (UN-Habitat, 2006). Most households who are, or are at risk of being, homeless have subjective security of tenure, at best. *De facto* security of tenure, backed by traditional documentation, political patronage, promises or the sheer weight of numbers, is essentially subjective. In cities where subjective security has sufficed over the medium to long term, legal rights to land are probably unnecessary to most low-income households in the informal sector. Indeed, as Payne (2002a) points out, legal tenure can be a short-lived benefit for poorer households. Where the graph of increasing legal rights to land is not parallel to the graph of increasing income, richer people with less tenure approach poorer people with more and buy them out, usually at much less than the market price because the latter lack market information.[21] This 'raiding', as it is commonly called, tends to restore the parallelism in the distributions of legal tenure and income, in the face of policy attempts actively to help the poor. If they had been granted improved rights, but not such improvements that they were more secure than better-off households, they would probably not have been bought out.

To the question of whether it means that the footpath dweller under a tarpaulin in Mumbai has the right to secure tenure where he is, however, we would posit a nuanced approach in line with Payne's (2001) typology. Secure tenure would be interpreted as meaning that the footpath dweller has a right to own the piece of footpath on which he dwells. It would involve dividing up public highway into privately owned parcels and is clearly impractical. However, he would be entitled to secure tenure somewhere as close as possible to his footpath site, he would have the right to be involved in the decision on where to be resettled, and would be treated fairly and humanely in the way the law would require for someone whose property was being sequestered under a compulsory purchase order.

Enforce existing women's and children's rights legislation

Current legal interventions seem unable to protect women and children from being homeless. There is a need now for a better understanding of exactly how countries have interpreted international women's and children's rights legislation and what the cultural and institutional barriers are to embedding rights in practice.

Some countries have begun to recognise this inequality and the fact that broad-based legislation is insufficient to overcome cultural attitudes and protect women's and children's rights. In India, for example, the Metropolitan Council of Delhi (MCD) has taken to giving land titles in its slum-upgrading schemes in the names of couples, rather than solely in the name of the man. Thus, it is more difficult for an errant husband to sell the property (Kundu, 2002). The 1994 National Housing Policy Act also confers joint or exclusive title on poor or disadvantaged women.

Similarly, in Brazil, the Concession of the Real Right to Use (CRRU) is a mechanism of allocating legal security of tenure (although not ownership). In terms of both policy and practice, CRRU is gender sensitive and, under it, title to land is given in the names of both partners, regardless of their marital status. Indeed, there have been cases of the title reverting solely to the woman's name after the couple separated because of domestic violence (Fernandez, 2002).

Nevertheless, these legal interventions will not work if they are not enforced. Enforcement requires the legal and political will to bring about social and cultural change and to end the deeply entrenched discrimination and disempowerment of women in many countries. In part, this means recognising and addressing women's weaker economic position through education, training and employment.

End forced evictions and inappropriate resettlement

The practice of forcibly evicting people from their dwellings and settlement, however poor, informal or illegal, is counterproductive in terms of addressing homelessness at all levels. Apart from the trauma it causes to the individual household, it undermines what is often a considerable investment in the physical and social development of the settlement.

Wherever possible, informal settlements should be upgraded in situ. The release of valuable land for development without moving the occupants off might also be achieved through land sharing. This device requires mediation between informal settlers and a land owner to exchange the use of most of the site for improved housing for the residents on part of the site, usually involving increased densities achieved by multi-storey construction. It has been used successfully in Thailand (Angel and Boonyabancha, 1988; Islam and Yap, 1989) but less successfully in Cambodia where mediation was not available and each side simply tried to maximise its own gains at the expense of the other (Rabé, 2005). While the land-sharing solution may not transfer to other places, the idea of negotiation between land owners and occupants, with an honest broker mediating, should be a better start to the process than simply bringing in the bulldozers and armed police to evict and destroy.

Where in-situ solutions are not possible, the process of moving people should be done in participation with those affected. Resettlement schemes are often established with little or no consultation and without any legitimate participation of the settlers. There are, however, good examples and new approaches to participatory upgrading and relocation to be drawn on worldwide which tackle both settlement upgrading or relocation and poverty in a holistic way (Patel et al., 2002). However, it is important to sound a note of caution as not all that is good practice in one local or national context is replicable more widely. The most important points are to ensure that those to be resettled are fully consulted and that they have the opportunity to participate in their relocation. Alternatives to eviction should be offered, especially those that energise the potential of residents to save and participate in housing themselves (Du Plessis, 2005).

Improve incomes

Just as improved housing supply helps homeless people in developing countries, so improved income potential can be a great boost to reducing homelessness. With the growth of micro-credit in the last decade, more governments and NGOs can be directly involved in improving incomes of households living in poverty. Many of the countries in the CARDO study have interventions which include micro-credit and other assistance to small enterprises that are aimed at people living in poverty. The story of micro-credit is generally a very positive one and many millions of households have been assisted to grow out of poverty or enabled to survive through the businesses they have been able to set up, both individually and cooperatively (Counts, 1996). Not only have household incomes been raised but also other benefits are found, for example, school attendance of both boys and girls has risen among beneficiary households and female empowerment measures have improved (Kevane and Wydick, 2001). However, there are also problems arising. Mosley and Hulme (1998) found that micro-credit helps the lowest income households the least. In addition, although there was a feeling at first that micro-finance would create significant employment, it has rarely done so (Prugl, 1996). There are also issues of indebtedness, intimidation and increasing family violence as some members of society manipulate others (usually men manipulating their wives) especially when only some (usually women in groups) qualify for the loans and others (usually men) do not (Rogaly, 1996). Mahmud (2003) argues that empowerment through micro-credit is severely constrained by male-dominated gender relations. Thus, although the borrowers are women, Rahman (1999) and Mallick (2002) point out that, in Bangladesh, the users of the loans are mainly the men (husbands or relatives) who encourage the women to join and borrow on their behalf. None of this denies the need to assist people living in the most extreme poverty to help themselves to improve. It does, however, caution against seeing micro-credit and business development as the only way forward.

UNCHS/ILO (1995) and Tipple (1995) argue that housing and infrastructure supply can be very beneficial for income generation, especially for households living in extreme poverty, but it must be done using local materials and labour-intensive technologies. Housing construction through labour-based technologies using local materials generates more jobs per unit of expenditure than most other forms of activity. In addition, construction is one of the most effective investments in creating informal sector jobs in other sectors such as food processing (for feeding the workforce), transportation, components manufacturing, etc. In addition, each dwelling built generates jobs in furnishings and fittings industries and maintenance. The money earned by workers in construction tends to stay in the local economy, generating high income multipliers.

Ways of delivering water, sanitation, waste collection, etc., that generate employment should be preferred over those which use capital-intensive methods.[22] Governments and local authorities can make a real difference to the amount of employment by adopting such technologies and considering how much work can be created not only in the construction of housing and infrastructure but also in its lifetime. Thus, mitigating the shortfall of housing and infrastructure can generate the wealth in an economy that is required to afford better housing.

Support for NGOs

It is the role and responsibility of governments to address homelessness at a strategic levels, by developing enabling environments to encourage the supply of housing, ensuring the regulatory frameworks do not penalise the poor, and adopting and enforcing rights legislation concerning housing and property. However, much of the practical support which either minimises the distress of homelessness or reduces vulnerability to it can only realistically be undertaken by NGOs.

Unencumbered by bureaucracy, NGOs are able to respond rapidly to urgent need. They frequently work in ways more supportive and non-judgemental than official agencies can and are more able to gain the respect of the community. However, if they are to be entrusted to deliver services, some important points about what helps or hinders NGO activity need to be acknowledged (Edwards and Fowler, 2002).

First, NGOs require sustainable funding if they are to avoid the difficulties inherent in the project cycle. It serves no one well if months or years spent learning about local needs and building up trust are wiped out because funding is cut short. Moreover, cyclical funding encourages rapid rather than logical spending decisions. Thus, flexibility in their funding and budgeting cycles is crucial for addressing issues of homelessness.

Second, NGOs often focus on process rather than outputs. In most cases this is, ultimately, more beneficial. It is unhelpful for their funding to depend on their hitting predetermined targets or quantifiable measures of success, for example, numbers of children enrolled in sheltered education schemes. Most often, especially in the context of homelessness in developing countries, it is virtually impossible to assess the sustainability of quantifiable outputs. It is better to embrace measurements of success based on the improvement to lives of homeless people as they themselves see them.

Third, in the spirit of empowerment it is important that homeless people are involved in the development and delivery of services themselves. NGOs have been particularly good at this in comparison to governments. However, it should not be assumed that all NGOs or all empowered people within them are without personal agendas. Recent problems at one well-known NGO in southern Africa arose when leaders began to behave as if their position privileged them above their members and above the common population. The idea of working for the common good was replaced by personal aggrandisement and rent-seeking behaviour.

Conclusions

The discussion on interventions highlights that there is no 'one size fits all' answer to homelessness. This is true whether the unhoused person is a child or an adult, alone or with others. Interventions are needed at a number of levels to address current homelessness and future vulnerability.

At housing policy level, interventions are needed to ensure an adequate supply of affordable land for the poor with a range of appropriate tenure systems to ensure security. Regulatory frameworks should be adopted which encourage rather than discourage housing development by and for the poor.

In relation to practical support for currently unhoused people, interventions need to dispel myths and educate the public about the realities of unhoused people's lives and their valuable role in the city's development. Basic services must be provided to assist unhoused people to live with dignity and maintain basic health and hygiene. Shelter should be provided when and where needed, either free or at a very affordable price. Unhoused people should be recognised and supported as productive members of society and be assisted to maximise and protect the fruits of their labours, thus assisting them to help themselves out of their predicament.

In terms of human rights, interventions are required to encourage the adoption of housing, property and inheritance rights and enforce these where they exist already. People must be educated about their rights and what can be done to ensure they are upheld, for example, making wills. Above all, unhoused people should be empowered and involved in services for them and decisions about their circumstances and interventions therein.

The examination of unhousedness contained in this book shows that it is an issue requiring urgent attention by governments not only because unhoused people have rights to better treatment but also to prevent the waste of human resource which current policies represent. Finally, what is most needed is education of the housed to bring about a change of public perception and remove the stigma associated with homelessness. Only then might unhoused people be recognised as equals and as productive individuals in need of support and encouragement, rather than misplaced, disempowering sympathy, marginalisation or social control.

Notes

Foreword

1 ESCOR Research No.ESA343, 2001–2003. The UK Department for International Development (DFID) supports policies, programmes and projects to promote international development. DFID provided funds for the study as part of that objective, but the views and opinions expressed are those of the authors alone.

1 Current understandings of homelessness

1 Based on a report written by Graham Tipple.
2 O. A. Labeodan is O. A. Olufemi before her marriage.
3 There are, however, many traditional social safety nets to aid the survival of the weakest in society, the 'family house' in Nigerian and Ghanaian cities being one such (Amole et al., 1993).

2 Homelessness and international housing policy

1 Some of this discussion draws on a draft written by Graham Tipple for Chapter 2 of the Global Report on Human Settlements (UN-Habitat, 2005) and by Graham Tipple and Michael Majale for UN-Habitat (2006).
2 The following provisions of the Habitat Agenda also address human rights and housing rights considerations:
Para. 40: a) Ensuring consistency and coordination of macroeconomic and shelter policies and strategies;
b) Providing legal security of tenure and equal access to land to all people, and undertaking legislative and administrative reforms to give women full and equal rights to property;
c) Promoting access for all people to safe drinking water, sanitation and other basic services, facilities and amenities, especially for people living in poverty, women and those belonging to vulnerable and disadvantaged groups;
d) Ensuring transparent, comprehensive and accessible systems in transferring land rights and legal security of tenure;
e) Promoting broad, non-discriminatory access to open, efficient, effective and appropriate housing financing for all people;
h) Increasing the supply of affordable housing, including through encouraging and promoting affordable home ownership, rental, communal, cooperative and other housing;

i) Promoting the upgrading of existing housing stock;

j) Eradicating and ensuring legal protection from discrimination in access to shelter and basic services;

l) Promoting shelter and supporting basic services and facilities for education and health for vulnerable people including homeless people;

m) Protecting the legal traditional rights of indigenous people;

n) Protecting all people from and providing legal protection and redress for forced evictions.

Para. 41: Providing continued international support to refugees.

Para. 43: a) Promoting socially integrated and accessible human settlements.

3 Pronounced H'rootboom.

4 These included school meals for poor children and grants to protect house foundations from erosion. Similarly targeted interventions with a variety of names were implemented in other countries.

5 Under which there are targeted programmes like the Credit Assistance Fund (CAF) and the Poverty Alleviation Fund (PAF).

6 In their study of 10 African countries: Cameroon, the Gambia, Ghana, Guinea, Madagascar, Malawi, Mozambique, Niger, Tanzania and Zaire (now DR Congo).

7 As economies develop they are seen to require lessening proportions of female labour at first and then increasing proportions. Thus, there is said to be a U-shaped curve of feminisation of labour force participation with development (Çagatay and Özler, 1995).

3 The continuing urban housing shortfall and affordability crisis

1 The issues thrown up by inappropriate use of terms and units are demonstrated in the context of West Africa where there are no words for 'household' and 'dwelling' in many local languages (Tipple et al., 1994)

2 In India, a slum is one step up from an unauthorised settlement in that the designation is given where *de facto* security is accepted by the municipality.

3 As we discussed in Chapter 2, the intention of the enabling approach was certainly not to let governments 'off the hook' by allowing them to cut back on expenditure on housing provision. Indeed, the interventions in the five supply markets and the regulatory framework proposed in the enabling approach (World Bank, 1993) are potentially more challenging to government resources.

4 The supply level of 10 dwellings per 1,000 population has been regarded as a policy aim by countries intent on 'solving' housing problems. In the authors' youth, the Wilson government in the UK used 10 per 1,000 as a policy aim to wipe out slums and house everyone decently. Thus, 44 per 1,000 belongs in the realms of ultra-intensive housing supply alongside the 'Million Houses Programme' in Sri Lanka.

5 When a household wants a rent-controlled flat, the landlord demands a very large up-front non-returnable payment (key money). The longer the subsequent residence in the flat, the better value is extracted from the key money by the tenants: long tenancies and little mobility are encouraged by this practice.

6 As about 70 per cent of urban households occupy a single room (Tipple et al., 1999), the unit may be anything from a room in a multi-habited house to a whole detached villa, but this is rarely articulated.

7 Dwellings in India are classified as follows. '*Pucca*' is a structure whose walls and roof are made of materials such as cement, concrete, oven bricks, stone, stone blocks, jackboards (cement plastered reeds), iron and other metal sheeting, timber, tiles, slate, corrugated iron, zinc or other metal sheets, asbestos cement sheet, etc. '*Kutcha*' is a structure which has walls and roof made of unburnt bricks, bamboo, mud, grass, leaves, reeds and/or other thatch. 'Semi-*pucca*' are the remaining dwellings: usually their walls are *pucca* and the roofs are *kutcha* (Bannerjee Das, 2002).

8   It is the positive aspects of this process to which John Turner pointed to develop the early theory of informal housing supply (1972, 1976). On the other hand, the exploitative aspects of expecting the poor to provide for themselves the water, sanitation, power and access that are supplied to the rich at public expense formed the context in which Burgess (1982) and others criticised the new theories in what came to be known as the Turner–Burgess debate.

9   Further details can be found in Chapter 13.

10 Formally known as the Pay for Your House Scheme, this was a fund in which prospective owners made a fixed monthly contribution and would have a house allocated to them when their turn came. It was discontinued after major irregularities were exposed.

11 Figure calculated by Amin Kamete from statistics by Chenga (1993), MPCNH (1991) and National Housing Task Force (Zimbabwe) (2000).

12 Various figures are quoted for the total housing deficit in Zimbabwe. The popular figure is 2,000,000 (Government of Zimbabwe, 1995) but it has no empirical basis (Kamete, 2001). The 2005 mass eviction and clearances of informal housing added an estimated 92,460 housing structures to that (Tibaijuka, 2005).

13 In that document, slum housing is more extensive than just informal sector housing in that it is defined as an area which 'combines, the various extents … inadequate access to safe water, inadequate access to sanitation and other infrastructure, poor structural quality of housing, overcrowding, and insecure residential status' (UN-Habitat, 2003: 12).

14 See Tipple and Willis (1992) for a discussion of this in Ghana.

15 Plus what small amount can be added in cash by the new occupant – probably up to a maximum cost of R50,000 in all but a very few cases.

4   Defining homelessness in developing countries

1   The text of this section draws extensively from a recent paper (Tipple and Speak, 2006).

2   A similar influence has been discussed with reference to the words 'house', dwelling', 'family' and 'household' by one of the authors in the context of West Africa (Amole et al., 1993).

3   Fédération Européenne d'Associations Nationales Travaillant avec les Sans-Abri (Federation of European National Associations Working with the Homeless).

4   From the work of Ray Forrest and Jim Kemeny, cited in Williams and Cheal (2001).

5   For instance, the UN Global Shelter Strategy from 1987 referred to aspects of home as a site for adequate privacy, space, security, lighting and ventilation, basic infrastructure and location with regard to work and basic facilities – 'all at a reasonable cost'.

6   We use numbers per 1,000 rather than percentages because homeless populations tend to be assessed in this way.

7   Within the quotations, percentage numbers are changed to per 1,000 for consistency within this chapter.

8   By not fulfilling the first half of the Habitat Agenda's definition of adequate housing, above.

9   A similar plan for an area a few kilometres to the north was discussed in Kasongo and Tipple (1990).

10 See Chapter 3, note 7.

11 Non-serviceable seems to mean not fit for service rather than not able to be provided with services such as water supply.

12 This section draws on Tipple and Speak (2005).

13 With a measure of security thrown in for completeness!

14 These include the backyard shacks that are almost ubiquitous in the former 'Black Townships'.

15 High density only in local terms, with plots of 250 m^2.

16 Though living on houseboats may be quite a highly regarded strategy in some countries, both Indonesia and Egypt regard those who dwell on boats to be homeless.

17 *Hukou* was not simply a means of limiting rural–urban migration but was also the centre of a larger political and economic system through which essential rations and other benefits could

be distributed and controls maintained by various arms of the state (Chan and Zhang, 1999). There was an occasional relaxation of *hukou* controls when labour was very scarce for newly developing industries (especially in the late 1950s) which resulted in temporary influxes to the cities of non-registered people as employers scrambled for people to fill jobs (Cheng and Selden, 1994). There are many similarities to the *Propiska* stamp in the internal passport necessary in the past for migration within the Soviet Union (Spence, 1997).

18 It can also be interpreted as 'blindly floating' but we have recently been advised that 'aimlessly flowing' is probably a better translation in this context.

19 The pejorative meaning of *mangliu* is assisted by its linguistic relationship with words such as *liumang* (hooligan/rogue/vagabond/gangster/one of immoral behaviour) and *xialiu* (low-class/vulgar).

20 The cemeteries in question consist of dwelling-like structures but without doors or (frequently) roofs. These may be occupied by a caretaker who lives there with his household (and informal lodgers and renters), or by squatters. When the family of the deceased wish to come and remember the dead, the occupants may move out temporarily.

21 Anyone who has lived in Ghana can hardly fail to notice that there is frequent reference in conversation to what is and what is not 'Ghanaian', even though the various population groups differ quite markedly in many ways.

22 As there are no words for a household in at least some of the major local languages of Ghana, the meaning here is unclear. In *twi*, the *lingua franca* in Kumasi, the nearest concept is *fie nipa*, literally 'house people', members of the owner's lineage. It is almost unheard of for a Ghanaian to have no home as all originate from what is called, in *twi*, an *abusua fie* (a family root home) to which they can go and find accommodation as of right (Tipple et al., 1994).

23 Such hostels are not homeless people's hostels but the dormitories built for single male workers by the apartheid regime and now occupied by households. See Home (2000) for a discussion of their origins.

24 Inadequate housing is the converse of adequate housing which is defined earlier in this chapter.

5 Accommodation conditions and differentiating between homeless people and those in inadequate housing

1 Either because windows are too small or because they have been boarded up to prevent burglary as poor preys on poor.

2 And of our previous writing (Tipple and Speak, 2006).

3 In low-income compound housing in Ghana, for example, households in the same house may have very different access to the services therein. The owner is likely to have full access to any services and may have a tap, bathroom and toilet for exclusive use of his/her household. Relatives living in the house and favoured tenants may have good access, but some tenants may have to use public taps and latrines and wash in their rooms (Andreasen et al., 2005).

4 The following material draws heavily on Tipple and Speak (2006).

5 Writers too numerous to name have contributed to the cataloguing of this process. The pedigree starts with Abrams (1964) and Turner (1972, 1976) and continues through Peil (1976), Peattie (1980), Hardoy and Satterthwaite (1989), Schlyter (1987), Ward (1976) and many others.

6 Estimating the hidden millions

1 Doubling-up includes sharing accommodation and sleeping on someone's floor or sofa as a temporary guest. In Canada, staying with friends is called 'sofa-surfing' (Social Planning and Research Council of BC, 2005).

Notes

2 Numbers per 1,000 are used instead of percentages as that is the way homelessness figures have generally been expressed in the literature.

3 National and city populations in this section are taken from the tables in UN-Habitat (2003).

4 Defining homeless people as having no fixed abode (known as *bomzhi*) – the official status of those lacking the *propiska*, the stamp in the internal passport that verifies official place of residence (Spence, 1997). This is equivalent to the Chinese *hukuo* registration system.

5 These reception centres were set up in the communist era to give homeless people new documents, check for criminal activity and help them start a new life with job training and a place to live (usually hostels supported by factories and enterprises). The police were responsible for supervision of this process. This accords with the Chinese system of repatriation centres which have now become more humane in intent.

6 If such a description as 'definition' is not too ambitious for some countries.

7 The total official population of Shanghai is 16.7 million, Beijing is 12.8 million and Guangzhou 3.9 million.

8 Out of the 5.3 million households in Shanghai in 2000.

9 They are not included in the Census definition of homeless.

10 COFOPRI is a highly centralised government organisation created by the Fujimori government to design and execute a programme for the formalisation of property rights in urban invasion settlements.

11 However, it should be noted that, for people in informal settlements, the concept of 'tenure security' is relative. For those who live in a squatter settlement, their security originates from the construction of at least a room of the house itself rather than the registered property title.

12 Because they are very different in scale from their nearest neighbours.

7 Who are the hidden millions?

1 This is an ideal example of how data based on inadequate housing as homelessness distorts the picture for those we would include in homelessness from the discussion in Chapter 5.

2 In 2006, demographic data was reported by over 115 countries, hosting more than 75 per cent of the total population of concern to UNHCR. Not all countries, however, were able to provide a complete breakdown by sex and age. In fact, a complete breakdown by sex is available for only 70 countries, representing 10.3 million persons of concern.

3 In this case, enterprises with less than 11 employees.

4 Botswana, Kenya, Lesotho, Malawi and Swaziland.

5 It is not long since this was the norm in Europe also, as witnessed by the English term for skilled tradesmen as 'journeymen' from the French word for day.

6 Given the number of 'floating' prostitutes in major cities in Bangladesh, it is surprising that prostitution is absent from the 1997 census as a form of employment.

7 This contradicts the 15,000 for the whole 'floating' population of Dhaka (BBS, 1999, and Table 6.1), which is probably too low. In 2008, a woman who washes dishes for one or more middle-class households in Delhi receives Rs500 (£6) per month from each.

8 Based on expenditure required for a daily calorie intake of 2,100 per person in urban areas at 1999–2000 prices.

9 Only 8 per cent on a 30-day recall period and 5 per cent on a 7-day recall period.

10 There is still a common compulsion for those who die in urban areas to be buried in their rural homes.

8 Economic, social and cultural causes

1 According to Payne (2002), Mumbai had some of the most expensive land in the world by the mid-1990s. Land in Delhi is said to be as expensive as in London in 2008.

2   Bangladesh Institute of Development Studies and many other studies, however, use 2,112 cal./ person/day and 1,950 cal./person/day to define absolute and extreme poverty (BIDS, 2001).

3   In 1996, Indonesia's debt was 30 per cent of its GDP; in 2000, following the crisis, it stood at 128 per cent of GDP. The government had to allocate 40 per cent of the total expenditure of the 2000 state budget to paying loan instalments (INFID, 2000).

4   The UN Committee Against Torture has expressed concern about reports of violence towards workers by Indonesian military personnel, allegedly for security reasons (*Kompas*, 24 Nov. 2001).

5   Some analysts, however, believe that the number of unemployed people might actually have decreased, not because there has been more job opportunities open in the formal sector, but because there are fewer people who can afford to be unemployed. Being unemployed has become a luxury and people have no alternative but to work since there is no social security system in Indonesia (Wirakartakusumah and Hasan, n.d.).

6   The National Bureau of Statistics (Badan Pusat Statistik, 1984) set the poverty line at the cost of a basket of goods comprising food containing 2,100 calories per capita per day and a range of essential non-food items (Rahardjo, 2002). The daily *Republika* (29 July 1998) reported that the number of *gepeng* (beggars) in Jakarta increased by 30 per cent, prostitutes by 30 per cent, street vendors by 75 per cent and street children by 200 per cent after the crisis.

7   INEI defines poor people in Peru as those in households which have a total per capita monthly expenditure less than the value of basic food staples.

8   Other transferred funds for specific programmes (e.g. Vaso de Leche Program) may have increased it to 8 per cent (Miranda and Salazar, 2002).

9   In Zimbabwe, the poor are people who earn incomes below the Total Consumption Poverty Line (TCPL), while the very poor earn below the Food Poverty Line (FPL) (Kamete, 2001).

10 Minimum wage was Z$70 and the cost of a two bed-roomed house was Z$2,600.

11 Average annual urban incomes in 2002 were less than Z$42,000 (£420), while the lowest priced house in Harare was Z$300,000 (£3,000).

12 It is worth noting here that there is a suggestion that this trend in rural outmigration might be slowing in some African countries, most notably in Côte d'Ivoire, where the proportion of the population living in urban areas is falling (Beauchemin et al., 2004).

13 For an overview of land rights in a number of developing countries see de Janvry (2001).

14 One report observes that Zimbabweans are becoming 'more concerned with their immediate families with some even failing to adequately feed and clothe their spouses and children' (Musengeyi, 1999).

15 A similar trend in the UK is discussed by Haws (1999).

9 Political and legal issues

1   The major exception to this occurred in West Africa where a combination of a climate unsuited to European settlement and long-established urban settlements confined European land-take to prime urban land, usually on hill-tops.

2   The cost of services is influenced by plot size; the larger the plot, the longer are pipe runs and road frontages per plot.

3   For an excellent discussion of the importance of flexible regulatory frameworks, see Payne and Majale (2004).

4   Clientelism is defined as 'transactions between politicians and citizens whereby material favours are offered in return for political support at the polls' (Wantchekron, 2003: 400).

5   Such promotion in India turns a squatter settlement into a 'slum', a term used to denote a poor-quality settlement in which the residents have a right to be allocated a plot in a resettlement area if clearance takes place. Squatters in India have no rights whatsoever.

6   The State Ministry of Popular Housing Decision No. 06/KPTS/1994 aptly sums this up in the following statement: 'without a home or a permanent place to stay it would be difficult for a

person's formal existence to be recognised (to have a KTP)' *(tanpa rumah atau tempat bermukim yang tetap keberadaan seseorang secara formal sulit diakui (memiliki KTP))*.

7 These organisations are legacies of the Japanese occupation (1942–5) when they were used to organise the people in war efforts (Jellinek, 1995). In 1969, Ali Sadikin, the governor of Jakarta, revived them to promote community participation in the city's development. A *rukun tetangga* (RT) consists of around 30 households, while a *rukun warga* (RW) consists of around 10 RTs (300 households).

10 Disaster and conflicts

1 There seems to have been a similar urge among agencies following the Indian Ocean tsunami. Moving a tearful household into a new home provides great publicity.
2 In reality, many self-builders employ artisans to do most of the work (Laquian, 1983; UNCHS/ ILO, 1995).
3 As we write, the news pictures following the earthquake in Sichuan province, China, once again show likely flaws in reinforced concrete construction that are all too familiar.
4 For example a person who paid Z$100 in taxes would pay a drought levy of Z$3.

11 Exclusion, perceptions and isolation

1 The three-generation household is traditional and still very common in China.
2 These organisations are a legacy of the Japanese occupation (1942–45) when they were used to organise the people for the war effort (Jellinek, 1991). In 1969, Ali Sadikin, the governor of Jakarta at that time, revived them to promote community participation in the city's development. A *rukun tetangga* (RT) consist of around 30 households, while a *rukun warga* (RW) consist of around 10 RTs.
3 These are free-standing ranges of rooms built in the plots of formal dwellings to provide rental accommodation or just extra space for large households. They may be rudimentary assemblies of recycled materials or masonry constructions. Households occupying them usually share services with the main dwelling (Crankshaw et al., 2000).

12 Children and homelessness

1 Children are also protected from capital punishment and life imprisonment.
2 *Eet* is a Bengali term for brick; *eetalian* hotel is a situation where one eats sitting on an *eet*, often in the open air.

13 Towards strategic interventions for homeless people

1 In which a young family is tragically split up when they lose their accommodation and cannot find a replacement. Written by Jeremy Sandford, *Cathy Come Home* was screened by BBC1 on 16 December 1966, within the regular 'Wednesday Play' slot. After the screening, the issue of homelessness became more prominent in public and political discussion and the housing action charity Shelter was formed. For the younger generation, it is probably hard to understand the importance of this black-and-white television play. Like both the authors, large numbers of British people of a certain age can remember *Cathy Come Home* more than 40 years after its screening.
2 As we write, the result of the presidential election of 2008 is still to be announced.
3 Ownership in common means that the share of the property held by one of the owners can be bequeathed to another person rather than passing in full to the other joint owners.

4 The Holy See (the Papal State of Vatican City) uses its seat in the United Nations to protect families by examining all proposals against how they affect the family as an institution.

5 The subsidised housing programme undoubtedly has advantages and disadvantages. It has provided about two million dwellings but has not provided for the majority nor for many of the very poor. It is not our purpose here to detail these or make a case for or against the approach in the special situation of post-apartheid South Africa.

6 There are a few night shelters for children operated by NGOs in Dhaka.

7 Land formed from river delta sand deposits.

8 Nautical language is the root of much of colloquial English, including 'toeing the line', 'to the bitter end', 'at loggerheads' and 'by and large'.

9 This association has its limits, however. The reference to cargo, etc., which is adrift is less helpful in our context as anything not fixed down (housed) would be a nuisance and could be dangerous in rough seas. The expression 'loose cannon' comes from this context as several tonnes of metal on wheels, loose on a pitching deck, were a dangerous and unpredictable companion. The extension of the loose cannon metaphor to homeless people is not recommended!

10 We gratefully acknowledge the contribution of Sheela Patel in developing this insight.

11 Approximately US$656,000 (1.00 P (Philippines Peso) = US$0.0187441).

12 This occurs when the staircase of transition is turned into a staircase of exclusion, generating (new metaphor) 'revolving door effects' in which an entrance to a new level can be quickly followed by an exit back to a lower level (Sahlin, 1998; Busch-Geertsema, 1999).

13 Currently, many street sleepers can afford a room in the cheapest informal settlements but prefer not to live there as the cost, location, environment and accommodation combination they offer is less attractive than living free on the street and finding hostel space when the weather is particularly poor.

14 A rest house or *sarai* provided by a religious organisation.

15 This is being done in a context of rapid commercial development of studio apartments and $5,500 per month penthouses in the old buildings on The Bowery (Hevesi, 2002).

16 In the days when capsule hotels are quite popular in Japan and may be moving to Europe, the idea that people could occupy relatively small spaces with shared bathrooms and sitting areas might not be as alien as it might have been a decade or so ago.

17 Although they don't tend to in industrialised countries.

18 It is important that the savings are banked because cash is vulnerable to loss in disasters. Similarly, the ability to lodge title documents in a secure place would be very helpful in recovery from cyclonic surge disasters in Bangladesh (Sorrill, 1998).

19 Known as 'panhandling' in the USA.

20 Though the institutions are usually referred to using more euphemistic language such as rehabilitation centres.

21 There is an argument that this is not a problem as low-income households should be entitled to capitalise on the windfall benefits accruing from their tenure security by choosing to sell and go back into poorer accommodation. However, because of their ignorance of a fair market price, the cost of providing the benefit is likely to be many times higher than the income they secure, making it a very inefficient way for the state to pass benefits to the poor. For example, Tipple was told by a South African NGO in East London that beneficiaries of 22,500 rands-worth of subsidised housing had been known to sell it for a few hundred rands worth of beer.

22 Within the bounds of decent work (ILO, 1999; Ghai, 2003).

Bibliography

Aashray Adhikar Abhiyan (2001). *The Capital's Homeless: A Preliminary Study,* New Delhi: Aashray Adhikar Abhiyan.

Abdelgalil, S., R. G. Gurgel, S. Theobald and L. E. Cuevas (2004). 'Household and family characteristics of street children in Aracaju', *Brazil Archives of Disease in Childhood,* 89: 817–20.

Abdulai, R. T. and I. E. Ndekugri (2007). 'Customary landholding institutions and housing development in urban centres of Ghana: case studies of Kumasi and Wa', *Habitat International,* 31: 257–67.

Aboderin, I. (2004a). 'Modernisation and ageing theory revisited: current explanations of recent developing world and historical Western shifts in material family support for older people', *Ageing and Society,* 24: 29–50.

Aboderin, I. (2004b). 'Current explanations of recent developing world and historical Western shifts in material family support for older people', *Ageing and Society,* 24 29–50.

Abrams, C. (1964). *Man's Struggle for Shelter in an Urbanizing World,* Cambridge, MA: MIT Press.

ADAMHA (1983). *Alcohol, Drug Abuse and Mental Health Problems of the Homeless,* Proceedings of a round table, Washington, DC: United States Alcohol, Drugs Abuse and Mental Health Administration.

ADB, GOB and LGED (1996). *A Report on the Survey of Street Dwellers of Dhaka City: Final Report. Urban Poverty Reduction Project,* Dhaka: Government of Bangladesh (GOB) and Asian Development Bank (ADB).

Adler, M. (1999). 'Public attitudes to begging: theory in search of data', in H. Dean (ed.). *Begging Questions: Street-level Economic Activity and Social Policy Failure,* Bristol: Policy Press.

Afolayan, A. A. (1988). 'Immigration and expulsion of ECOWAS aliens in Nigeria', *International Migration Review,* 22(1): 4–27.

Africa News (2007). 'Homeless man freezes to death in Johannesburg after snow', *Africa News,* 27 June, accessed 5 Sept. 2007 from <http://news.monstersandcritics.com/africa/news/article_1323283.php>.

Afsar, R. (2001). *The State of Urban Governance and People's Participation in Bangladesh,* Dhaka: CARE International.

Agbola, T. and A. M. Jinadu (1997). 'Forced eviction and forced relocation in Nigeria: The experience of those evicted from Maroko in 1990', *Environment and Urbanisation,* 9(2): 271–88.

Ahmed, S. A., D. L. Mallick, L. Ali and A. A. Rahman (2002). *Literature Review on Bangladesh Shrimp, Project PORESSFA No.IC4–2001–10042*, Dhaka: Bangladesh, University of Portsmouth UK and BCAS.

AITEC (1994). 'AITEC declaration on land occupation and regularisation with regard to rights to housing and to the city in the developing countries', accessed 24 Feb. 1999 from <http://www.globenet.org/aitec/urbain/Mexgb.html>.

Alarcon, J. J. (1998). 'Comercializacion de la Papa para Consumo: El caso de eje Valle del Mantaro-Lima', in J. Escobal (ed.), *Comercialization Agricola en el Peru,* Lima: IEP Library.

Albertyn, R., S. W. Bickler, A. B. van As, A. J. W. Millar and H. Rode (2003). 'The effects of war on children in Africa', *Pediatric Surgery International,* 19(4): 227–32.

Ali, M. and A. de Muynck (2005). 'Illness incidence and health seeking behaviour among street children in Rawalpindi and Islamabad, Pakistan: A qualitative study', *Child: Care, Health and Development,* 31(5): 525–32.

Amole, B., D. Korboe and A. G. Tipple (1993). 'The family house in West Africa: A forgotten resource for policy makers?', *Third World Planning Review,* 15(4): 355–72.

Amuyunzu-Nyamongo, M. (2006). 'Declarations upon declarations: When shall women experience real change?', *CODESRIA Bulletin,* 1 and 2, Nairobi, Kenya: African Institute for Health and Development (AIHD).

Anderson, I. and J. Christian (2003). 'Causes of homelessness in the UK: A dynamic analysis', *Journal of Community and Applied Social Psychology,* 13: 105–18.

Anderson, I. and D. Tulloch (2000). *Pathways through Homelessness: A Review of the Research Evidence*, Edinburgh: Scottish Homes.

Andreasen, J., J. Eskemose and G. Tipple (2005). *The Demise of the Compound Houses: Consequences for the Low Income Population in Kumasi*, RICS Research Paper, 6/1, accessed 24 Sept. 2007 from <http://www.rics.org/ricsweb/getpage.aspx?p=kav8edhaikg4wqeg7lpj7a>.

Andrienko, Y. and S. Guriev (2004). 'Determinants of interregional mobility in Russia', *Economics of Transition,* 12(1): 1–27.

Anerfi, K. (1996). *Street Children in Accra, Sexual Behaviour Factors and HIV/AIDS: A Survey Report*, Accra: UNICEF.

Angel, S. (2000). *Housing Policy Matters: A Global Analysis,* Oxford: Oxford University Press.

Angel, S. and S. Boonyabancha (1988). 'Land sharing as an alternative to eviction: The Bangkok experience', *Third World Planning Review,* 10(2): 107–27.

Anthropology Today (2005). Front cover photograph, 21(4).

Aoki, H. (2003). 'Homelessness in Osaka: Globalisation, *Yoseba* and disemployment', *Urban Studies,* 40(2): 361–78.

Aparajeyo-Bangladesh (2000). *Need Assessment Survey of the Street Children in the Sayedabad and Jatrabari Areas of Dhaka City,* Dhaka: Aparajeyo-Bangladesh (AB).

Aparajeyo-Bangladesh and Terre des hommes (2000). *A Baseline Survey on the Street Children of Chittagong City, Bangladesh,* Dhaka: Aparajeyo-Bangladesh (AB) and Terre des hommes (Tdh).

Apt, N. A. (1993). 'Care of the elderly in Ghana: An emerging issue', *Journal of Cross-Cultural Gerontology,* 8(4): 301–12.

Apt, N. A. (1999). *Rapid Urbanization and Living Arrangements of Older Persons in Africa,* New York: Population Division, Department of Economic and Social Affairs, United Nations Secretariat.

Aptekar, L. (1988). *Street Children of Cali,* Durham, NC, and London: Duke University Press.

Aptekar, L. (1994). 'Street children in the developing world: A review of their condition', *Cross-Cultural Research,* 28(3): 195–224.

Aptekar, L. and P. Heinonen (2003). 'Methodological implications of contextual diversity in research on street children', *Children, Youth and Environments,* 13(1).

Aries, P. (1962). *Centuries of Childhood,* Harmondsworth: Penguin.

Arndt, C. and J. D. Lewis (2001). 'The HIV/AIDS pandemic in South Africa: Sectoral impacts and unemployment', *Journal of International Development. Special Issue: AIDS and Development in Africa,* 13(4): 427–49.

Asian Coalition for Housing Rights (1989). *Battle for Housing Rights in Korea,* Bangkok: ACHR.

Asian Development Bank (1999). *The Bank's Urban Sector Strategy (Draft),* Manila: Agricultural and Social Sectors Department (West), Asian Development Bank.

Aspinall, E. (2005). 'Indonesia after the tsunami', *Current History,* 104: 105–9.

Association for Development (2002). *A Study on the Problems of Street Children Living at Railway Stations in Delhi,* New Delhi: Association for Development.

Audefroy, J. (1994). 'Eviction trends worldwide and the role of local authorities in implementing the right to housing', *Environment and Urbanisation,* 6(1): 8–24.

Australian Institute of Health and Welfare (1999). *Australia's Welfare 1999: Services and Assistance,* Canberra: Australian Institute of Health and Welfare.

Avi-Yonah, R. S. (2000). 'Globalization, tax competition, and the fiscal crisis of the welfare state', *Harvard Law Review,* 113(7): 1573–1676.

Avramov, D. (1995). *Homelessness in the European Union: Social and Legal Context of Housing Exclusion in the 1990s,* Brussels: FEANTSA.

Avramov, D. (1996). *The Invisible Hand of the Housing Market,* Fourth Research Report of the European Observatory on Homelessness, Brussels: FEANTSA.

Badan Pusat Statistik. (2000). 'Statistics by sector', BPS Statistics Indonesia, accessed 7 July 2001 from <http://www.bps.go.id/statbysector/population/method.shtml>.

Baker, R. and C. Panter-Brick (2000). 'A comparative perspective on children's "careers" and abandonment in Nepal', in C. Panter-Brick and M. Smith (eds), *Abandoned Children,* Cambridge: Cambridge University Press.

Bamberger, M., B. Sanyal and N. Valverde (1982). *Evaluation of Sites and Services Projects: The Experience from Lusaka, Zambia,* Washington, DC: World Bank.

Banerjee, A. and S. Sengupta (2000). 'Socio-economic and cultural determinants of high risk sexual behaviors among street children: West Bengal Sexual Health Project, Calcutta', XIII International AIDS Conference, Durban, South Africa. 9–14 July.

Banerjee, R. (2000). 'Poverty and primary schooling', *Economic and Political Weekly* (4 March): 795–802.

Bannerjee Das, P. (2002). *The Nature, Extent and Eradication of Homelessness in India: Country Report for the CARDO Project on Homelessness in Developing Countries,* New Delhi: PK-Peu Das.

Barnett, A. and A. Whiteside (1999). 'HIV/AIDS and development: Case studies and a conceptual framework', *European Journal of Development Research,* 11: 200–34.

Bartlett, S., R. Hart, D. Satterthwaite, X. de la Barra and A. Missair (1999). *Cities for Children: Children's Rights, Poverty and Urban Management,* London: Earthscan, UNICEF.

BAWO Projekt Büro (n.d.). *Östereich, Grundsatzprogramm,* Vienna: BAWO Bundesarbeits-gemeinschaft Wohnungslosenhilfe, accessed 10 Jan. 1999, from <http://www.bawo.at/>.

BBS (1999). *Census of Slum Areas and Floating Population 1997*, Dhaka: Bangladesh Bureau of Statistics (BBS).

BBS (2000). *Statistical Pocketbook*, Dhaka: Bangladesh Bureau of Statistics.

Beata, D. and T. A. B. Snijders (2002). 'Estimating the size of the homeless population in Budapest, Hungary', *Quality and Quantity,* 36(3): 291–303.

Beauchemin, C., S. Henry and B. Schoumaker (2004). 'Rural–urban migration in West Africa: Toward a reversal? Migration trends and economic conjuncture in Burkina Faso and Côte d'Ivoire', Paper submitted for the 2004 PAA Annual Meeting, Session 608: Internal Migration in Developing Countries, Boston, 1–3 April.

Beauchemin, E. (1999). *The Exodus: The Growing Migration of Children from Ghana's Rural Areas to the Urban Centres*, Accra: Catholic Action for Street Children (CAS) and UNICEF, Ghana.

Beavis, M. A., N. Klos, T. Carter and C. Douchant (1997). 'Aboriginal peoples and homelessness', Executive Summary. Institute of Urban Studies, University of Winnipeg, accessed Jan. 1999, from <http://www.cmhc-schl.gc.ca/Research/Homeless/F_aborig.html>.

Beazley, H. (1999). *'A Little but Enough': Street Children's Subcultures in Yogyakarta, Indonesia*, Canberra: Australian National University.

Beazley, H. (2000). 'Street boys in Yogyakarta: Social and spatial exclusion in the public spaces of the city', in S. Watson and G. Bridges (eds), *Companion to the City,* London: Blackwell.

Beazley, H. (2002). 'Vagrants wearing makeup: Negotiating spaces on the streets of Yogyakarta, Indonesia', *Urban Studies,* 39(9): 1665–83.

Begum, A. (1997). *The Socio-economic Conditions of Pavement Dwellers of Dhaka City*, Dhaka: Bangladesh Institute of Development Studies (BIDS).

Benjamin, S. (2000). 'Governance, economic settings and poverty in Bangalore', *Environment and Urbanization,* 12(1): 35–56.

Benschop, M. (2002). *Rights and Reality: Are Women's Rights to Land, Housing and Property Implemented in East Africa?*, Nairobi: UN-Habitat.

Benschop, M. (2004). 'Women in human settlements development – challenges and opportunities – women's rights to land and property', Paper for the Commission on Sustainable Development, Nairobi, UN-Habitat.

Beresford, S. (1998). 'Law and urban change in the new South Africa', in E. Fernandes and A. Varley (eds), *Illegal Cities*, London: Zed Books.

Berke, P. (1995). *Natural Hazard Reduction and Sustainable Development: A Global Assessment*, Working Paper Number S95–02, Chapel Hill, NC: University of North Carolina at Chapel Hill, Center for Urban and Regional Studies.

Bernasconi, O. and G. Puentes (2006). 'Inhabiting the streets: Self-portraits of Chilean homeless people', GURU International Conference on Homelessness: a Global Perspective, New Delhi, 9–13 Jan.

Berner, E. (1997). 'Opportunities and insecurities: Globalisation, localities and the struggle for urban land in Manila', *European Journal of Development Research,* 9: 167–82.

Berner, E. (2000). 'Poverty alleviation and the eviction of the poorest: Towards urban land reform in the Philippines', *International Journal of Urban and Regional Research,* 24(3): 554–66.

Berner, E. (2001). 'Learning from informal markets: Innovative approaches to land and housing provision', *Development in Practice,* 11(2–3): 292–307.

Bhaumik, S. and V. Srivastava (2002). *Volunteering to Make Delhi Aware*, Delhi: Multiple Action Research Group.

Bibars, I. (1998). 'Street children in Egypt: From home to street to inappropriate institutions', *Environment and Urbanization*, 10(1): 201–16.

BIDS (2001). *Fighting Human Poverty: Bangladesh Human Development Report 2000*, Dhaka: Bangladesh Institute of Development Studies (BIDS).

Blanchet, T. (1996). *Lost Innocence, Stolen Childhood*, Dhaka: University Press.

Blau, J. (1992). *The Visible Poor: Homelessness in the US*, New York: Oxford University Press.

Bolnick, J. (1996). 'uTshani Buyakhuluma (The grass speaks): People's dialogue and South African Homeless People's Federation (1994–6)', *Environment and Urbanisation*, 8(2): 153–70.

Boston Partnership for Older Adults (2003). '100,000 voices on growing older in Boston', accessed 6 June 2008, from <http://www.bostonolderadults.org/pdf/voices.pdf>.

Boyden, J. and P. Holden (1991). *Children of the Cities*, London: Zed Books.

Bracher, M., G. Santow and S. C. Watkins (2003). 'A microsimulation study of the effects of divorce and remarriage on lifetime risks of HIV/AIDS in rural Malawi', Paper prepared for Session 20, Health Status and Mortality over the Life Course in Developing Countries, Population Association of America Annual Meeting, Minneapolis, MN, 1–3 May.

Bracking, S. (2005). 'Development denied: Autocratic militarism in post-election Zimbabwe', *Review of African Political Economy*, 32 (104–5): 341–57.

Brinkhoff, T. (2003). 'City population: The principal agglomerations of the world', <city population.de>, accessed 1 Sept. 2003, from <http://www.citypopulation.de/Country. html?E+World>.

Bristol City Council (1998) *Audit of Homelessness Services for Single People in Bristol: Initial Findings*, Bristol: Housing Services, BCC.

Brown, A. and T. Lloyd-Jones (2002). 'Spatial planning, access and infrastructure', in C. Radoki and T. Lloyd-Jones (eds), *Urban Livelihoods: A People-Centred Approach to Reducing Poverty*, London and Sterling, VA: Earthscan.

Brown, J. (1997). 'Working toward freedom from violence: The process of change in battered women', *Violence Against Women*, 3(1): 5–26.

Browne, A. and S. S. Bassuk (1997). 'Intimate violence in the lives of homeless and poor housed women: Prevalence and patterns in an ethnically diverse sample', *American Journal of Orthopsychiatry*, 67(2): 261–78.

Budiman, A. (1993). 'Stabilitas Politik dan Pertumbuhan Ekonomi', in INFID (ed.), *Pembangunan di Indonesia: Memandang dari Sisi Lain*, Jakarta: Yayasan Obor Indonesia

Burgess, R. (1982). 'Self-help housing advocacy: A curious form of radicalism. A critique of the work of John F. C. Turner', in P. M. Ward (ed.), *Self-Help Housing: A Critique*, London: Mansell.

Burgess, R. (1985). 'The limits of self-help housing', *Development and Change*, 16(2): 271–312.

Burra, S., S. Patel and T. Kerr (2003). 'Community-designed, built and managed toilet blocks in Indian cities', *Environment and Urbanization*, 15(2): 11.

Busch-Geertsema, V. (1999). 'Homelessness and support in housing in Germany. Solution or problem?', *National Report 1998 for the European Observatory on Homelessness*, Brussels: FEANTSA.

Bustamante, D. O. (1999). 'Family structure problems, child mistreatment, street children and drug use: A community-based approach', in Consortium for Street Children (ed.),

Prevention of Street Migration: Resource Pack, Cork: Consortium for Street Children and University College.

Buvinic, M. and G. R. Gupta (1997). 'Female-headed households and female-maintained families: Are they worth targeting to reduce poverty', *Economic Development and Cultural Change,* 45(2): 259–80.

Çagatay, N. and S. Özler (1995). 'Feminization of the labor force: The effects of long-term development and structural adjustment', *World Development,* 23(11): 1883–94.

Cai, Y. (2001). 'Cheap-rent housing project in Shanghai', *Urban Development,* 18(47–8).

Caplow, T., H. M. Bahr and D. Sternberg (1968). 'Homelessness', in D. L. Sills (ed.), *International Encyclopedia of the Social Sciences*, vol. 6, New York: Free Press.

CAPMAS (1996). *Census of Egypt*, Cairo: CAPMAS.

Carrizosa, S. O. and J. Poertner (1992). 'Latin American street children: Problem, programmes and critique', *International Social Work,* 35: 405–13.

Carter, M., P. Little, T. Mogues and W. Negatu (2007). 'Poverty traps and natural disasters in Ethiopia', *World Development,* 35(5): 835–56.

Central Statistical Office (1998). *Poverty in Zimbabwe*, Harare: CSO.

Centre for Disease Control (2004). *HIV/AIDS Surveillance Report, 2004*, Atlanta, GA: US Department of Health and Human Services, Centre for Disease Control.

Centre for Media Studies (CMS) (2000). *An In-Depth Study of Problems, Control and Prevention of Beggary and Rehabilitation of Beggars in NCT of Delhi*, New Delhi: Ministry of Social Justice and Empowerment, Government of India.

Chabal, P. and J.-P. Daloz (1999). *Africa Works: Disorder as Political Instrument,* London and Bloomington, IN: James Currey and Indiana University Press.

Chamberlain, C. (1999). *Counting the Homeless, 1996*, Canberra: Australian Bureau of Statistics, accessed 22 Feb. 2007 from <http://www.abs.gov.au/Ausstats/abs@.nsf/525a1b 9402141235ca25682000146abc/f26f9a1fc5d22f89ca256889000d02fd!OpenDocument>.

Chan, K. W. and L. Zhang (1999). 'The hukou system and rural–urban migration in China: Processes and changes', *China Quarterly,* 160: 818–55.

Chant, S. (1996). *Gender, Urban Development and Housing*, New York: United Nations Development Programme.

Chaudhuri, D. P. (1997). 'A policy perspective on child labour in India with pervasive gender and urban bias in school education', *Indian Journal of Labour Economics,* 40(1): 789–808.

Chen, M. A. (2007). *Rethinking the Informal Economy: Linkages with the Formal Economy and the Formal Regulatory Environment*, United Nations Department of Economic and Social Affairs Working Paper No. 46 ST/ESA/2007/DWP/46, New York: United Nations.

Cheng, T. and M. Selden (1994). 'The origins and consequences of China's hukuo system', *China Quarterly,* 139: 644–68.

Chenga, M. M. (1993). 'Provision of housing in Zimbabwe', in L. M. Zinyama, D. S. Tevera and S. D. Cumming (eds), *Harare: The Growth and Problems of the City,* Harare: University of Zimbabwe.

Chicago Coalition for the Homeless (2006). *How Many People are Homeless in Chicago? An FY 2006 Analysis*, Chicago, IL: Chicago Coalition for the Homeless and Survey Research Laboratory, University of Illinois at Chicago.

China Daily (2005). 'Moving millions rebuild a nation', 17 Jan, accessed 5 March 2007 from <http://www.china.org.cn/english/BAT/118112.htm>.

Chinaka, C. (2000). 'Zimbabwe floods leave 250,000 homeless', *The Guardian*, 26 February, accessed 13 Nov. 2008 from <http://www.guardian.co.uk/world/2000/feb/26/zimbabwe>.

Choguill, C. L. (1993). 'Housing policy trends in Bangladesh: Meeting the needs of a low-income population', *Cities,* 10(4): 326–36.

Choguill, M. B. G. (1996). 'A ladder of community participation for underdeveloped countries', *Habitat International,* 20(3): 431–44.

Christian, J. (2003). 'Homelessness: Integrating international perspectives', *Journal of Community and Applied Social Psychology,* 13(2): 85–90.

Clapham, D. (2002). 'Housing pathways: A post modern analytical framework', *Housing, Theory and Society,* 19(2): 57–68.

Clapham, D. (2003). 'Pathways approaches to homelessness research', *Journal of Community and Applied Social Psychology,* 13(2): 119–27.

Clarke, C. and D. Howard (2006). 'Contradictory socio-economic consequences of structural adjustment in Kingston, Jamaica', *Geographical Journal,* 172(2): 106–29.

Cleveland, D. A. (1991). 'Migration in West Africa: A savanna village perspective', *Africa: Journal of the International African Institute,* 61(2): 222–46.

Cloke, P., P. Milbourne and R. Widdowfield (2000). 'Partnerships and policy networks in rural governance: Homelessness in Taunton', *Public Administration,* 78: 111–33.

Cloke, P., P. Milbourne and R. Widdowfield (2001). 'Making the homeless count? Enumerating rough sleepers and the distortion of homelessness', *Policy and Politics,* 29(3): 259–79.

CMDA (1987). *A Study on Pavement Dwellers,* Calcutta: Calcutta Metropolitan Development Authority.

Comerio, M. C. (1997). 'Housing issues after disasters', *Journal of Contingencies & Crisis Management;* 5(3, Sept.): 166–79.

Consortium for Street Children (2001). *A Civil Society Forum for South Asia on Promoting and Protecting the Rights of Street Children, 12–14 December 2001,* Colombo, Sri Lanka, accessed 22 June 2007, from <http://www.streetchildren.org.uk/resources/details/?country=64&type=country>.

Consortium for Street Children (2004a). *A Civil Society Forum for North Africa and the Middle East on Promoting and Protecting the Rights of Street Children,* Cairo, 3–6 March.

Consortium for Street Children (2004b). 'Information about street children: Indonesia', accessed 11 March, 2008 from <http://www.streetchildren.org.uk/>.

Cooley, A. and J. Ron (2002). 'The NGO scramble: Organizational insecurity and the political economy of transnational action', *International Security,* 27(1): 5–39.

Cooper, B. (1995). 'Shadow people: The reality of homelessness in the '90s', accessed 14 June 1999 from <gopher://csf.colorado.edu:70/00/hac/homeless/Geographical-Archive/reality-australia>.

Cotton, A. and R. Franceys (1991). *Services for Shelter: Infrastructure for Urban Low Income Housing,* Liverpool: Liverpool University Press.

Counts, A. (1996). *Give us Credit: How Muhammad Yunus's Micro Lending Revolution is Empowering Women from Bangladesh to Chicago,* New York: Random House.

Crane, M. (1997). *Homeless Truths: Challenging the Myth about Older Homeless People,* London: Help the Aged and Crisis.

Crankshaw, O., A. Gilbert and A. Morris (2000). 'Backyard Soweto', *International Journal of Urban and Regional Research,* 24(4): 841–54.

Croll, E. J. and H. Ping (1997). 'Migration for and against agriculture in eight Chinese villages', *China Quarterly,* 149: 128–46.

Csikszentmihalyi, M. and E. Rochberg-Halton (1981). *The Meaning of Things: Domestic Symbols and the Self,* Cambridge: Cambridge University Press.

CSIR and Department of Housing (1999). *The State of the Human Settlements, South Africa 1994–1998*, Pretoria: CSIR and Department of Housing.

D'Monte, D. (1989). 'The pavement dwellers of Bombay', in D. de Silva (ed.), *Against all Odds, Breaking the Poverty Trap*, London: Panos.

D'Lima, H. and R. Gosalia (1992). *Situational Analysis of Street Children in Bombay*, Bombay: UNICEF.

Daly, G. (1996). 'Migrants and gatekeepers: The links between immigration and homelessness in Western Europe', *Cities*, 13(1): 11–23.

Daly, M. (1993). *Abandoned: Profile of Homeless Persons in Europe*, Second Report of the European Observatory of the Homeless, Brussels: FEANTSA.

Daly, M. (1994). *The Right to a Home, the Right to a Future*, Brussels: FEANTSA.

Daly, M. (2002). 'Care as a good for social policy', *Journal of Social Policy*, 31(2): 251–70.

Daniels, L. (1999). 'The role of small enterprises in the household and national economy in Kenya: a significant contribution or a last resort?', *World Development*, 27(1): 55–65.

De Haan, A. (1999). 'Livelihoods and poverty: The role of migration. A critical review of the migration literature', *Journal of Development Studies*, 36(2): 1–47.

De Janvry, A. (2001). *Access to Land, Rural Poverty, and Public Action*, Oxford: Oxford University Press.

De Janvry, A. and E. Sadoulet (2000). 'Rural poverty in Latin America: Determinants and exit paths', *Food Policy*, 25(4): 389–409.

De Soto, H. (2000). *The Mystery of Capital: Why Capitalism Triumphs in the West and Fails Everywhere Else*, New York: Basic Books.

DeVerteuil, G. (2006). 'The local state and homeless shelters: Beyond revanchism?', *Cities*, 23(2): 109–20.

De Vos, P. (2001). 'Grootboom, the right to access to housing and substantive equality as contextual fairness', *South African Journal on Human Rights*, 17(2): 258–76.

De Wit, M. J. (1992). 'The slums of Bangalore: Mapping a crisis in overpopulation', *Geographic Information Systems*, 2(1): 33–45.

Deacon, B. (2000). 'Eastern European welfare states: The impact of the politics of globalization', *Journal of European Social Policy*, 10(2): 146–61.

Dehavenon, A. (1996). *From Bad to Worse at the Emergency Assistance Unit: How New York City Tried to Stop Sheltering Homeless Families in 1996*, New York: Action Research Project on Hunger, Homelessness and Family Health.

Demusz, K. (2003). 'From relief to development: Negotiating the continuum on the Thai–Burmese border 1', *Journal of Refugee Studies*, 11(3): 231–44.

Dennis, C. (1997). 'Truck pushers, grain pickers and grandmothers: Street children and some gender and age aspects of vulnerability in Tamale, Northern Ghana', in S. Jones and N. Nelson (eds), *Urban Poverty in Africa: From Understanding to Alleviation*, London: IT Press.

Department for Communities and Local Government (2003). *Homelessness Statistics, December 2002, and Bed & Breakfast Policy Briefing*, London: Department of Communities and Local Government.

Department for Communities and Local Government (2006). *Homelessness Research Summary No. 3, Evaluating Homelessness Prevention*, London: Department of Communities and Local Government.

Department for Communities and Local Government (2008). 'Rough sleeping 10 years on: From the streets to independent living and opportunity', accessed 12 May 2008 from <http://www.communities.gov.uk/documents/housing/doc/Disscussionpaper.doc>

Bibliography

Department of Housing (2006). *Annual Report 2005–2006*, Pretoria: Department of Housing, Republic of South Africa.

Department of Housing and Planning Research (2002). *The Nature, Extent and Eradication of Homelessness in Developing Countries: ESCOR Project R7905: Ghana Case Study*, Kumasi, Ghana: Department of Housing and Planning Research, Kwame Nkrumah University of Science and Technology.

Department of Social Services and Population Development (2000). *Draft Green Paper: Towards a National Child Labour Action Programme*, Pretoria: Department of Social Services and Population Development.

Department of Welfare and Population Development (1998). *Draft Document on Policy Issues and Strategic Guidelines on Street Children in South Africa*, Pretoria: Department of Welfare and Population Development.

Despres, C. (1991). 'The meaning of home: Literature review and directions for future research and theoretical development', *Journal of Architectural and Planning Research*, 8(2): 96–115.

DFID (2005). 'Making markets systems work better for the poor (M4P): An introduction to the concept', Discussion Paper prepared for the ADB–DFID 'learning event', Manila: DFID.

Doherty, J. (2001). 'Gendering homelessness', in B. Edgar and J. Doherty (eds), *Women and Homelessness in Europe*, Bristol: Policy Press.

Douglass, M. (2000). 'Mega-urban regions and world city formation: globalisation, the economic crisis and urban policy issues in Pacific Asia', *Urban Studies*, 37(12): 2315–35.

Dovey, K. (1985). 'Home and homelessness', in I. Altman and C. Werner (eds), *Home Environments*, New York: Plenum Press.

DRC (2007). *Democratic Republic of the Congo: Poverty Reduction Strategy Paper*, Washington, DC: International Monetary Fund.

Drever, A. (1999). *Homeless Count Methodologies: An Annotated Bibliography*, Los Angeles, CA: Institute for the Study of Homelessness and Poverty, University of California.

Drew, R., G. Foster and J. Chitima (1996). 'Cultural practices associated with death in the North Nyanga District of Zimbabwe and their impact on widows and orphans', *Journal of Social Development in Africa*, 11(1): 79–86.

Drimie, S. (2003). 'HIV/Aids and land: Case studies from Kenya, Lesotho and South Africa', *Development Southern Africa*, 20(5): 647–58.

Driver, F. (2004). *Power and Pauperism*, Cambridge: Cambridge University Press.

DSS (1999a). 'A review of existing services relating to street children (Khulna, Barisal and Jessor): Appropriate resources for improving street children's environment (ARISE) (BGD/97/028)', *ARISE*, vol. 3, Dhaka: Department of Social Services (DSS), Ministry of Social Welfare.

DSS (1999b). 'A review of existing services relating to street children (Narayangonj, Tongi and Mymensingh): Appropriate resources for improving street children's environment (ARISE) (BGD/97/028)', *ARISE*, vol. 2: Dhaka: Department of Social Services (DSS), Ministry of Social Welfare.

Du Plessis, J. (2005). 'The growing problem of forced evictions and the crucial importance of community-based, locally appropriate alternatives', *Environment and Urbanization*, 17(1): 123–34.

Dupont, V. (1998). 'Mobility pattern and economic strategies of houseless people in Old Delhi', Paper presented to the International Seminar 'Delhi games: Use and control of the urban space. Power games and actors' strategies', New Delhi, 3–4 April.

Dupont, V. (2000). 'Mobility patterns and economic strategies of houseless people in Old Delhi', in V. Dupont, E. Tarlo and D. Vidal (eds), *Delhi: Urban Space and Human Destinies*, New Delhi: Manohar.

Durand-Lasserve, A. (1997). 'Regularizing land markets', *Habitat Debate*, 3(2): 11–12.

Durand-Lasserve, A. and L. Royston(2002). *Holding their Ground: Secure Land Tenure for the Urban Poor in Developing Countries*, London and Sterling, VA: Earthscan.

Ebigbo, P. O. (2003). 'Street children: The core of child abuse and neglect in Nigeria', *Children, Youth and Environments*, 13(1), accessed 14 April 2004 from <http://cye.colorado.edu/>.

The Economist (1998a). 'Indonesia's agony and the price of rice', 347 (8090): 51–2.

The Economist (1998b). 'Raising the Rupiah', 347 (8079): 64.

The Economist (2000). 'A tale of two giants: Why Indonesia has beaten Nigeria hands down', 354 (8153) 104–6.

Edgar, B. (2001). 'Women, the housing market and homelessness', in B. Edgar and J. Doherty (eds), *Women and Homelessness in Europe: Pathways, services and experiences*, Bristol: Policy Press.

Edgar, B. and J. Doherty (2001). 'Introduction', in B. Edgar and J. Doherty (eds), *Women and Homelessness in Europe: Pathways, Services and Experiences*, Bristol: Policy Press.

Edgar, B., J. Doherty and A. Mina-Coull (1999). *Services for Homeless People: Innovation and Change in the European Union*, Bristol: Policy Press.

Edgar, B., J. Doherty and H. Meert (2002). *Access to Housing: Homelessness and Vulnerability in Europe*, Bristol: Policy Press.

Edwards, M. and A. Fowler (2002). *The Earthscan Reader on NGO Management*, London: Earthscan.

EERI (1997). 'The Nazca, Peru, Earthquake of November 12th 1996', *Learning from Earthquakes: Special Earthquake Report*, Oakland, CA: Earthquake Engineering Research Institute, accessed 23 Jan. 2008, from <http://www.eeri.org/lfe/pdf/peru_nazca_eeri_preliminary_report.pdf>.

El Baz, S. (1996). *Children in Difficult Circumstances: A Study of Institutions and Inmates*, New York: UNICEF.

El-Masri, S. and G. Tipple (2002). 'Natural disaster, mitigation and sustainability: The case of developing countries', *International Planning Studies*, 7(2): 157–75.

El-Sheikh, T. (2002). *The Nature, Extent and Eradication of Homelessness in Developing Countries: Egypt Case Study*, Cairo: Urban Training and Studies Institute.

El-Waly, M. (1993). *Residents of Shacks and Squatter Settlements* (in Arabic), Cairo: Rosa El-Youssef Press. Ellis, F. (2000). *Rural Livelihoods and Diversity in Developing Countries*, London: Oxford University Press.

Ellis, S. and S. Barakat (1996). 'From relief to development: The long-term effects of "temporary" accommodation on refugees and displaced persons in the Republic of Croatia', *Disasters*, 20(2): 111–24.

Elson, D. (1995). 'Gender awareness in modeling structural adjustment', *World Development*, 23(11): 1851–68.

EM-DAT (2008). 'EM-DAT: Emergency Events Database', Louvain/Leuven, Centre for Research on the Epidemiology of Disasters, Université Catholique de Louvain, accessed 22 Jan. 2008 from <http://www.emdat.be/Database/DisasterProfile/profiles.php>.

Ennew, J. (1994). 'Parentless friends: A cross-cultural examination of networks among street children and street youth', in F. Nestman and K. Hurrelman (eds), *Social Networks and Social Support in Childhood and Adolescence*, London: de Gruyter.

Ennew, J. and J. Swart-Kruger (2003). 'Introduction: Homes, places and spaces in the construction of street children and street youth', *Children, Youth and Environments*, 13(1, Spring), accessed 12 Aug. 2004 from <http://cye.colorado.edu/>.

ESCAP (2001) *Synthesis of National Reports on the Implementation of the Habitat Agenda in the Africa Region, Economic Commission for Africa Region Report to Istanbul+5*, accessed 15 Feb. 2002 from <http://www.unhabitat.org/istanbul+5/eca2.doc.htm>.

Espínola, B. (1988). *In the Streets: Working Street Children in Asunción: A Book for Action*, Bogota: Gente Nueva.

Ezawa, A. (2002). 'Japan's "new homeless"', *Journal of Social Distress and the Homeless*, 11(4, Oct.): 279–91.

Fahmi, W. S. (2005). 'The impact of privatization of solid waste management on the Zabaleen garbage collectors of Cairo', *Environment and Urbanization*, 17(2): 155–70.

FEANTSA (1999). *Strategies to Combat Homelessness in Western and Eastern Europe: Trends and Traditions in Statistics and Public Policy*, Nairobi: prepared for UNCHS (Habitat).

Fekade, W. (2000). 'Deficits of formal urban land management and informal responses under rapid urban growth, an international perspective', *Habitat International*, 24(2): 127–50.

Fernandes, D. (2006). 'The unseen and unheard', GURU International Conference on Homelessness: A Global Perspective, New Delhi. 9–13 Jan.

Fernandes, E. and A. Varley (1998). *Illegal Cities: Law and Urban Change in Developing Countries*, London: Zed Books.

Fernandez, E. (2002). 'Combining tenure policies, urban planning and city management in Brazil', in A. Durand-Lasserve and L. Royston (eds), *Holding their Ground: Secure Land Tenure for the Urban Poor in Developing Countries*, London: Earthscan.

Ferreira, M. L. (1996). *Poverty and Inequality during Structural Adjustment in Rural Tanzania*, World Policy Research Working Paper, 1641, Washington, DC: World Bank.

Firozuddin, M. (1999). 'Urban low-income housing: Reality and need for change' (in Bengali), Paper presented to the IAB seminar on the occasion of the World Habitat Day, Dhaka, 29 Oct.

Fisher, B., M. Hovell, C. R. Hofstetter and R. Hough (1995). 'Risks associated with long-term homelessness among women: Battery, rape, and HIV infection', *International Journal of Health Services: Planning, Evaluation and Administration*, 25(2): 351–69.

Fitzpatrick, S. (1999). *Young Homeless People*, Basingstoke: Macmillan.

Fitzpatrick, S. and D. Clapham (1999). 'Homelessness and young people', in S. Fitzpatrick and D. Clapham (eds), *Homelessness: Public Policies and Private Troubles*, London: Cassell.

Fitzpatrick, S. and C. Kennedy (2001). 'The links between begging and rough sleeping: A Question of legitimacy?', *Housing Studies*, 16(5): 549–68.

Forrest, R. (1999). 'The new landscape of precariousness', in P. Kennett and A. Marsh (eds), *Homelessness: The New Terrain*, London: Policy Press.

Forster, L. M. K., M. Tannhauser and H. M. T. Barros (1996). 'Drug use among street children in southern Brazil', *Drug and Alcohol Dependence*, 43(1–2): 57–62.

Foster, C. and F. J. Plowden (1996). *The State Under Stress*, Buckingham: Open University Press.

Foster, G. (2000). 'The capacity of the extended family safety net for orphans in Africa', *Psychology, Health and Medicine*, 5(1): 55–62.

Foster, G., C. Makufa, R. Drew and E. Kralovec (1997). 'Factors leading to the establishment of child-headed households: the case of Zimbabwe', *Health Transitions Review* Supplement 2 to Volume 7: 155–68.

Freeman, P. K. (2004). 'Allocation of post-disaster reconstruction financing to housing', *Building Research and Information*, 32(5): 427–37.

Frijns, J. and B. Van Vliet (1999). 'Small-scale industry and cleaner production strategies', *World Development*, 27(6): 967–83.

Fry, E. M. and J. B. Drew (1964). *Tropical Architecture in the Dry and Humid Zones,* London: Batsford.

Fuhrer, U. and F. G. Kaiser (1992). 'Bindung an das Zuhause: Die emotionalen Ursachen', *Zeitschrift für Sozialpsychologie*, 23(2): 105–18.

Funkhouser, E. (1996). 'The urban informal sector in Central America: Household survey evidence', *World Development*, 24(11): 1737–51.

Gallagher, R. (1992). *The Rickshaws of Bangladesh*, Dhaka: University Press.

Gang, I. N. and R. C. Stuart (1999). 'Mobility where mobility is illegal: Internal migration and city growth in the Soviet Union', *Journal of Population Economics*, 12(1): 117–34.

García-Moreno, C., H. Jansen, M. Ellsberg, L. Heise and C. Watts (2005). *WHO Multi-country Study on Women's Health and Domestic Violence against Women: Initial Results on Prevalence, Health Outcomes and Women's Responses*, Geneva: World Health Organization, accessed 25 Jan. 2008 from <http://www.who.int/gender/violence/who_multicountry_study/en/index.html>

Gardner, D. (2007). *Access to Housing Finance in Africa: Exploring the Issues. Zambia*, Pretoria: FinMark Trust.

Garg, R. (1999). 'Night shelters programmes for homeless: A case study of Delhi', School of Planning and Architecture, New Delhi, Master of Planning dissertation.

Ghafur, S. (1999) 'For whom are our cities?', *Daily Star* (Dhaka, 7 Oct.)

Ghafur, S. (2001). 'Beyond homemaking: The role of slum improvement in home-based income generation in Bangladesh', *Third World Planning Review*, 23(2): 111–35.

Ghafur, S. (2002). *The Nature, Extent and Eradication of Homelessness in Bangladesh*, Newcastle upon Tyne: Bangladesh Report for CARDO/ESCOR project on Homelessness in Developing Countries.

Ghai, D. (2003). 'Decent work: Concept and indicators', *International Labour Review*, 142(2, Summer): 113–45.

Ghana Statistical Service (2000). *Poverty Trends in Ghana in the 1990s*, Accra: Ghana Statistical Service.

Gilbert, A. (1999). 'A home is for ever? Residential mobility and home ownership in self-help settlements', *Environment and Planning A*, 31(6): 1073–91.

Gilbert, A. (2002). 'On the mystery of capital and the myths of Hernando de Soto: What difference does legal title make', *International Development Planning Review*, 24(1): 1–19.

Gilbert, A., O. O. Camacho, R. Coulomb and A. Necochea (1993). *In Search of a Home: Rental and Shared Housing in Latin America,* London: UCL Press.

Gilbert, R. (2001). *Doing More for Those Made Homeless by Natural Disasters*, Washington, DC: World Bank.

Gilborn, L. Z., R. Nyonyintono, R. Kabumbuli and G. Jagwe-Wadda (2000). *Making a Difference for Children Affected by AIDS: Baseline Findings from Operations Research in Uganda*, Washington, DC: Population Council.

Glasser, I. (1994). *Homelessness in Global Perspective,* New York: G. K. Hall.

Glendinning, C. and J. Millar (1992). *Women and Poverty in Britain: The 1990s*, Hemel Hempstead: Harvester Wheatsheaf.

GOB and ADB (1993). *Housing Sector Institutional Strengthening Project Final Report*, Dhaka: Government of Bangladesh (GOB) and Asian Development Bank (ADB).

Gonzalez Lopez, M. J. and M. Solsona (2000). 'Households and families: Changing living arrangements and gender relations', in S. Duncan and B. Pfau-Effinger (eds), *Gender, Economy and Culture in the European Union*, London: Routledge.

Gough, K. V., A. G. Tipple and M. Napier (2003). 'Making a living in African cities: The role of home-based enterprises in Accra and Pretoria', *International Planning Studies*, 8(4): 253–77.

Government of Bangladesh (2000). *Bangladesh Economic Survey 2000*, Dhaka: Ministry of Finance. Government of India (1991). *National Census of India*, New Delhi: Registrar General and Census Commissioner.

Government of Bangladesh (2005). *Unlocking the Potential: National Strategy for Accelerated Poverty Reduction*, Poverty Reduction Strategy Paper, Dhaka: General Economics Division, Planning Commission.

Government of India (1996). *NBO Handbook of Statistics Part 1: Excluding Assam and Jammu and Kashmir. 1991*, New Delhi: Ministry of Urban Affairs and Employment, National Building Organisation.

Government of India (2000). *Ninth Five Year Plan 1997–2002*, vol. 1, New Delhi: Nabhi Publication.

Government of India (2001). *Census of India 2001*, New Delhi: Registrar General and Census Commissioner, accessed 12 Sept. 2007, from <www.censusindia.net/>.

Government of Malaysia (2006). *Ninth Malaysia Plan 2006–2010*, Kuala Lumpur: Government of Malaysia.

Government of Peru (1998). *Habitat in Peruvian Cities, 1997–1998: Two Years After Habitat II*, Lima: Habitat Commission.

Government of Peru (2001). *National Report of Perú, Habitat II +5*, Official National Commission to Habitat II, Lima: Habitat Commission.

Government of South Africa (1997). *White Paper on Social Welfare*, Gazette number 18166, vol. 386, Pretoria: Government of South Africa.

Government of South Africa (2001). *State of the Nation's Children Report (2001): A Report on the State of the Nation's Children*, Pretoria: National Programme of Action for Children in South Africa, Office on the Rights of the Child, The Presidency, Union Buildings.

Government of Zimbabwe (1995). *Global Strategy for Shelter to the Year 2000*, Harare: Government Printers.

Gray, M. and A. Bernstein (1994). 'Pavement people and informal communities: Lessons for social work', *International Social Work*, 37: 149–63.

Gregson, S., P. R. Mason, G. P. Garnett, T. Zhuwau, C. A. Nyamukapa, R. M. Anderson and S. K. Chandiwana (2001). 'A rural HIV epidemic in Zimbabwe? Findings from a population-based survey', *International Journal of STD and AIDS*, 12(3): 189–96.

Grifa, M. A. (2006). *The Construction Industry in Libya, with Particular Reference to Operations in Tripoli*, Newcastle upon Tyne: School of Architecture, Planning and Landscape, Newcastle University.

GTZ (2006). 'Two years on: GTZ looks back on tsunami recovery process', Eschborn: Deutsche Gesellschaft für Technische Zusammenarbeit, accessed 23 Jan. 2008, from <http://www.gtz.de/en/aktuell/18119.htm>.

Guirguis-Younger, M., T. Aubry and V. Runnels (2004). *A Study of the Deaths of Persons Who are Homeless in Ottawa: A Social and Health Investigation. Presentation to the*

National Secretariat on Homelessness on 'Homelessness and Death: A Social Autopsy Study', Ottawa: Center for Research on Community Services, University of Ontario.

Gurgel, R. Q., J. D. C. da Fonseca, D. Neyra-Castañeda, G. V. Gill and L. E. Cuevas (2004). 'Capture–recapture to estimate the number of street children in a city in Brazil', *Archives of Disease in Childhood*, 89: 222–4.

Haggerty, R. (2006). 'Making a flophouse a home, and a decent one at that', 13th Annual Housing Conference: Housing Washington, Meydenbauer Center, Bellevue, WA, 11–12 Sept.

Hamdi, N. and M. Majale (2004). *Partnerships in Urban Planning: A Guide for Municipalities*, Oxford: DataPrint.

Hampshire, K. (2002). 'Fulani on the move: Seasonal economic migration in the Sahel as a social process', *Journal of Development Studies*, 38(5): 15–36.

Handa, S. and D. King (1997). 'Structural adjustment policies, income distribution and poverty: A review of the Jamaican experience', *World Development*, 25(6): 915–30.

Hardoy, J. E. and D. Satterthwaite (1989). *Squatter Citizen: Life in the Urban Third World,* London: Earthscan.

Harris, R. and G. Arku (2007). 'The rise of housing in international development: The effects of economic discourse', *Habitat International*, 31(1): 1–11.

Harris, R. and M. Wahba (2002). 'The urban geography of low-income housing: Cairo (1947–96) exemplifies a model', *International Journal of Urban and Regional Research*, 26(1): 58–79.

Hartley, D. (1999). *Begging Questions: Street-level Economic Activity and Social Policy.* Bristol: Policy Press.

Hashimoto, A. (1991). 'Living arrangements of the aged in seven developing countries: A preliminary analysis', *Journal of Cross-Cultural Gerontology*, 6(4): 359–81.

Haws, D. (1999). 'Older and homeless: "A double jeopardy"', in P. Kennett and A. Marsh (eds), *Homelessness: Exploring the New Terrain*, Bristol: Policy Press.

Hecht, T. (1998). *At Home in the Street: Street Children of Northeast Brazil*, New York: Cambridge University Press.

Heckert, U., L. Andrade, M. J. M. Alves and C. Martins (1999). 'Lifetime prevalence of mental disorders among homeless people in a southeast city in Brazil', *European Archives of Psychiatry and Clinical Neuroscience*, 249(33): 150–5.

Heise, L. L. (1994). *Violence Against Women: The Hidden Health Burden*, World Bank Discussion Paper, 225, Washington, DC: World Bank.

HelpAge International and International HIV/AIDS Alliance (2003). *Policy Report: Forgotten Families. Older People as Carers of Orphans and Vulnerable Children*, London: HelpAge International, accessed 3 June 2008, from <http://www.helpage.org/Resources/Policyreports/>.

Hernandez, F. and P. Kellett (2008). *Rethinking the Informal City: Radical Perspectives from Latin America,* London and New York: Berghahn.

Hertzberg, E. L. (1992). 'The homeless in the United States: Conditions, typology and interventions', *International Social Work*, 35: 149 61.

Hestyanti, R. (2006). 'Children survivors of the 2004 tsunami in Aceh, Indonesia: A study of resiliency', *Annals of the New York Academy of Sciences*, 1094(1): 303–7.

Hevesi, D. (2002). 'On the new Bowery, down and out mix with up and coming', *New York Times* (14 April), accessed 11 April 2007 from <http://query.nytimes.com/gst/fullpage.html?res=9C02E0DC163CF937A25757C0A9649C8B63>.

Hill, R. P. and M. Stamey (1990). 'The homeless in America: An examination of possessions and consumption behaviors', *Journal of Consumer Research*, 17(3): 303–21.

Hoek-Smit, M. (1998). *Housing Finance in Bangladesh: Improving Access to Housing Finance by Middle and Lower Income Groups*, Dhaka: GOB/UNDP/UNCHS.

Hoek-Smit, M. (2002). 'Implementing Indonesia's new housing policy: The way forward', *Findings and Recommendations of the Technical Assistance Project 'Policy Development for Enabling the Housing Market to Work in Indonesia'*, Washington, DC: World Bank.

Hogar de Cristo (n.d.). 'Integral development: housing', Guayaquil: Hogar de Cristo, Ecuador, accessed 5 March 2008, from <http://www.hogardecristo.org.ec/en/NuestrosProyectos/vivienda.shtml>.

Holland, P. (1992). *What is a Child?* London: Virago.

Holloway, S. and G. Valentine (2000). *Children's Geographies*, London: Routledge.

Holmes, C. A. (2006). 'Living homeless in Darwin: Resilience, resourcefulness and determination', GURU International Conference on Homelessness: A Global Perspective, New Delhi, 9–13 Jan.

Holzmann, R. and S. Jorgensen (2001). 'Social risk management: a new conceptual framework for social protection and beyond', *International Tax and Public Finance*, 8(4), 529–56.

Home, R. K. (2000). 'From barrack compounds to the single-family house: Planning worker housing in colonial Natal and Northern Rhodesia', *Planning Perspectives*, 15: 327–47.

Honig, M. and R. K. Filer (1993). 'Causes of intercity variation in homelessness', *American Economic Review*, 83(1): 248–55.

Hoogeveen, J. G. and B. Özler (2005). *Not Separate, Not Equal: Poverty and Inequality in Post-Apartheid South Africa*, Working Paper, 75, Ann Arbor, MI: William Davidson Institute at the University of Michigan Business School.

Housing and Urban Development Department (HUD) (1999). *Homelessness: Programs and the People they Serve,* Washington, DC: Housing and Urban Development Department Summary Report, accessed 10 Dec. 1999, from <http://www.huduser.org/publications/homeless/homelessness/>.

HPFP (n.d.). *Financial Model*, Manila: Homeless People's Federation Philippines.

Huchzermeyer, M. (2003). 'Housing rights in South Africa: Invasions, evictions, the media, and the courts in the cases of Grootboom, Alexandra, and Bredell', *Urban Forum,* 14(1): 80–107.

Hulchanski, J. D. (2000). *A New Canadian Pastime? Counting Homeless People*, Toronto: University of Toronto, accessed 16 Feb. 2007 from <http://www.urbancenter.utoronto.ca/pdfs/researchassociates/Hulch_CountingHomelessPeople.pdf>.

Hunter, A. (1985). 'Private, parochial and public social orders: The problem of crime and incivility in urban communities', in G. D. Suttles and M. N. Zald (eds), *The Challenge of Social Control: Citizenship and Institution Building in Modern Society. Essays in Honor of Morris Janowitz,* Norwood, NJ, Ablex.

Hunter, S. and J. Williamson (2000). *Children on the Brink: Executive Summary. Updated Estimates and Recommendations for Intervention*, Washington, DC: USAID.

Hutson, S. and D. Clapham (1999). *Homelessness: Public Policies and Private Troubles*, London: Cassell.

Hutton, S. and M. Liddiard (1994). *Youth Homelessness: The Construction of a Social Issue,* Basingstoke, Macmillan.

Hyden, G. (1999). 'The governance challenge in Africa', in G. Hyden, D. Oluwu and H. Ogendo (eds), *African Perspectives on Governance*, Trenton, NJ: Africa World Press.

IDNDR (1996). *Cities at Risk; Making Cities Safer before Disaster Strikes*, Geneva: International Decade for Natural Disaster Reduction.

ILO (1999). 'Decent work', Report of the Director-General, International Labour Conference, 87th Session, Geneva, June.

ILO (2001a). *In-depth Analysis of the Situation of Working Street Children in Moscow*, Geneva: International Labour Office.

ILO (2001b). *Working Paper: Analysis of the Situation of Working Street Children in Moscow*, Moscow: International Labour Organisation.

INEI (1998). *National Census and Survey of Municipalities*, Lima: National Statistics Institute.

INFID (2000). 'Background paper: Hutang Luar Negeri Indonesia: Penjara bagi rakyat Indonesia?', Tanggapan terhadap, CGI Meeting, Tokyo, INFID, 17–18 Oct.

IFRC (International Federation of Red Cross) (2000). 'Homeless and forgotten in Zimbabwe', accessed from <http://www.ifrc.org/docs/news/00/00032401/>.

Institute for War and Peace Reporting (IWPR) (2005). 'Clearance victims left in limbo', accessed 11 July 2005, from <http://www.reliefweb.int/rw/RWB.NSF/db900SID/MIRA-6E24C5?OpenDocument>.

Inter-American Development Bank (n.d.). 'Hogar de Cristo and housing options for the poor', accessed 6 March 2008, from <http://www.iadb.org/sds/FOROMIC/IXforo/Material/es_tgonzalez_e.pdf>.

Invernizzi, A. (2003). 'Street-working children and adolescents in Lima', *Childhood*, 10(3): 319–41.

Iraqi Constitutional Committee (2005). *The Constitution of Iraq*, Baghdad: Iraqi Constitutional Committee.

IRIN (2007). 'South Africa: Government housing project excludes poorest of the poor', New York: IRIN Humanitarian News and Analysis, UN Office for the Coordination of Humanitarian Affairs, accessed 19 Nov. 2007 from <http://www.irinnews.org/Report.aspx?ReportId=75102>.

Islam, P. P. and K. S. Yap (1989). 'Land sharing as a low income housing policy: An analysis of its potential', *Habitat International*, 13(1): 117–26.

Ito, H. and L. I. Sederer (1999). 'Mental health services reform in Japan', *Harvard Review of Psychiatry*, 7(4, Nov.): 208–15.

Jacobs, K., J. Kemeny and T. Manzi (1999). 'The struggle to define homelessness: A constructivist approach', in S. Hutton and D. Clapham (eds), *Homelessness: Public Policies and Private Troubles*, London: Cassell.

Jagannathan, N. V. and A. Halder (1988) 'Income-housing linkages: a case study of pavement dwellers in Calcutta', *Economic and Political Weekly*, 23(23, June. 4): 1175–8.

Jagannathan, N. V. and A. Halder (1990). 'Income housing linkages: A case study of pavement dwellers in Calcutta', in M. Raj and P. Nientied (eds), *Housing and Income in Third World Urban Development,* London and New Delhi: Aspect Publishing, pp 141–8.

Jain, A. K. (2006). 'Shelter for the homeless in Delhi', GURU International Conference on Homelessness: A Global Perspective, New Delhi, 9–13 Jan.

James, A., C. Jenks and A. Prout (1998). *Constructing and Reconstructing Childhood*, London: Falmer Press.

Jejeebhoy, S. J. (1995). *Women's Education, Autonomy, and Reproductive Behaviour: Experience from Developing Countries*, London: Oxford University Press.

Jellinek, L. (1991). *The Wheel of Fortune: The History of a Poor Community in Jakarta*, Sydney: Allen & Unwin.

Jellinek, L. (1995). *Seperti Roda Berputar: Perubahan Sosial Sebuah Kampung di Jakarta*, Jakarta: LP3ES.

Jellinek, L. and B. Rustanto (1999). 'Survival strategies of the Javanese during the economic crisis', Jakarta, unpublished preliminary draft.

Jencks, C. (1994). *The Homeless*, Cambridge, MA: Harvard University Press.

Jordan, B. (1996). *A Theory of Poverty and Social Exclusion*, Cambridge: Polity Press.

Juliá, M. and H. P. Hartnett (1999). 'Exploring cultural issues in Puerto Rican homelessness', *Cross-Cultural Research*, 33(4): 318–40.

Kabachenco, N. (2006). 'The problem of homelessness in Ukraine', GURU International Conference on Homelessness: A Global Perspective, New Delhi, 9–13 Jan.

Kabir, Z. N., M. Szebehely and C. Tishelman (2002). 'Support in old age in the changing society of Bangladesh', *Ageing and Society*, 22(5): 615–36.

Kakita, Y. (n.d.). *Homeless People in Japan: Characteristics, Processes and Policy Responses*, Oita: Oita University, accessed 14 June 2007 from <http://www.lit.osaka-cu.ac.jp/soc/zasshi/No.5kakita.pdf>.

Kamete, A. Y. (1997). 'Constraints to housing delivery in Zimbabwe: A comprehensive re-evaluation', Paper prepared for the National Housing Convention, 22–27 Nov., Victoria Falls.

Kamete, A. Y. (2000). *The Urban Housing Crisis in Zimbabwe: Some Forgotten Dimensions?*, Harare: Department of Rural and Urban Planning, University of Zimbabwe.

Kamete, A. Y. (2001). *The Nature, Extent and Eradication of Homelessness in Zimbabwe: Report for the CARDO/ESCOR Project on Homelessness in Developing Countries*, Harare: University of Zimbabwe.

Kamete, A. Y., M. Sidambe and M. Ndubiwa (2000). *Managing the Interface between Urban Councils and the Surrounding Rural District Councils: The Case of Bulawayo City Council and Umguza Rural District Council*, Harare: Municipal Development Programme.

Kamete, A. Y., A. Tostensen and I. Tvedten. (2001). *From Global Village to Urban Globe: Urbanisation and Poverty in Africa: Implications for Norwegian Aid Policy*, Bergen: Chr. Michelsen Institute.

Kamruzzaman, M. and N. Ogura (2006). 'Urbanization and housing crisis in Dhaka city', GURU International Conference on Homelessness: A Global Perspective, New Delhi. 9–13 Jan.

Kasongo, B. A. and A. G. Tipple (1990). 'An analysis of policy towards squatters in Kitwe, Zambia', *Third World Planning Review*, 12(2, May): 147–65.

Kaur, P. (1997). 'The Indian statistical story of Indian street children, my name is today', *Children in News* (Documentation, Research and Advocacy Centre), 5(1, Jan.–March).

Keare, D. H. and S. Parris (1982). *Evaluation of Shelter Programs for the Urban Poor: Principal Findings*, Washington, DC: World Bank.

Kellett, P. and J. Moore (2003). 'Routes to home: homelessness and home-making in contrasting societies', *Habitat International*, 27: 123–41.

Kelly, M. (n.d.). *The Impact of HIV/AIDS on Schooling in Zambia: Bulletin 42*, Lusaka: Jesuit Centre for Theological Reflection, accessed 2 June 2008 from <http://www.jctr.org.zm/bulletins/impact%20of%20AIDS%20on%20educa.htm>.

Kennett, P. and A. Marsh (1999). *Homelessness: Exploring the New Terrain*, Bristol: Policy Press.

Kevane, M. and B. Wydick (2001). 'Microenterprise lending to female entrepreneurs: Sacrificing economic growth for poverty alleviation?', *World Development*, 29(7): 1225–36.

Khair, S. and S. Khan (2000). *Shoshur Bari: Street Children in Conflict with the Law*, Dhaka: Save the Children (UK).

Khan, S. (1999). 'Through a window darkly: Men who sell sex to men in India and Bangladesh', in P. Aggleton (ed.), *Men Who Sell Sex: International Perspectives on Male Prostitution and HIV/AIDS*, London: University College London.

Kilbride, P. L., A. Collette, S. Suda, E. Njeru and E. H. N. Njeru (2000). *Street Children in Kenya: Voices of Children in Search of a Childhood*, Westport, VA: Greenwood Publishing Group.

Kishwar, M. (2001). 'License-quota-raid raj: Economic warfare against rickshaw owners and pullers', *Manushi*, 125 (July–Aug.).

Kisor, A. J. and L. Kendal-Wilson (2002). 'Older homeless women: Reframing the stereotype of the bag lady', *Affilia*, 17(3): 354–70.

Koegel, P., M. A. Burnam and S. C. Morton (1996). 'Enumerating homeless people: Alternative strategies and their consequences', *Evaluation Review*, 20(4): 378–403.

Koenigsberger, O. (1973). *Manual of Tropical Housing and Building,* London: Longman.

Korboe, D. (1996). *A Profile of Street Children in Kumasi*, Kumasi: UNICEF and RESPONSE.

Kothari, M. (2005). *Women and Adequate Housing: Study by the Special Rapporteur on Adequate Housing as a Component of the Right to an Adequate Standard of Living*, Report presented to UN Economic and Social Council, New York: UN Economic and Social Council

Kuhn, R. (2003). 'Identities in motion: Social exchange networks and rural–urban migration in Bangladesh', *Contributions to Indian Sociology*, 37(1–2): 311–37.

Kulsudjarit, K. (2004). 'Drug problem in Southeast and Southwest Asia', *Annals of the New York Academy of Sciences*, 1025(1): 446–57.

Kundu, A. (1993). *National Trends in Housing Production Practices in India*, Case study prepared for UNCHS (Habitat), Nairobi: UNCHS

Kundu, A. (2002). 'Tenure security, housing investment and environmental improvement: The case of Delhi and Ahmedabad, India', in G. Payne (ed.), *Land, Rights and Innovation: Improving Tenure Security for the Urban Poor,* London: ITDG Publishing.

Labeodan, O. A. (1989). 'The homeless in Ibadan', *Habitat International*, 13(1): 75–85.

Lall, S. (2001). 'Settlements of the poor and guidelines for urban upgrading: A case study of Alwar, a secondary town', Paper prepared for ITDG Regulatory Guidelines for Urban Upgrading Research Project by the Society of Development Studies (SDS), New Delhi.

Lalor, K. J. (1999). 'Street children: A comparative perspective', *Child Abuse and Neglect*, 23(8): 759–70.

Lanegran, K. and D. Lanegran (2001). 'South Africa's national housing subsidy programme and apartheid's urban legacy', *Urban Geography*, 22(7): 671–87.

Laquian, A. A. (1983). *Basic Housing: Policies for Urban Sites, Services and Shelter in Developing Countries*, Ottawa: International Development Research Centre.

Law, R. (2001). '"Not in my city": Local governments and homelessness policies in the Los Angeles metropolitan region', *Environment and Planning C: Government and Policy,* 19(6): 791–815.

Le Roux, J. and C. S. Smith (1998). 'Public perceptions of, and reactions to, street children', *Adolescence*, 33(132): 901–13. Lee, B. A. (1978). 'Residential mobility on skid row: Disaffiliation, powerlessness, and decision making', *Demography*, 15(3): 285–300.

Lee, Y. J., W. L. Parish and R. J. Willis (1994). 'Sons, daughters, and intergenerational support in Taiwan', *American Journal of Sociology*, 99(4): 1010–41.

Leus, X., J. Wallace and A. Loretti (2001). 'Internally displaced persons: Special report', *Prehospital and Disaster Medicine*, 16(3, July–Sept.): 75–83.

Levison, D. (1991). 'Children's labor force activity and schooling in Brazil', University of Michigan, doctoral dissertation.

Lewis, O. (1969). 'The culture of poverty', in D. P. Moynihan (ed.), *On Understanding Poverty*, New York: Basic Books.

Li, H. (2002). *The Nature, Extent and Eradication of Homelessness in China*, Shanghai: China Report for CARDO/ESCOR project on Homelessness in Developing Countries.

Liang, Z. (2001). 'The age of migration in China', *Population and Development Review*, 27(3): 499–524.

Lucchini, R. (1996). 'The street and its image', *Childhood*, 3(2): 235–46.

Lusk, M. W. (1989). 'Street children programs in Latin America', *Journal of Sociology and Social Welfare*, 16(1): 55–77.

Lyssiotou, P., P. Pashardes and T. Stengos (2004). 'Estimates of the black economy based on consumer demand approaches', *Economic Journal*, 114(497): 622–40.

Ma, Z. (2001). 'Urban labor force experience as a determinant of rural occupation change: Evidence from recent urban–rural return migration in China', *Environment and Planning A*, 33(2): 237–55.

McAuslan, P. (2000). 'Land tenure, the urban poor and the law in Bangladesh: Implementing the Habitat Agenda', in N. Islam (ed.), U*rban Land Tenure and Housing Finance in Bangladesh*. Dhaka: CUS and UNCHS.

McGray, D. (2002). 'Images of home: Rosanne Haggerty reinvents the flophouse as a clean, well-lighted place', *The Metropolis Observed* (April), accessed 11 April 2007 from <http://www.metropolismag.com/html/content_0402/ob/ob03_0402.html>.

MacGregor, S. (1999). 'Welfare, neo-liberalism and new paternalism: Three ways for social policy in late capitalist societies', *Capital and Class*, 67: 91–118.

McIntosh, G. and J. Phillips (2000). '"There's no home-like place": Homelessness in Australia', accessed 16 Jan. 2007 from <http://www.aph.gov.au/library/intguide/sp/homeless.htm>.

MacKenzie, D. and C. Chamberlain (2003). *Homeless Careers: Pathways in and out of Homelessness*, Melbourne: RMIT University and Swinburne University of Technology.

Mackenzie, P. W. (2002). 'Strangers in the city: The hukou and urban citizenship in China', *Journal of International Affairs*, 56(1): 305–19.

Madon, S. (2004). 'Bangalore: Internal disparities of a city caught in the information age', in S. Graham (ed.), *The Cybercities Reader*, London: Routledge.

Mafico, C. J. C. (1991). *Urban Low-income Housing in Zimbabwe*, Aldershot: Avebury.

Mahmud, S. (2003). 'Actually how empowering is microcredit?', *Development and change*, 34(4): 577–605.

Majale, M. (2002). 'Tenure regularisation in informal settlements in Nairobi', in W. Olima and V. Kreibich (eds), *Urban Land Management in Africa*, Spring Research Series, 40, Dortmund: Technische Univeristät Dortmund.

Majale, M. and G. Tipple (2007). *Provision of Affordable Land and Housing in Africa and Asia: Successful Policies and Practices*, scoping paper prepared for UN-Habitat, Newcastle upon Tyne: UN-Habitat.

Mak, S. W. K., L. H. T. Choy and W. K. O. Ho (2007). 'Privatization, housing conditions and affordability in the People's Republic of China', *Habitat International*, 31: 177–92.

Malinowski, B. (1920). 'War and weapons among the natives of the Trobriand Islands', *Man*, 20: 10–12.

Mallick, R. (2002). 'Implementing and evaluating microcredit in Bangladesh', *Development in Practice*, 12(2): 153–63.

Maloney, C. (1991). *Behaviour and Poverty in Bangladesh*, 3rd edn, Dhaka: Dhaka University Press.

Malpezzi, S. J. (1986). 'Rent control and housing market equilibrium: Theory and evidence from Cairo, Egypt', George Washington University, Washington, DC, doctoral dissertation.

Malpezzi, S. J. (1990). 'Urban housing and financial markets: Some international comparisons', *Urban Studies*, 27(6): 971–1022.

Malpezzi, S. J., A. G. Tipple and K. G. Willis (1989). *Costs and Benefits of Rent Control: A Case Study in Kumasi, Ghana*, Washington, DC: World Bank.

Mamun, N. A. (2001). *Ghar Nai* [*Homeless*] (in Bengali), Dhaka: Mowla Brothers.

Manninen, H. (2006). 'Opening intervention at the conference on Housing Rights in Europe', Helsinki, <www.environment.fi>, accessed 11 Jan. 2007 from <http://www.ymparisto.fi/default.asp?contentid=201560&lan=EN>.

Marquette, C. M. (1997). 'Current poverty, structural adjustment, and drought in Zimbabwe', *World Development*, 25(7): 1141–9.

Marshall, T. H. (1950). *Citizenship, Social Class and Other Essays,* Cambridge: Cambridge University Press.

Martell, D. A. (2005). 'Homeless mentally disordered offenders and violent crimes: Preliminary research findings', *Law and Human Behaviour*, 15(4): 333–47.

Matchinda, B. (1999). 'The impact of home background on the decision of children to run away: The case of Yaounde City street children in Cameroon', *Child Abuse and Neglect*, 23(3): 245–55.

Mayo, S. K. and D. Gross (1987). 'Sites and services – and subsidies: The economics of low-cost housing in developing countries', *World Bank Economic Review*, 1(2): 305–35.

Mayo, S. K., S. J. Malpezzi and D. J. Gross (1986). 'Shelter strategies for the urban poor in developing countries', *World Bank Research Observer*, 1(1): 183–203.

Mayrhofer, A. M. and S. L. Hendriks (2003). 'Service provision for street-traders in Pietermaritzburg, KwaZulu-Natal: Comparing local findings to lessons drawn from Africa and Asia', *Development Southern Africa*, 20(5): 595–604.

Millar, K. (2006). 'A human security analysis of the war in Iraq', *Sécurité Humaine/Human Security Journal,* 2 (June): 47–63.

Mills, S. (2007). 'The Kuyasa Fund: Housing microcredit in South Africa', *Environment and Urbanization*, 19(2): 457–69.

Ministry of Municipalities and Public Works, Ministry of Construction and Housing and UN-HABITAT (2005). *Final Report: Discussion Paper for a Slum Upgrading Strategy for Iraq,* Baghdad and Nairobi: Government of Iraq and UN-Habitat.

Ministry of Public Construction and National Housing (1991). *Report on Development of Human Settlements in Zimbabwe*, Harare: Ministry of Public Construction and National Housing.

Ministry of Public Construction and National Housing (1995). *Zimbabwe Shelter and Urban Indicator Study*, Harare: Ministry of Public Construction and National Housing.

MIPTC (Zimbabwe) (1992). *Zimbabwe: The Facts*, 12, *Housing*, Harare: MIPTC, Ministry of Information, Posts and Telecommunication.

Miranda, L. and L. Salazar (2002). *Homelessness and Street Children in Peru: Peru Country Report*, CARDO Project on Homelessness in Developing Countries, Lima: ECOCITY.

Mital, R. (2006). 'Houseless by choice in New Delhi', GURU International Conference on Homelessness: A Global Perspective, New Delhi. 9–13 Jan.

Mizuuchi, T. (2004). 'Transformation of recent homelessness issues and policies for them in capitalist metropolises of the East Asia: The case of Hong Kong, Seoul, Osaka and Taipei', International Conference on Urban Change in the 21st Century, East China Normal University, Shanghai, China, 30 June–1 July.

Moberly, C. (1999). 'Creating policies which address the "voluntary separation" of children in Angola', in A. Schrader and A. Veale (eds), *Prevention of Street Migration: Resource Pack*, London: Consortium for Street Children, UK.

Mody, S. (2001). 'Makeshift homes of construction workers', *Labour File* (Chennai, June–July).

MOF (2000). *Bangladesh Economic Survey 2000*, Dhaka: Ministry of Finance.

Mohamed, S. I. (1997). 'Tenants and tenure in Durban', *Environment and Urbanization*, 9(2): 101–18.

Moore, B. and I. Begg (2001). 'Urban growth and competitiveness in Britain: A long-run perspective', in M. Boddy and M. Parkinson (eds), *City Matters: Competitiveness, Cohesion and Urban Governance*, Bristol: Policy Press.

Moser, C. O. N. (1993). 'Domestic violence and its economic causes', *Urban Age*, 1(4): 13.

Mosley, P. and D. Hulme (1998). 'Microenterprise finance: Is there a conflict between growth and poverty alleviation?', *World Development*, 26(5): 783–90.

Mosse, D., S. Gupta, M. Mehta, V. Shah and J. Rees (2002). 'Brokered livelihoods: Debt, labour migration and development in tribal Western India', *Journal of Development Studies*, 38(5, June): 59–88..

MPCNH (1991). *Report on Development of Human Settlements in Zimbabwe*, Harare: Ministry of Public Construction and National Housing.

MPSLSW (1999). *Study on Street Children in Zimbabwe*, Harare: Ministry of Public Service, Labour and Social Welfare.

MPSLSW (2000). *Study on Street Children in Zimbabwe*, Harare: Ministry of Public Service, Labour and Social Welfare.

Mubvami, T. and A. Y. Kamete (2000). *The Contribution of Co-operatives to Shelter Development in Zimbabwe*, Harare: Report prepared for the UNCHS (Habitat) report on the Contribution of Co-operatives to Shelter Development in Developing Countries.

Mubvami, T. and O. Musandu-Nyamayaro (1996). *Procedural Impediments to the Low-Income Housing Land Delivery Process in Cities of Zimbabwe*, Harare: Department of Rural and Urban Planning, University of Zimbabwe.

Munoz, M. and C. Vazquez (1999). 'Homelessness in Spain: Psychosocial aspects', *Psychology in Spain*, 3(1): 104–16.

Musengeyi, I. (1999). 'Extended family breaking up fast in Zimbabwe', Pan-African News Agency.

Mutenje, M. J., C. Mapiye, Z. Mavunganidze, M. Mwale, V. Muringai, C. S. Katsinde and I. Gavumende (2008). 'Livestock as a buffer against HIV and AIDS income shocks in the rural households of Zimbabwe', *Development Southern Africa*, 25(1, March): 75–82.

Nangia, S. (1987). 'Spatial reorganisation of low income urban communities and its impact on the quality of housing and income: A case of metropolitan Delhi', Paper presented at the International Seminar on Income and Housing in Third World Development, New Delhi, 30 Nov.–4 Dec.

Napier, M., G. Tipple, N. Majija, R. Bean and K. Wall (2003). *Global Report for the Period January 2000 to December 2003: Mid-term Evaluation of Financing Agreement*

(SA/73200–99/20) between the European Community and the Urban Sector Network, Pretoria: Council for Scientific and Industrial Research and University of Newcastle upon Tyne.

National Coalition for the Homeless (2007). *Homelessness among Elderly Persons,* NCH Fact Sheet, 15, Washington, DC: National Coalition for the Homeless, accessed 7 Feb. 2008, from <http://www.nationalhomeless.org/publications/>.

National Coalition for the Homeless and National Law Center on Homelessness and Poverty (2006). *A Dream Denied: The Criminalisation of Homelessness in US Cities*, Washington, DC: National Coalition for the Homeless and the National Law Center on Homelessness and Poverty.

National Housing Task Force (Zimbabwe) (1998). *Public Private Partnerships: Proceedings of the National Housing Convention*, Harare: National Housing Convention, Victoria Falls, National Housing Task Force.

National Housing Task Force (Zimbabwe) (2000). *National Housing Policy for Zimbabwe (Final Draft)*, Harare: Ministry of Local Government and National Housing.

National Literacy Mission – India (n.d.). *Literacy Rates for Total Population, Scheduled Caste Population and Scheduled Tribe Population by Sex – 1991*, accessed 10 May 2004, from <http://www.nlm.nic.in/tables/f_scst.htm>.

National Programme of Action (1994). *A National Programme of Action for Children in South Africa: An Outline*, Pretoria: National Children's Rights Committee.

Neale, J. (1997). 'Homelessness and theory reconsidered', *Housing Studies*, 12(1): 47–61.

Nedoroscik, J. A. (1997). *The City of the Dead: A History of Cairo's Cemetery Communities*, Westport, CT: Bergin & Garvey.

Newell, P. (1997). 'Children and violence', *Innocenti Digest 2,* Florence: UNICEF International Child Development Centre.

Newman, O. (1972). *Defensible Space: Crime Prevention through Urban Design,* New York: Macmillan.

Neysmith, S. M. and S. Edward (1984). 'Economic dependency in the 1980s: Its impact on Third World elderly', *Ageing and Society*, 4(1): 21–44.

Nkomo, M. and O. A. Olufemi (2001). 'Educating street and homeless children in South Africa: The challenge of policy implementation', *International Journal of Educational Policy, Research and Practice*, 2(4): 337–56.

Nochlezhka (n.d. [post-1996]). 'Home page', Nochlezhka St Petersburg Regional Humanitarian Organisation for the Homeless, accessed 19 Jan. 2007 from <http://www.homeless.ru/en/index_en.php>.

Novac, S., J. Brown and B. A. Bourbonnais (1996). *No Room of her Own: A Literature Review on Women and Homelessness*, Toronto: Canadian Housing Information Centre.

Nyakazeya, P. (2001). 'Up to 60% resort to walking to work', *Zimbabwe Standard* (19 Aug.).

O'Connell, J. (2005). *Premature Mortality in Homeless Populations: A Review of the Literature*, Nashville, TN: National Health Care for the Homeless Council.

O'Toole, T. P., A. Conde-Martel, J. L. Gibbon, B. H. Hanusa and M. J. Fine (2003). 'Health care of homeless veterans', *Journal of General Internal Medicine*, 18(11): 929–33.

Office on the Rights of the Child (2001). *Children in 2001: A Report on the State of the Nation's Children*, Pretoria: Office on the Rights of the Child, Republic of South Africa.

Ohlemacher, S. (2007). 'Study: 744,000 are homeless in U.S.', Associated Press, accessed 15 Dec. 2008 from <http://www.washingtonpost.com/wp-dyn/content/article/2007/01/10/AR2007011001362.htm>.

Okongwu, A. F. and J. P. Mencher (2000). 'The anthropology of public policy: Shifting terrains', *Annual Review of Anthropology,* 29: 107–24.

Olufemi, O. A. (1997). 'The homelessness problem: Planning, phenomenology and gender perspectives', PhD, Faculty of Architecture, University of the Witwatersrand, Johannesburg, South Africa.

Olufemi, O. A. (1998). 'Street homelessness in Johannesburg inner-city: A preliminary survey', *Environment and Urbanisation*, 10(2): 223–34.

Olufemi, O. A. (1999). 'Health of the homeless street women in South Africa', *Habitat International*, 23(4): 481–93.

Olufemi, O. A. (2000). 'Feminisation of poverty among the street homeless women in South Africa', *Development Southern Africa*, 17(2): 221–34.

Olufemi, O. A. (2001). *The Nature, Extent and Eradication of Homelessness in South Africa,* Report for CARDO/ESCOR project on Homelessness in Developing Countries, Johannesburg: University of Witwatersrand.

Olufemi, O. A. (2002). 'Images of homelessness in Johannesburg, South Africa', CARDO E-Conference on Homelessness, accessed 21 Dec. 2004 from <http://www.campus.ncl.ac.uk/cardo/virtualconf/asp/listpaperscom.asp?subject=Perceptions%20of%20homelessness>.

Omenya, A. (2006). 'A thin veil of protection: Fragility of informal tenure in Nairobi and Johannesburg', GURU International Conference on Homelessness: A Global Perspective, New Delhi, India. 9–13 Jan.

Oswald, F. and H. W. Wahl (2005). 'Dimensions of the meaning of home in later life', in G. D. Rowles and H. Chaudhury (eds), *Home and Identity in Late Life: International Perspectives*, New York: Springer.

Overwien, B. (2000). 'Informal learning and the role of social movements', *International Review of Education/Internationale Zeitschrift für Erziehungswissenschaft/Revue internationale l'éducation*, 46(6): 621–40.

Pallen, D. (2001). *Reinventing the City: The Role of Small Scale Enterprise,* Ottawa: Canadian International Development Agency.

Pande, R. (1993). *Street Children of Kanpur: A Situational Analysis*, New Delhi: Child Labour Cell, Ministry of Social Welfare.

Pannell, J. and G. Palmer (2004). *Coming of Age: Opportunities for Older Homeless People under Supporting People*, London, New Policy Institute.

Parker, D. L. (2002). 'Street children and child labour around the world', *The Lancet,* 360 (21/28 Dec.): 2067–71.

Parnell, S. (1997). 'South African cities: Perspectives from the ivory tower of urban studies', *Urban Studies*, 34(5): 891–906.

Pascall, G. (1991). *Social Policy: A Feminist Analysis*. London: Routledge.

Patel, I. V. and A. Kleinman (2003). 'Poverty and common mental disorders in developing countries', *Bulletin of the World Health Organisation*, 81(8): 608–15.

Patel, S. (1990). 'Street children, hotel boys and children of pavement dwellers and construction workers in Bombay: How they meet their daily needs', *Environment and Urbanization*, 2(2): 9–26.

Patel, S., S. Burra and C. D'Cruz (2001). 'Slum/Shack Dwellers International (SDI): Foundations to treetops', *Environment and Urbanisation*, 13(2): 45–59.

Patel, S., C. D'Cruz and S. Barra (2002). 'Beyond evictions in a global city: People-managed resettlement in Mumbai', *Environment and Urbanisation*, 14(1): 159–72.

Patrinos, H. A. and G. Psacharopoulos (1997). 'Family size, schooling and child labor in Peru: An empirical analysis', *Journal of Population Economics,* 10: 387–405.

Paul, B. K. and S. A. Hasnath (2000). 'Trafficking in Bangladeshi women and girls', *Geographical Review*, 90(2): 268–76.

Payne, G. (1999). *Making Common Ground: Public–Private Partnerships in Land for Housing*, London: Intermediate Technology Publications.

Payne, G. (2001). 'Urban land tenure policy options: Titles or rights?', *Habitat International*, 25(3): 415–29.

Payne, G. (2002a). 'Introduction', in G. Payne (ed.), *Land, Rights and Innovation: Improving Tenure Security for the Urban Poor*, London: ITDG.

Payne, G. (2002b). *Land, Rights and Innovation: Improving Tenure Security for the Urban Poor*, London: ITG Publishers.

Payne, G. and M. Majale (2004). *The Urban Housing Manual: Making Regulatory Frameworks Work for the Poor*, London: Earthscan.

Peattie, L. R. (1980). 'Anthropological perspectives on the concepts of dualism, the informal sector and marginality in developing urban economies', *International Regional Science Review,* 5(1): 1–31.

Peil, M. (1976). 'African squatter settlements: A comparative study', *Urban Studies*, 13: 155–66.

Peralta, F. (1992). 'Children of the streets of Mexico', *Children and Youth Services Review*, 14: 347–62.

Peressini, T., L. McDonald and D. Hulchanski. (1995). 'Estimating homelessness: towards a methodology for counting the homeless in Canada: Executive Summary', Centre for Applied Social Research Faculty of Social Work, University of Toronto, accessed December 1998 from <http://www.cmhc-schl.gc.ca/Research/Homeless/F_estima.html>.

Perras, F. and J. Huyder (2003). *Interagency Shelter Count for 2002*, Calgary: Interagency Committee for the Absolute Homeless.

Pilbeam, K. (2001). 'The East Asian financial crisis: Getting to the heart of the issues', *Managerial Finance*, 27(1–2): 111–33.

The Pioneer (2000) 'For whom the streets are their home', 20 July.

Plaatjies, C. (1999). 'Tales of Johnny Louw', *Homeless Talk*, 6(3): 7.

Pleace, N. (1998). 'Single homelessness as social exclusion: The unique and the extreme', *Social Policy and Administration*, 32(1): 46–59.

Pomodoro, L. (2001). 'Trafficking and sexual exploitation of women and children', in P. Williams and D. Vlassis (eds), *Combating Transnational Crime: Concepts, Activities and Responses*, London: Frank Cass.

Porteous, D. (2004). *Making Markets Work for the Poor*, Pretoria/Tshwane: FinMark Trust.

Posel, D. (1991). 'Curbing African urbanisation in the 1950s and 1960s', in M. Swilling, R. Humphries and K. Shubane (eds), *Apartheid in Transition*, Cape Town: Oxford University Press.

PREDA (1999). 'PREDA's Campaign against the shooting of streetchildren in Davao City, Philippines', accessed 3 Nov. 2007 from <http://www.preda.org/archives/1999/r9909251.htm>.

Prugl, E. (1996). 'Biases in labour law: A critique from the standpoint of home-based workers', in E. Boris and E. Prugl (eds), *Homeworkers in Global Perspective: Invisible No More,* New York, and London: Routledge.

PUCL (2000). *Homeless Migrants in Delhi: Findings from a PUCL Investigation*, New Delhi: People's Union for Civil Liberties (PUCL).

Rabé, P. E. (2005). *Land Sharing in Phnom Penh: An Innovative But Insufficient Instrument of Secure Tenure for the Poor,* UN-ESCAP Expert Group Meeting on Secure Land Tenure: New Legal Frameworks and Tools, Bangkok, 8–9 Dec.

Radley, A., D. Hodgetts and A. Cullen (2005). 'Visualizing homelessness: A study in photography and estrangement', *Journal of Community and Applied Social Psychology,* 15(4): 273–95.

Rafaelli, M. (1997). 'The family situation of street children in Latin America: a cross national review'. *International Social Work,* 40: 89–100.

Rahardjo, T. (2002). *The Nature, Extent and Eradication of Homelessness in Developing Countries: Indonesia,* Report for the CARDO/ESCOR project on homelessness in developing countries, Semarang: Centre for Urban Studies, Soegijapranata Catholic University.

Rahardjo, T. (2006). 'Forced eviction, homelessness and the right to housing in Indonesia', Paper presented at the conference on Homelessness: A Global Perspective, New Delhi, 9–13 Jan.

Rahman, A. (1999). 'Micro-credit initiatives for equitable and sustainable development: Who pays?', *World Development,* 27(1): 67–82.

Rahman, M. M. (2001). 'Bastee eviction and housing rights: A case of Dhaka, Bangladesh', *Habitat International,* 25(1): 49–67.

Rahman, T. (1993). *The Rural Homeless in Bangladesh,* Dhaka: UNICEF-Bangladesh.

Rahman, W. (1997). *Child Labour Situation in Bangladesh: A Rapid Assessment,* Dhaka: ILO and UNICEF.

Rajkumar, V. (2000). *Vulnerability and Impact of HIV/AIDS on Children in Selected Areas of Delhi, Rajasthan, Tamil Nadu and Maharashtra,* London: Save the Children.

Ramet, S. P. (1992). 'War in the Balkans', *Foreign Affairs,* 71(4): 79–98.

Randall, G. and S. Brown (2001). *Trouble at Home: Family Conflict, Young People and Homelessness,* London: Crisis.

Ray, S. K., R. Biswas, S. Kumar, T. Chatterjee, R. Misra and S. K. Lahiri (2001). 'Reproductive health needs and care seeking behaviour of pavement dwellers of Calcutta', *Journal of the Indian Medical Association,* 99(33): 142–3, 145.

Razani, R. (1978). 'Seismic protection of un-reinforced masonry and adobe low-cost housing in less-developed countries: Policy issues and design criteria', *Disasters,* 2(2–3): 137–47.

READ (2000). *Need Assessment Survey of the Disadvantaged Women and Children In the Urban Areas of Bangladesh,* Report prepared for CONCERN Bangladesh by Research Evaluation Associates for Development (READ), Dhaka: READ

Republic of Ghana (2006). *Ghana: Poverty Reduction Strategy Paper,* Washington, DC: International Monetary Fund.

Republic of Kenya (2002). *Report of the Commission of Enquiry into the Land Law System of Kenya on the Principles of a National Land Policy Framework and New Institutional Framework for Land Administration,* Nairobi: Government of Kenya.

Republic of Mozambique (2006). *Action Plan for the Reduction of Absolute Poverty, 2006–2009 (PARPA II),* Maputo: Republic of Mozambique.

Republic of South Africa (1996). *The Constitution of the Republic of South Africa,* Act No. 108 of 1996.

Resource Information Service (2000). 'Homelessness', accessed 28 Feb. 2007 from <http://www.homelesspages.org.uk/subs/subjects.asp?sbid=10>.

Ribeiro, M. O., T. Ciampone and M. Helena (2001). 'Homeless children: The lives of a group of Brazilian street children', *Journal of Advanced Nursing,* 35(1): 42–9.

Ritchie, M. (1999). 'Children in especially difficult circumstances: Children living on the street. Can their special needs be met through specific legal provisioning?' Consultative paper prepared for the South African Law Commission.

Rizzini, I. (1996). 'Street children: An excluded generation in South America', *Childhood*, 3(1): 215–34.

Rizzini, I. and M. W. Lusk (1995). 'Children in the streets: Latin America's lost generation', *Children and Youth Services Review*, 17(3): 391–400.

Rogaly, B. (1996). 'Micro-finance evangelism, "destitute women" and the hard selling of a new anti-poverty formula', *Development in Practice*, 6(2): 100–12.

Rogaly, B. (2003). 'Who goes? Who stays back? Seasonal migration and staying put among rural manual workers in Eastern India', *Journal of International Development*, 5(5): 623–32.

Rogaly, B. and C. Coppard (2003). '"They used to go to eat, now they go to earn": The changing meanings of seasonal migration from Puruliya District in West Bengal, India', *Journal of Agrarian Change*, 3(3, July): 395–433.

Rosenthal, R. (2000). 'Imaging homelessness and homeless people: Visions and strategies within the movement', *Journal of Social Distress and the Homeless*, 9(2): 111–26.

Rotberg, R. I. (1999). *Creating Peace in Sri Lanka: Civil War and Reconciliation,* Washington, DC: Brookings Institution Press.

Roy, S. and S. Ray (2000). 'Prevention of malnutrition', *Journal of the Indian Medical Association*, 98(9): 510–11.

Rust, K. (2007). *Analysis of South Africa's Housing Sector Performance*, Pretoria/Tshwane: FinMark Trust

Ruthven, O. and R. David (1995). 'Benefits and burdens: Researching the consequences of migration in the Sahel', *IDS Bulletin*, 26(1): 47–53.

Sack, A. L. and Z. Suster (2000). 'Soccer and Croatian nationalism: A prelude to war', *Journal of Sport and Social Issues*, 24(3): 305–20.

Sahlin, I. (1998). *The Staircase of Transition*, European Observatory on Homelessness, National Report from Sweden, Brussels: FEANTSA.

Sahn, D. E., P. Dorosh and S. Younger (1996). 'Exchange rate, fiscal and agricultural policies in Africa: Does adjustment hurt the poor?', *World Development*, 24(4): 719–47.

Salazar, A. (1999). 'Disasters, the World Bank and participation: Relocation housing after the 1993 earthquake in Maharashtra, India', *Third World Planning Review*, 21(1): 83–108.

Salinas, F. (1990–2). *Sans-abri en Espagne,* Observatoire National des Sans-abri en Espagne: Annual Reports, Brussels: FEANTSA.

Samara, T. R. (2003). 'State security in transition: The war on crime in post apartheid South Africa', *Social Identities*, 9(2): 277–312.

Sancio, R. (2000). 'Disaster in Venezuela: The floods and landslides of December 1999', *Natural Hazards Observer*, 24(4, March): 1–2.

Sato, H. (2006). 'Housing inequality and housing poverty in urban China in the late 1990s', *China Economic Review*, 17(1): 37–50.

Satterthwaite, D. (2003). 'The links between poverty and the environment in urban areas of Africa, Asia, and Latin America', *Annals of the American Academy of Political and Social Science*, 590: 73–92.

Schatz, S. (1994). 'Structural adjustment in Africa: A failing grade so far', *Journal of Modern African Studies*, 32(4): 679–92.

Bibliography

Schilderman, T. (2004). 'Adapting traditional shelter for disaster mitigation and reconstruction: Experiences with community-based approaches', *Building Research Information*, 32(5): 414–26.

Schildkrout, E. (1978). *People of the Zongo: The Transformation of Ethnic Identities in Ghana*, Cambridge: Cambridge University Press.

Schleiter, M. K. and A. Statham (2002). 'US welfare reform and structural adjustment policies', *Anthropological Quarterly*, 75(4): 759–64.

Schlyter, A. (1987). 'Commercialisation of housing in upgraded squatter areas: The case of George, Lusaka, Zambia', *African Urban Quarterly*, 2: 287–97.

Schuler, S. R., S. M. Hashemi, A. P. Riley and S. Akhter (1996). 'Credit programs, patriarchy and men's violence against women in rural Bangladesh', *Social Science & Medicine*, 43(12): 1729–42.

Schutz, E. (1989). 'Para festejar el dia: Actualmente son desaslojados miles de familias en Santo Domingo', *Medio Ambiente y Urbanizacion*, 25: 78–81.

Searfoss, K. (2000). 'Saving children from the streets', *Presbyterian Today online*, accessed 22 Nov. 2001 from <http://www.pcusa.org/pcusa/today>.

Seth, R., A. Kotwal and K. K. Ganguly (2005). 'Street and working children of Delhi, India, misusing toluene: An ethnographic exploration', *Substance Use and Misuse*, 40(11): 1659–79.

Sethuraman, S. V. (1997). *Urban Poverty and the Informal Sector: A Critical Assessment of Current Strategies*, ILO and UNDP, accessed 1 Dec. 2003 from <http://www.ilo.org/public/english/employment/recon/eiip/publ/1998/urbpover.htm>.

Shafi, S. A. (1998). *Study on Financing of Urban Low-income Housing, Draft Final Report*, Dhaka: Asian Development Bank (ADB).

Shahmanesh, M. and S. Wayal (2004). 'Targeting commercial sex-workers in Goa, India: Time for a strategic rethink?', *The Lancet*, 364(9442, 5–9 Oct.): 1297–9.

Shakur, M. T. and T. A. Khan (1986). 'Changing attitudes of the "concerned groups" toward squatter settlements in Dhaka: A case study', *Journal of Local Government*, 15(2): 35–50.

Shamim, I. (2001). *Mapping of Missing, Kidnapped and Trafficked Women: Bangladesh Perspective*, Dhaka: International Organisation of Women (IOM).

Shamim, I. and K. Salahuddin (1995). *Widows in Rural Bangladesh: Issues and Concerns*, Dhaka: Centre for Women and Children.

Shaw, M., D. Dorling and N. Brimblecombe (1999). 'Life chances in Britain by housing wealth and for the homeless and vulnerably housed', *Environment and Planning A*, 31(12): 2239–48.

Sherman, D. J. (1992). 'The neglected health care needs of street youth', *Public Health Report*, 107: 433–40.

Siddiqui, K., S. R. Qadir, S. Alamgir and S. Huq (1990). 'The informal sector poor of Dhaka City', in K. Siddiqui, S. R. Qadir, S. Alamgir and S. Huq (eds), *Social Formation in Dhaka City*, Dhaka: University Press.

Sihlongonyane, M. F. (2006). 'Images of homelessness in the inner city of Johannesburg: Hillbrow, Kotze Street', GURU International Conference on Homelessness in a Global Perspective, New Delhi, Newcastle University, 9–13 Jan.

Singh, A. M. and A. de Souza (1980). *The Urban Poor, Slum and Pavement Dwellers in Major Cities of India*, New Delhi: Manohar.

Singh, S., K. Dahal and E. Mills (2005). 'Nepal's war on human rights: A summit higher than Everest', *International Journal for Equity in Health*, 4: 9–15.

Sinha, D. (1994). *Stopping Evictions in Asia: Report from Bangladesh,* Bangkok: Housing by People in Asia, Asian Coalition for Housing Rights.

Snow, D. A. and M. Mulcahy (2001). 'Space, politics, and the survival strategies of the homeless', *American Behavioral Scientist*, 45(1): 149–69.

Social Planning and Research Council of BC (2005). 'On our streets and in our shelters . . . Results of the Greater Vancouver Homeless Count', *Homeless Count 2005, Bulletin* (Sept.), Vancouver, BC: Social Planning and Resarch Council of BC, accessed 16 Jan. 2007 from <www.gvrd.bc.ca/homelessness/pdfs/HomelessCount2005Bulletin.pdf>.

Somerville, P. (1992). 'Homelessness and the meaning of home: Rooflessness or rootlessness?', *International Journal of Urban and Regional Research*, 16(4): 529–39.

Sorrill, D. (1998). 'The permanent emergency shelter cum roofing unit for Bangladesh', unpubl. MPhil thesis, Department of Architecture, University of Newcastle upon Tyne.

SOS Children's Villages (2008) 'AIDS orphans in Lesotho' accessed 21 January 2009 from <http://www.soschildrensvillages.org.uk/aids-africa/>.

Sossou, M. A. (2002). 'Widowhood practices in West Africa: The silent victims', *International Journal of Social Welfare*, 11(3): 201–9.

SPARC (1985). *We, the Invisible: A Census of Pavement Dwellers*, Mumbai: Society for the Propagation of Area Resource Centres.

Speak, S. (2004). 'Degrees of destitution: A typology of homelessness in developing countries', *Housing Studies*, 19(3): 465–82.

Speak, S. (2005). 'The relationship between children's homelessness in developing countries and the failure of women's rights legislation', *Housing Theory and Society,* 22(3): 129–46.

Speak, S. and A. G. Tipple (2006). 'Perceptions, persecution and pity: The limitations of interventions for homelessness', *International Journal of Urban and Regional Research*, 30(1): 172–88.

Spence, J. (1997). 'Homeless in Russia: A visit with Valery Sokolov', *Share International Archives*, accessed on 19 Jan. 2007 from <www.share-international.org/archives/homelessness/hl-jsRussia.htm>.

Springer, S. (2000). 'Homelessness: A proposal for a global definition and classification', *Habitat International*, 24(4): 475–84.

Sriyuningsih, N. (2001). *Profil Kemiskinan dan Gender Kota Semarang*, Kota Semarang, Semarang: Urban Management Programme.

Statistics South Africa (2004). *Primary Tables South Africa: Census '96 and 2001 Compared*, Pretoria: Statistics South Africa, accessed 15 Jan. 2007 from <http://www.statssa.gov.za/census01/html/RSAPrimary.pdf>.

Stoecker, S. (2001). 'Homelessness and criminal exploitation of Russian minors: Realities, resources and legal remedies', *Demokratizatsiya*, 9(2): 319–36.

Stoecklin, D. (2000). 'In-depth study (qualitative survey) on the street children of Chittagong City, Bangladesh', in Aparajeyo-Bangladesh and Terre des hommes (eds), *A Baseline Survey on the Street Children of Chittagong City, Bangladesh*, Dhaka: Aparajeyo-Bangladesh and Terre des hommes.

Subbarao, K., J. Braithwaite and J. Jalan (1995). *Protecting the Poor during Adjustment and Transitions*, HCO Working Papers, 58, Washington, DC: World Bank.

Suda, C. (1997). 'Street children in Nairobi and the African cultural ideology of kin-based support system: Change and challenge', *Child Abuse Review*, 6(3): 199–217.

Suliman, M. (n.d. [*c.*1992]). *Civil War in Sudan: The Impact of Ecological Degradation*, Environment and Conflicts Project ENCOP Occasional Papers 1992–1995, Zurich and

Berne: Swiss Peace Foundation, Center for Security Studies and Conflict Research/Swiss Federal Institute of Technology ETH-Zentrum.

Summerfield, D. (1997). 'The social, cultural and political dimensions of contemporary war', *Medicine, Conflict and Survival*, 13(1): 3–25.

Susman, P., P. O'Keefe and B. Wisner (1983). 'Global disasters, a radical interpretation', in K. Hewitt (ed.), *Interpretations of Calamity*, London: Allen & Unwin.

Swaminathan, M. (1995). 'Aspects of urban poverty in Bombay', *Environment and Urbanization*, 7(1): 133–43.

Swart, J. (1988). 'An anthropological study of street children in Hillbrow, Johannesburg, with special reference to their moral values', unpubl. MA dissertation in anthropology, University of South Africa, Pretoria.

Swart-Kruger, J. and L. M. Richter (1997). 'AIDS-related knowledge, attitudes and behaviour among South African street youth: Reflections on power, sexuality and the autonomous self', *Social Science and Medicine*, 45(6): 957–66.

Syagga, P., W. Mitullah and S. Karirah-Gitau (2001a). *Nairobi Situation Analysis: Consultative Report*, Nairobi: Government of Kenya and UN-Habitat.

Syagga, P., W. Mitullah and S. Karirah-Gitau (2001b). *GOK/UNCHS Slum Upgrading Initiative: Nairobi Situational Analysis*, Nairobi: Government of Kenya and UNCHS (Habitat).

Szekely, M. (1995). 'Poverty in Mexico during adjustment', *Review of Income and Wealth*, 41(3): 331–48.

Tait, G. (1993). 'Re-assessing street-kids: A critique of subculture theory', *Child and Youth Care Forum*, 22(2): 83–93.

Taylor, E. J. (1999). 'The new economics of labour migration and the role of remittances in the migration process', *International Migration*, 37(1): 63–88.

Tessler, R. (2003). 'Homeless veterans of the all-volunteer force: A social selection perspective', *Armed Forces and Society*, 29(4): 510–24.

Thomas de Benitez, S. (2003). 'Reactive, protective and rights-based approaches in work with homeless street youth', *Children, Youth and Environments*, 13(1, Spring): 1–16.

Tibaijuka, A. K. (2005). *Report of the Fact-Finding Mission to Zimbabwe to Assess the Scope and Impact of Operation Murambatsvina*, Nairobi: UN-Habitat.

The Times of India (2001) 'Night shelters make way for fountains', 27 October.

Times Online (2008). 'Burma cyclone: Up to 50,000 dead and millions homeless, but still no call for aid', London, 7 May, accessed 5 June 2008, from <http://www.timesonline.co.uk/tol/news/world/asia/article3883123.ece>.

Tipple, A. G. (1987). 'Ghana: Revolution in property rights', *West Africa* (27 Jan.): 179–80.

Tipple, A. G. (1994a). 'A matter of interface: The need for a shift in targeting housing interventions', *Habitat International*, 18(4): 1–15.

Tipple, A. G. (1994b). 'The need for new urban housing in sub-Saharan Africa: Problem or opportunity', *African Affairs*, 93: 587–608.

Tipple, A. G. (1995). 'Dear Mr President, housing is good for your economy', *Norsk Tidsskrift Geografisk*, 49(4): 175–86.

Tipple, A. G. (2000). *Extending Themselves: User-Initiated Transformations of Government-Built Housing in Developing Countries,* Liverpool: Liverpool University Press.

Tipple, A. G. (2005a). 'Housing and urban vulnerability in rapidly-developing cities', *Journal of Contingencies and Crisis Management*, 3(2): 66–75.

Tipple, A. G. (2005b). 'Pollution and waste production in home-based enterprises in developing countries: Perceptions and realities', *Journal of Environmental Planning and Management,* 48(2, March): 275–98.

Tipple, A. G. (2006). 'Employment and work conditions in home-based enterprises in four developing countries: Do they constitute "decent work"?', *Work, Employment and Society*, 19(4): 841–53.

Tipple, A. G. and M. S. Ameen (1999). 'User initiated extension activity in Bangladesh: "Building slums" or area improvement', *Environment and Urbanisation*, 11(1): 165–83.

Tipple, A. G. and D. Korboe (1998). 'Housing policy in Ghana: Towards a supply-oriented approach', *Habitat International*, 22(3): 245–57.

Tipple, A. G. and S. Speak (2005). 'Definitions of homelessness in developing countries', *Habitat International*, 29(2): 337–52.

Tipple, A. G. and S. Speak (2006). 'Who is homeless in developing countries: Differentiating between inadequately housed and homeless people', *International Development Planning Review*, 28(1): 57–84.

Tipple, A. G. and K. G. Willis (1991). 'Tenure choice in a West African city', *Third World Planning Review*, 13(1): 27–45.

Tipple, A. G. and K. G. Willis (1992). 'Why should Ghanaians build houses in urban areas?', *Cities* (Feb.): 60–74.

Tipple, A. G., B. Amole, B. Korboe and H. Onyeacholem (1994). 'House and dwelling, family and household: Towards defining housing units in West African cities', *Third World Planning Review*, 16(4): 429–50.

Tipple, A. G., D. Korboe, G. Garrod and K. Willis (1999). 'Housing supply in Ghana: A study of Accra, Kumasi and Berekum', *Progress in Planning*, 51: 253–324.

Toole, M. J. and R. J. Waldman (1993). 'Refugees and displaced persons: War, hunger, and public health', *Journal of the American Medical Association*, 270(5): 600–5.

Turner, B., S. (1993). *Citizenship and Social Theory*, London: Sage.

Turner, J. F. C. (1968). 'Housing priorities, settlement patterns, and urban development in modernizing countries', *Journal of the American Institute of Planners*, 34 (Nov.): 354–63

Turner, J. F. C. (1972). 'Housing issues and the standards problems', *Ekistics*, 196: 152–8.

Turner, J. F. C. (1976). *Housing by People: Towards Autonomy in Building Environments,* London: Marion Boyars.

Turner, J. F. C. and R. Fichter (1972). *Freedom to Build*, London: Macmillan.

UNAIDS and WHO (2006). *AIDS Epidemic Update: December 2006*, Geneva: UNAIDS.

UNAIDS, UNICEF and USAID (2004). *Children on the Brink 2004: A Joint Report of New Orphan Estimates and a Framework for Action*, New York: UNICEF.

UNCED (1992). *Agenda 21, Chapter 7: Promoting Sustainable Human Settlement Development*, United Nations Conference on Environment and Development, Rio de Janeiro, 14 June.

UNCESCR (1991). *General Comment 4: The Right to Adequate Housing (Art 11 (1)),* United Nations Committee on Economic, Social and Cultural Rights, 13 Dec.

UNCHS (1976). *The Vancouver Declaration on Human Settlements and the Vancouver Action Plan*, Nairobi: UNCHS (Habitat).

UNCHS (1990). *The Global Strategy for Shelter to the Year 2000*, Nairobi: UNCHS (Habitat).

UNCHS (1991). *Evaluation of Experience with Initiating Enabling Shelter Strategies*, Nairobi: UNCHS (Habitat).

UNCHS (1994). *Sustainable Human Settlements Development: Implementing Agenda 21: Report Prepared for the Commission on Sustainable Development*, Nairobi: UNCHS (Habitat).

UNCHS (1995). *The Right to Adequate Housing: Final Report Submitted by Mr. Rajindar Sachar, Special Rapporteur*, Nairobi: UNCHS (Habitat).

UNCHS (1996). *An Urbanising World: Global Report on Human Settlements*, Oxford: Oxford University Press.

UNCHS (1997). *The Habitat Agenda*, Nairobi: United Nations Centre for Human Settlements.

UNCHS (1999). *Guidelines on Practical Aspects in the Realisation of the Human Right to Adequate Housing Including the Formulation of the United Nations Housing Rights Programme*, Nairobi: Progress Report of the Executive Director to the Seventeenth Session of the Commission on Human Settlements (CH/C/17/INF/6).

UNCHS (2000). *Strategies to Combat Homelessness*, Nairobi: UNCHS (Habitat).

UNCHS (2001a). *Cities in a Globalizing World: Global Report on Human Settlements, 2001*, London: Earthscan.

UNCHS (2001b). *The State of the World's Cities 2001*, Nairobi: UNCHS (Habitat).

UNCHS (n.d.). *Practical Aspects in the Realization of the Human Right to Adequate Housing: Guidelines for the Formulation of the United Nations Housing Rights Programme (UNHRP) (Draft)*, Nairobi: UNCHS (Habitat).

UNCHS and ILO (1995). *Shelter Provision and Employment Generation*, Nairobi and Geneva: United Nations Centre for Human Settlements (Habitat) and International Labour Office.

UNDP (1991). *Cities, Poverty and People: Urban Development Cooperation for the 1990s*, New York: UNDP.

UNDP (2006). 'Mongolia at a glance', Youandaids: the HIV/AIDS portal for Asia and the Pacific, accessed 10 Jan. 2007 from <http://www.youandaids.org/Asia%20Pacific%20at%20a%20Glance/Mongolia/index.asp>.

UNDP and GOB (1993). *Bangladesh Urban and Shelter Sector Review*, New York, and Dhaka: United Nations Development Programme and Government of Bangladesh.

UNEP Youth Xchange (n.d.). *Homelessness: A Growing Phenomenon*, Nairobi and Geneva: UNEP and UNESCO, accessed 11 Jan. 2007 from <http://www.youthxchange.net/main/b236_homeless-a.asp>.

Ungerson, C. (1990). *Gender and Caring: Work and Welfare in Britain and Scandinavia*, Hemel Hempstead: Harvester Wheatsheaf.

UN-Habitat (2001). 'Declaration on cities and other human settlements in the new millennium', accessed 10 Dec. 2004 from <http://www.unchs.org/istanbul+5/declaration_cities.htm>.

UN-Habitat (2002). *Housing Rights Legislation: Review of International and National Legal Instruments*, Nairobi: UN-Habitat and Office of the High Commissioner for Human Rights.

UN-Habitat (2003). *The Challenge of Slums: Global Report on Human Settlements 2003*, London and Sterling, VA: Earthscan.

UN-Habitat (2005). *Financing Shelter and Urban Development: Global Report on Human Settlements 2005*, Nairobi and London: UN-Habitat and Earthscan.

UN-Habitat (2006a). *Enabling Shelter Strategies: Review of Experience from Two Decades of Implementation*, Nairobi: UN-Habitat.

UN-Habitat (2006b). *The State of the World's Cities 2006/2007*, Nairobi and London: UN-Habitat and Earthscan.

UN-Habitat (2007a). *Global Report on Human Settlements 2007: Enhancing Urban Safety and Security,* Nairobi and London: UN-Habitat and Earthscan.

UN-Habitat (2007b). *The State of Iraqi Cities Report*, Nairobi and Baghdad: UN-Habitat and Ministry of Municipalities and Public Works.

UNHCHR (1989). 'Convention on the Rights of the Child', UN General Assembly Resolution 44/25 of 20 Nov.

UNHCR (2006). *Statistical Yearbook 2006*, Geneva: United Nations High Commissioner for Refugees. UNHCHR (n.d.). *Fact Sheet No.21: The Human Right to Adequate Housing*, Geneva: Office of the High Commissioner for Human Rights, accessed 10 March 2007 from <http://www.unhchr.ch/html/menu6/2/fs21.htm>.

UNICEF (1996). *Country Profile: Brazil*, Geneva: UNICEF.

UNICEF (2002). *Priorities for Children 2002–2005*, Geneva: UNICEF.

UNICEF (2003). *UNICEF Bolivia: The Children. The Situation of Children in Bolivia*, La Paz: UNICEF Bolivia, accessed 6 Feb. 2007 from <http://www.unicef.org/bolivia/children_1540.htm.>

UNICEF (2008a). *Children Living in Poverty*, Geneva: UNICEF, accessed 16 March 2008 from <http://www.unicef.org/sowc05/english/poverty.html>.

UNICEF (2008b). *Peru at a Glance*, Geneva: UNICEF, accessed 2 April 2008 from <http://www.unicef.org/infobycountry/peru.html>.

UNICEF (n.d.). 'UNICEF in emergencies: Displaced children', accessed 19 Feb. 2007 from <http://www.unicef.org/emerg/index_displacedchildren.html>.

United Nations (1948). 'The Universal Declaration of Human Rights', United Nations Resolution 217A, 10 Dec.

United Nations (1959). 'Declaration of the Rights of the Child', UN General Assembly Resolution 1386 (XIV) of 20 Nov.

United Nations (1966). 'International Covenant on Economic, Social and Cultural Rights', General Assembly Resolution 2200A (XXI) of 16 Dec.

United Nations (1976). *Report of Habitat: United Nations Conference on Human Settlements*, New York: United Nations.

United Nations (1979). *The Convention on the Elimination of All Forms of Discrimination against Women (CEDAW)*, New York: United Nations.

United Nations. (1982). 'International Year of Shelter for the Homeless', General Assembly Resolution A/RES/37/221, accessed 21 Mar. 2007 from <http:// www.un.org/documents/ga/res/37/a37r221. htm>.

United Nations (1995). *The Copenhagen Declaration and Programme of Action, World Summit for Social Development, 6–12 March*, New York: United Nations.

United Nations (1998). *Principles and Recommendation for Population and Housing Censuses*, New York: United Nations.

United Nations (2000). 'United Nations Millennium Declaration', Resolution 55/2.

United Nations (2004). *World Population Prospects: The 2002 Revision*, vol. 3, *Analytical Report*, New York: Population Division, Dept. of Economic and Social Affairs.

United Nations (2005). 'UN Millennium Development Goals: Keep the promise', accessed 17 March 2007 from <http://www.un.org/millenniumgoals/>.

United States Conference of Mayors (2005a). 'Hunger and homelessness survey 2005', Long Beach, CA, accessed 9 Sept. 2007 from <http://www.usmayors.org/uscm/hungersurvey/2005/HH2005FINAL.pdf>.

United States Conference of Mayors (2005b). 'Hunger and homelessness survey 2005: A status report on hunger and homelessness in America's cities, December 2005', Sodexho,

Inc, accessed 9 Feb. 2008 from <http://www.usmayors.org/uscm/hungersurvey/2005/HH2005FINAL.pdf>.

USA (1994). *Priority: Home! The Federal Plan to Break the Cycle of Homelessness*, Washington, DC: US Government.

USAID, UNICEF and UNAIDS (2002). *Children on the Brink 2002: A Joint Report on Orphan Estimates and Program Strategies*, Washington, DC: USAID/UNICEF/UNAIDS.

Uy, W. J. (2006). 'Medium-rise housing: The Philippine experience', 5th Asian Forum, Tokyo, Japan, 18–20 Jan.

Vasquez, D. (1997). *Registro único computarizado de niños y adolescentes intervenidos por la administración de justicia*, Lima: CEDRO.

Veale, A. and G. Dona (2003). 'Street children and political violence: A socio-demographic analysis of street children in Rwanda', *Child Abuse and Neglect*, 27: 253–69.

Veale, A., A. Aderfrsew and K. Lalor (1993). *A Study of Street Children in Four Regional Towns in Ethiopia,* Report for UNICEF in conjunction with the Ministry for Labour and Social Affairs, Ethiopia, Cork: University College.

Vissing, Y. M. (1996). *Out of Sight, Out of Mind: Homeless Children and Families in Small-Town America*, Lexington, KY: University Press of Kentucky.

Waddington, C. (2003). *Livelihood Outcomes of Migration for Poor People*, Brighton: Development Research Centre on Migration, Globalisation and Poverty, University of Sussex.

Walker, A. (1996). *The New Generational Contract: Intergenerational Relations, Old Age, and Welfare*, London: Routledge.

Walter, J. (2003). 'Disasterproofing: Reducing the impact of natural disasters', *ID21 Society and Economy*, accessed 20 Jan. 2005 from <http://www.id21.org/society/s10ajw1g1.html>.

Walter, T. R., R. Wang, B.-G. Lühr, J. Wassermann, Y. Behr, S. Parolai, A. Anggraini, E. Günther, M. Sobiesiak, H. Grosser, H.-U. Wetzel, C. Milkereit, K. Sri Brotopuspito, H. Prih and J. Zschau (2007). 'Soft volcanic sediments compound 2006 Java earthquake disaster', *Eos Transactions, American Geographical Union,* 88(46): 486.

Wang, F. and X. Zuo (1999). 'Inside China's cities: Institutional barriers and opportunities for urban migrants', *American Economic Review*, 89(2): 276–80.

Wang, G. and J. Shen (2001). 'Research on external and local labor forces of Shanghai', *Population Research (China),* 25(1): 9–19.

Wang, Y. P. (2004). *Urban Poverty, Housing and Social Change in China*, London: Routledge.

Wantchekron, L. (2003). 'Clientelism and voting behaviour: A field experiment in Benin', *World Politics*, 55(3): 399–422.

Ward, P. M. (1976). 'The squatter settlement as slum or housing solution: Evidence from Mexico City', *Land Economics*, 52: 330–46.

Ward, P. M. (1982). *Self-help Housing: A Critique*, London: Mansell.

Watson, S. (1987). 'Ideas of the family in the development of housing form', in M. Loney (ed.), *The State or the Market*, London: Sage.

Watson, S. (1988). *Accommodating Inequality: Gender and Housing*, Sydney: Allen & Unwin.

Watson, S. (1999). 'A home is where the heart is: Engendered notions of homelessness', in P. Kennett and A. Marsh (eds), *Homelessness: Exploring the New Terrain,* Bristol: Policy Press.

Watson, S. and H. Austerberry (1986). *Housing and Homelessness: A Feminist Perspective*, London: Routledge & Kegan Paul.

West, A. (2003). *At the Margins: Street Children in Asia and the Pacific*, Poverty and Social Development Papers, 8, Manila: Asian Development Bank.

Wheaton, W. C. (1980). 'Development and infrastructure in the Greater Cairo Region', Mimeo prepared for the World Bank, Cambridge, MA.

Whitbeck, L. B., D. R. Hoyt and K. A. Ackley (1997). 'Families of homeless and runaway adolescents: A comparison of parent/caretaker and adolescent perspectives on parenting, family violence, and adolescent conduct', *Child Abuse and Neglect,* 21(6, June): 517–28.

Whitbeck, L. B., D. R. Hoyt and K. A. Yoder (1999). 'A Risk-Amplification Model of Victimization and Depressive Symptoms Among Runaway and Homeless Adolescents', *American Journal of Community Psychology*, 27(2): 273–96.

Whitbeck, L. B., D. R. Hoyt, K. A. Yoder, A. M. Cauce and M. Paradise (2001). 'Deviant behavior and victimization among homeless and runaway adolescents', *Journal of Interpersonal Violence*, 16(11): 1175–1204.

Williams, M. (2005). 'Definition, measurement and legitimacy in studies of homelessness', in M. Romero and E. Margolis (eds), *The Blackwell Companion to Social Inequalities*, Malden, MA, Blackwell.

Williams, M. and B. Cheal (2001). 'Is there any such thing as homelessness? Measurement, explanation and process in "homelessness" research', *Innovations*, 14(3): 239–53.

Wirakartakusumah, M. D. and I. Hasan (n.d.). 'Krisis Moneter di Indonesia, Dampak Sosial yang Ditimbulkan dan Strategi Penanggulangannya', accessed 26 Nov. 2001 from <http://psi.ut.ac.id/Jurnal/91djuhari.htm>.

Wisner, B. (1998). 'Marginality and vulnerability: Why the homeless of Tokyo don't "count" in disaster preparations', *Applied Geography*, 18(1): 25–33.

World Bank (1980). *Shelter*, Washington, DC: Urban Projects Department, World Bank.

World Bank (1991). *Urban Policy and Economic Development: An Agenda for the 1990s*, A World Bank Policy Paper, Washington, DC: World Bank.

World Bank (1993). *Housing: Enabling Markets to Work,* Washington, DC: World Bank.

World Bank (1998). *Bangladesh 2020: A Long-run Perspective Study*, Dhaka: University Press.

World Bank (1999). *Toward an Urban Strategy for Bangladesh*, Report no. 20289-BD, 30 Sept., Infrastructure Sector Unit, South Asia Region, Washington, DC: World Bank.

World Bank (2001). *World Development Report 2000/2001: Attacking Poverty*, London and Washington, DC: Oxford University Press and World Bank.

World Bank (2002). *Algeria: World Bank to Support Development of Mortgage Loan Market*, Washington, DC: World Bank.

World Bank (2003). *World Development Report 2004: Making Services Work for Poor People*, Washington, DC: World Bank.

World Bank (2007). *PovertyNet: Poverty Reduction Strategies*, Washington, DC: World Bank, accessed 22 May 2007 from <http://web.worldbank.org/WBSITE/EXTERNAL/TOPICS/EXTPOVERTY/EXTPRS/0,,menuPK:384207~pagePK:149018~piPK:149093~theSitePK:384201,00.html>.

World Health Organisation (2002). *Impact of AIDS on Older People in Africa,* Geneva: WHO 11: World Health Organisation.

World Resources Institute (1999). 'Population and human well-being: Urban growth', accessed 11 May 2004 from <http://www.wri.org/wr-98–99/citygrow.htm>.

Wright, J. D. and J. Devine (1995). 'Housing dynamics of the homeless: Implications for a count', *American Journal of Orthopsychiatry*, 65(3): 320–9.

Bibliography

Wright, J. D. and J. A. Devine (1999). 'Counting the homeless: The Census Bureau's 'S-Night" in five US cities', *Evaluation Review*, 16(4): 355–64.

Wright-Howie, D. (2007). 'An Australian blueprint to reduce and eliminate homelessness', accessed 12 May 2008 from <http://www.chp.org.au/public_library/>.

Wu, W. (2002). 'Migrant housing in urban China: Choices and constraints', *Urban Affairs Review*, 38(1): 90–119.

Yasmeen, G. (2001). 'Stockbrokers turned sandwich vendors: The economic crisis and small-scale food retailing in Southeast Asia', *Geoforum*, 32: 91–102.

Yin, H. and C. Li (2001). 'Human impact on floods and flood disasters on the Yangtze River', *Geomorphology*, 41(2–3): 105–9.

Young, L. and N. Ansell (2003). 'Young AIDS migrants in Southern Africa: Policy implications for empowering children', *AIDS Care*, 15(3): 337–45.

Young, L. and H. Barrett (2001). 'Adapting visual methods: Action research with Kampala street children', *Area*, 33(2): 141–52.

Yudohusodo, S. and S. Salam (1991). *Rumah Untuk Seluruh Rakyat*, Jakarta: Unit Percetakan Bharakerta.

Zanger, M. (n.d.). 'Refugees in their cwn country', *Middle East Report*, accessed 29 March 2006 from <http://www.merip.org/mer/mer222/222_zanger.html>.

Zhang, L., S. X. B. Zhao and J. P. Tian (2003). 'Self help in housing and *chengzhongcun* in China's urbanisation', *International Journal of Urban and Regional Research*, 27(4): 912–37.

Zimbabwe Congress of Trade Unions (1999). *Position Paper: Focus for the 1999/2000 Negotiations*, Harare: ZCTU.

Zong, Y. and X. Chen (2000). 'The 1998 flood on the Yangtze, China', *Natural Hazards*, 22(2): 165–84.

Zvauya, C. (2001) 'Farm workers face bleak future', *Zimbabwe Standard* (27 Aug.).

Index

Index

and conflict/disaster 218; and crime/
authority 220–2; diversity of 234; and
education 222–3; and food 226–7; and
health/healthcare 226–8; and HIV/
AIDS 217–18; interventions 230–4;
and lifestyles 222–8; locations of
homelessness 209; and making an
income 223–4; numbers of 210–13;
perceptions/characterisations 228–30;
as planned/temporary 215, 222; and
poverty 214–15; and sexual activity
224–5; socio-economic factors 214–15;
and substance abuse 225; and survival/
coping strategies 222–8; and toilets/
washing facilities 227; *see also*
children; street children
Homeless International 66, 100
homeless people: accommodators 60–1;
and age 125–6; as anti-citizen 202–3;
and assisted returns to rural areas
240–2; as beggar 198–9; causes of
141; and crime 137–9; definition of
121–2; economic dimension 126–32,
141, 142–50; and food distribution
242; and gender 123–4; and health
133–7; as helpless 203; and household
formation 122–3; as immoral 199–200;
and income 132–3; as loner 201–2; as
mentally ill 199; and minority groups
139–40; as 'others' 197–8; political
dimension 141, 179; and poverty
126–32; and race/ethnicity 139–40;
resistors 60–1; social dimension 141,
154–63; strategic interventions for
235–71; teeterers 60–1; as transient
200–1; as villain 198
homelessness: and adequate housing 54–6;
agency/structuralist approach 4, 5–6,
204; assessment of 53; causes of 4–8;
change of term 245–8; circumstances
of 51–2; complexity continuum 49–50;
conditions of 47–8; counting 8–10;
definitions of 4, 47–79, 121, 158,
201; divisions of 52; dynamic nature
of 6–7, 50–1; gender differences
53; and gender vulnerabilities 7–8;
and government dilemmas 6; and
housing market deficiencies 7;
ideological/political continuum 49,
50; individualist approach 4, 5–6;
and inter-agency systems 25–6; lack
of literature on 1; market approach
28–9; minimalist/maximalist approach

4–5; national understandings of 77–8;
pathway metaphor 6–7; and personal
crisis 33; potential for 59–60; risk
continuum 6; security continuum
5; social context 57, 59; and social
exclusion 52–3; structural causes of 33;
time component 54; typologies of 8–9;
understanding of 10, 100–1; and urban
poverty 1
Honduras 194
Hong Kong 107
Honig, M. and Filer, R.K. 6
Hoogeveen, J.G. and Özler, B. 149
Household Expenditure Survey (HES,
1995/6) 150
household formation: breakdown in 154–7,
216; changes in 126; and families as
homeless 201–2; and family groups
122; and homeless families 211; and
mother/child groups 122–3, 124; and
single people 122; and weakening of
extended family support 157–60
Household Income Expenditure and
Consumption Survey (HIECS) 147–8
housing career/pathway approach 6–7, 50,
152
housing interventions: and access to
land 260–1; and access to services
262–3; and disaster mitigation
263–5; enabling approach 258–65;
and formalisation process 261–2;
and inadequately housed 258–65;
and lumpiness of supply 260; and
making life on the street more bearable
257–8; and non-housing interventions
265–9; and progressive improvement in
accommodation 252–4; and provision/
improvement of shelters 254–5; and
reintroducing the flop-house 255–6;
and treating unhoused as special cases
249–58; and unhoused-inadequate
housing duality 248–9; *see also*
interventions
housing need 116–17
housing rights 46, 243; and government
responsibilities 22–3; national
interpretations 23–5; realising
programmes for 20–2; UN Declarations
on 19–20
housing shortfall: and affordability 33,
36–7, 42–5; and building/planning
regulations 32; calculating 31–2,
35–9; and economic conditions 34;

Index

Japan 33, 52, 146
Java 223
Jejeebhoy, S.J. 154
Jellinek, L. and Rustanto, B. 145, 148
Jencks, C. 256
Jordan, B. 196
Julià, M. and Hartnett, P. 5, 201

Kabachenco, N. 212
Kabir, Z.N. et al. 161
Kakita, Y. 52, 143
Kamete, A.Y. 38, 39, 72, 77, 111, 117, 124, 138, 140, 149, 150, 158, 159, 171, 192, 236
Kampung Improvement Project (KIP) 177–8
Kamruzzaman, M. and Ogura, N. 147
Kasongo, B.A. and Tipple, A.G. 101
Kaur, P. 226
Kellett, P. and Moore, J. 2, 3
Kennett, P. and Marsh, A. 5, 121, 142, 154
Kenya 124, 127, 155, 156, 166, 170
Kevane, M. and Wydick, B. 269
Khair, S. and Khan, S. 221
Khan, S. 132
Kilbride, P.L.A. et al. 220
Kisor, A.J. and Kendal-Wilson, L. 160
Koenigsberger, O. 14
Korboe, D. 124, 152, 213, 214, 215, 223, 224
Kothari, M. 123, 124
Kuhn, R. 152
Kulsudjarit, K. 224
Kurdistan 172
Kuyasa Fund (South Africa) 251–2

Labeodan, O.A. 1
Lall, S. 166
Lalor, K.J. 221
land: access to 166–7, 260–1; allocation of 187; and colonialism 166; and corruption/land-grabbing 170; cost of 166–7; and improvement in legal/other rights to 267; informal building on 168; and minimum plot size 168; ownership of 219; and racial/class patterns 166; tenure/allocation as political tool 169–70
Lanegran, K. and Lanegran, D. 176
language/labelling: and change of terminology 245–8; and construction of 'other' 204; exclusionary 207; and false/negative perceptions 203,
205; and images/names 204; national examples 204; and public conditioning 204–5; and reinforcement of individual pathology approach 206–7; and self-perception 205–6
Laquian, A.A. 192
Law, R. 195
Lee, Y.J. et al. 160
Lesotho 217
Leus, X. et al. 194
Levison, D. 223
Lewis, O. 147
Li, H. 234, 241
Liang, Z. 152
local government 266
Lucchini, R. 209
Lusk, M.W. 215
Lutheran World Service 240
Lyssiotou, P.P. 127

Ma, Z. 152
McAuslan, P. 36
McGray, D. 256
MacGregor, S. 8
McIntosh, G. and Phillips, J. 51, 54, 56, 78, 105, 107
Mackenzie, D. and Chamberlain, C. 125
Mackenzie, P.W. 178
Madon, S. 144, 145
Mafico, C.J.C. 179
Mahmud, S. 269
Majale, M. 170; and Tipple, G. 42, 43
Mak, S.W.K. et al. 114
Making Markets Work for the Poor (MMW4P) 28–9, 42, 46, 250
Malawi 217
Malinowski, B. 193
Mallick, R. 269
Maloney, C. 157
Malpezzi, S.J. 16, 37; et al. 171
Mamun, N.A. 132
marginal housing units 114–15
Marmara earthquake (1999) 188
Marquette, C.M. 27
Martell, D.A. 2
Massachusetts Housing and Shelter Alliance 'Census of Homeless Elders' 125
Matchinda, B. 216, 217
Mayrhofer, A.M. and Hendriks, S.L. 127
Mexico 27
Mibanco (Peru) 251
Middle East 155

Index

Index

becoming 10; and food distribution
242; as homeless 32, 51, 52, 53, 57,
60, 67–8, 77, 100; and making life
more bearable 257–8; and rural-
urban migration 151–2; types of
75; and urban employment 51; and
use of shelters 91; and versions of
accommodation 86–7, 88
street sleepers 48, 100, 178–9, 200;
definition 48, 49, 72, 73; need of 57;
negativity of 61; and security of tenure
84; vulnerability of 90
street-homeless 87, 95, 97, 121, 122,
200–1, 202–3
structural adjustment programmes (SAPs)
26–7, 143
Sub-Saharan Africa 127, 155, 217
Subbarao, K. et al. 26
substance abuse 225
Sudan 194
Sumatra 223
Summerfield, D. 193
Supported Accommodation Assistance
Program (SAAP) (Australia) 54, 56,
154–5
Susman, P. et al. 185
Swaminathan, M. 1, 196
Swart-Kruger, J. and Richter, L.M. 135,
224
Syagga, P. et al. 166, 170
Szekely, M. 27

Tait, G. 2
Tanzania 155, 156, 219–20
Taylor, E.J. 150
Temporary Assistance for Needy Families
(TANF) 142
Tessler, R. 193
Thailand 145
Tibaijuka, A.K. 173
Tipple, A.G. 40, 45, 66, 80, 131, 168,
169, 186, 260, 261, 263, 266, 269; and
Ameen, M.S. 238; and Korboe, D. 157;
and Speak, S. 100; and Willis, K.G. 65,
156
transient homeless 69–73, 200–1
Trobriand Islands 193–4
Turner, B.S. 2
Turner, J.F.C. 14, 32, 73, 88, 90, 243; and
Fichter, R. 88
typologies: and choice/trajectory 61–2;
as continuums 49, 50; and exclusion
61; and homeless people's perceptions

60–1; quality-oriented 50; quality/
type of accommodation 56–9; and
responsibility for alleviating action 62;
and risk 59–60

Uganda 219–20
UK Housing (Homeless Persons) Act
(1977) 235
Ukraine 212
UN-Habitat 1, 17, 18, 23, 34, 39, 40, 42,
57, 64–5, 113, 122, 168, 170, 183, 187,
251
UNAIDS 217
UNCED 19–20
UNCESCR 55
UNCHS/ILO 269
UNDP 107
UNDP-GOB 35
UNEP Youth Xchange 211
Ungerson, C. 8
UNHCR 20, 23, 123, 218
unhoused 246, 247; decriminalisation of
266–7; and financial arrangements
251–2; and flop-houses 255–6; and
inadequate housing duality 248–9;
and intervention framework 249–58,
271; and minimum size of units
250–1; and privacy 257–8; progressive
improvement in accommodation for
252–4; and role of shelters 254–5; and
security issues 257; special approach to
249–58; and standards/regulations 250;
and subsidised housing 250
UNICEF 208, 211, 213, 215, 218, 231
United Kingdom 33, 103, 104, 122–3, 124,
125, 154, 195, 196, 202, 211
United Nations 15, 19, 22, 52, 160
United Nations Centre for Human
Settlement (UNCHS) 9, 14–15, 16, 17,
19, 20, 21–2, 43, 48, 55, 79, 81, 106,
113, 133, 141–2, 151, 157, 180, 197,
243, 246, 257
United Nations Commission on Human
Rights 172
United Nations Convention on the Rights
of the Child (UNCRC) 218–19, 221
United Nations Declaration of the Rights
of the Child (1959) 19
United Nations Housing Rights
Programme (UNHRP) 20–1
United States 102, 104, 107, 125, 142, 195
United States Conference of Mayors, The
123, 127, 211

326